REPAIR, BROKENNESS, BREAKTHROUGH

Politics of Repair

Series Editors:
Francisco Martínez, University of Leicester
Patrick Laviolette, *Anthropological Journal of European Cultures*

Politics materialises in buildings lacking maintenance, disrepair infrastructures, and potholes on the road. But what kind of politics, precisely? The volumes in this series put an emphasis on repair and maintenance as an analytical means for studying how we think about and imagine social relations.

Volume 1
Repair, Brokenness, Breakthrough: Ethnographic Responses
Edited by Francisco Martínez and Patrick Laviolette

Repair, Brokenness, Breakthrough

Ethnographic Responses

Edited by

Francisco Martínez and Patrick Laviolette

berghahn
NEW YORK • OXFORD
www.berghahnbooks.com

First published in 2019 by
Berghahn Books
www.berghahnbooks.com

First paperback edition published in 2022

Library of Congress Cataloging-in-Publication Data

Names: Martínez, Francisco, 1982- editor. | Laviolette, Patrick, editor.
Title: Repair, brokenness, breakthrough : ethnographic responses / edited by Francisco Martínez and Patrick Laviolette.
Description: New York : Berghahn Books, 2019. | Series: Politics of repair ; Volume 1 | Includes bibliographical references and index.
Identifiers: LCCN 2019028708 (print) | LCCN 2019028709 (ebook) | ISBN 9781789203318 (hardback) | ISBN 9781789203325 (ebook)
Subjects: LCSH: Material culture–Cross-cultural studies. | Repairing–Social aspects–Cross-cultural studies. | Applied anthropology–Cross-cultural studies.
Classification: LCC GN406 .R44 2019 (print) | LCC GN406 (ebook) | DDC 306–dc23
LC record available at https://lccn.loc.gov/2019028708
LC ebook record available at https://lccn.loc.gov/2019028709

British Library Cataloguing in Publication Data

A catalogue record for this book is available from the British Library

ISBN 978-1-78920-331-8 hardback
ISBN 978-1-80073-643-6 paperback
ISBN 978-1-78920-332-5 ebook

https://doi.org/10.3167/9781789203318

CONTENTS

ILLUSTRATIONS

INTRODUCTION

Insiders' Manual to Breakdown

FRANCISCO MARTÍNEZ

> From a certain point on, there is no more turning back. That is the point that must be reached.
>
> —Franz Kafka, *The Zurau Aphorisms*

Lose something that you highly appreciate, try hard in the art of failing, be obdurate in the error, persist in the awkwardness, and then think of what you have learnt. We relapse and fall, and then we stand up again. Also things fail and slip back. They get broken again and again; they persist in falling apart. We all know about failed conjugal lives, about fallen ice creams, hair and porcelains. A good companion gets sick; a teenager falls in love, again and again, merciless. Out of this (increasingly fragmented) combination – of system and error, of silence and noise, of dirt and cleanness – we make music, art, business and politics. If you have read to this point, it is because you also share our interest in accidents and people who have failed, those who don't do things as they are told, who don't follow straight lines, champions of the accident, insiders to failure and mistakes. I am sorry to insist, but systems fail. Weak states are prone to violent coups and revolutions. The financial market follows patterns of boom, bust, kaboom! Vehicles crash. Buildings and infrastructures crack. Smartphones run out of battery. We also know that our body can react strangely sometimes.

Ordinary life is made up of eventful junctures, constant surprises and adjustments that go beyond all attempts to rigorously plan things and manifest a gap between how the world is and how it should be. Indeed, I felt so good in the morning; I expected to take a shower and then to drink a coffee. However, today the hot water did not work, the coffee pot appeared empty, and the internet was slow. And then the day continues and life does not stop. Failure can be both – embedded in and disruptive of everyday life. It is hard though to measure the depth of a failure, and also of our altered mood, but it is worth examining instances of error and failure, as an exercise of critical breaking. The world touches us through failures. Brokenness feels like something, but one does not know what it looks like, and even less how to verbalise that something. Modern societies lack a language in which to discuss failure beyond economic reasoning. In a way, it is like Roland Barthes' argument (1978) regarding the lack of a verbal system capable of interpreting amorous experiences. Current discourses about failure are misleading, if not annoying. They ignore the fact that failure provides space for thinking and self-assessment by interrupting the expected flow of things. Also, they overlook how wasted time can be socially and culturally productive, especially in contexts where we are impelled to avoid what is inefficient, distorted, outside of the straight line (Ahmed 2006; Martínez 2018b).

Nonetheless, accidents and brokenness do not always involve mistakes and misbehaviour, but rather use, testing and tinkering. Likewise, failure does not have to be understood necessarily as the end of knowledge; it can also be considered as an experiential process integral to learning (Miyazaki and Riles 2005), hard to replicate or reproduce, having patina and an aura (Boym 2017). Indeed, failures do not occur twice in the same way, they offer many lessons, and give rise to other forms of life. Ordinary failures open up the potential for organising our lives differently, and for stepping where we are not expected, generating disordering affects that are resistant to categorisation.

Hardly Ever Final

What is gained from an ethnography of repair and breakage? What does it mean to claim that something is broken? Who measures the value of fixing up, and how? This anthology explores the conditions of brokenness and repair in different social and cultural settings. It is, thus, about people doing things, handling situations: holding on, letting go. Also, it studies how both people and institutions develop strategies of maintaining, repairing and fixing up – from objects to concepts, social relations and feelings. The focus on repair opens up a wide range of questions about responsibility, care-taking and sustainability. To repair is an act on the world: to engage in mending and fixing entails a relational world-building that materialises affective formations. It also settles endurance, material sensitivity and empathy, as well as more altruistic values oriented towards the sustainability of life.

Brokenness, in turn, is seen as a pervasive condition of disarray and disorder, an offence against the neat and tidy. Any breakage puts an end to a time and to an order. Hence, it implies some sort of adjustment, a generative tension and a measure of entropy. Yet breakdown can also be part of a continuum, ordinary and normal, full of activity and exchange (see Drazin in this volume). Breakage is hardly ever absolute and final. Neither is repair. Repair has continually to be worked at and is not necessarily pleasant. It rather hurts, while simultaneously it liberates the practitioner from the tyranny of that voracious king called Breakdown. Things are constantly falling out of place, deteriorating, malfunctioning, falling into disrepair, in some cases losing their status as objects and always attesting to the fallibility and fracturability of the world. To keep things as objects and in order is thus a process without end (Domínguez Rubio 2016). Repairing equally involves a degree of normalisation, as it recognises a certain 'fixed' state to which the failing system should evolve as well as the accepted strategies to reach unbrokenness (Ureta 2014).

For a productive dialogue between 'breakage' as an analytical trope and as an ethnographic fact, we might also be interested in introducing a few nuances about the difference between all the terms used: breakdown relates to a failure of functioning; breakage refers rather to the act of breaking and what is left over; while brokenness alludes to the quality of being broken. All three conditions bring a failure of relationships to the forefront, as value is reproduced or lost owing to all-too-human choices, such as repair interventions, investment and care. Breakdown and the death of things is thus contingent to situated decisions, grounded in specific contexts and structures (Cairns and Jacobs 2014). One of the key differences between them is that brokenness testifies to negligence, while repair appears as a generative experience of care and potentiality: to repair is a form of passing through and carrying out, a way of lending continuity to discontinuity, despite the utter impossibility of a whole, complete, absolute restoration.

We Are All Repairers

Collectively, the research presented here reconsiders the dialectics of repair and brokenness by exploring how attempts at mending influence wider social processes. The anthology moves the reader across a mosaic of discussions on the dynamics of material production and cultural mediation, creating synergies across themes of 'breakage' and 'repair'. We aim at providing a device for questioning what it means to fix something, as well as exploring the learning potential that breakdown entails and how the design of things also manifests a view on their maintenance and repairability. In this way, we hope to set out a fecund cross-disciplinary meeting ground for the empirical and the conceptual study of responses to brokenness, contributing to crafting the field of repair studies, recalibrating ideologies of failure, challenging innovation as the dominant paradigm, and strengthening alternate views of affect theory, critical heritage, anthropology, archaeology, material culture and media studies.

By starting with a mundane object or situation, the contributors work with seemingly trivial details and show how they can create an understanding of large issues and political problems. It can be a malfunctioning elevator or a worn out trolleybus line in post-Soviet settings, a pothole in the road, a sunken warship, a broken favourite toy, a stalled snowmobile in arctic Siberia or a group of Norwegian villagers trying to use American retro bric-a-brac for a local festival. There is a good pedagogy but also a creative analytical strategy in such approaches. With a focus on the materiality of these processes of maintenance and repair, there is also much on the haptic dimensions of everyday life, so often forgotten. However, what makes repair relevant is not that things break, but that we care if they do (Spelman 2002; Puig de la Bellacasa 2011)

Our ethnographic responses engage with these matters, developing an open-ended combination of empirical and theoretical questions, which include: At what point is something broken repairable? How much tolerance for failure do our societies have? Where and when do the social relationships that occur during the act of repairing something manifest themselves? What are the social relationships that take place around repair? Our first answer would be that the relevance of repair is not its occurrence, but the values attached, as well as its aesthetic and moral implications (see also Alexander 2012). The effects of restoring things extend far beyond the physical facet; they enable the recreation of social relationships.

Repair is also a practice of placing, entangled in a number of localised relationships that contribute to creating transcendental narratives of reconstitution after abandonment, or of recuperation after breakdown. This understanding of repair updates the Western idea that the healing of past wrongs and empowerment can happen through verbal recounting, suggesting material repair as permeating synchronisation and public recuperation. We can also take repair as an enactment of care, a matter of everyday interaction, manifested in the form of affirmative interventions and affective transmissions that have significance as public feelings (Laviolette 2006; Stewart 2007; Martínez 2017). Activities such as inhabiting, gardening and refurbishing actively change our surrounding material landscapes and shape the meanings associated with them (Strebel 2011). These practices show that other elements and people have been here before us, and also that some new ones will come.

Fixing Is a Political Aspiration

The book's affect-informed ethnographies account for how attempts to lengthen the lives of things allow people to construct a moral self, and/or connect with others and their environment. Overall, talking about the values associated with repair requires understanding people's ideas about their society, their standards, frames of behaviour and orders of worth (Boltanski and Thévenot 2006). Repair and fixing interventions have become matters of public concern. Arguably, this is due to the appreciation of the limits and fragility of the worlds we inhabit and a recognition that many of the orders of modernity are in the process of coming apart (Jackson 2014). Failures and breakdowns are crucial situations in the production of sociotechnical inequities (Graham 2010). We can observe that breakdowns have an impact on a large number of people simultaneously (Graham and Thrift 2007). Indeed, feelings of uselessness have become an intrinsic aspect of contemporary life (Bauman 2004).

In turn, the recovery of past things appears as one of the most symbolic instruments used in negotiating abrupt changes and belonging. It helps to connect generations and ensure stability in the material world, demonstrating a relationship between things and human security (Cherrier and Ponner 2010). Material relations are central to the process of political participation and the production of knowledge (Latour 2005; Marres 2012). For instance, we can relate the recuperation of social bonds with the reworking of things and the engagement in practices beyond the capitalist culture of competition, consumption, expenditure and excess. The mending of things recreates value in objects and resources that have been wasted, reconnecting personal biographies to public and private materiality (Martínez 2018a). In so doing, repair demonstrates concern with continuity and change, and with the interaction between the two, becoming a way of 'preservation without permission' (Brand 2012), and establishing a dialectic relation between necessity and freedom (Oroza 2009).

Our possessions, the tools we use, and the built environment around us are everyday elements of sense-making. Material and temporal considerations redefine the realm of possibility, generating specific meanings and affects, thus making certain experiences and narratives more viable (Kracauer [1927] 1995; Barthes 1957; Simmel 1997). Such considerations are always conjectural to a society, and hence affect the actual power relations, values and representations (Miller 2005). By accounting for quotidian practices of fixing and breakdown and how these acts help to construct multidimensional connections and stabilise matter (Edensor 2016), previous studies on repair and maintenance have made visible the multiple temporalities that shape things (Houston 2017), the politics of recuperating (Guyer 2017; Sánchez Criado 2019) and different regimes of maintenance (Denis and Pontille 2017). Prosaically, fixing is a practice that restores the pragmatic or symbolic function of things (Gerasimova and Chuikina 2009). But in this project, we want to approach repair in a broader sense, as a theory-making practice, focusing on mending as works of adaptation, reconnection and recuperation, which generate in turn a rich array of physical transformations as well as new aesthetic and intellectual genres.

Talent for Destruction

My anthropological interest in repair appeared accidentally, yet with some biographical projections, as psychoanalysts would say. My grandfather is known for his hoarding and tinkering, and I always envied the mechanic skills of my father. Also, my ex, before our rupture, used to tell me that I have a facility for breaking things and relationships. 'You have talent for destruction', she insisted. Then, I could not come up with a good answer, but now I can say that breakage is just a way of changing things and seeing what happens next. A failure, an accident, a breakdown is a new beginning and a liminal point of assessment. It is like an adventure: an intense exploration in which we move away from a centre, going east, going south, going off, breaking through, and feeling the adrenaline rush from 'being in the edge'.

Failures make evident the possibility of breakthrough, of becoming something else, telling us about accidental findings, gaps, tricksters and hackers. This volume calls into question the assumption that creativity always leads to novelty; in many cases, breakthroughs occur through non-heroic acts such as tinkering, material manipulations and the rearrangement of things (Latour 2008; Farías and Wilkie 2016). Breakthrough is a copy-error exercise with a durable impact. Hence, we can also take breakdown, erosion and decay as the starting points of our designs, instead of novelty, growth and progress (Jackson 2014). Failures and lapses do not always materialise a systemic breakdown or a point of disequilibrium; they can also be an asset, if they happen in the early stages of a process, thus becoming an element of learning, experimentation and innovation (Birla 2016), or a window of opportunity characterised by potentiality (Latour 1996; Miyazaki and Riles 2005). In this sense, failure can be understood not simply as a crisis, but also as a terrain of interstitiality, which can also exist as a modality of planning or as a way of keeping people busy (Abram and Weszkalnys 2013; Ssorin-Chaikov 2016).

Systems are organised by defining why some things are proper and others failures (Douglas 1966).1 However, in our life, we most often encounter fragments of repair and brokenness and of failure and success, instead of absolutes (Murawski 2018). Defining the contours of brokenness is, therefore, an anthropological problematic, a vantage point for making sense of the connections and disconnections, continuities and ruptures, subtractions and additions. As Arjun Appadurai points out (2016), no society or culture lacks a word for failure, being always presented through the prisms of language, context and tradition. He also notes how failure – or brokenness, in our case – tends to appear as a self-evident fact, even if it is most often a judgement made. Error, breakage and failure exist in different languages showing distinct nuances, reflective of the societies that produce them (Carroll, Jeevendrampillai and Parkhurst 2017), and yet the notion of failure and success currently hegemonic in the West seems to have been translated-imposed from the language of business. Our work and our minds are measured through financial models, ranging from credit ratings (a number 1) to investments (good for nothing). As a consequence, failure has been redefined, appearing not as an outright misfortune, but as an attribute of those behind the action, who become failures themselves (Sandage 2005).

No Future for Archaeologists

Fixing interventions combine an assessment of something from the past with a sought consequence towards the future. In its Latin etymology, *reparare* refers to a process that starts by going back, yet entailing two meanings: 'making ready' and 'paying attention to'. We can thus say that through repair both people and things grow new, not in the sense of being completely new again, but rather an experience of going through, of being reshaped and modified, having changed from one state to another, hence suggesting transition, intersection, transfer, transmission – a becoming with character (Haraway 2008). Sensuous engagements with the past and efforts to stitch things in time demonstrate the importance of repair as a form of passing through and carrying out (König 2013), thus healing entropic pathologies of desynchronicity (Rosa 2013).

In its etymology, also Latin, *obsolēscere* means 'to grow old', 'be accustomed' and 'to fall into disuse'. Nonetheless, things generate meaning not just in their preservation and repair, but also in their destruction and breakage – as another mode of going through and being in time (DeSilvey 2017). Not surprisingly, the study of waste and decay is receiving increasing attention as a complementary critical angle for the study of consumption and production (Edensor 2005; Gregson, Metcalfe and Crewe 2007; Alexander and Reno 2012; Reno 2015; Eriksen and Schober 2017). Things break and technologies become obsolete much faster than ever before, showing that late-capitalism learned well how to make profit out of accidents. The way in which actual cycles of consumption triturate materials and resources makes us believe, however, that we can dispose of things with total impunity. Likewise, recycling cannot keep pace with increased production, becoming also part of the current 'accelerated archaeology' (Stallabrass 1996) that characterises capitalist rationality and the rapid turnover of commodities. Only repair keeps open the possibility of future remains and ruins; if we recycle everything, there won't be work for archaeologists and all traces would be reduced to a digital archive.

What Lays beyond Repair?

What happens when design and planning meet the material world? What kind of epistemological and ontological gaps are generated? When is the next unruly failure to arrive? Each breakdown entails an emergency and calls for being fixed (Larkin 2016). In a way, this is what we have done from Antiquity (Gruzinski 2012). The richness of repair practices contrasts, however, with paradigms of planning, as well as standardised design procedures (Orr 1996). As designer Ernesto Oroza (2009) points out in his study of vernacularly produced design work in 1990s Cuba, every repaired object can also be understood as a declaration of necessity, often a technologically disobedient one.

Everybody knows that not all that is broken can be fixed or recuperated. Yet sometimes we forget that there are things in a state of repair that keep working zombie-like, sophisticated systems of auto-repair such as the body, or un-failed technologies with no possible repair (i.e. floppy disks or DVDs). The questions of skills of joining and competences are also foregrounded in this book, as well as how things might provide remission but not repair, satisfaction without resolution. Repair is constitutive of a particular embodied thinking and web of connections, a 'cognitive mindset' of being able to assess a problem and identify an appropriate remedy in a given context (König 2013).

Further on, repair cannot happen without sensory explorations and intellectual speculations, in order to ascertain what the problem might be (Denis and Pontile 2014a). Successful maintenance always anticipates failures and entails abstract thinking (Dant 2009). In their interventions, repair workers rely on improvisation and accidental wisdom (Henke 2000), a making-do characterised by alertness, adaptability and celerity (Pine 2012). The work of repair also shows a complex repertoire of gestures and sensual knowledge that involves emotions and is distinct from the experience generated during industrial manufacturing (Dant 2009). Bodily practices such as repair that entail skilled work with different materials become ingrained in your mind (Sennett 2008). This process is part improvisation, part knowledge of standards, reproducing a normative description of the world (Denis and Pontile 2014b).

Efforts to fix generate particular infrastructures, networks and environments of everyday life that often become a condition of existence for those involved (Larkin 2016). A distinct knowledge emerges through repair, often pointing to a discrepancy between the sense of desire and possibility. Such embodied practice is ingrained within personal experience and shaped by the historical and cultural circumstances of its implementation. For artist Kader Attia (2014), repair is an ethical answer to guilt, but also a form of reappropriation and translation, moving things along, a sort of transfer from one cultural space/time to another performed through different acts or stages. To repair is, therefore, to connect – times, people, things (Gruzinski 2012); it is a contemporary writing of history (Gauthier 2014). Hence, it is imperative to project onto repair not only as corrective of obsolescence, breakdown, waste, negligence, subtraction and excess, but also an ideo-praxeological ethos for recuperating us.

The Pervasive Effects of Repair and Breakage

Brokenness reveals fragile relations between people, and that material injuries aggravate immaterial ones. The acts of fixing and mending contain emotional states of being attached to things. These interventions are both defensive (responding to scarcity and facilitating adaptation to changes) and generative (reconnecting and producing new kind of affects that then circulate in public). Also, repair can be dynamic, transforming or modifying the artefact for a new function; or static, trying to make the object appear as it was, to rehabilitate it according to its previous condition. Otherwise, what is broken is not destroyed but rather exists in a state of unfinished disposal (Hetherington 2004). As a verb, to break refers to something being separated, inoperative, scattered, uncompleted, fractured, torn down; it also refers to an escape, trespass, interruption, changing directions, termination, pause and delay of continuity; and finally to a state of bankruptcy, disregard, ruin, failure to function, and good luck.

Through an attention to ethnographic observations and reflections, this volume discloses what the dictionary obviates, namely that disrepair and fixing are part of a particular structure of feeling (Williams 1977), showing affective features of shame and cynicism, or care and solidarity in turn. The set of contributions illustrates the strong affective power hidden in situations of disrepair and repair; broken objects often bring strong emotions into play: frustration, disappointment, feelings of care and love as well as loss and shame, but also energising reactions of creative action. Repair is an open-ended process with no clear boundaries. It refers to embodied acts of completing things that stand in a stage of in-betweenness, engaging with signs of use and giving to disassembled pieces the opportunity for recovered meaning.

The selected authors have been invited to reflect on the social implications of repair and breakage, as well as how they are inscribed in material forms, highlighting the rather invisible relationships between order/disorder, wound/stitch, bone/plaster, hole/cork, and system/error. Despite some recent research in fields such as material culture and urban studies, scholars examining sustainability, the museification of everyday life and the changing notions of value have not yet sufficiently explored how breakage as a phenomenon varies culturally. Nor have they comprehensively scrutinised the importance of repair as an affective generator of haptic learning, symbolic meaning and socio-psychological behaviours. This collection therefore fills a significant conceptual niche within the humanities and social sciences by: 1) setting the general framework for a theory of repair and bringing about a better understanding of the socio-aesthetic significance of these practices; 2) testing the applicability of this concept in relation to the complex processes of transmission; 3) discussing how material culture differs and the ability to define what value can be; 4) investigating the ways that breakage can be anticipated in advance and hence predicting certain possibilities in distinguishing between early/late failure in a plan or system; 5) studying how social contingencies are not themselves projectless; 6) considering what needs to be fixed – is it the world, is it us, is it our way of living, or rather our idea of failure and success?; and 7) countering discourses of innovation, success and technological heroes with actual invisible practices of maintenance and repair.

About This Book

This anthology explores some of the ways in which repair practices and perceptions of brokenness vary culturally and, as such, influence wider processes such as care-taking and projections towards the future. The idea of repairing herein appears as more than a technique; it entails responsibility, attention and a moral statement, making things visible and knowable (Puig de la Bellacasa 2011). Repair is considered as a cultural issue rather than simply a mindless mechanical procedure. This practice is part of a wider sub-architecture of maintenance, a backstage strategy to sustain social relations and constructions; without these reuse exchanges, skilled work and daily re-enactments of care, the world descends into dereliction (Sennett 2008; DeSilvey, Bond and Ryan 2013).

The volume also addresses how fixing and breakage have consequences for how we think about personal human prospections and retrospections. Rather than placing the emphasis on how infrastructures function, or how things get broken, our focus is instead on the affective responses to breakage and the vernacular ways of mobilising resources and generating value, often done as a patchwork of services and support networks without an active design or clear planning. During the editing process, we realised that some of these ideas would be better discussed if we provided authors with the possibility to contribute snapshots, which would then be placed between longer chapters. These shorter insights indeed help to explore many possible inter-articulations between knowledge and intervention, parallels between fieldwork and the practices of tinkering, as well as to acknowledge the role of anecdotalisation in the study of brokenness and repair. Likewise, the snapshot-chapter-snapshot structure relates to the research arguments about different material imaginings and the experimentality of social life, helping to better inform the volume by including topics such as breakage work on Chinese roads, digital telecare supporters in Madrid, consumption dilemmas with de-bobbling garments in Romania, clandestine repairers taking care of the Panthéon's clock in Paris, or a collection of puddles in different cities.

Overall, the book is organised in twelve chapters, intertwined with thirteen shorter snapshots. The variety in the length of each contribution type is also intended to break the textual monotony often present in such thematic compilations. The reader is taken through a wide range of situations and analytical understandings that go beyond the confines of specific disciplines. For example, we meet trash pickers in Istanbul, grassroots activists in Helsinki, people handling their belongings in London homes, luxury-watch repairmen in Hong Kong, a grandmother in Chile who stabilises kinship relations through object-maintenance, coin-operated elevators in Tbilisi, and a bike repair shop community in Brussels, to name just a few. At first glance, the range of examples could appear a bit too far-ranging and the number of topics included might seem chaotically eclectic. Nevertheless, much of the strength of the book lies precisely in this wide range of examples, because they illustrate the fascinating complexities of what is hidden behind labels like maintenance, brokenness and mending, making and breaking relations. The reader can emerge him or herself in a richness of settings, while appreciating the nuanced ways in which each text opens up a number of current theoretical and methodological debates in social and cultural research. The ways in which the contributions create a dialogue with a number of current interests in disciplines such as anthropology, sociology, STS and cultural studies also mean that it is a book of interest for several disciplines. Summing up, this volume shows the following key ideas:

- Social relations are sustained in relation to the maintenance and use of built forms; accordingly, the repair of broken and wasted artefacts helps to recover identities, histories and relations, thus broadening the considerations for the social and allowing a second opportunity.
- Any reparation has two dimensions: a practical attempt to fix what has been broken and the symbolic charge that honours care over wasting. Repair does not merely remake artefacts; the engagement with things shapes the social identities of the repairers and involves subtle shifts in the spatial, temporal, scalar and material processes, which, when combined, help constitute further social transformations.
- The act of breaking is contagious, generating the transmission of negative affects and a sense of failed relationship. Broken means damaged, in need of urgent attention, thus unusable for the initial design purpose.
- Brokenness is not meaningless; there is disordering power and an inherent energy level present in accidents, failures or mistakes, achieving what is understood as a breakthrough. Breakage is also a way of touching reality, of gaining direct access to our surroundings, of connecting to the ground. It thus harbours potentiality, becoming a catalyst, incentive or trigger for self-assessment.

Francisco Martínez is a lecturer in the School of Museum Studies, University of Leicester.

Note

1. The exclusion of the deviant (the noise, dirt, darkness, the negative and so on) informs us about a general order of things, which might, in turn, lead to negligence, discard, disinvestment or devaluation.

References

Abram, S., and G. Weszkalnys (eds). 2013. *Elusive Promises: Planning in the Contemporary World*. Oxford: Berghahn Books.

Ahmed, Sara. 2006. *Queer Phenomenology: Orientations, Objects, Others*. Durham, NC: Duke University Press.

Alexander, Catherine. 2012. '*Remont*: Work in Progress', in C. Alexander and J. Reno (eds), *Economies of Recycling*. London: Zed, pp. 255–75.

Alexander, C., and J. Reno. 2012. 'Introduction', in C. Alexander and J. Reno (eds), *Economies of Recycling*. London: Zed, pp. 1–33.

Appadurai, Arjun. 2016. 'Failure. Introduction', *Social Research* 83(3): xxi–xxvii.

Attia, Kader. 2014. *The Repair from Occident to Extra-Occidental Cultures*. Berlin: Green Box.

Barthes, Roland. 1957. *Mythologies*. Paris: Editions du Seuil.

——. 1978. *A Lover's Discourse: Fragments*. New York: Hill and Wang.

Bauman, Zygmunt. 2004. *Wasted Lives: Modernity and Its Outcasts*. London: Polity.

Birla, Ritu. 2016. 'Failure via Schumpeter: Market, Globality, Empire, and the End(s) of Capitalism', *Social Research* 83(3): 645–71.

Boltanski, L., and L. Thévenot. 2006. *On Justification: The Economies of Worth*. Princeton, NJ: Princeton University Press.

Boym, Svetlana. 2017. *The Off-Modern*. London: Bloomsbury.

Brand, Stewart. 2012. 'Preservation without Permission: The Paris Urban eXperiment'. Introduction to the Long Now Seminar, 13 November. Retrieved from 15 March 2019. http://longnow.org/seminars/02012/nov/13/preservation-without-permission-paris-urban-experiment.

Cairns, Stephen, and Jane M. Jacobs. 2014. *Buildings Must Die*. Cambridge, MA: MIT Press.

Carroll, T., D. Jeevendrampillai and A. Parkhurst. 2017. 'Introduction: Towards a General Theory of Failure', in T. Carroll, D. Jeevendrampillai, A. Parkhurst and J. Shaklesford (eds), *The Material Culture of Failure*. London: Bloomsbury, pp. 1–20.

Cherrier, H., and T. Ponner. 2010. 'A Study of Hoarding Behavior and Attachment to Material Possessions', *Qualitative Market Research: An International Journal* 13(1): 8–23.

Dant, Tim. 2009. *The Work of Repair: Gesture, Emotion and Sensual Knowledge*. Lancaster: Lancaster University Press.

Denis, J., and D. Pontille. 2014a. 'Maintenance Work and the Performativity of Urban Inscriptions: The Case of Paris Subway Signs', *Environment and Planning D: Society and Space* 32(3): 404–16.

——. 2014b. 'Une écriture entre ordre et désordre: Le relevé de maintenance comme description normative', *Sociologie du Travail* 56(1): 83–102.

——. 2017. 'Beyond Breakdown: Exploring Regimes of Maintenance', *Continent* 6: 13–17.

DeSilvey, Caitlin. 2017. *Curated Decay*. Minneapolis: University of Minnesota Press.

DeSilvey, C., S. Bond and J.R. Ryan. 2013. *Visible Mending*. Axminster: Uniform.

Domínguez Rubio, Fernando. 2016. 'On the Discrepancy between Objects and Things: An Ecological Approach', *Journal of Material Culture* 21(1): 59–86.

Douglas, Mary. 1966. *Purity and Danger*. London: Routledge & Kegan Paul.

Edensor, Tim. 2005. 'Waste Matter: The Debris of Industrial Ruins and the Disordering of the Material World', *Journal of Material Culture* 10(3): 311–32.
——. 2016. 'Incipient Ruination: Materiality, Destructive Agencies and Repair', in M. Bille and T.F. Sørensen (eds), *Elements of Architecture*. London: Routledge, pp. 348–64.
Eriksen, T.H., and E. Schober. 2017. 'Introduction: Waste and the Superfluous', *Social Anthropology* 25(3): 282–87.
Farías, I., and A. Wilkie (eds). 2016. *Studio Studies: Operations, Topologies and Displacements*. New York: Routledge.
Gauthier, Léa. 2014. 'Foreword', in L. Gauthier (ed.), *Kader Attia: RepaiR*. Paris: Blackjack, pp. 6–9.
Gerasimova, E., and S. Chuikina. 2009. 'The Repair Society', *Russian Studies in History* 48(1): 58–74.
Graham, Stephen. 2010. 'When Infrastructures Fail', in S. Graham (ed.), *Disrupted Cities*. London: Routledge, 1-14.
Graham, S., and N. Thrift. 2007. 'Out of Order: Understanding Repair and Maintenance', *Theory, Culture & Society* 24(3): 1–25.
Gregson, N., A. Metcalfe and L. Crewe. 2007. 'Moving Things Along: The Conduits and Practices of Divestment in Consumption', *Transactions of the Institute of British Geographers* 32(2): 187–200.
Gruzinski, Serge. 2012. 'From Holy Land to Open Your Eyes'. Leaflet accompanying Kader Attia's installation at dOCUMENTA. Retrieved 15 March 2019, from http://kaderattia.de/de-holy-lans-a-open-your-eyes/.
Guyer, Jane I. 2017. 'Aftermaths and Recuperation in Anthropology', *Hau: Journal of Ethnographic Theory* 7(1): 81–103.
Haraway, Donna J. 2008. *When Species Meet*. Minneapolis: University of Minnesota Press.
Henke, Christopher R. 2000. 'The Mechanics of Workplace Order: Toward a Sociology of Repair', *Berkeley Journal of Sociology* 44: 55–81.
Hetherington, Kevin. 2004. 'Secondhandedness: Consumption, Disposal, and Absent Presence', *Environment and Planning D: Society and Space* 22(1): 157–73.
Houston, Lara. 2017. 'The Timeliness of Repair', *Continent* 6(1): 51–55.
Jackson, Steven J. 2014. 'Rethinking Repair', in T. Gillespie, P.J. Boczkowski and K.A. Foot (eds), *Media Technologies*. Cambridge, MA: MIT Press, pp. 221–39.
Kafka, Franz. 2006. *The Zurau Aphorisms*. London: Harvill Secker.
König, Anna. 2013. 'A Stitch in Time: Changing Cultural Constructions of Craft and Mending', *Culture Unbound* 5(33): 569–85.
Kracauer, Siegfried. (1927) 1995. *The Mass Ornament: Weimar Essays*. Cambridge, MA: Harvard University Press.
Larkin, Brian. 2016. 'Ambient Infrastructures: Generator Life in Nigeria', *Technosphere*. Retrieved 15 March 2019, from https://technosphere-magazine.hkw.de/article1/cd07bf50-921e-11e6-9341-7d6509c7f586/76704180-91e7-11e6-8d22-0bf4eeadcfb0.
Latour, Bruno. 1996. *Aramis, or, The Love of Technology*. Cambridge, MA: Harvard University Press.
——. 2005. 'From Realpolitik to Dingpolitik or How to Make Things Public', in B. Latour and P. Weibel (eds), *Making Things Public: Atmospheres of Democracy*. Cambridge, MA: MIT Press, 14–41.

——. 2008. 'A Cautious Prometheus? A Few Steps toward a Philosophy of Design (with Special Attention to Peter Sloterdijk). Retrieved 15 March 2019, from http://www.bruno-latour.fr/sites/default/files/112-DESIGN-CORNWALL-GB .pdf.

Laviolette, Patrick. 2006. 'Ships of Relations: Navigating through Local Cornish Maritime Art', *International Journal of Heritage Studies* 12(1): 69–92.

Marres, Noortje. 2012. *Material Participation: Technology, the Environment and Everyday Publics*. Basingstoke: Palgrave Macmillan.

Martínez, Francisco. 2017. 'Waste Is Not the End: For an Anthropology of Care, Maintenance and Repair', *Social Anthropology* 25(3): 346–50.

——. 2018a. *Remains of the Soviet Past in Estonia: An Anthropology of Forgetting, Repair and Urban Traces*. London: UCL Press.

——. 2018b. 'Doing Nothing: Anthropology Sits at the Same Table with Contemporary Art in Lisbon and Tbilisi', *Ethnography*, online first, 1–19. https://journals .sagepub.com/doi/full/10.1177/1466138118782549.

——. 2019. 'Politics of Recuperation: An Introduction', in F. Martínez (ed.), *Politics of Recuperation: Repair and Recovery in Post-crisis Portugal*. London: Bloomsbury, in press.

Miller, Daniel (ed.). 2005. *Materiality*. Durham, NC: Duke University Press.

Miyazaki, H., and A. Riles. 2005. 'Failure as an Endpoint', in A. Ong and S.J. Collier (eds), *Global Assemblages: Technology, Politics, and Ethics as Anthropological Problems*. Malden, MA: Blackwell, 320-31.

Murawski, Michał. 2018. 'Actually-Existing Success: Economics, Aesthetics and the Specificity of (Still-)Socialist Urbanism. A Review Essay', *Comparative Studies in Society and History* 60(4): 907–37.

Oroza, Ernesto. 2009. *RIKIMBILI: Une étude sur la désobéissance technologique et quelques formes de réinvention*. Cité du design: Université de Saint-Étienne.

Orr, Julian. 1996. *Talking about Machines: An Ethnography of a Modern Job*. Ithaca, NY: Cornell University Press.

Pine, Jason. 2012. *The Art of Making Do in Naples*. Minneapolis: University of Minnesota Press.

Puig de la Bellacasa, Maria. 2011. 'Matters of Care in Technoscience: Assembling Neglected Things', *Social Studies of Science* 41(1): 85–106.

Reno, Joshua O. 2015. *Waste Away: Working and Living with a North American Landfill*. Los Angeles: University of California Press.

Rosa, Hartmut. 2013. *Social Acceleration*. New York: Columbia University Press.

Sánchez Criado, Tomás. 2019. 'Repair as Repopulating the Devastated Desert of Our Political and Social Imaginations', in F. Martínez (ed.), *Politics of Recuperation: Repair and Recovery in Post-crisis Portugal*. London: Bloomsbury, in press.

Sandage, Scott. 2005. *Born Losers: A History of Failure in America*. Cambridge, MA: Harvard University Press.

Sennett, Richard. 2008. *The Craftsman*. London: Penguin.

Simmel, Georg. 1997. *Simmel on Culture: Selected Writings*. London: Sage.

Spelman, Elizabeth. 2002. *Repair: The Impulse to Restore in a Fragile World*. Boston, MA: Beacon Press.

Ssorin-Chaikov, Nikolai. 2016. 'Soviet Debris: Failure and the Poetics of Unfinished Construction in Northern Siberia', *Social Research* 83(3): 689–721.

Stallabrass, Julian. 1996. *Gargantua: Manufactured Mass Culture*. London: Verso.

Stewart, Kathleen. 2007. *Ordinary Affects*. Durham, NC: Duke University Press.
Strebel, Ignaz. 2011. 'The Living Building: Towards a Geography of Maintenance Work', *Social & Cultural Geography* 12(3): 243–62.
Ureta, Sebastian. 2014. 'Normalizing Transantiago: On the Challenges (and Limits) of Repairing Infrastructures', *Social Studies of Science* 44: 368–92.
Williams, Raymond. 1977. *Marxism and Literature*. Oxford: Oxford University Press.

SNAPSHOT 1

HEAD, HEART, HAND

On Contradiction, Contingency and Repair

CAITLIN DESILVEY

For want of a nail the shoe was lost.
For want of a shoe the horse was lost.
For want of a horse the rider was lost.
For want of a rider the battle was lost.
For want of a battle the kingdom was lost.
And all for the want of a horseshoe nail.
—Proverb of unknown origins

Craft and the Corporate Imagination

Silas and Juliana Hubbard welcomed their son, Elbert Green, into the world on 19 June 1856 in Bloomington, Illinois. Elbert went on to make himself a small fortune selling soap for his brother-in-law, J.D. Larkin. Despite this success, by the last decade of the century Elbert became restless. In 1894 he introduced himself to William Morris on a tour of England; on his return he reinvented himself, leaving behind sales for a life of philosophising and socialist experimentation. Inspired by Morris's example, he set up a printing collective and craft workshops in the small town of East Aurora, near Buffalo in the State of New York. Hubbard's Roycroft commune espoused elements of Morris's Arts and Crafts ethos, but did so in a peculiarly American context that retained more than a trace of the self-promoting huckster salesman.

'Head, Heart, Hand' was the Ruskin-derived Roycroft motto, and Hubbard championed meaningful work with the hands as a stimulant for intellectual and social engagement. The commune's production eventually extended to pottery, hammered copper, wrought iron, leather goods, stained glass and furniture. Hubbard also wrote a series of quirky tracts on self-reliance, initiative and individualism. Their pronouncements (among them 'There is no failure except in no longer trying' and 'Never explain – your friends do not need it and your enemies will not believe you anyhow') were enthusiastically taken up by big business and absorbed into the nascent corporate management philosophy of the early twentieth century (Champney 1968).

Hubbard went down with the Lusitania in 1915 but the Roycroft brand survived his demise: Sears & Robuck briefly carried a line of its furniture. The original print shop was repurposed as an inn and restaurant, and his son Elbert II continued to manage the Roycroft shops until operations ceased just before the Second World War.

Entrepreneurs Herman Fisher and Irving Price founded another business in East Aurora in 1930, specialising in high-quality wood and steel pull toys. Fifteen years later, John and Betty DeSilvey moved to town with their small son, Dennis. My grandfather was an expert in the repair and rebuilding of turret lathes and milling machines. He started out with a shop in East Aurora, but eventually took his business on the road, travelling to factories and workshops across western New York and Ohio with his fine metal-working tools. He also played ragtime piano, visiting a circuit of road houses and bars on his rounds. On his increasingly infrequent visits back to East Aurora, he would sometimes stop in to play at the Roycroft Inn.

From Handicraft to Plastic Fantastic

Betty and John's son grew up in East Aurora and fell in love with a local girl, Kathy Selkirk, daughter of the local paediatrician. During the summers of their courtship in the early 1960s, when they were home from university, Dennis worked as a milkman and Kathy worked at the Fisher-Price Factory, where she earned $1.10 an hour assembling and packaging toys. The boredom of her job was relieved only by the salty gossip of the other women on the line, who were mostly full-time and long-term. Her assembly-line tasks included attaching the wings on Buzzy Bee, the first Fisher-Price toy to use plastic in its construction. She recalls that a few women collapsed from the heat back in the plastics section of the factory during her last summer: in 1962 Fisher-Price set up a plastics plant in Mexico.

Dennis and Kathy married in 1965, and a decade later, after a spell in Manhattan and New Jersey, they bought a farm in Vermont, becoming part of a back-to-the-land urban exodus of young professionals. They raised three children and many animals, while Dennis pursued his career as a cardiologist. Back in East Aurora, Dennis's mother, Betty, acquired an oak, slant-top Roycroft writing desk (c.1910), which she kept in the hallway of her split-level suburban ranch house. Every year the Vermont family returned to East Aurora to celebrate Christmas with the grandparents. We often received Fisher-Price toys as gifts, but at age two my favourite new acquisition was a toy tool belt. It may or may not have been a gift from my mother's sister Andrea, who, after training as a dancer, eventually became a plumber and maintenance worker. As a child I often helped my father with carpentry projects around the farm; on my twelfth birthday he gave me a proper contractor's steel toolbox and a full set of tools of my own.

After Betty died in 2005, I inherited her Roycroft writing desk and her vintage Fisher-Price 'Snoopy' pull toy. The Snoopy figure bears little resemblance to Charles Schultz's famous beagle, although they were contemporaries. The lithographic label attached to the wooden body reads: 'Made in USA c. 1961, Fisher-Price Toys, East Aurora, NY'. I have a photograph of my grandmother posing with a giant replica of the Snoopy pull toy on the lawn outside the Fisher-Price factory.

Resonance and Repair

The Roycroft desk was shipped to me in Montana on a long-haul moving van. It was badly damaged in transit: a gouge on the back panel scraped into the stained oak to reveal a patch of raw wood. Since its creation in the Roycroft workshops, the desk had taken on the status of an antique, and its value was estimated at $14,000. I had never owned an object of comparable worth, so I felt responsible for its repair. A friend recommended John Kjeland, whose past wood restoration projects included an antique backbar in Valdez, Alaska, a marquetry mural in Yellowstone National Park and an animatronic gypsy fortune teller (which David Copperfield offered to buy for $2 million). John did a fine job repairing the cosmetic damage to the desk, but I still had to be gentle with it; the brass hinges that connected the slant-top were worn, meaning the ratchets no longer caught properly.

When I packed the desk for a cross-Atlantic move in 2007, I unscrewed the hinges and ratchets and left them with John, who promised to rebuild them and ship them over, even though he didn't usually work with metal. I put the hinge screws in a little brown velvet sack and tucked them into the desk drawer for safe-keeping. The year 2008 found me living and working in Cornwall, in the southwest of the UK, trying to find my feet in a new place and in a new job. A chance opportunity to document the contents of an abandoned cobbler's shop led to my meeting of Steven Bond, a photographer and son of an ironmonger from Bridgwater, Somerset.

On the back of our work in the cobbler's shop, Steve and I came up with an idea for a collaborative project to visit places in the region where people repaired everyday things – shoes, clothes, books, tools, sewing machines, typewriters. We would talk to people about what they did and the objects they cared for, and take photographs of their workplaces. Steve was particularly fond of William Morris's adage: 'Have nothing in your houses that you do not know to be useful, or believe to be beautiful'. We called the project 'Small is Beautiful?' – with a nod to E.F. Schumacher (1975).

Meanwhile, the Roycroft desk languished topless, in need of repair. John decided he couldn't do the job, and the hinges were sent on to a 'father & son' company in Rockland, Maine which specialised in custom boat hardware. In 2010 the rebuilt hinges arrived in Cornwall, new ratchets gleaming. As I screwed them in and went to fasten the folding arms that held the edges of the desktop level, I realised I was missing one screw. I looked in the little brown velvet sack, in my generic screw collection, in my toolbox, and in all of the other places I could think of. No screw.

So began the search for a slot head no. 6 X ¾ inch screw – 'just an ordinary wood screw' – but remarkably hard to find. The man in the Falmouth hardware shop claimed they used to be standard, but he didn't have any in stock (he showed me the tiny drawers where they once lived in the shop). A local woodworker tested one of the sister screws with a magnet and surmised that it might be treated steel. I asked my father to root around in his home workshop and asked others to check their own collections. I ended up with a selection of screws, all roughly the right size and shape, but none an exact match for the missing screw.

The closest match came from Peter Bond, Steve's father, who found a candidate in the stock that was left over after the closure of his ironmonger's shop. Thompson Brothers had traded continuously in Bridgwater, Somerset for 210 years, until Peter decided he could no longer hold out against the undercut prices of the corporate DIY chains and closed his doors in August 2007. The screw that Peter provided was new, brass and shiny, while the old one was tarnished and steel. He suggested that I do some 'blueing' on the new screw – usually a process of heating and dipping in oil, but approximated with boot polish or cold tea. I decided it was more honest to leave the shine on as evidence of the substitution. When I screwed it into the desktop, I delighted in noting the word on the hinge fitting, set in a diamond shape: 'Process'.

The story might end there, except that a few months later Steve and I visited a shop in Colyton, Devon called The Tool Box, on the recommendation of his father. The shop sold only second-hand tools, lovingly restored and ready for reuse. Something about seeing the array of well-used tools all polished and poised on the shelves of the shop made me feel guilty about my own neglected toolbox. The same steel box my father gave me in 1983 now held a few tools from the original set alongside a rag-tag collection of other tools picked up along on the way. I spent part of a Sunday afternoon sorting out the box. In the red metal top tray I found, among bits of wire and stray washers and other detritus, the lost Roycroft desk screw – although I was certain that I had looked there already.

Figure S1.1. Desk. Photograph by Caitlin DeSilvey.

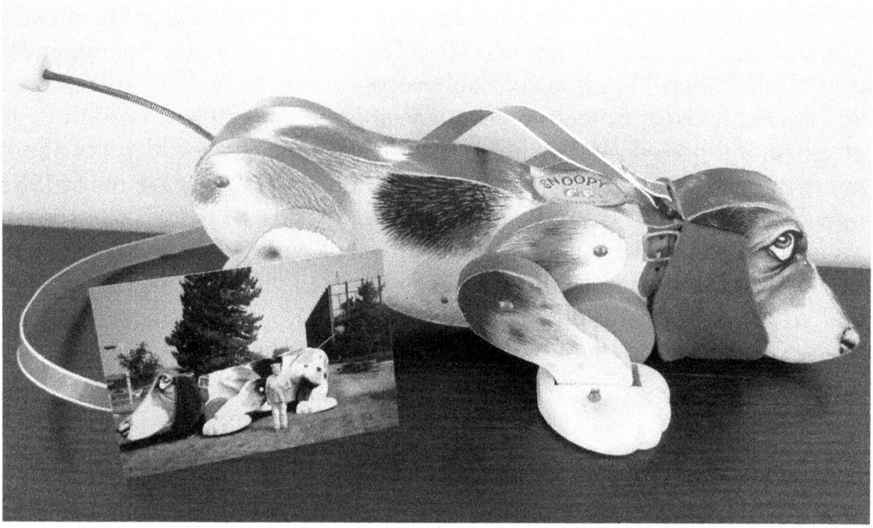

Figure S1.2. Snoopy. Photograph by Caitlin DeSilvey.

The desk is now whole again, and my Fisher-Price inheritance sat on top while I was thinking about how to tell this story. Fisher-Price is now a subsidiary of Mattel. They still make the 'Snoopy' pull toy, though it is now entirely plastic, and goes by the diminutive 'Lil' Snoopy'. It lacks the mournful charm of the original, and is made not in East Aurora but in China. Until a few years ago, one of the main manufacturing hubs for Fisher-Price was a toy factory in Foshan, owned by Lee Der Industrial. The head of operations was a man named Zhang Shuhong, who had started out as an errand boy and worked his way up to manage three factories. In 2007 an international scandal erupted when it was discovered that lead-based paint had been used in the manufacture of Fisher-Price toys at Lee Der, and a massive recall followed. In August of that year, the same month that Peter Bond closed up shop in Bridgwater, Zhang Shuhong took his own life by hanging himself on the third floor of one of his factories.

Epilogue

A few words of explanation and reflection on the story above – which admittedly has some of the elliptical and inconsequential qualities of a 'shaggy dog story' – might be welcome. I assembled this narrative out of threads of my own personal and family history, in relation to wider cultural (and corporate) histories that run along parallel tracks, sometimes switching into the path of my own story. In the process of assembly, I became aware of (occasionally tenuous) connections I hadn't been conscious of previously. As an auto-ethnographic exercise (Okely and Callaway 1992), the story teases out a formative tension between the attraction of things made or mended by hand (as part of a life lived in contact with materials and their properties) and the background swell of mass production and mass consumption that has been building for over a century, and is now threatening to crest and crash.

The story exposes nostalgia for an authentic mode of existence that never quite existed, tracked as a countercultural force through William Morris, Elbert Hubbard and E.F. Schumacher. But this is an attraction learned and honed through relationships with real people – fathers, friends and grandparents – and real objects – tools and toys. Equally, the story reveals that corporate entities enter personal biographies in curious ways. Fisher-Price's evolution from small-town operation to subsidiary of an indifferent multinational is a corporate 'any-story'. Yet there is equally a genuine affection for objects produced by this compromised system, not to mention their role in shaping our lives. There is no settled ending to a tale like this one, just an ongoing collection of contingent and sometimes contradictory storylines, some of which may be useful when the time comes.

Caitlin DeSilvey is Associate Professor of Cultural Geography at the University of Exeter.

References

Champney, F. 1968. *Art and Glory: The Story of Elbert Hubbard.* New York: Crown Publishers.

Okely, J., and H. Callaway (eds). 1992. *Anthropology and Autobiography.* London: Routledge.

Schumacher, E.F. 1975. *Small Is Beautiful: Economics as if People Mattered.* New York: Perennial Library/Harper & Row.

CHAPTER 1

Underwater, Still Life

Multi-species Engagements with the Art Abject of a Wasted American Warship

JOSHUA O. RENO

Introduction

For European Futurists the destructive war machines crafted from steel and iron were sublimely beautiful, no less than war itself.[1] Following Alfred Gell (1998, 1999), one needn't be a Futurist to associate the two domains. Both technical and artistic objects are products of artifice, which other thinking beings may recognise and be affected by in turn, and this gives them a similar capacity to extend the agency of their creators. What, then, can be made of machines when they disintegrate and fall to ruin? They are no longer potential weapons of war, but are they still art objects in Gell's sense? After all, their very neglect might suggest the absence of repair and maintenance rather than the presence of agentive care and creativity. Are they still beautiful in a Futurist sense? After all, their once sleek form of precise design is now lost to the inhuman designs of other beings and forces.

For the world's largest military, there are plenty of examples of wasted war machines to draw from. According to the CIA, the US Navy alone now has 430 ships in service and on reserve, some in a state that even the most enthusiastic Futurist would have trouble exalting. When they begin to wear, American ships become the responsibility of the Maritime Administration (MARAD). Since 1949, MARAD has decided whether to scrap, sink or 'mothball' old ships as part of the Naval Defense Reserve Fleet (NDRF). This Ghost Fleet, as it is known, consists of the Ready Reserve

Force and the Non-Ready Reserve Force. The latter do not meet standards for readiness and are docked in three sites to await disposal: the James River in Virginia, Beaumont in Texas, and Suisun Bay in California. NDRF ships awaiting disposal can generate tension between military and non-military interests that, for example, worn out planes stored at the Air Force's boneyard in the middle of the Sonoran Desert do not. Between 2000 and 2003, at least nine spills resulted from the Ghost Fleet docked on the James River. Even more controversial has been Suisun Bay, where in the last decade environmental activists have produced evidence that the reserve fleet was leaking toxic pollutants not far from where civilians lived and worked. After a protracted legal battle, the US government decided to remove and scrap the remaining ships, a process that is still ongoing.

But mothballed vessels can be reimagined in many ways. Another member of the Ghost Fleet is the USNS *Vandenberg*, an 11,000-ton transport ship that served in the Navy and Air Force off and on from 1963 to 1984. After it left the service, the ship was still used for various films, including the 1999 movie *Virus* starring Jamie Lee Curtis. After being mothballed, the *Vandenberg* was eventually scuttled off the coast of Key West Florida in 2009 to create an artificial coral reef, the largest in the Keys. Not long after, the *Vandenberg* was also the setting for an underwater art exhibit, to display photographs that used the ship itself as a background and the growing coral reef as curator and co-creator of the artwork. This art is notable for two reasons. First, non-human oceanic processes and beings are involved in the ongoing transformation of the art; these pieces will decay and rot with the ship. Second, the sunken military ship is repurposed as both a gallery space and as a setting to frame the photographs. In other words, it is both directly incorporated into the art, and used to display it.

But what does it mean to have coral as a collaborator in one's artwork? To explore this question, I combine the insights of Gell with those of Hannah Arendt and Julia Kristeva, who offer tools to investigate the typically hidden regimes of care that maintain durable artwork. This is what is intentionally lacking in the *Vandenberg* gallery. Corrupting Gell's key concept, I refer to the *Vandenberg* and similar projects as the *art abject*, artworks deliberately given over to the 'countersignature' (Marder 2009) of non-human forces and forms. Put simply, and utilising Arendt's terms, the art abject is what is left over when the artlabour of maintenance and repair is subtracted from artwork. In the absence of repair, non-humans leave their indelible imprint on the work and remind witnesses that this is the fate of all human creations, that each art object we make and maintain is destined to exhaust and exceed our labours and become, or reveal itself as having always already been, art abject.

I start by describing the social context of the Florida Keys and of artificial reefing of naval vessels. This is in keeping with Gell's important insight that all art objects be understood in terms of the social interactions they presuppose as well as those they entail (Myers 2001; Chua and Elliott 2013). Outlining the value (and limitations) of Gell's anthropology, Born writes: 'Through the art object . . . social relations are distributed and dispersed both temporally and spatially. But in the process the social relations are also relayed and transformed, as are the objects themselves' (2005: 16). After describing the *Vandenberg* project, I explain the art abject and its relevance to interpret Franke and supplement Gell by pointing attention to the role of reparative and restorative artlabour. As such, the *Vandenberg* project simultaneously recuperates a dying ship for artistic representation and bears witness to its inevitable failure.

Artificial Reefing in the Florida Keys: A Brief History

> My family's going to eat as long as anybody eats. What they're trying to do is starve you Conchs out of here so they can burn down the shacks and put up apartments and make this a tourist town. That's what I hear. I hear they're buying up lots, and then after the poor people are starved out and gone somewhere else to starve some more they're going to come in and make it into a beauty spot for tourists.
>
> —Ernest Hemingway, *To Have and Have Not*

As Hemingway notes, residents of Key West (or Conchs) are no strangers to the creative destruction of capitalism. The use of old naval ships as coral reefs offers a case in point. The *Vandenberg* is a primary attraction for divers and a source of multiple forms of revenue for the region of Key West. It survived even the devastation of Hurricane Harvey in the summer of 2017. This is from Key West's Dive Center:

> A diver's delight, the massive General Hoyt S. Vandenberg is the newest compelling addition to the Florida Keys Shipwreck Heritage Trail . . . At 524 feet long, the Vandenberg is almost two football fields long and stands 10 stories tall. The ship's structure begins at depths of about 40 feet and continues to a depth of 145 feet, offering so many great nooks, masts and radar dishes to explore that it cannot all be seen in a single dive.

Accidental shipwrecks have a long and storied history in the Florida Keys. But ships deliberately sunk to serve as coral reefs, less so.

Conchs live much of their lives in, on and under the water. Water also drew European colonists who found the Straits of Florida a convenient way to return with what they had taken from people in the West Indies. If it is the water that brings many people to Florida, then it is the only barrier coral reef in the US, and more specifically the shipwrecks they cause, that made Key West prosperous. If not for the waste of the Spanish colonial war machine, in fact, Key West would not exist. Many Conchs are aware that their city's history has its origins in maritime predation and celebrate this fact.[2] In this way, Key West residents are similar to those of Cornwall, as discussed by Patrick Laviolette, whose analysis of recycled maritime vessels parallels my own. The fact that 'death and regeneration are so important in Cornwall', he writes, 'has to do with the relationship that these notions have with a legacy of maritime tragedies and mortalities' (2006: 83).

Still today, stories of treasure hunters, pirates and famous wrecks circulate within the diving community. In 1977, Florida archaeologists discovered eight wrecks from the 1733 Fleet, one of many ill-fated convoys to Spain. The same year that the 1733 Fleet was found, Jimmy Buffet's breakthrough hit 'Margaritaville' described tourists descending on Key West in waves. With a growing population and tourist industry, naturally existing coral reefs began to suffer, as did biodiversity in the Keys in general. In the 1960s and 1970s, Conchs were encouraged by the municipal government to dump trash in the water, especially tyres, in order to generate artificial reefs to supplement those in decline. This proved unsuccessful and is remembered as a foolish mistake. Among other things, tyres are unstable and roll around the ocean floor, disturbing and killing coral in the process. Artificial reefing clearly had an inauspicious beginning. So, despite the history of wrecks and their importance to Key West, the idea of sinking ships to restore the coral coastline was not automatically appealing.

Throughout the world, ruins and relics of the Cold War lie in various states of decay. In some cases, they may represent heritage to be reclaimed and/or offer challenges to official narratives of global crisis (see Burström, Karlsson and Gustafsson 2012; Gustafsson et al. 2017). Artificial reefing of naval vessels in particular is a contentious enterprise. During the Reagan administration, the American fleet was expanded to some six hundred vessels. At the conclusion of the Cold War, this once highly valued fleet suddenly seemed unnecessary. Congress passed a new act requiring that MARAD speed up the process of scrapping the 'non-ready' ships of the Ghost Fleet and, in the two decades since, the number of ships was reduced by over 25 per cent. The National Maritime Heritage Act of 1994 gave MARAD five years to dispose of surplus ships. Since the 1980s, the primary means of doing so had been to export ships to be broken up abroad, usually where it could be done cheaply. After the Cold War, however, there were also growing concerns about wealthy countries exporting hazardous waste to poorer parts of the world. Just a few years later, the 1999 deadline had to be extended to 2006, when it became difficult for MARAD to continue exporting NDRF ships abroad. At the time, there was growing awareness about how toxic and dangerous ship-breaking was for the people who did it and the places in which they live. These concerns became formalised with the Basel Convention agreements of the early to mid 1990s. These forbade the transfer of hazardous waste from Organisation for Economic Co-operation and Development (OECD) to non-OECD countries.[3] What Basel does not do is prevent OECD countries from exporting hazardous materials to one another. So, responding to the growing global discourse around ship-breaking, the Environmental Protection Agency (EPA) and MARAD eventually chose to export thirteen ships from the James River to Teesside in the United Kingdom. However, this was never completed after it was challenged by the Sierra Club and an NGO representing the Basel Convention, Basel Action Network (BAN). After Basel, BAN's efforts have mostly been directed to identifying 'green-washed' businesses that disguise polluting practices as recycling, among them ship-breaking and ship disposal at sea. With the Sierra Club they filed a successful action accusing MARAD and the EPA of environmental wrongdoing. According to Puthucherril (2010: 50), the primary result of this was to create a robust domestic ship-dismantling operation, primarily centred in Brownsville, Texas.

But there was yet another loophole that MARAD could use to avoid violating Basel and other environmental regulations. Since the Liberty Ship Act was passed in 1974, the government has donated NDRF vessels for use in the creation of artificial reefs. The SINKEX programme sank naval ships off the east and west coasts for years. It was only in the twenty-first century that artificial reefing became a civilian enterprise. The SINKEX programme represents an unwanted comparison to the efforts of those who sank the *Vandenberg*. As a result of this government programme, BAN released a 2011 report entitled 'Dishonorable Disposal' (Self 2011). The primary target for the 2011 report was the SINKEX programme of the US Navy, which has used old ships for target practice for many years, leaving hundreds to leak toxic materials at the bottom of the ocean. The same year that the report was published, BAN joined the Sierra Club in a lawsuit against the EPA, in an effort to force the agency to forbid the practice, but dropped the suit in 2013 due to lack of funds. The US government has repeatedly claimed that the Navy satisfies regulatory requirements but that it is also exempt from national and international environmental regulations anyhow. The sinking of the *Vandenberg* has come under fire from BAN and other groups by association. Joe Weatherby is the Key West resident and entrepreneur most responsible for sinking the *Vandenberg*. He was interviewed as part of a research project I conducted with Priscilla Bennett in 2015 and counters BAN's claims by emphasising how clean and careful his company's deployment of artificial reefs is by comparison. He also accuses BAN of being 'wolves in NGOs' clothing' who work on behalf of the scrapping industry. In addition to contesting Joe's environmental claims, BAN alleges that it would be more cost effective to scrap the ships domestically rather than let them go to waste on the ocean floor. Both claims frustrate Joe. To date, there is no evidence that the *Vandenberg* is a source of pollution, though this is admittedly a hard thing to prove or disprove definitively.

For these and other reasons, the private group that sank the *Vandenberg*, led by Joe, sought out ways to legitimise the wreck as more than an ecological solution to the problems of marine biodiversity and more than an economic opportunity for fishing and diving. According to them, it is also a form of cultural heritage. If one takes the *Vandenberg* to be an art object, in Gell's sense, its presence off the coast of the Florida Keys could be regarded as evidence of the agency of the US military and its efforts to avoid shipping wastes overseas while also meeting demands to eliminate them. This is how BAN tends to see the ship. It could be regarded as evidence of the foolhardy agency of local politicians and entrepreneurs who seek convenient solutions to more profound problems. This is how some locals see the ship, based on past efforts at restoring the reef that they remember well. But there are other ways to abduct or hypothesise about the agency behind the *Vandenberg*. It could instead be regarded as evidence of former human occupation; finally, as a home for sailors and a weapon of war. This is how the artificial reefers have routinely framed the ship, characterising it at the start of their campaign as a 'Cold Warrior' that served the nation and its service members well.

But Gell insists that art objects also create new social possibilities; they are not reducible to the past agentive acts they presuppose. Consequently, none of these semiotic accounts exhausts what the ship can yet become in the hands, fins and polyps of others. As some fear, namely the people behind BAN, it can lead to pollution. As those who sank the *Vandenberg* hope, it can lead to greater legitimacy for artificial reefing in the Keys and in general. It is within this contentious social context that the artwork of Austrian photographer Andreas Franke enters the picture.

Coral Collaborators

In an interview published in *Ecotone*, Franke explains how he came to take photos of the *Vandenberg*:

> In search of a new diving challenge a few years ago, I planned to photograph the *Baron Gautsch*, a former Austrian passenger ship that sank ninety-nine years

> ago and lies off the Croatian peninsula of Istria. I would have a good time, relax, and return home. But afterward, I could not stop thinking about the peculiar emptiness and tragic stillness of the photos. Something was missing. I decided then to use ships as a stage and animate the wrecks with scenes photographed in a studio.
>
> Since you can travel to the Red Sea from Austria without crossing half the planet, I next photographed the *Thistlegorm*, a British freighter that sank during World War II. I took over one hundred pictures, but it did not have that special mystical thing a wreck can have. Aboard the lifeboat that carried me there, I found a magazine and, on its cover, a picture of the USNS *General Hoyt S. Vandenberg*. I knew it would be the ship. (Franke 2013: 96)

Franke is very clear that his artwork is meant to destabilise the relationship between reality and fantasy. On his website, he writes: ‘With my photographs of The Sinking World, I want to pull the spectators into unreal and strange worlds. Ordinary scenes of the past play within a fictional space and become dreamworlds you can get lost in or you can identify with’. I cannot reprint Franke’s work here, but much of it can be accessed online at thesinkingworld.com. An image of the *Vandenberg* is the first one visible under the Underwater Art Projects heading on the main page. A long shot of the ship’s deck with five large photographs arranged in a row, each one with washed out colour and no borders. Each one depicting photo-realistic scenes of people doing ordinary things – hanging up clothing on a clothes line, dancing in a studio, boxing, waiting in line at the cinema – only set against the backdrop of the sunken *Vandenberg* and its sea life. The subjects of the photos are often in what are ordinary mid-twentieth-century, Western European clothing and settings, but none are reacting to the fish, the water, the ghostly ship.

The unusual scenes depicted in these photographs are already notable. But they not only contain moments taking place on the ship as a background, but as artworks are also displayed in the ship as a gallery. Visitors to thesinkingworld.com can also see divers moving around the Vandenberg to view the exhibit, and this, more than the content of the photos *per se*, is one of the more remarked upon dimensions of Franke’s work. It is such an immersive context to engage with art, in fact, that it can distract from the way content and form interact. This is most obvious in the second element of Franke’s exhibit: not only are the photos arranged on the *Vandenberg*, but they are meant to break down and age with the ship itself, as it is taken over by the artificially grown coral reef. The coral, Franke insists, become collaborators in the art as a result. As the reef grows, so too will the art transform, the images distort and warp as the ship itself will gradually merge with the surrounding marine ecosystem. This is, after all, the point of an artificial reef.

To describe this coral collaboration as mere 'decay' would be to render the design and development of the artwork as Franke's and his alone, one which other beings, all with their own specific agendas and ways of perceiving the world, could only corrupt. In this regard, Franke can be compared to other artists, most obviously British sculptor Andy Goldsworthy. Consider this passage, taken from a collection of his art installations entitled *Time*:

> Sunny and cold. Returned to the same place. I feel bound to this place by the work I have already made here. It is so interesting to watch leaves dry up and blow off the slab of rock. It would be wrong to describe it as decay – the work is changing and becoming something else. (Goldsworthy 2000: 169)

Here Goldsworthy describes returning to photograph a site-specific sculpture he made out of fallen yellow leaves, arranged in a pattern along a long flat rock he found on a walk in Ithaca, New York.[4]

Goldsworthy is notable for incorporating local materials in his work and allowing the local surroundings and beings that inhabit them to participate in their gradual rearrangement. Andreas Franke is most different from Goldsworthy in that he is happy to make use of deracinated materials, subjects and ideas that transcend the specific environmental settings he works within. Though it is tempting to imagine how a site-specific art installation would work a hundred or more feet below the ocean's surface, Franke does not constrain himself in this way. As a consequence, the designs that Franke starts with are simultaneously more representational and more abstract. More representational in that he begins with direct renderings of subjects in staged and photo-realistic postures and settings. More abstract in that the juxtaposition between the materials and subjects and the setting in which they are placed could not be more glaring and, in this sense, suggest additional interpretive work that could be done, metaphorical associations beyond the direct image itself. Even basic co-constructed patterns like Goldsworthy's can manage to allude to an individual artist's signature style, but the combination of photographs of historically staged scenes, with an unusual setting and gallery space, provides even more possibilities for interpreting Franke's work.

Where Franke and Goldsworthy overlap is in their shared commitment to using artwork to put transformation on display, where what might ordinarily be classified as decay is presented alternatively as the artwork changing and becoming something else, perhaps what it always was. As in Anna Tsing's (2015: 27) reassessment of 'contamination' as multi-species collaboration, in the situational transformation of the artwork something is gained rather than lost. I propose to characterise this contaminated and emergent aesthetics as the *art abject*. The abject, in the radical psychoanalytic reading of Julia Kristeva, is a reaction to the drama of contact and separation associated with the archaic maternal figure. Hence, 'neither subject nor object, the abject lies between the two' (Smith 1998: 33). As something abject, a thing fits neither category precisely, because it is both too far from and too close to the bodily sensorium and its unconscious fantasies. When something is considered an object, this tends to presuppose that it can be perceived as a discrete form, an entity that can be clearly categorised as a distinct sort of being. By association, this presupposes a subject doing the perceiving and categorising that does both successfully and is therefore reliably discrete and distinct, rather than distributed in its cognition or divided in its attention. For Kristeva, the abject is neither discrete nor distinct, and therefore troubles both object and subject. At the same time, she privileges artists, alongside analysts and religious practitioners, as those capable of speaking the unspeakable of the abject. Kristeva writes that the 'artistic experience . . . is rooted in the abject it utters and by the same token purifies' (1982: 17).[5]

By art abject, I am referring to the abjection of art itself, meaning art not as mastery or mediation of the abject, but a figure of aesthetic experience that does not quite fit the category of art or promote a straightforward understanding of the singular artist. Experiments and other engagements with coral literally complicate perception and relation, in a similar way as does the abject for Kristeva. Partly for this reason, Eva Hayward proposes the figure of 'fingereyes' as a way to relay how corals and people sensorially accommodate to novel environments and multi-species engagements, 'becoming more than ourselves' in the process (2010: 593). Complementing Hayward's more ethnographic account, Stefan Helmreich traces a genealogy of 'figurations of coral' among scientists and artists that ends in a contemporary focus on their readability: 'for today's environmentalists, biotechnologists, and would-be coral geneticists, coral is something to be read – for climate change, for potentially patentable genes, for representativeness' (2016: 60).

If coral is being increasingly 'read' by these scientists, for Franke it could instead be described as writing, that is, as a full-fledged author of artistic experience. Graham Harman echoes conventional wisdom when he writes that 'aesthetics is generally regarded as belonging solely to humans, or at most to certain favoured animals such as beautiful songbirds and mournful humpback whales' (2007: 30). But, Harman argues, insofar as aesthetics is about allusion, rather than direct causation, it involves non-human relations as much as human ones.[6] This allure of the object, as he calls it, is not (only) about the unthinkable or sublime from the standpoint of a subject with aesthetic judgement, but about the ungraspable in a purely ontological sense, that which one object cannot 'touch' or reach in another when they interact. In a sense, for Harman every object has an abject quality about it, since it can never be fully represented by any other entity with which it interacts, human or non-human. But this, in turn, would mean that abjection does not require Kristeva's unconscious and desiring all-too-human mind (which Kristeva [1999] faults Arendt for dismissing). Whatever categories that the art abject may disrupt for (some) human beings, the art abject also exists as such insofar as it involves allusive or incomplete and open-ended relations between non-human entities beyond anyone's or anything's reckoning.

Artwork - Artlabour = Art Abject

There are many ways to interpret Franke's sinking world. The one I pursue is to consider what artworks tend to mean, in contrast to what I call the art abject. For this it is helpful to consider what artworks like Goldsworthy's and Franke's intentionally lack, which I will call artlabour, the acts of repair and maintenance that artworks normally depend on to remain permanent fixtures of our social environments.

To distinguish between artwork and labour, I am relying on Hannah Arendt's *The Human Condition*. Unlike ancient Greeks or Marxists with whom she is in dialogue, these are not distinguished on the basis of assumptions about how worthwhile actions are (their relative 'slavishness' or 'nobility', 'productivity' or 'unproductivity'), but according to the different degrees to which they partake in and therefore represent the 'worldliness' of the human condition. As Arendt writes, 'Human life, in so far as it is world-building, is engaged in a constant process of reification, and the degree of worldliness of produced things, which all together form the human artifice, depends upon their greater or lesser permanence in the world itself' (1958: 96). Labour refers to necessary activities that humans and non-human living things engage in (eating, excreting, reproducing). Because the being labouring must do so, it is harder to interpret as if it stemmed from their freedom or, better said, as if it were an expression of *who they are*. If labour represents repetitive regimes of care, for Arendt, work refers to products of human creation that index freedom (akin to Gell's art object), namely the production of some thing that can be taken to index the freedom from instinct and basic fulfilment of needs. Artwork, by most definitions, is used as a way to index a peculiarly *human* ability to produce things unnecessary for survival. Indeed, Arendt sees artworks as exemplifying work:

> Because of their outstanding permanence, works of art are the most intensely worldly of all tangible things; their durability is almost untouched by the corroding effect of natural processes, since they are not subject to the use of living creatures, a use which, indeed, far from actualizing their own inherent purpose – as the purpose of a chair is actualized when it is sat upon – can only destroy them. (Arendt 1958: 167)

Here Arendt's existential phenomenology exposes its anthropocentrism. For Arendt, art objects are not useful *as art objects* for any living things besides humans. It is for this reason that the apparent presence of cave art painting or aesthetic tradition in burial is enough for some archaeologists and biological anthropologists to attribute human-like cognition to Neanderthals or other early humans. It is seen as a break between the seeming necessity of animal life and its labours and the relative freedom of human community and culture.

This freedom would not be adequate were it simply about human freedom from constraint, since we can never cease to be worldly in that we will eventually decay and die. Rather, it is only the durability of art objects that unmoors them from base worldly existence. 'Thus, their durability is of a higher order than that which all things need in order to exist at all; it can attain permanence throughout the ages' (Arendt 1958: 167). Like Kristeva, Arendt characterises this process as a form of purification of worldly things to a quasi-sacred status:

> Nowhere else does the sheer durability of the world of things appear in such purity and clarity, nowhere else therefore does this thing-world reveal itself so spectacularly as the non-mortal home for mortal beings. It is as though worldly stability had become transparent in the permanence of art, so that a premonition of immortality, not the immortality of the soul or of life but of something immortal achieved by mortal hands, has become tangibly present, to shine and to be seen, to sound and to be heard, to speak and to be read. (Arendt 1958: 167–68)

Gell would seem to agree. For him, art, and aesthetics more broadly, are exemplified by the power of the art object. This is why they seem to index the specifically human ability to freely choose to do something technically clever or inessential (i.e. not mere labour). Gell is actually more fluid on this point than is Arendt. While the latter sticks to an essentially Aristotelian tradition, Gell shifts between a more epistemological and ontological definition of agency. According to Liana Chua and Mark Elliott (2013), the first part of Gell's *Art and Agency* is devoted to *the recognition* of causal effect (for example, our individuating folk-recognition that it 'is' Joe Weatherby who sank the *Vandenberg* and 'is' Andreas Franke who assembled the artwork for it). The second part makes agency something more distributed, the direct or indirect effect that some entity – including non-human beings and inorganic objects – can have on others. This is evident, for instance, when the form of the material an artist works with exerts some influence over the creation of the final product, like a knot in the block of wood being carved.

Artists do 'work' insofar as it must be done and finished (Arendt 1958: 169), and yet the immortal permanence of artwork would not be possible without the care of what we might call *artlabour*. The most obvious example would be the people who feed and care for 'starving artists' (who of course are not starving if they actually complete 'work'). But it would also include any cleaners who care for their workspaces or do repetitive necessary labour that does not create a reified 'work' but sustains the life of the artist. Once the art is created, this would include the labour of preserving and caring for the artwork itself, without which it could not be 'immortalised' in the way that Arendt assumes.[7] Consider not only art restorers but the janitor who routinely sweeps the museum in which the art is displayed. Without such artlabour, artworks become what I have called the art abject. Franke's sinking world, like the work of Andy Goldsworthy, is a testament to this truism.

Conclusion

What does all of this mean for understanding the work of Franke or Goldsworthy? First, by letting his artwork decay underwater, Franke is drawing attention to the broader conditions that are necessary to immortalise art as artwork. The artlabour of coral reefs, unlike the artlabour of museum cleaners, preserving and restoration crews and janitors, is similarly about necessary, repetitive and reproductive labour, but it is done for the purpose of restoring reef life, which the artwork submits to as does the entire ship. Franke highlights the worldliness of all art, as Arendt argues, by bringing to the forefront the fact that all art decays, which means it always relies on usually hidden labour to restore and maintain it. The labour done by the coral is not hidden but brought to the forefront, which could be taken as an implicit commentary on what the production of exclusively human art (and, by extension, the fame of artists) entails. This is not simply about indexing a uniquely human trait, for example agency, in other words, but about staging the absence of the kinds of labours that normally make enduring artworks possible. What is absent from the *Vandenberg* gallery is arguably just as important as what is co-present and indexed directly. The necessary, artlabour, the regime of care that lies behind artwork, is just as essential as the creative work of the artist or the imaginative work of art critics, dealers, consumers and anthropologists.

Second, whether or not it was Franke's intent, it is arguably a very political work. Gell is insistent that art objects be placed in social context and appreciated for their broader impacts. 'The task of the anthropology of art', he argues, 'is to understand the sometimes very dominant role that competition in the realm of aesthetic expression (underwritten by sophisticated artistic techniques) plays in many societies, even to the possible detriment of their material productivity' (Gell 1999: 231). One can interpret the *Vandenberg* exhibit, following Gell, in an indexical fashion by comparing it to normal scenes (what Gell might call the prototype) from which it is derived. In this indexical comparison, thinking about normal scenes of Austrian life, work and family, one might initially think that they are utterly disconnected from the bottom of the sea and from military vessels. One possible interpretation, which Franke may or may not have intended, is that there is something similarly decaying and abject about this way of life, that it is in the past and fading from memory taphonomically. One could go even further, and suggest that this iconic connection belies an indexical, causal relationship that is generally hidden from view: that everyday Austrian life was somehow made possible by an unspoken violence, perhaps of American global hegemony.

In this reading, the *Vandenberg* exhibit can be compared, for instance, to James Rosenquist's instalment painting *F-111*, portraying a US Air Force fighter-bomber 'interrupted' by American consumer items: 'By exemplifying the relationship between an assortment of American made products and activities to the military-industrial complex, Rosenquist demonstrates the way consumerism and militarism coincide and he suggests the violence underlying these American images' (Martucci 2007: 127). Franke interrupts not only the consumption of the image (as in *F-111*), but the consumption of the art object itself. You need to work to see it, to consume something else – the experience of diving an underwater tour – and this is no easy task since it requires significant preparation and investment in diving. In Nigel Thrift's words, the *Vandenberg*, as art abject diving experience for sale, would be one of many contemporary efforts to slow things down for consumption of natural wonder, 'to foreground the background of bare life – to make it comprehensible and therefore able to be apprehended and so made more of' (2000: 49). In its relatively extreme inaccessibility, the *Vandenberg* project could be seen as a commentary, not only on the *Vandenberg* itself, on bourgeois Austrian life, but on the privilege of accessing and appreciating art, the inequality and competition that is the social precondition of the aesthetic field of art practice.

It is not only through deliberately disintegrated artworks, like Goldsworthy's or Franke's, that the usually hidden infrastructure of art preservation and repair is rendered visible. Arguably, all art evinces some connection with process and change. For Derrida, as explained by philosopher Michael Marder, there is an 'enigmatic kinship' between waste and any artwork, whether knockoff or masterpiece (quoted in Marder 2009: 129). Every artwork's fall into entropic disrepair, as paper, paint, clay gradually dissolve and merge with their surroundings, is an inevitability that is as much a part of artistic practice as is the eventual death of the artist. Art restorers know this well (see Spelman 2002: 24). But, as Marder is quick to point out, the idea that, 'in such a return, the prior unity of organic nature is restored is as absurd a proposition as the claim that the recycling of paper regenerates the very cut tree from which it was produced' (2009: 129). The deformation of art is a creative event, in other words, not a passive loss. It would be similarly absurd to interpret the sinking of the *Vandenberg* as a restorative activity that returns this ship to a prior unity from which it was rendered separate. Among other things, such an interpretation would absolve the US military for deliberately producing and sinking so many (at least potentially) toxic objects. The ship is an emergent event, in Marder's sense, not a foregone conclusion but a process and promise. As the setting for Franke's artwork, the *Vandenberg* is already developing what Harman calls allure, already creating new and unfinished relations between beings, organic and inorganic. These entanglements cannot exhaust the *Vandenberg* as art abject, since there are aspects of it that are of no account to the water, the coral, the fish, the divers and so on. Arguably, Franke is just one more added agent here and not necessarily the most aesthetically attuned.

Alfred Gell's approach to art helps remind any analyst to attend to the many ways that humans and non-humans do things with art objects, including using them as indices to help appreciate and recognise one another's doings. Where the existential phenomenology of Julia Kristeva and Hannah Arendt is additionally helpful, I would argue, is as a reminder that there are many ways to regard and dismiss the doings of others as more or less noteworthy. It is for this reason that the person who dusts a priceless portrait or restores it is never as prominent a figure, never as indexically rich an agent, as the artist who painted it or the owner who displays it proudly, even though all might be causally tied to the art object's storied career. The art abject is, for this reason, a testimony to the agency of these doings, of humble acts of repair and maintenance, precisely because it calls attention to their absence. Better said, in the case of the *Vandenberg* at least, it calls attention to the replacement of restorative acts by the allusive aesthetics of coral collaborators.

Joshua O. Reno is Associate Professor in Anthropology at Binghamton University.

Notes

1. On the complicated relationship between the Italian Futurist movement and the First World War, see Daly (2016).
2. Blackbeard and other infamous pirates used the Keys as a base of operations, which initially attracted the relatively new American Navy (originally financed to battle 'Algerian corsairs') to occupy the Keys. Once Caribbean pirates were rooted out, Conchs continued to exploit shipwrecks that littered the ruin-scape, many from the Spanish fleet. Before lighthouses were built in the early nineteenth century, shipwrecks were very common and the primary source of revenue.
3. On the timeline and debate surrounding the disposal of American ships, see Puthucherril (2010). On the global market in recycled materials and the Basel Convention in general, see Gregson and Crang (2015); in terms of e-waste, see Lepawsky and McNabb (2011) and Lepawsky (2015).
4. Thanks to Hunter Claypatch for drawing my attention to the work of Goldsworthy. For more on Goldsworthy's approach, see Matless and Revill (1995).
5. In this respect, Kristeva resembles Mary Douglas (1966), whom she draws upon and who also identifies religious practice as a method for purifying the unspeakable and unthinkable.
6. Comparing Harman's idea of allusion and Gell's central notion of indexicality is potentially fruitful, but I do not have space to do so here. Suffice to say that allusion could be seen as a kind of abduction, or a hypothesis about the qualities and relations of an object we encounter. The difference is that, for Harman, there is a central failure or gap that always interferes in any process of interpreting or engaging with objects; every object is simultaneously abject.
7. I am leaving out considerations of the benefactors of artwork, for instance the rich or royalty who seek to be immortalised through depiction. On the association between kingship and immortality, see Graeber and Sahlins (2017).

References

Arendt, Hannah. 1958. *The Human Condition*. Chicago: University of Chicago.

Born, Georgina. 2005. 'On Musical Mediation: Ontology, Technology and Creativity', *Twentieth-Century Music* 2(1): 7–36.

Burström, Mats, Håkan Karlsson and Anders Gustafsson. 2012. *World Crisis in Ruin: The Archaeology of the Former Soviet Nuclear Missile Sites in Cuba*. Gothenburg: Bricoleur Press.

Chua, Liana, and Mark Elliott. 2013. 'Introduction: Adventures in the Art Nexus', in L. Chua and M. Elliott (eds), *Distributed Objects: Meaning and Mattering after Alfred Gell*. New York: Berghahn Books, pp. 1–24.

Daly, Selena. 2016. *Italian Futurism and the First World War*. Toronto: University of Toronto Press.

Douglas, Mary. 1966. *Purity and Danger*. New York: Routledge.
Franke, Andreas. 2013. 'The Sinking World', *Ecotone* 9(1): 96–112.
Gell, Alfred. 1998. *Art and Agency: An Anthropological Theory*. New York: Clarendon Press.
———. 1999. *The Art of Anthropology: Essays and Diagrams*. London: The Athlone Press.
Goldsworthy, Andy. 2000. *Time*. New York: Harry N. Abrams.
Graeber, David, and Marshall Sahlins. 2017. *On Kings*. Chicago: HAU Books.
Gregson, Nicky, and Mike Crang. 2015. 'From Waste to Resource: The Trade in Wastes and Global Recycling Economies', *Annual Review of Environment and Resources* 40: 151–76.
Gustafsson, Anders, Javier Iglesias Camargo, Håkan Karlsson and Gloria M. Miranda González. 2017. 'Material Life Histories of the Missile Crisis (1962): Cuban Examples of a Soviet Nuclear Missile Hangar and US Marston Mats', *Journal of Contemporary Archaeology* 4(1): 39–58.
Harman, Graham. 2007. 'Aesthetics as First Philosophy: Levinas and the Non-Human', *Naked Punch* 9: 21–30. Retrieved 7 April 2018 from http://dar.aucegypt.edu/bitstream/handle/10526/3073/AetheticsFirstPhilosophy.pdf?sequence=1.
Hayward, Eva. 2010. 'Fingereyes: Impressions of Cup Corals', *Cultural Anthropology* 25(4): 577–99.
Helmreich, Stefan. 2016. *Sounding the Limits of Life: Essays in the Anthropology of Biology and Beyond*. Princeton, NJ: Princeton University Press.
Hemingway, E. 1937. *To Have and Have Not*. New York: Charles Scribner's Sons.
Kristeva, Julia. 1982. *Powers of Horror: An Essay on Abjection*. New York: Columbia University Press.
———. 1999. *Hannah Arendt*. New York: Columbia University Press.
Laviolette, Patrick. 2006. 'Ships of Relations: Navigating through Local Cornish Maritime Art', *International Journal of Heritage Studies* 12(1): 69–92.
Lepawsky, Josh. 2015. 'The Changing Geography of Global Trade in Electronic Discards: Time to Rethink the E-Waste Problem', *The Geographical Journal* 181(2): 147–59.
Lepawsky, Josh, and Chris McNabb. 2011. 'Mapping International Flows of Electronic Waste', *The Canadian Geographer* 54(2): 177–95.
Marder, Michael. 2009. *The Event of the Thing: Derrida's Post-Deconstructive Realism*. Toronto: University of Toronto Press.
Martucci, Elise A. 2007. *The Environmental Unconscious in the Fiction of Don DeLillo*. New York: Routledge.
Matless, David, and George Revill. 1995. 'A Solo Ecology: The Erratic Art of Andy Goldsworthy', *Ecumene* 2(4): 423–48.
Myers, Fred. 2001. 'Social Agency and the Cultural Value(s) of the Art Object', *Journal of Material Culture* 9(2): 205–13.
Puthucherril, Tony George. 2010. *From Shipbreaking to Sustainable Ship Recycling: Evolution of a Legal Regime*. Leiden: Martinus Nijhoff Publishers.
Self, Colby. 2011. *Dishonorable Disposal: The Case Against Dumping U.S. Naval Vessels at Sea*. Seattle, WA: Basel Action Network.
Smith, Anne-Marie. 1998. *Julia Kristeva: Speaking the Unspeakable*. London: Pluto Press.

Spelman, Elizabeth. 2002. *Repair: The Impulse to Restore in a Fragile World.* Boston, MA: Beacon Press.

Thrift, Nigel. 2000. 'Still Life in Nearly Present Time: The Object of Nature', *Body and Society* 6(3–4): 34–57.

Tsing, Anna. 2015. *The Mushroom at the End of the World: On the Possibility of Life in Capitalist Ruins.* Princeton, NJ: Princeton University Press.

SNAPSHOT 2

Beyond the Sparkle Zones

Kathleen Stewart

Last summer, in my turbo-engine Hyundai that's prone to explosive road dramas, I drove across country listening to NPR's podcast, *S-Town*. An hour into the drive, the landscape suddenly dropped out of the sparkle zone of Austin into a surprise desolation. The bubble of economic boom, population pouring in, architectural pop, foodie yoga paradise, candy bar delivery in the middle of the night, and all of that, stopped as abruptly as the edge of the simulated world in *The Truman Show* (1998). Or, to go much further back in American pop culture, it was like stepping behind the curtain in *the Wizard of Oz*'s (1939) Emerald City.

I thought, when did *this* happen? *This* new hard shift, different from and beyond the old fakery of the lure from which you returned home, or the early shock of the simulacra-felted world out of which you might awake with effort and attention. *This thing* now where the clichés of a downturn got surreally real and were written onto matter as if the possibility of image itself had failed, as if the promise of self-propelled buoyant mood had gone slack. Ruined strip malls, vast empty parking lots, even the gas station gone, and way down at the end, where you can barely see it, a failing Chinese restaurant. *This* racially mixed no-man's land extending to the horizon with a dull thud. Places barely connected to the sparkling territories of ongoing, high-speed, harsh development. Places in sad decomposition only ever so slightly still shored up by the way things were just a little while ago, maybe the habit of a certain standing that gave you a national link. Places that might have the utopia of a church that worked, or where people might have the booster-club thought that their town was right and in the middle – not too much of anything, not too little, not too close to the city, not too far. Places that had a single gesture at middle-class feminine pomp in an after-store selling ice cream, Crabtree & Evelyn lotion and cloth shoulder bags. Places where the only speciality coffee shop was called something like 'Espresso Yourself'.

Of course, the drama of country and city, of upsurge and its decay, is not exactly new; I remember towns that had the multipurpose fancy store with deli foods, greetings cards and arty earrings from decades ago. Certainly, within all towns, within all lives, things happen that drag and propel. But now, driving through it, the crazy contrast between pop and decomp seemed like a brokenness, as if the poles were too close, too easily converging on the notes of a brutal dirge. Maybe just because now, all of a sudden, the world is an ecological shitstorm and everything seems to have come loose from its moorings. Now that the landscape seems to be a testimony to widespread leakage, now that the pinched faces and the impatience with the possibility of otherness and otherwise are an almost autonomic response to the way money, power and industry now work, when they work at all, all of it a wound that stinks, a raw aggression. Now that all the longstanding national sacrifice zones cordoned off to extract oily combustibles, rock and trees have leaked everywhere and lodged in bodies as cancer or asthma. Now that the detritus of once-was generative machineries of countless forms of living languishes all around. What comes through in *this* place, *this* now, *this thing*, is the atmospheric residue of money's unclaimed voraciousness, the floating affects of the super-hardened, now caste-like, vortex of race, class and gender, the explosive moments and ordinary non-events of rampant mental illness and drugs in all quarters, with all the dreams corralled into the puny remainder of hope, now, for just a moment of safety in private, or the dream of just drifting.

Now the sparkle zones are a machinery of speeds, intensities and tones – a sparking, spitting experiment surging towards a finished aesthetic and the zones of desolation have their own frictions, an unrest, matter and meaning clumping and sheering off, tracks laid to move with less labour of living or left standing, the accidental traces of whatever. Even passing through, you can catch the glimpse of trajectories that dug in or took off in flights chasing possibilities. What you're seeing is the fractal this and that of the business of living through a present splitting up and reeling, detouring into the emergent and skidding back into what might have been solid once for a little while.

The Econolodge in Dickson, Tennessee is so plastered in Christianity that they gave me a replacement room key without even asking my name. Because they were being Christian, meaning, in this case, because I have a white smile, because I'm a woman of a harmless age, because I was paying attention to them, because matter aligns with idea in a recognisable body.

And because the Bible tracts on display right next to the check-in desk (but not quite touching) announced the felt knowledge that 'freedom of religion' in this country is code for the establishment of a foundational state religion.[1] The tracts had been run off on whatever the equivalent of a mimeograph machine is now; they were all low-brow business, like the fliers the next rack over for Busy Bee Traders, Johnny Cash's Museum and Hideaway Farm, and the Las Fajitas menu.

Coming into Pigeon Forge the next day, the billboards[2] suddenly became as graphic as fresh kill and there were huge white crosses everywhere; we were in the land of stark choices between being a Christian or being a sinner. Three rangy, sinewy young guys came into the convenience store in homemade tats and bandanas, high on a hard day's work in the heat, talking too loud, 'Ya, me and Jake have to go to *probation* tomorrow'. Their eyes cut around to see their audience. The crew boss made an avuncular show of telling me how to get out of my parking spot because they had me blocked in.

The African-American utopian hotel in Texarkana is a high-efficiency comfort zone, open smiles, staff gathering in clusters to get the stories of the road. They help us find Ariana's grandmother's mood ring when she loses it near the pool. The lobby's full of truck drivers waiting on their trucks; one's been staying there for three weeks. They speculate about an exhaust manifold, a weak seal, anything's possible. They're gingerly with each other but puffed up too, things could go bad, they have kinds of expertise so specific they signal them in shorthand. It's not sympathy they want; I don't know *what* it is though.

In the Comfort Inn, a mass of people, not ageing well. Fox News is on in the breakfast room like that's nothing and there's automatic chatter at contact. Not deep, not an opening, just the kind of talk of people noticing that they are *in it* together. The staff member in charge of sugar-carb breakfast tells a little girl she can't be barefoot in there, then tells the mother she'll have to go get shoes for the kids. Someone says I told you, not a word from the pissed-off mother. Even families here are on their own, not funded institutions like on parents' weekend at the Dartmouth Hotel. Five big bikers are in our elevator. 'How's your day?' they ask. They've got something to say. 'Today was beautiful', they say, 'but yesterday flooded big time'. 'It *did*?'

A father coming out of the pricey aquarium asks his teenage son, 'How did you like *that*?' 'It was sort of good.' 'Well how about if I sort of slap you?'

Beyond the sparkle zones there's plenty going on, a circuit of reactions caving in on itself claustrophobically, a series of gestures floating by, roosting, splintering off.

Kathleen Stewart is Professor in the Department of Anthropology at the University of Texas at Austin.

Notes

1. Personal communication with Susan Harding (see Harding 2001).
2. See also the film *Three Billboards Outside Ebbing*, Missouri (Fox Searchlight Pictures, 2017).

References

Fleming, Victor et al. (dir.). 1939. *The Wizard of Oz*. Hollywood, CA: Metro-Goldwyn-Mayer.

Harding, Susan. 2001. *The Book of Jerry Falwell: Fundamentalist Language and Politics*. Princeton, NJ: Princeton University Press.

S-Town. 2017. Podcast from *Serial and This American Life*. Hosted by Brian Reed.

Weir, Peter (dir.). 1998. *The Truman Show*. Hollywood, CA: Scott Rudin Productions, Paramount Pictures.

CHAPTER 2

'Till Death Do Us Part'

The Making of Home through Holding on to Objects

TOMÁS ERRÁZURIZ

Things, Time and Love

Going through some old family albums, I stopped at some photographs of my father's older sister's wedding in 1967. As was usual at that time, after the religious ceremony in the church, the celebration took place in the house of the bride's parents (my grandparents). The bride and groom posed with their close family and friends in the public areas of the house. While not the objective of the photographer, my attention and interest were diverted to the context that surrounded those who posed. What was left between and around the figures was disconcerting. The living room, the dining room, the main hall, the library, the bar and the terrace were practically the same as they are today. Every single piece of furniture, including curtains, rugs, sofas, chairs and so on, still exists in the house, and most of them remain in the same room and in the exact same place. More than fifty years have passed since the wedding and the only difference seems to be that I am used to seeing the place in colours and not in the grey tones shown in the photographs.

This first discovery led me to analyse in detail the furniture and objects that were visible in each room. My surprise was greater when I realised that not only did objects persist in time and space, but also their material conditions did not seem to have changed much. Many of the tapestries and carpets, surfaces that usually suffer great wear, remained unchanged, as if they had not been used in a half-century. Unlike the historical distance alluded to by Roland Barthes (1981) when he describes his non-existence in his mother's dresses in an old photograph, in the images described above, objects function as bridges between different generations.

After noticing that this obduracy of things was present in different ways in most of the house, my attention was drawn to how different the trajectories of objects and materials in my grandmother's house are when comparing them to these same trajectories in my own house. Not only have I moved several times, but I also seem to have lost, thrown away or given away many of the things I used to have only a few years ago. My house is constantly and rapidly changing. Most things have short lives at home, and when something arrives I rarely expect it to last for good. My impression is that things have been wearing out in another way, existing in different temporal regimes, if not cosmologies.

But what is the point of comparing? Today, consumption practices have dramatically shortened the path from new to obsolescence, and multiplied the number of objects passing through our houses. Disposal and replacement are common practices through which we usually understand the process of homemaking (Gregson 2007). Here I argue, however, that holding onto old domestic objects has become a sort of subaltern practice, rather defensive among groups and territories remote from capitalism (Errázuriz 2019).

The abysmal difference in the fate of objects in both houses, mine and my grandma's, is related to a series of given conditions. Among these we can mention the size of her house for today's parameters (which allows the accumulation of 'stuff'); the possibility of having only one house for a lifetime; the better quality of things and their materials; an economic stability that guarantees the maintenance of living conditions over time; a certain disconnection from networks of capital; and a strong family identity that prevents changes in response to new styles and changes in habits.

However, not all is difference. There is one last condition that is vital to understanding why things last, one condition that can be reached eventually by anybody at home. This is the possibility and willingness to dedicate time to the house and its things. Returning to the photos of the wedding, and specifically the state in which carpets, tapestries and furniture have been preserved, it is evident that for such persistence to occur, the investment of time and work was necessary. The long life of things also depends on a relationship, a kind of contract of duties and rights between two entities, commonly understood as a person and a thing. Now, what is this relationship based on?

My grandmother, born in 1922, has lived in the same house since the late 1940s, after she married my grandfather. Received as an inheritance from her parents, the three-storey house is located in what used to be an exclusive residential area of downtown Santiago. Since her husband passed away in 1989, her sons and daughter have worried about how the neighbourhood was changing and have done everything possible to move her to an apartment closer to where they live. She always responds that the only way in which she will leave the house will be in a coffin. At some point, they stopped insisting and assumed that she would stay there. So, the question is this: how can someone be so attached to a house to the point of not being able to imagine life without it? I believe the answer in my grandmother's case is love. Of course, I am not the first to mention that we should consider love when trying to understand our relationship with objects.

The Search for Enduring Love

In the middle of the 1990s, the Dutch foundation 'Eternally Yours' was founded with the purpose of analysing the problem of the durability of products in a context of environmental crisis. The diagnosis that motivates this group is the absolute lack of what they call a '"psychological life span": the time products are able to be perceived and used as worthy objects' (Van Hinte 1997: 19). The cover and the pages of their book work as a manifesto of the foundation, showing images of couples embracing and kissing each other. The analogy is clear: the durability of things depends on our relationship with them, having as an ideal those loving relationships that we could have with someone else. One of the articles included in the book asks, 'What kinds of things would we love so much, that we would want to keep them, eternally?' While the object may vary from person to person, the specific relationship we generate with it is of particular interest. It is suggested, in this regard, that perhaps if we learned to love, protect and care for our possessions, then we would do everything possible to keep them by our side as long as possible (Koskijoki 1997).

Perhaps where the importance of a person's emotional ties with an object have been more clearly pointed out is in the case of collectors. The contemplation and physical handling of the pieces of a collection is a habitual experience among collectors and a cause for satisfaction. Some people even refer to collectors as eccentric because they treat their objects as if they were part of their family (Danet and Katriel 1994). The love of the collector towards his objects, which translates into appreciation and appropriation, prevents him from buying in un-thought and un-loved ways (Koskijoki 1997).

From another perspective (and although the goal is not to understand the emotions that unite people and objects), in *Aramis, or the Love of Tech-*

nology, Bruno Latour (1996) equates our bond with technology to a loving relationship. The dream of materialising Aramis (an automated train system that promised to transform public transportation in Paris) and all of the complex network that sustains it endures as different parties declare their love for it. On the other hand, the epilogue, 'Aramis unloved', refers to the breakdown, incomprehension and oblivion that, at the end, leads to replacement. 'No, no, you didn't love me. You loved me as an idea. You loved me as long as I was vague' (Latour 1996: 294). The last words of Aramis, charged with the spite of the unloved one, not only question the barriers between what has traditionally been understood as human and nonhuman, but suggest that more important than these categories and their differences are the relationships that are forged between different entities.

The possibility of uniting subjects and their objects through love is analysed by Jonathan Chapman (2005). Inspired by the Freudian idea that the person who falls in love perceives that the limits with his beloved vanish, forming a single unit, Chapman believes that our eagerness to consume and surround ourselves with meaningful things has a similar origin. This author suggests that strong feelings of empathy, and even love, arise towards those objects that have accumulated healthy narratives over time. However, he warns that today this type of attachment is less and less habitual, as the love relationship is reduced to what the author calls 'the honeymoon period'. Then, the discrepancies between the real and the imagined of the object generate a break in the relationship. Mirroring this idea, Jean Baudrillard stated some years earlier that the 'period of newness is, in a sense, the sublime period of the object and may, in certain cases, attain the intensity, if not the quality, of the emotion of love' (2012: 114). He compares this experience to the way a child relates to his objects and toys.

Tim Cooper (2010), expert in sustainable design, similarly argues that consumers are in great part responsible for overcoming this first break, guaranteeing a healthy accumulation of narratives. Purchasing choices, the care, frequency and intensity with which products are used, and decisions regarding repair, reuse or disposal can all determine life-span and longevity. The clearest proof that these habits are becoming less common is the number of products that are thrown away even though they remain functional (Cooper and Mayers 2000).

Paradoxically, although several authors point to the importance of love – or of the feelings we experience towards the material world that surrounds us – as fundamental to move towards a more sustainable environment, this approach has not received much attention. In part, this is due to the lack of a theoretical framework and methodological strategies that allow transformation of this 'loving' experience into a research variable. The lack of a theoretical discussion and definitions is present in most of the literature reviewed. This is crucial if we consider that in English, the meaning of the word love covers a wide semantic spectrum, ranging from liking something to profound loving, from passion and charm to security and certainty, from commitment to excitement, and so on. One way to move forward in this understanding is to leave, for a moment, the world of objects and analyse some of the main theories of love that have been raised by scholars, especially social psychologists, since the 1960s. Such theoretical frameworks may offer clues to analyse how we relate to objects.

The Social Psychology of Love

One early theory of love was the 'mere-exposure effect'. Developed by Robert Zajonc (1968), the theory argues that there is a tendency to like people to whom we are exposed more frequently, those who are familiar to us. In other words, there is a propensity for interpersonal attraction when there is physical proximity. A few years later, Zick Rubin (1973) was the first to develop an instrument to measure love empirically, establishing scales of intensity that allowed him to distinguish between liking and loving. While liking can lead to appreciation, admiration and desire to be with another, loving is a much more intense, deep feeling and involves a strong desire for physical intimacy and contact with the other. The variables that, in his opinion, make up romantic love are: (1) attachment or need to receive care, approval and physical contact; (2) caring and appreciation for the needs of the other; (3) intimacy, understood as the possibility of sharing thoughts, wishes and feelings with another person.

Overcoming the distinction between liking and loving, John Lee (1973) proposes that there are different types of love and these can be understood as a colour wheel, with primary, secondary and tertiary classifications. Making use of Greco-Latin terms associated with love, he has established several categories. *Eros* describes passionate, physical, sensual and intense love; *ludus* distinguishes a type of love based on games and excitement; *storge* is a form of love that slowly emerges over time and privileges stability and friendship; *pragma* is based on practical considerations and convenience; *mania* arises from the mixture between *ludus* and *eros* and implies obsession, dependence, jealousy and instability; and *agape* refers to a kind of disinterested love that arises through altruism and compassion.

Drawing upon these possible combinations of variables, Robert Sternberg (2004) suggests that intimacy, passion and commitment are the three components of love. As in the colour wheel theory, these three components are combined in different ways to give rise to new types of love. Consequently, Sternberg suggests that 'romantic love' is based primarily on intimacy and passion and not on commitment, and is common among younger groups. 'Companionate love' involves intimacy and commitment, without passion, being habitual among close friends and sometimes in couples who have been together for many years. Others, like 'infatuated love', imply only passion; 'empty love' is only commitment, without intimacy or passion; and finally, 'fatuous love' is passion and commitment, without intimacy.

In an attempt to change the focus, from what love is to why we stay in relationships, Caryl Rusbult (1980) has done profound organisational research on 'commitment'. She has suggested that our ability to maintain a relationship over time with another person depends on three factors: (1) how much has been invested in the relationship (what has been sacrificed and what are the costs to end the relationship); (2) how much is obtained from the relationship; and (3) if there are any attractive alternatives. With a clear influence of economic theory, Rusbult proposed an understanding of commitment as the result of investment plus rewards, minus attractive alternatives.

We cannot finish this brief account without considering the differentiation that Elaine Hatfield has made between two forms of love: compassionate and passionate. While the first is characterised by being based on mutual respect, attachment, affection and trust, and implies a relationship of respect and mutual understanding, the second is distinguished by being sustained in intense emotions, sexual attraction, anxiety and affection. Unlike compassionate love, the passionate sort is transitory and fades with the passage of time, although it can eventually lead to developing the compassionate kind (see Hatfield and Rapson 1993).

Objects as Expression of Love

Although there are many contemporary authors who have contributed to theoretical discussions about the concept of love, it is rare to find references to relationships other than among humans. So, let us return to my grandmother's house. If we believe that love can be the answer to why someone can become so attached to her house and cannot imagine life without it, how can these theories contribute to understanding this particular relationship?

From the different readings that social psychology has done on the concept of love, recently reviewed, there are several elements to highlight in order to think about the relationship with non-human environments. In the first place, it is common to recognise the different intensities through which love can manifest itself. This includes not only the difference between loving and liking, but also the variations in each category according to the weight of the variables that define them. Second, there is a certain coincidence in the importance of closeness, physical contact and intimacy as factors whose relevance is transversal to different types of love. Third, a kind of split between two forms is recognised. On one hand, there are certain manifestations that rest mainly on physical attraction, sexual desire, play and passion (see: *eros/ludus/mania*, passionate love, romantic love, infatuated love). On the other, there are other forms that are based on affection, attachment, empathy, compassion, caring for others and so on (see: compassionate love, companionate love, *storge/agape/pragma*, exposure effect, commitment equation).

Not only is there clarity regarding the break between these two forms of love, but there is also consistency among most authors who consider that they usually do not occur simultaneously. While the first form of love could be labelled as more unstable in terms of time, space and actors involved, the second tends to stability and permanence. The idea of an intense, fleeting and unstable love is probably similar to what authors such as Baudrillard (2012) or Chapman (2005) refer to when alluding to the strong attraction that a desired appearance (usually new and bright) can arouse, as well as the short honeymoon that usually follows this connection. The pre-eminence of appearance and the lack of significant narratives foretell the quick disenchantment and break in the relationship. The ideas of Rusbult (1980) are especially clarifying to interpret these breaks between people and objects. The inability to persist in the relationship with objects would be directly related to the low costs of ending the relationship, the decreasing retribution by objects, and the existence of a large number of more attractive alternatives.

Helga Dittmar (2008), who investigates the relationship between consumer culture, identity and well-being, argues that the act of impulsive consumption, increasingly common in contemporary societies, represents a scenario where passion takes over our capacity for deliberation. Studies on impulsive buyers show that 80 per cent of them later discover those negative aspects of what they have bought, whereas 55 per cent regret having acquired it in the first place (Rook 1987; Dittmar 2001). In the popular jargon on love relationships, these meetings could be understood as a 'one night stand', or as the literal meaning of the phrase 'touch and go', sometimes used to refer to a sneaky love encounter whose only motor is the sexual pleasure of physical contact.

Without a doubt, the relationship that my grandmother has established with her objects is far from any 'passionate love' model. There is little room for the transitory or untimely wishes in a material world whose relevance is confirmed daily through a strict domestic routine. Through the repetition of this routine, the object is recognised and respected. It is taken care of and its needs are met, in such a way that the relationship persists, so that both can continue together. There is a constant investment of time and resources, and those who make that investment are later rewarded with confidence and security. Unlike the short and fragmented times of the 'one night stand', in my grandmother's house, objects seem to accompany the rhythms of those living in the house, be a part of the different life cycles, and share the process of ageing and death.

Complementary to the importance of time as a determining factor in the relationship with the domestic material world, Daniel Miller's approach to the concept of 'stuff' suggests another entry of interest. By stating that the best way to understand our humanity is by paying attention to our materiality, Miller (2010) challenges the relationship between subject and object, person and thing, animate and inanimate. Once the limits have blurred and the focus rests on everyday practices, a dialectic is proposed between objects and subjects of devotion or love, where each constitutes and affects the other. The object is not only a manifestation of social relations, but also has the capacity to generate social values that affect people. Consumption and its processes of appropriation (the purchase, time of possession, and use) would favour the inalienability of objects, which, in turn, is directly linked to the construction of individual and/or collective identities. Miller (1998) starts from the idea that if people and relationships are the main means through which we get a sense of transcendence, any object in which these relationships can be expressed can become an object of devotion or love.

A True Love Story

How can we analyse time in a relationship? If the relationship that my grandmother has established with her things can be understood as a long love story based on commitment, recognition and the passage of time, it is essential to attend to the trajectory of this relationship in order to identify practices and milestones through which it has been built and consolidated. As in any romantic relationship between a couple that has been together for a long time, there are memorable moments or milestones that define the relationship. Such moments (i.e. when they met, when they moved in together, when they bought their own place, the arrival of a son or daughter, the illness or death of someone close) encapsulate significant experiences that not only trace a sort of navigation chart of the relationship, but also provide an occasion for evaluation and re-signification. Besides these memorable moments, there is the day-to-day, the small gestures, attitudes and affection, which many refer to as fundamental for the persistence of a relationship over time.

Which are these moments, both the memorable and small gestures of everyday life, that allow my grandmother to establish lasting bonds with her material environment? The first encounter is marked by the *arrival* of objects or the first memories that a person has of those things that inhabited a place before she arrived. The day-to-day will depend largely on the systematic repetition of a set of actions that ensure the proper *use, care and maintenance* of an object. But care is not a guarantee of stability and permanence. Change, and therefore crisis, is inherent in matter and in human relationships and, therefore, is inevitable. Faced with this destiny, the moment of *repair*, as the main response, implies a re-evaluation and re-signification. *Storing* the object is also a possibility that can determine the relationship between two entities. Objects' isolation from everyday life is a kind of pause, a distancing without breaking, with all the risks that this can entail (sometimes even an end and a forgetting). Finally, the *leaving* of the object, which may be relocated to another house or place, represents different forms of closure.

In order to better understand the importance of these moments for the construction of lasting and significant love relationships, the pages that follow are an invitation to delve into the most intimate and mundane aspects of the history of a house, its things, and those who inhabit it. With no interest in transforming this case study into a model, this journey seeks to reflect on certain ways of relating to our domestic things that are less and less common in contemporary societies.

Arrival

So how did this love story begin? What was that first encounter like – the excitement and expectations? Unlike the apartment where I live, very few things have been bought in my grandmother's house. Instead most were received as gifts, exchanged, inherited or manufactured. The global industry of goods, advertisement and the mysterious supply chain only appears in some isolated artefacts of the house. On the other hand, the vast majority of things have left visible traces of their journeys undertaken to reach the house. They come from her parents, grandparents or siblings; they were made at home, or they were wedding gifts. Or they were continually reproduced, shared and 'organically' transferred, as we witness with most of the plants in the house.

Unlike buying something at Ikea or at a supermarket, the things in her house come from different places and there is a particular history linked to them. Therefore, the value given to them does not reside exclusively in the object and its functional or symbolic qualities. Rather, it is often associated with a previous history, to other people and/or past lives. As Michael Mc-

Coy states, 'Especially enduring are those things that belonged to or were given to us by a loved one or a friend. Enduring objects of this kind possess the special condition of having been touched or chosen by someone close to you. A sense of their presence is triggered' (1997: 192).

If we had domestic photos of my paternal great-grandparents and their parents, we would recognise several items of furniture that are present today in my grandmother's house. Paintings, vases, pendulum clocks, cabinets, armchairs, tableware, chairs and rugs are not only household objects; they constitute a significant part of a family's heritage, things that store over a century of history. Both economic and symbolic value here are evident. The bed on which my grandmother sleeps today was the same bed on which her father died more than sixty years ago. The big painting that hangs in the living room is the same one that hung in the house of my great-great-grandfather. Having belonged to an elite that for several generations has remained in the same city allows, in part, for this persistence and identity construction through things. The houses deteriorate, and in a seismic country like Chile, they usually fall. Nevertheless, many things are kept in the family, moving and persisting through kinship connections, acquiring status as heirlooms. In the logic of the 'gift economy' or the inalienable goods, the transfer of these objects between the members of a family and from generation to generation implies that, along with the gift itself, something of the person who had the object before is passed on to those who receive it. The result is that the objects that are received in this way always maintain links with other places and known people (Mauss 1954).

Although lower life expectancies anticipated the time at which a family could receive an inheritance, the transfer of goods occurred many times while family members were still living. This could be the natural condition that occurred between different generations sharing spacious houses or the transfer of goods as wedding gifts. Weddings are probably the foundational moment for that long-lasting relationship between a house and the dwellers. The love relationship that my grandmother maintains today with her house goes back to the loving commitment that in 1945 she made with my grandfather when they got married.

Furniture not inherited or received as gifts was bought by my grandfather at auctions or from well-known furniture makers. In the case of the latter, it was common that they were fabricated only after being ordered. Consequently, the time before delivery was long enough to generate great expectations among the members of the household. On the other hand, the simplest furniture, that in which the functional value predominated over the symbolic, was mostly made by household members or by a carpenter well known to the family for many years, who provided all kinds of wood services needed in the house.

In a place where things seem to last forever and replacement is rare, arrivals may become an important event – something long expected that the family then remembers over time. This is even the case for many home appliances. Their arrival mobilises the family. Something anticipated, which usually comes to replace another home appliance that may have been in use for twenty or thirty years. My father remembers with great clarity the arrival of the Westinghouse refrigerator in the late 1960s. It was first selected by catalogue and then ordered from the United States. Several months passed before the refrigerator reached the port of Valparaíso, was transported to Santiago, and finally arrived at my grandmother's house. It would be another thirty-five years before this device was finally discarded as a refrigerator and replaced with a new one.

Care and Maintenance

The apparent inalterability of things – which can be deduced from the comparison between photos of my grandmother's house fifty years ago and the same house today – is not a phenomenon that is clear-cut and easy to define. The house and the things that are contained within it are far from existing as stable matter, unaffected by the forces of the environment. They are, instead, matter in evolution, objects of becoming, artefacts with a physical life that entail and make possible a set of practices (Gregson, Metcalfe and Crewe 2009). As Tim Edensor (2016) explains in the case of buildings, the capacities and properties of matter are permanently altered by non-human and human agents. In response to these processes, strategies for the stabilisation of matter, commonly known as maintenance and repair, arise. Maintenance practices refer to a need for stabilising not only the physical appearance of objects, but the human relationship with them as well. In this sense, appearances may vary, but function and meaning are maintained, keeping an intrinsic value that will certainly change along with maintenance practices over time. Care, on the other hand, although like maintenance initiatives also recognises instability and change as the basis of social and material life, does not necessarily seek stabilisation. Annemarie Mol (2008) refers to the logic or rationale of care, as a shared work in which a set of local, specific practices – and in which bodies are actively involved – take place. Along with suggesting the importance of mobilising the logic of good care in other fields, Mol warns about the disadvantage of continuing to promote the moral and dis-involved judgement that characterises individual choice. Instead, her invitation is to stop planning and controlling, and invest more time in getting involved with our social and material environment from a collaborative approach.

This silent logic of good care, which is evident only in practice, is probably what has allowed for the commitment between my grandmother and her house to persist. A strong bond, which is renewed and transformed over time, arises due to the constant investment of energies in care practices over an environment that is real and not imagined. This logic contrasts without a doubt with the questioning rationality that evaluates, selects and discards, in order to achieve a more idealistic scenario to later develop. The short stays that characterise many of the objects that pass through my apartment are surely related to the importance my partner and I give to our ability to decide exactly where and how we want to live.

I have never heard my grandmother deliberate about which habits, objects or spaces lead to a correct way of living. There is no questioning involved, you just do what you have to do, based on the real environment and according to knowledge that is inherited, acquired and eventually changed during repeated daily practice. Care and maintenance are, therefore, all about commitment in action. They require periodic activities and attitudes that need to be accomplished (daily, weekly, monthly, annually), a matter of everyday interaction, generating in turn a shift of values (Martínez 2017).

The house needs and receives constant attention. Or at least this was the general rule some years ago, when my grandmother was still active. Different agents are involved in its care and maintenance. The clothes are kept with mothballs to prevent them from being infested; shoes and boots are kept in their boxes with newspaper and rags, placed so that they do not lose their shape; delicate tapestries are protected with a cover removed only on special occasions; mattresses are filled; sofa springs are straightened; furniture and ornaments are shielded from direct sunlight by curtains and shutters; wood and leather articles are moistened and polished; chair and table joints are tightened whenever they show signs of letting go; cutlery and metal items are polished in December before Christmas; wine glasses are stored separately from the rest of the dishes; everything has a place that provides certain conditions of security and access, according to its value and function; pest control is undertaken every year to keep insects and rodents away; the interior of the house is painted every eight to ten years. In other words, anything for your beloved, or whatever is necessary to keep the house in tip-top shape (or at least to keep it going).

The routine of care and maintenance generates a co-dependence between people and objects that guarantees a longer-lasting relationship based on trust and need. Sometimes it can also generate deep feelings of cohesion, attachment and even love (Chapman 2005). A set of Chinese cups, or other extremely delicate objects, pass from one generation to another, thanks to care, hence making their possession something to be proud of, a triumph of human will over chaos (Csikszentmihalyi and Rochberg-Halton 1981). Another example is when someone takes care of houseplants. Care and attention to these plants (water, light, nutrients and protection against pests) result in new leaves and flowers. In case this does not happen, the person will modify the treatment and invest more energy to reverse the situation (Chapman 2005).

Repair

Care and maintenance on a daily basis implies a recognition of an object's instability and permanent transformation. Things never look like new because they rarely are, not even when they arrive home. They have a life, a history. Wear is accepted, as long as functionality is maintained. The worn wooden floor, the opaque aluminium pot, the tablecloth with stripes and stains. As Tanizaki (1994) argues for pre-war Japanese architecture, the visibility of the passage of time on things and spaces allows those who inhabit the place to feel calm and secure. Far from the anonymity of serial production, the accumulation of a patina gives signs regarding the life history of things. The use and care are printed on the objects, forming layers of narratives. Thus, insofar as things are allowed to show the passage of time in their surfaces and mechanisms, their biographies are also visible (Kopytoff 1986; Hoskins 1998).

On top of the patina that covers the objects in my grandmother's house, the marks that repairs leave are added. When the passage of time is visible, it becomes evident that objects, at some point, fail, decompose or break. As in any relationship, it is expected that there will be breaks and restoration processes. There does not seem to be any fear of this happening among those who inhabit the house. The flawless relationship is an illusion.

This correspondence between the projected image and its physical history contrasts, without a doubt, with the desire and search for environments where the pristine and smooth appearance of the new extends unlimitedly. The disruptive condition that is currently associated with the process in which something breaks, mismatches or decomposes (Graham and Thrift 2007) loses intensity in a house where these dynamics are intrinsically incorporated into daily life. Reparation, like care and maintenance, is a never-ending activity in the routine that takes place in my grandmother's house. There is always something that needs to be fixed, and no direct link between damage and disposing.

Contrary to the general trend of disposal and replacement (Cooper 2010), repair is usually the only possible solution in my grandmother's house. Purchasing an alternative product could only occur after several failed attempts and only if it is absolutely necessary. These attempts are undertaken first by people who live or work daily in the home. The house has a special room for manual work, where tools are stored and some of the repair work is carried out. This room also houses all those parts and materials that may eventually be useful for future repair challenges. Repairing is artisanal work in which a repertoire of gestures, emotional commitment and sensual knowledge appear, all under a logic other than the repetition and systematisation that distinguishes industrial productive processes (Dant 2010). Among those who participate in this process – generally the men of the family – there is a positive perception of manual labour and a pride in their ability to solve a problem and restore the function of something. When the task goes beyond the capabilities of the home, there is always a network of people specialised in fixing different objects (toilets, electrical appliances, machines, clothes, the house itself). These are people well known to my grandmother and they periodically visit her.

The arrangements that are made in this house could not be classified in either of the two categories identified by Gregson, Metcalfe and Crewe (2009). The restoration of the object is not sought to return it to a pristine state that leads to its preservation and increase of value. Nor are they quick, temporary and visible repairs that do not require greater knowledge or skill and that end up devaluing the object. The reparation taking place in my grandmother's house, rather than being a means for favouring the devaluation or revaluation, works as a strategy for the conservation of value. And above all, it works to affirm the function and place that the object receives in the house. There is little interest if this repair increases or decreases its potential commercial value. Repair is undertaken, first, because in the logic of care, it is what has to be done, and second, because failures, breaks and damage are understood as an inherent part of the relationship with a good. In this house, to consume is also to repair.

Storage

In the closets of the sewing room, located on the third floor, all the fur coats that my grandmother used to wear are gathered together. One can also find party costumes and hats. In the pantry, there are suitcases, trunks and boxes with different things that have not moved for decades. Downstairs in the garage, in an mezzanine built to store larger things, terrace furniture, chairs, beds and other objects that are no longer used pile up. Inside the locked cabinet under the bookshelves of the library, my grandfather used to have his carving tools, many important documents, a portable typewriter and several audio recordings on micro cassettes. In a medicine cabinet located in the main bathroom of the third floor, syringes and doses of insulin were left untouched for more than thirty years. On a shelf in the landing of the same floor, the complete collection of *Hoy* magazine – one of the few publications opposing the military regime and which arrived periodically at the house for more than twenty years – is kept.

The house contains things, and some of those things contain more things inside. In this house, to live means to store. Storage is about organising, protecting, preserving and, sometimes, forgetting. Daily, weekly, seasonal or undetermined storage. Some things never come out again. Storage occurs in every room, in unthoughtful places. Most of the things that are used in the house have a place where they are kept. Just as happens with books in a library, value, wear, frequency of use, and contents or purpose determine where things are, and to whom and when they are available.

Although my grandmother's house is full of things – and my father is afraid of the day when it will be necessary to vacate it – it is a completely different accumulation than what happens in my apartment or my friends' homes. In the latter, the tendency is for the storage spaces to be problematic areas that generate recurrent concern among those who inhabit the place. This feeling has its origin in the permanent threat of disorder that occurs due to the constant flow of new acquisitions and the always unattainable desires of a simpler, minimalist and more austere house (Boscagli 2014; Löfgren 2017). The feelings of guilt and even shame that this disorderly and unnecessary accumulation of things leads to has even led some experts to talk about 'obese houses', full of things we do not really need. Paradoxically, before cleaning or throwing out, many end up buying new things to deal with the excess of things (Fear 2008; Löfgren 2017).

The controlled flow of objects that enter and leave my grandmother's house ensures the stability of what is stored. In this sense, the approach of Shannon Mattern is interesting to consider. She presents the house and its spaces for storage as a large personal or family archive, curated by the inhabitants themselves. This author suggests that 'behind the doors, closets are also active, generative spaces where media are made, where imaginaries and anxieties are formulated, where knowledges and subjectivities are born and transformed' (2017: 2). The analogy with the archive leads us to consider stored things as sources that allow us to understand a family history and reinforce a temporal consciousness or a spatialised memory (Makovicky 2007).

Understood as a kind of material correlate of memory, storage is about keeping and not throwing away. In a certain way, the relationship with the object is paused. It is no longer there, but it is available, it is potentially present. It is like moving without breaking up. Relationships change over time and things become more or less available. Similar to what happens with memories, some things come out again and others are simply forgotten. As my grandmother ages and her activity decreases, the house gradually moves from spaces of availability to spaces of storage and memories. With time, rooms are transformed into closets and then the whole house feels like a large cellar. Although this is not the case with my grandmother, it is usual for this process to be interrupted when older people move to smaller places. This produces the reduction, selection and relocation of many of the domestic objects that have accompanied the dwellers throughout their lives (Marcoux 2001).

Leave

Getting an object to physically disappear forever, without leaving many signs, is a normal circumstance in the homes of the modern age. Once the rubbish truck takes the bags away, whatever was left will never be part of our daily environment again. It is not usual for this to happen in my grandmother's house. A quick look at the size of the rubbish dumps leads us to understand that objects that lose value and meaning follow alternative paths. The idea of waste or rubbish is usually reduced to the organic that is not consumed by the animals in the house (a dog, a parrot and a canary). It is not a possibility to dump or discard things in which so much has been invested – things that belonged to her parents, to her husband, or that may be useful sometime in the future.

On the other hand, the rules of obsolescence that generally apply to consumer goods seem not to apply. Technological obsolescence is rare when the needs of a home do not change significantly with time. Functional obsolescence may lead to repair, disassembly or the discovering of other functions (the old fridge can store groceries, the oven is a good place for pots and pans, etc.). Aesthetic obsolescence does not exist at my grandma's house.

Objects do not disappear, but they leave. The difference is relevant. Disappearance is predominantly physical, it happens from one moment to another, in an instant, and the space-time break is significant. On the other hand, leaving is a variable process that can extend in time, it can be suspended, start again, and even never be fully realised. Under this logic, disposal is not about waste, but about absence and its way of acquiring meaning.

Just as most of the objects that arrive at my grandmother's house have particular histories of their previous trajectories, those that leave or are forgotten also have a recognisable path. There are several ways in which objects decrease their availability in the home. Storing things is probably one of the most common. As previously explained, closets, shelves, cabinets, drawers and even complete rooms are spaces for suspension, transition, memory and forgetting. This is possible insofar as there is availability of space and a disposition not to let go easily. More or less available, things have different value, and this value may change over time. Apparently important heirlooms may lose their value for us. Likewise, the reverse process may occur with what we thought was not worth enough. Therefore, some things never come out again. Although they have lost all value, they remain because of inertia, forgetfulness, or simply because there are no other replacements waiting to occupy their space. Contrary to the suggestion of Kevin Hetherington (2004), it happens with some objects that, while they are physically still present, oblivion leads to semiotic absence.

Relocation is another strategy in which the objects of my grandmother's house can move away until they lose their availability. The few things that leave the house do not always make it into the rubbish. Instead, they frequently end up with other owners, for new purposes. On one hand, within the logic of care, there is an ethic and responsibility to the durability of the object that goes beyond the home itself. The transfer to new homes is sought because this relocation allows for the object's survival or an increase of its value (Gregson and Crewe 2003; Cooper 2005). Destinations and people are generally known. Some grandchild or younger family member, a worker in the house, or, eventually, some charity institution to which my grandparents were connected.

The second way in which things leave the house is when they move into the homes of close relatives who used to live in the house. Just as many of my grandmother's pieces of furniture and ornaments left other homes, over time some of her furniture left for other houses too. Far from disposal, this relocation implies that things remain tied to the house. In fact, the proof is that they eventually come back. This movement of things between households of the same family is, in a certain way, a strategy of preservation of the patrimony and family identity (Marcoux 2001).

When my grandmother visits the house of one of her children, she finds things that were previously in her place. Just as the children leave to form new homes, eventually the objects do the same. When she visits her younger sister, she finds things that she grew up with or saw as a child in the homes of her parents and grandparents. There are other things that she remembers fondly and, although she never saw them again, she knows which branch of the family has received them. When we are in the living room, she always comments that there were two vases of Sèvres porcelain in her grandparents' house – one that she keeps on the cabinet and a second one that her elder brother inherited. Several sets of chairs and armchairs were also distributed among her brothers and sisters after her parents passed away.

The objects of my grandmother's house can be kept forgotten or they can leave the house to be integrated into new homes. However, unlike the objects that pass through my house, the bond is rarely lost. The degrees of availability of the object and the proximity of those who receive it may vary, but there is rarely a total and definitive separation.

The End

What happens then? How does this love story end? After more than sixty years together, it is difficult to distinguish between my grandmother and her house. She situates herself, her identity and her culture in a spatial way (Gaffin 1996). My grandmother is her house and that house is my grandmother. Still today my grandmother tells me that there is no better place to be than in her house. This place is a guarantee of freedom, autonomy and security, the certainty that her story belongs to her only while she is able to inhabit it.

It is common to hear people say that when we get old we begin to live more and more in our memories. I believe that there is a similar process happening with this house. While familiar people living in the house move out and my grandmother loses mobility, there are fewer and fewer spaces that are physically inhabited, and those spaces that are remembered increase. Although rooms and places keep the names of the functions they had, or of the people who inhabited them, they no longer serve their old purpose.

The last three decades represent a one-way path. In 1989, my grandfather got sick and could not keep his bedroom on the third floor, so the decision was made to move him to the second floor. The following year he died. From then onwards, the third floor became a place to which my grandmother went only occasionally, mainly to make sure that everything was in order. In 2005, together with my parents and my brothers, we left the first floor of the house, where we had lived since 1989, and moved to another house. The first floor was rented as an independent apartment and my grandmother never visited it again. In 2006, my grandmother was no longer able to drive, and since then the car (and the garage area overall) has not been used. A couple of years later, the woman who had attended the grocery store located on the first floor for more than forty years passed away. The place had always been managed by my grandmother, who used to go down every weekday between 6 and 7 p.m. The store closed and there are no intentions of opening it again.

During the following years, she got older, lost mobility, and some of her memories were lost. The house resents this decay, intensifying the wear and deterioration due to the lack of maintenance, care and repair. In 2014, my grandmother fell down the stairs and since then has not been able to go up and down the stairs on her own. Therefore, she stopped maintaining the third floor and visiting the garden, and only left the house to go to the doctor and on other unpostponable occasions. A short while later, she began to be taken care of by different nurses. Her sons and her daughter, to prevent the disappearance of valuable things in the house, locked the library, the bar and the living room and took away many valuable objects that were placed around the house. This year, after a few days during which my grandmother was in very bad health, her sons and her daughter decided to take the couch out of her bedroom and install a second bed, so that there would always be a person accompanying her.

Today the house is only her bed, the bedroom, the adjacent bathroom, and the sum of micro routes that are undertaken from there. She knows each step takes time, each foot patiently waits its turn to move, under the watchful eye of whoever directs them. The rest of the house is left aside, waiting, showing the signs of a new moment, probably the last. There are rooms that are forgotten, for which there is no longer any reason to enter. Others seem unreachable in her current state of health. As Gaston Bachelard points out, 'as soon as we become motionless, we are elsewhere; we are dreaming in a world that is immense' (1994: 184).

The living house contracts and decay is the natural response when resistance has disappeared. My grandmother is aware that the minute she stays in bed and stops moving through her things will be the end of her life. To live is to dwell with her things in her house. In tune with a long-lasting companionate love relationship based on co-dependence, once my grandmother is gone, the days of the house will be numbered. Her home as we know it will no longer exist. The value of things will change and a significant part of what is now contained will probably be thrown away.

In a bond that is sustained by the investment of time and care in things, and in the value that is given to the passage of time and accumulation of narratives, death constitutes the main interruption, unavoidable, forced and imposed. Death, not as an instant but as a process, which in this particular case has as a turning point the death of my grandfather in 1989. 'Till death do us part' is the end of an implicit promise, the termination of a contract that has been guarded by the daily time of doing and being. It is the end of a shared existence. This break also represents the freedom for objects (and subjects) to initiate other paths that may end up in new relationships.

Accustomed today to numerous objects passing through our homes, the possibility that things can have long lives seems strange. Although the quality of materials and the variability of needs and functions are undoubtedly crucial to define durability, long life also has a direct relationship with routines that persist over time. In other words, unconscious habits that are acquired by repeating the same task tirelessly influence the trajectory of objects. Far from an eternal monotony, these routines suppose the repetition of cycles, seasons and rites that order and qualify the daily time. Unlike the fleeting surprise, excitement and anxiety that many objects cause us today, the long time of things is guarded by the foreseeable action of those who know the origin, anticipate the effects, accompany the deterioration, arrange, reuse, keep and occasionally let go. These routines have the potential to generate attachment, empathy, compassion and even love. When this happens, we rescue the objects from that modern perception that separates them as something different from the subject and the place and disparagingly throws them away, and we recover their possibility of being a constituent part of something beyond themselves.

Tomas Errázuriz is Assistant Professor at the Creative Campus of Universidad Andres Bello.

References

Bachelard, G. 1994. *The Poetics of Space*. Boston, MA: Beacon Press.
Barthes, R. 1981. *Camera Lucida: Reflections on Photography*. New York: Hill and Wang.
Baudrillard, J. 2012. *The Consumer Society: Myths and Structures*. Los Angeles: Sage.
Boscagli, M. 2014. *Stuff Theory: Everyday Objects, Radical Materialism*. London: Bloomsbury.
Chapman, J. 2005. *Emotionally Durable Design: Objects, Experiences, and Empathy*. Sterling: Earthscan.
Cooper, T. 2005. 'Slower Consumption: Reflections on Product Life Spans and the "Throwaway Society"', *Journal of Industrial Ecology* 9(1/2): 51–67.
—— (ed.). 2010. *Longer Lasting Products: Alternatives to the Throwaway Society*. Burlington, VA: Ashgate.
Cooper, T., and K. Mayers. 2000. *Prospects for Household Appliances*. Halifax: Urban Mines.
Csikszentmihalyi, Mihaly, and Eugene Rochberg-Halton. 1981. *The Meaning of Things: Domestic Symbols and the Self*. Cambridge: Cambridge University Press.
Danet, Brenda, and Tamar Katriel. 1994. 'Collecting, Metaphor, and the Romantic Ethic', in S. Riggins (ed.), *The Socialness of Things*. Berlin: Mouton de Gruyter, pp. 23–61.
Dant, T. 2010. 'The Work of Repair: Gesture, Emotion and Sensual Knowledge', *Sociological Research Online* 15(3): 7.
Dittmar, H. 2001. 'Impulse Buying in Ordinary and "Compulsive" Consumers', in E. Weber, J. Baron and G. Loomes (eds), *Conflicts and Tradeoffs in Decision Making*. Cambridge: Cambridge University Press, pp. 110–35.
——. 2008. *Consumer Culture, Identity, and Well-being*. London: Psychology Press.

Edensor, T. 2016. 'Incipient Ruination: Materiality, Destructive Agencies and Repair', in M. Bille and T. Flohr (eds), *Elements of Architecture*. London: Routledge, pp. 348–64.
Ekerdt, D., J. Sergeant, M. Dingel and M. Bowen. 2004. 'Household Disbandment in Later Life', *Journal of Gerontology, Social Sciences* 59B: S265–73.
Errázuriz, T. 2019. 'Estación Terminal: La vida de las cosas en la vivienda rural', in F. Alarcón (ed.), *Catastro y rescate de la arquitectura popular en la vivienda rural en el valle central*. Santiago: ARQ, in press.
Fear, J. 2008. 'Stuff Happens: Unused Things Cluttering Up Our Homes'. The Australia Institute for a Just, Sustainable, Peaceful Future, Research Paper no. 52.
Gaffin, D. 1996. *In Place: Spatial and Social Order in a Faeroe Islands Community*. Prospect Heights, NY: Waveland Press.
Graham, S., and N. Thrift. 2007. 'Out of Order: Understanding Repair and Maintenance', *Theory, Culture & Society* 24(3): 1–25.
Gregson, N. 2007. *Living with Things: Ridding, Accommodation, Dwelling*. Wantage: Sean Kingston.
Gregson, N., and L. Crewe. 2003. *Second-hand Cultures*. Oxford: Berg.
Gregson, N., A. Metcalfe and L. Crewe. 2009. 'Practices of Object Maintenance and Repair: How Consumers Attend to Consumer Objects within the Home'. *Journal of Consumer Culture* 9(2): 248–72.
Hatfield, E., and R.L. Rapson. 1993. *Love, Sex, and Intimacy: Their Psychology, Biology, and History*. New York: HarperCollins.
Hetherington, K. 2004. 'Secondhandedness: Consumption, Disposal, and Absent Presence'. *Environment and Planning D: Society and Space* 22(1): 157–73.
Hoskins, J. 1998. *Biographical Objects: How Things Tell the Stories of People's Lives*. New York: Routledge.
Kopytoff, I. 1986. 'The Cultural Biography of Things: Commoditization as a Process', in A. Appadurai (ed.), *The Social Life of Things*. Cambridge: Cambridge University Press, pp. 64–91.
Koskijoki, M. 1997. 'My Favourite Things', in E. van Hinte (ed.), *Eternally Yours: Visions on Product Endurance*. Rotterdam: 010 Publishers, pp. 132–43.
Latour, B. 1996. *Aramis, or the Love of Technology*. Cambridge, MA: Harvard University Press.
Lee, J.A. 1973. *Colours of Love: An Exploration of the Ways of Loving*. Toronto: New Press.
Löfgren, O. 2017. 'Mess: On Domestic Overflows', *Consumption Markets & Culture* 20(1): 1–6.
Makovicky, N. 2007. 'Closet and Cabinet: Clutter as Cosmology', *Home Cultures* 4(3): 287–309.
Marcoux, J.-S. 2001. 'The "Casser Maison" Ritual: Constructing the Self by Emptying the Home', *Journal of Material Culture* 6(2): 213–35.
Martínez, F. 2017. 'Waste Is Not the End: For an Anthropology of Care, Maintenance and Repair', *Social Anthropology* 25(3): 346–50.
Mattern, Shannon. 2017. 'Closet Archive', *Places Journal*. Retrieved July 2017, from https://placesjournal.org/article/closet-archive/.
Mauss, M. 1954. *The Gift: Forms and Functions of Exchange in Archaic Societies*. London: Cohen & Wes.

McCoy, M. 1997. 'Angling for Endurance', in E. van Hinte (ed.), *Eternally Yours: Visions on Product Endurance*. Rotterdam: 010 Publishers, pp. 190–200.
Miller, D. 1998. *A Theory of Shopping*. Malden, MA: Polity
——. 2010. *Stuff*. Malden, MA: Polity.
Mol, A. 2008. *The Logic of Care: Health and the Problem of Patient Choice*. London: Routledge.
Rook, D.W. 1987. 'The Buying Impulse', *Journal of Consumer Research* 14: 189–99.
Rubin, Z. 1973. *Liking and Loving: An Invitation to Social Psychology*. New York: Harvard University Press.
Rusbult, C.E. 1980. 'Commitment and Satisfaction in Romantic Associations: A Test of the Investment Model', *Journal of Experimental Social Psychology* 16: 172–86.
Sternberg, R.J. 1988. *The Triangle of Love: Intimacy, Passion, Commitment*. London: Basic.
Tanizaki, J. 1994. *El elogio de la sombra*. Madrid: Siruela.
van Hinte, E. (ed.). 1997. *Eternally Yours: Visions on Product Endurance*. Rotterdam: 010 Publishers.
Zajonc, R.B. 1968. 'Attitudinal Effects of Mere Exposure', *Journal of Personality and Social Psychology* 9: 1–27.

SNAPSHOT 3

'The Lady Is Not Here'

Repairing Tita Meme as a Telecare User

Tomás Sánchez Criado

In the summer of 2009, I went on holiday to southern Cádiz (Spain), close to Gibraltar, together with Raquel, my partner at the time. There I met her parents, and Tita Meme (her grandma's sister, who had been for her the closest thing to a grandmother). They all knew that since late 2007 I had been working on my PhD, an ethnographic study of how telecare services – which had spread all over Spain as part of the public social services portfolio – might entail a change in formal and informal practices of care for older people. In fact, on many occasions they reminded me that Tita Meme, a very lively and vigorous older woman herself, was also a telecare user. Hence, I ended up interviewing her in her flat, where she lived with only the company of Jacky, a nervous little dog, constantly barking and sniffing everything.

By then, I had spent more than seven months following different workers of a telecare service in Madrid (providing support at a distance through a series of information technologies, comprising 'social alarm' pendants to call for help through a gadget, terminal or hub installed in the house; also, they were prototyping other technologies, such as video assistance and home sensors to monitor older people in their homes). Accompanying social workers or emergency phone operators and, mainly, the installation, maintenance and repair technicians daily, I had been going in and out of many older people's homes. Hence, I had witnessed all kinds of material-technical and emotional issues in dealing with how a new gadget irrupts in established modes of dwelling, changing older people's perceptions of their autonomy, as well as the ways in which people wanted to take care and be taken care of.

Figure S3.1. Tita Meme posing with her telecare pendant (picture taken by the author with permission in August 2009).

In the very enjoyable interview I had with her, Tita Meme told me she only had the pendant in case of an emergency, and that she was not usually wearing it (in fact, it was usually placed on her bedside table). The main reason she gave, joking the whole time, was that if she fell, she would ask for help, dragging herself across the floor if needed. She even jokingly called some of her friends who also have telecare 'chickens' (*cagonas*) as she argued they are always afraid something might happen to them. She argued that she wishes to continue living in the flat where she has lived most of her life, and was not planning on moving anywhere (not to a residential

Figure S3.2. The pendant in its usual place, on top of Tita Meme's bedside table (picture taken by the author with permission in August 2009).

facility, and definitely not to her niece's house). In fact, she also told me, it had been her niece (Raquel's mother) who had pushed her to request the service, as there was a worry in the family that something might happen to her: her small dog Jacky could easily trip her up, or because she was already an aged person (eighty-five at the time) she could develop any sort of complex condition, limiting her movements at any time. Telecare, hence, was giving Tita Meme's relatives a certain peace of mind, while at the same time 'supporting her autonomy' (as the services frequently advertise).

A few weeks later, I returned alone to Madrid. One day Raquel called me and told me an intriguing story. Apparently, the telecare service had been trying to contact Tita Meme via their regular phone checks for several weeks, but were met with a puzzling female voice at the other end of the phone, stating 'La señora no está' (the lady is not here) and abruptly hanging up the phone. Telecare workers were astonished, as no record in their databases showed that Tita Meme had anyone working for or living with her. They demanded to know whether this was the case (mainly so they could have the phone number of that person, and register her as a 'contact'). As it turned out, after Raquel's parents became involved in dealing with the situation, it had been Tita Meme herself who had replied to those calls, resulting in a quite hilarious family drama: why was she answering the service in this way? Why wasn't she wearing the pendant at all times, as the service requested? Tita Meme replied to all these questions that she was fit, and that whenever she felt something was not working, she would of course use the pendant.

This tension (which continued for a long time afterwards) proved very interesting food for thought, since in behaving like this Tita Meme was testing the limits of telecare services as such. Telecare services have to constantly monitor not only the technical equipment, but also the contractual borders of the service (made up of particular behaviours by the users and the people nearby whom they have defined as 'contacts', who should be activated in case there is a need, for example, to open the doors of the flat). In this regard, the work of these services' operators, technicians and social workers is to repair the service. Repair has indeed been addressed in the growing body of literature in the social sciences either as a restoration of social order (Henke 1999) or as a form of care for fragile things (Denis and Pontille 2015). But in Tita Meme's case, repair mainly addresses the 'flesh and bones' side of it, not a restorative form of medical rehabilitation, but a constant restoration of a web of embodied, legal and technical practices so that she could be considered a user of a service, and, hence, for the service to 'tele-care' for Tita Meme in meaningful ways.

Telecare is a biopolitical strategy for older people, premised upon constant self-screening and monitoring activities. This requires that older users always practise themselves as beings potentially in danger, according to each individual's bodily and environmental proclivities and vulnerabilities (from having a chronic illness or a particularly dangerous condition to being at risk because of loneliness). However, Tita Meme rather unfolded as an intermittent user: now she took the pendant and put it around her neck, now she didn't; now she felt insecure and bad, and placed the pendant on her bedside table, now she forgot. These behaviours caused multiple problems, since for telecare companies to be able to provide their service, a certain 'continuity of the (tele)cares' is needed. In fact, all providers struggle in connecting the dots, the intervals, the segments of any gap in the functioning of such a complex legal, technical and behavioural ecology. And they engage in a constant supervision of what might put the service in jeopardy, since this is what makes them able to respond and provide immediate care, should it be needed (López and Domènech 2008).

Are these activities of the telecare providers a form of repair of a broken social order, or instead its technical support? In my view, what the service workers and Tita Meme's relatives were together doing was maintaining an *infrastructure of usership* (Sánchez Criado et al. 2014), that is, creating and ensuring the conditions for (tele)care to happen or take place in compliance with contractual terms. Rather than as a form of 're-instauration' (going back to square one, revitalising and polishing in practice the terms of the contract), this form of repair that I call 'underpinning' entails going with the flow, and acting thereon. For Tita Meme to be a user (indeed, she could be rejected from the service because of a breach of contract), and for that to be meaningful in her care as a woman living alone in her flat, with her little dog, she has to be constantly dammed like an overflowing river. In these underpinning efforts, it not only matters what the telecare provider, relatives or contacts do to ensure that Tita Meme keeps acting as a user, but also what she herself does. Thus, underpinning could be described as a form of repair that addresses habits as things going beyond the skin, in and through different mediators that connect uneven events and places. To underpin, hence, is to ensure on the go that a certain topology of habit – a *habitality* (López and Sánchez Criado 2009) – can take place; or, to put it briefly, that Tita Meme is held in her own way of practising herself as a telecare user, whatever may happen, and in case anything happens. . .

Tomás Sánchez Criado is Senior Researcher at the Institute of European Ethnology, Humboldt-University of Berlin.

Note

This text is an abridged version of a chapter published in Spanish: Sánchez Criado, T. 2012. '¿Cómo se mantiene una usuaria? Prácticas de apuntalamiento en la teleasistencia para personas mayores', in F.J. Tirado and D. López (eds), *Teoría del actor-red: más allá de los estudios de ciencia y tecnología*. Barcelona: Amentia, pp. 111–55.

References

Denis, J., and D. Pontille. 2015. 'Material Ordering and the Care of Things', *Science, Technology & Human Values* 40(3): 338–67.

Henke, C.R. 1999. 'The Mechanics of Workplace Order: Toward a Sociology of Repair', *Berkeley Journal of Sociology* 44: 55–81.

López, D., and M. Domènech. 2008. 'On Inscriptions and Ex-inscriptions: The Production of Immediacy in a Home Telecare Service', *Environment and Planning D: Society and Space* 26(4): 663–75.

López, D., and T. Sánchez Criado. 2009. 'Dwelling the Telecare Home: Placeness, Location, and Habitality', *Space and Culture* 12(3): 343–58.

Sánchez Criado, T., D. Lopez, C. Roberts and M. Domènech. 2014. 'Installing Telecare, Installing Users: Felicity Conditions for the Instauration of Usership', *Science, Technology & Human Values* 39(5): 694–719.

CHAPTER 3

In the House of Un-things

Decay and Deferral in a Vacated Bulgarian Home

MARTIN DEMANT FREDERIKSEN

Directions

Gnawing to be gone. Less no good. Worse no good. Only one good. Gone. Gone for good. Till then gnaw on. All gnaw on. To be gone.

—Samuel Beckett, *Worstward Ho*

When the Keskins moved out and left an empty house behind, Kemal went in and took a doorknob that his beloved had touched every day for eighteen years; a doll's arm; an old marble; a piece of wallpaper; and a porcelain handle that was hanging off the toilet chain. But he wasn't yet thinking of setting up a museum.

—Orhan Pamuk, *The Innocence of Objects*

Ceramic ornament: Hanging on entrance door. rectangular ceramic tile with engraved figure in various colours (tuscan red, princeton orange, maize yellow, powder blue and pistachio green). attached to the door with weathered, blue plastic clothes peg. Below a keyhole. made of gilded metal. does not serve a purpose as door is un-locked.

—Fieldnotes, Plovdiv/Bulgaria (March 2015)

Admissions

Out of the hundreds of items present in the abandoned house, the plastic-wrapped lump of clay – lying in the corner of what would have been the living room – is the only thing Drago pays any real attention to. He even steps on it from time to time, to check whether it is still soft enough to be used one day. Drago owns this house along with the adjacent one. The two houses share a small yard in between them, with roses below and vines above. They were built at the same time, in the early 1990s, yet while one has been vacated for a period of years, the other is being rented out, currently to me. I had been curious about the insides of the vacated house for some time. And so, as Drago one day came to visit, I joined him on his clay-check.

Inside the vacated home, we are met by an immediate mess. Aside from cobwebs, dust and a vast variety of tools, scattered on the floor is a variety of stuff. Items such as coloured paper, pens, a pair of shoes, a plastic clock, paint stripper, stacks of tiles, decorated cups, oven gloves, lighters, an unopened letter, a partly withered plant, greetings cards, anti-bacterial wipes, cushions, a plastic duck and old Christmas decorations. We make our way through the various piles to the lump of clay, which Drago determines is still doing just fine. Afterwards I ask him whether it would be okay if I, once in a while, go into the house alone, promising not to break anything. Drago laughs and says everything in there is already broken, that I am free to spend as much time inside as I want. And so, over the next weeks I make daily visits to the vacated house across the yard and in a notebook I eventually build up an inventory of every item inside.[1]

The house is located in Stariya Grad – the Old Town – in Bulgaria's second-largest city, Plovdiv. Stariya Grad is a neighbourhood in which a series of so-called 'Museum Houses' are scattered along cobbled streets. They are either restored historical buildings or monument protected ruins that seek to convey the history of the city. In what follows, I consider Drago's vacated house as one of these. That is, as a Museum House, yet one that represents the contemporary situation rather than the distant past, with remnants and artefacts reflecting a broken present, particularly in relation to the question of depopulation.

Based on my fieldwork in Plovdiv in 2015, this chapter consists of two main parts, or arguments. While in the first part I seek to locate the vacated house among the regular Museum Houses in terms of the similarities they share, in the second part I will focus on how the items or artefacts inside the vacated house differ from the artefacts of Museum Houses in terms of the quality of their decay or brokenness. On an overall level, the chapter departs from what one might call an anthropology of negativity (Frederiksen 2017; O'Neill 2017), taking inspiration from contemporary archaeology in a focus on present-day remnants, along with recent anthropological studies of decay, rubble and unfinished buildings (Gordillo 2014; Pétursdóttir and Olsen 2014; Ulfstjerne 2016, 2017). More specifically, I situate my empirical material in relation to Olga Shevchenko's study of 'durables' (Shevchenko 2002) and Ringel's study of 'shrinkage' (2018). Through this, I argue that the fragments and broken or decaying objects in the house serve as a deferral of a desired situation that seeks to circumvent the otherwise negative attitudes towards, and lack of representation of, such empty or vacated buildings in urban space. This indefinite postponement, however, is fraught with frailty. Drawing on Samuel Beckett's writing on unwords, I argue that the un-things in the vacated house are suspended between a situation of upholding a desire for *something*, while simultaneously sliding towards *nothing*.[2]

Museum Houses and the Architecture of National Revival

In many respects, Plovdiv may be seen as a city of ruins. As one of the oldest cities in Europe, human settlements in and outside of the city can be traced back to the sixth millennium BCE. Remnants of different or overlapping historical periods are scattered throughout the seven hills that the city is built on and around. Of the numerous historical events and periods that have left their marks on Plovdiv, it is the National Revival period that mainly dominates the Stariya Grad neighbourhood in terms of architecture. With its position in the European part of the Ottoman Empire, Plovdiv became a central site for craftmanship and trade between Asia Minor and Western Europe in the eighteenth and nineteenth centuries. The export and import of frieze, rice, wool, silk, cotton, leather, fur and timber saw the rise of a local commercial bourgeoisie, and as the Treaty of Adrianople that followed the Russian-Ottoman war of 1828–29 saw a strengthening of Bulgarian national spirit, these families came to symbolise the National Revival period, not least through their houses.

In 1848, large parts of Plovdiv were devastated in a fire and subsequently the new wealthy elite built a series of extravagant new, private homes. Later known as Bulgarian Baroque and locally as Plovdiv Houses, these were most often two- or three-storey houses separated from their neighbours by massive walls. They featured bay windows facing the streets and richly decorated interiors, with wood-carved staircases and wall paintings. In the words of a local guidebook, 'the houses and the trim yards around them remind us of a small family paradise that must not only suggest the financial means of the owner, but also inspire people with respect' (Strandzhev 2004: 52).

The majority of these new homes were named after the families who had built them, as 'The House of'. There was the House of Stepan Hindliyan, the House of Nikola Nedkovich, the House of Veren Stambolyan, the House of Luka Balabanov, the House of Artin Gidikov, the House of Kirkor

Mesrobovich, and so on. Today, none of these names represent people or families who presently occupy the premises, but people and families who once did. And the items of these former residents are what is now being displayed to the public.

Taken together, the Museum Houses of Stariya Grad represent a time of economic growth and, just as significantly, of population growth. Crammed in between these Museum Houses is where we find Drago's house. Drago is a sculptor by profession but he has not done any artworks for almost six years due to a series of accidents and injuries. First he cut off the thumb of his right hand. It was sewn back onto his hand but left him incapable of working for a long time. Later he had a fire in the kitchen, which resulted in massive burns to his face and body. Around one year ago he was ready to begin working on his art again, but then a third accident happened. It was on Palm Sunday and he was in the church across the street with his wife. He met his friend there and they decided to go to the house and do some work on the sauna they were building in the basement at the time. They were going to cut a few pieces of material so that everything would be ready for more extensive work being initiated the following day. As they started work, however, Drago suffered a cut right across one of his hands with a circular saw blade. 'I have the blade over there in the house', he tells me over a cigarette in the yard, 'Some day I'm going to put it in one of the old frames and hang it up on one of the walls out here'. He laughs. For now, all he does is check the bag of clay, making sure that it is soft enough to one day be used.

Drago has one child, a daughter. She is grown now and a parent herself, but she no longer lives in Plovdiv. Her husband is one of Drago's best friends, and in fact the man with whom Drago rebuilt the two houses in the yard. It is Drago's hope that one day the currently vacated house will at last be completed and his daughter and grandchild will come and live there, as had been the original intention. Or, rather, the original intention had been that Drago's daughter and her family would be living with him, but since she married his friend, she would be living just across the yard in a house of their own, and that was just as good. However, the daughter and her husband decided at some point to move elsewhere, and thus the second house was never finished. The interior reveals that the abandonment was relatively sudden: tools have been left as if work was to be resumed the very next day. Although Drago's house was finished, he and his wife decided to move to another apartment that they own in Plovdiv. The idea was to then rent out the finished house until their daughter's potential return, although now they do not know when, or if, that will ever happen. Consequently, the items inside the vacated house are slowly decaying; rust is emerging on the left-behind tools that will soon be too broken to be of any use, should work eventually be resumed.

Countdowns to Emptiness

That Drago has a daughter who has left her hometown is not a unique story, but reflects a larger tendency in Bulgaria. On various online sites, one can find different world clocks, world-o-meters or countrymeters that present estimated real-time counts of the world population. Second by second, the numbers of births and deaths on a global scale are compared, often along with overviews of people either leaving or entering particular countries. One can also zoom in on particular regions and countries, yet whereas most country clocks follow the global trend of counting 'up' populations, other clocks are counting down. Bulgaria is a case in point.

On www.countrymeters.info, the live clock not only counts births and deaths, but also net migration. A look at the screen on 15 December 2017 at 08.28 a.m. reveals the current population in Bulgaria to be 7,026,027 people. There have, on this particular day, been sixty-six births and 106 deaths, and net migration shows that over the last hours ten more people have left the country compared to the number of people entering. This leaves a population 'growth' of minus forty-nine. Numbers continue to change throughout the day. Two hours later, at 10.28 a.m., the population is 7,026,016. By now, eighty-one children have been born, 130 people have passed away, and net migration is at minus twelve. Population growth is now at minus sixty-one, meaning twelve people less than only two hours ago.

There is nothing remarkable about this particular day when compared to the year 2017 as a whole. With 64,649 births, 103,684 deaths and a net migration of minus 9,382, the population growth is at minus 48,418 on 15 December. By 31 December, the number has reached minus 50,016. And even 2017 is not remarkable. The population growth rate in Bulgaria has been negative since the mid 1980s, with almost two million fewer people residing in the country since then. At this rate, the country would statistically be almost empty in some seventy years' time.

Depopulation has had significant consequences for those still living in the country. As Gerald Creed has observed in his study of cultural dispossession in rural Bulgaria, 'massive migration ultimately removed a number of social relations from the social field, which gradually simplified some village relations while complicating family relations that were now at a distance' (Creed 2011: 11). Proportionally, rural areas have been affected much more, in many places devastatingly so, by depopulation, losing both to urban areas within Bulgaria and abroad. The vast majority of people are leaving in order to seek out job opportunities not found in their original place of residence. While the transition from socialism to market economy caused a steep increase in unemployment throughout the country, the tourism sector was one of the few to fare relatively well in creating work (Ghodsee 2005), yet tourist sites were also affected (Bethmann 2013: 304). As the second largest city in Bulgaria, a hub of transportation and economy, and a site of tourism, one would imagine Plovdiv to be among the success stories. And the city did fare slightly better than many of the rural areas of the country in terms of depopulation. But the tendency is still felt. 'There is a constant decline in the number of students enrolling', a university teacher tells me as we sit in her office. The main reason, she suspects, is the substantial drop in birth rates since the 1980s and 1990s. Moreover, she notes, tourism in Plovdiv has not been booming in the way that many had hoped for.

This is particularly evident during winter and there is a peculiar air to Stariya Grad as an out-of-season tourist site. Neon signs are never lit and advertisements hang in front of closed doors. During off-season, Stariya Grad itself has a feeling of abandonment. Nobody clears the streets after a snowfall, and during the hours after new snow has fallen, the lack of footprints makes it appear as if Stariya Grad in its entirety is empty. Even here, though there are actual residents in the neighbourhood, the off-season creates an atmosphere of a *citta morte*, a ghost city. 'Usually', a custodian in one of the Museum Houses tells me as I visit, 'people only come to Plovdiv for a few hours'. She goes on to explain how they either come here from Sofia or from one of the Black Sea beach resorts in Varna or Burgas for a day or afternoon trip. 'They spend a little time walking through Stariya Grad, see a few museums, enjoy the view from one of the hills, take a look at the Roman Theatre, buy a few trinkets, and then they go back to where they came from. Often they don't even have lunch here, it's just hit-and-run.' And that, she continues, is even during summer. Now, off-season, there is little else for her to do than sit and read the newspaper. Nearby, in a trinket shop, the owner is playing his guitar, waiting for a customer to walk in. But there are none.

In her ethno-sociological study of Plovdiv, Meglena Zlatkova has examined the urban palimpsests of the city. That is, the ways in which 'different temporal and spatial layers might "meet up" to throw into relief the "pieces of the city"' (Zlatkova 2012: 217). Underneath each ideological or historical layer, she argues, there are other layers representing former urban formations. While this attests to the heterogeneity of Plovdiv as a historically multicultural place, it does not mean that all layers come into view: 'depending on the various political and socioeconomic contexts, this heterogeneity is not necessarily allowed in the "official text"' (ibid.: 216). This manifests itself particularly in official (self-)representations of the city aimed at tourists where things such as sight-seeing options condense certain layers or aspects of history 'in order to reproduce [a] here-and-now model of the city and to turn the physical traces of different epochs into a well-exhibited heritage' (ibid.: 221; see also Yukov 2008).

Distinctions between good and bad architecture and historical legacy, as well as questions of exclusion and inclusion in the selection of what is to be part of official representations of multiculturalism, cosmopolitanism or heterogeneity, are of course not particular to Plovdiv.[3] What is of particular interest to me here, and also touched upon by Zlatkova, is the layers that are not represented or illuminated, but still visibly very present. With its perpetually unopened window shutters facing the street, the vacated house in Drago's yard is one such example, and only one of many. Unfinished houses falling into decay are scattered around Stariya Grad, some being more directly visible than others. And although being unintended representations, they do actually represent themes similar to those of the regular Museum Houses, namely questions of economy and demography. What they make visible, however, are matters of decline rather than revival. As with many of the out-of-season Museum Houses, Drago's house is vacated and the reason for its emptiness reflects one instance out of many in which depopulation has left a mark, thus sharply mirroring the contemporary situation. The question is, how do the objects present in the vacated house relate to the artefacts on display in the regular Museum Houses? That is, what is the quality of the slowly decaying objects scattered around the premises?

Ruins, Rubble and Decay

Gastón Gordillo, in his overview of perspectives on ruins and their relation to the modernity that invented them, notes how heritage industries tend to manufacture and reorder rubble into orderly, positive objects. 'The modernist preoccupation with ruins', he writes, 'has included a long and sustained struggle against the uncoded negativity of rubble' (Gordillo 2014: 9). He goes on to argue against Simmel's famous attempt to separate ruins from rubble, with the latter being viewed by Simmel as a 'mere heap of stones'. In that perspective, Gordillo observes, one can trace a hierarchy of debris where the formlessness and perceived insignificance of rubble places it at the bottom.[4]

As previously noted, Plovdiv may in its entirety be seen as a city of ruins. And the ruins of Plovdiv have a clear place in the kind of hierarchy Gordillo speaks of, namely in terms of what is repaired or preserved in order to attract the gaze of tourists, and what is left abandoned or negated as not being part of national heritage. This has been clear in ongoing public debates about the role of specific historical periods and their corresponding monuments (Valiavicharska 2014), particularly when Plovdiv was a candidate to become European Capital of Culture (Pehlivanova 2015). During my fieldwork, individuals attached to particular historical places, such as the custodians working in various Museum Houses, were particularly vocal about such concerns.

An example is the House of Nikola Nedkovich, which is located just around the corner from Drago's place. It belonged to a merchant who lived there with his wife and daughter. As the daughter did not establish a family of her own, the house was left to a servant after her death. During the socialist period, the state offered the servant an apartment somewhere else in the city so that the house could be turned into a museum. Now visitors can walk around in the main room downstairs and upstairs, but all adjacent rooms can only be observed from behind a piece of rope. Some of the furniture is from France, but most was locally produced, the custodian tells me upon a visit, such as the grand Kelim carpet upstairs in the main dining room. Various artists have decorated the different rooms in individual styles, with painted walls and ceilings, rendering this a typical house of the Revival period. Currently, most of the rooms have been restored, the custodian continues, except for the toilet, which has not been touched (and is the only room not on display). Restorations are an ongoing activity and they faced a problem recently, namely that the house in its entirety had started tilting, but a grant from the EU ensured that the foundation was repaired last year. Now, however, they have realised that the ceiling also needs restoration in order to be preserved, but that will be both expensive and difficult as the house has the status of a national monument of culture. If nothing is done, however, the ceiling will at some point be broken beyond repair. In this particular aspect, the House of Nikola Nedkovich differs significantly from the House of Drago in that Drago seemed deliberately not to be repairing anything. This leads us to the question of deferral.

Unwords and Un-things, Decay and Deferral

Decay, as Stephen Cairns and Jane Jacobs observe (2014), is a part of life, most often, though, as a negative index of disintegration. Þóra Pétursdóttir and Bjørnar Olsen nonetheless argue (2014) that portrayals of urban decay often tend to turn social and material misery into something seductive and aesthetically pleasing. Consequently, there remains a tendency to stop disintegration as a process in terms of preservation or restoration rather than letting objects or buildings decay completely (DeSilvey 2017). People who were working in the Museum Houses of Stariya Grad were, for instance, preoccupied with repair, such as the custodian in the House of Nikola Nedkovich hoping that money would soon arrive so that the ceiling could be restored. Drago, on the other hand, had few such concerns. Even though on the one hand the tools scattered around his vacated house gave an appearance that work at some point was intended to be resumed, the continuously thickening layers of dust testified to the fact that the population clock was still ticking downwards, that the house would remain unpopulated for some time to come. Yet clearing the premises of all the objects lying around in order to either rent it out or sell it to someone else would be an acknowledgement of his daughter never returning. Deferring that action – in terms of not repairing for someone else or selling it to someone else – meant that a small spark of hope could still be kept alive. This equally meant that everything inside decayed a little more with each passing day, rust slowly appearing on the tools, paint slowly drying out, objects slowly becoming broken beyond repair.

It is through this aspect that the objects inside Drago's house come to resemble the principle of 'unwords' found in the writing of Samuel Beckett. The literature of the unword, as read by Kathryn White, is a process of advancing through nothingness, 'to write words out of existence', or letting words decay (White 2011: 31; see also Weller 2010; Frederiksen 2018). Beckett had an antimonious perception of nothing as something that cannot exist, yet something which one still can (and perhaps even should) move towards. It is simultaneously a void and a core, and it simultaneously involves both hope and despair (e.g. Beckett 1983, 1996). This can be exemplified, writes David Kleinberg-Levin, in the story *Worstward Ho*, which is 'all about longing for something forever unapproachable, something belonging to the future of a past long lost' (Kleinberg-Levin 2015: 149).

The same dialectic, I believe, is figuratively at stake for the objects in the vacated house in terms of them being objects disintegrating in the process of becoming something; un-things that slowly decay through deferral, slowly move towards nothingness exactly because of the hope that they will someday become something. Similar to the rubble described by Gordillo, they are figures of negativity while still exerting 'positive pressure on human practice' (Gordillo 2014: 11). As such, they share an affinity with examples found in other recent anthropological studies of materiality, time and brokenness, whether in terms of places that are emptied out, such as Jean-Sébastien Marcoux's depiction of elderly citizens in Canada 'breaking the house' when moving from their home to a care environment through divesting themselves of their belongings (2001), or Michael Ulfstjerne's depiction of ghost cities in China that are barely even inhabited (2016, 2017).

More specifically, however, I want to draw a comparison with two examples that more closely resemble what I believe to be at stake here. Firstly, in her article on consumption and durables in Russia, Olga Shevchenko recounts the story of an elderly couple in Western Siberia who purchase a second refrigerator. This purchase puzzles their adult son Nikolai, as they had not really been using their old refrigerator (one that they keep alongside the new one). Yet 'none of the cooling devices . . . liberates Nikolai's parents from their life-long habit of hanging frozen products out of their windows during the long Siberian winters. Thus, despite the abundance of refrigerators, the family news Nikolai receives from Siberia is still full of accounts of food spoiled by sudden thaws or frosts' (Shevchenko 2002: 148). Maintenance and repair are even carried out to ensure the continuing functioning of the old refrigerator, despite the fact that it is never used. Both refrigerators are kept as durables, just in case.

Consider also Felix Ringel's more recent study of Hoyerswerda, 'Germany's fastest shrinking city'. Similar to Bulgaria, Hoyerswerda is slowly being depopulated and marked by a lost future, in this case the socialist future of East Germany. Hope in this context of shrinkage, Ringel notes, takes on a particular character. Despite a lost future looming over the city, it is not necessarily a matter of radical redirection (towards an imagined different future) but may just as well entail 'particular incitements to *maintaining* practices' (2018: 25, emphasis in original); it is a matter of staleness rather than emergence (see also Dalsgaard and Frederiksen 2013). In both cases, as in the case of Drago's house, we see aspects of holding onto something that is already broken, left unused or in the process of either breaking or being emptied out.

Working alongside the clock counting down the population – in terms of objects in time slowly turning into nothing through decay – the un-things of the house are simultaneously working against the clock, seeking to defer it. If the objects, and the house at large, were actually repaired, they would lose their 'un-ness', they would be turned into something but also lose the purpose of them being broken or decaying in the first place. Yet for the un-things it is at the same time the positivity – Drago's deferral, his not repairing the broken – that allows them to slide towards negativity. Thus, decay stands forth here as simultaneously a state of potentiality and a state of disintegration.

Exit

Drago's house is of course not a museum. Aside from the saw blade that cut his hand, Drago is not putting anything on display. As a thought-experiment, or as a mode of representation, it is more akin to Michael Taussig's *Cocaine Museum* (2004) and his exploration of how one might set up alternative representations of a particular (hi)story or reality. Contrary to Taussig's fictional construction, however, Drago's house is a place that actually does exist. As such, it shares an affinity with another make-believe museum, namely Orhan Pamuk's *Museum of Innocence*, a place that was at first an idea and a novel and later became an actual museum exhibiting the clutter that adheres to everyday life (Pamuk 2009, 2012). As such, the Museum of Innocence is rare. Indeed, as Taussig notes, museums most often abhor clutter (2004: xii), which is one reason why Drago's house differs from the Museum Houses. Yet his house, along with other houses like it, is still part of the vista of the Plovdiv cityscape, testament to a particular period of time. It is nevertheless a part of the artifice that one has to overlook in order to see the city the way that it officially wants to be seen in tourist brochures – representing parts of the city that dys-appear (Frederiksen 2016), scattering urban space with what Cairns and Jacobs refer to as 'obsolete buildings' (2014: 103) and Nick Yablon (2010) depicts as instances of 'untimely decay'. Also, within the framework of this volume, the introduction reflects on the frail line between that which is broken *without* repair and that which is broken *beyond* repair.

As mentioned, during winter Stariya Grad often gives the appearance of being a *citta morte*, not unlike the emptied Bulgarian villages in the countryside, represented better by the un-things present in Drago's house than any of the other Museum Houses. Yet even though they represent, or are representative, they are not being represented. And even though they are supposed to become something, or rather exactly because of this, they are becoming less and less. Rather than being *some*-things or *no*-things, they remain *un*-things. Unfinished. Unintended. Unrepresented. Gnawing on to be gone.

Martin Demant Frederiksen is a Postdoctoral Researcher in Social Anthropology at the University of Oslo.

Notes

1. For similar examples of this methodological approach, see Buchli and Lucas (2001). For studies of home cultures, see Carsten and Hugh-Jones (1995), Hecht (2001), Helliwell (1996), Laviolette (2008), Leivestad (2018) and Marcoux (2001).
2. As such, my use of the notion of 'un-things' represents what Daniel Miller (2005) refers to as a particular nuance of thing-ness. See also Frederiksen and Dalsgård (2014).

3. See, for example, the work done on Astana (Buchli 2007), Tbilisi (Frederiksen 2012), Tallinn (Martínez 2018), Warsaw (Murawski 2012) and Odessa (Skvirskaja 2012).
4. See also Augé (2003) and Edensor (2005).

References

Augé, Marc. 2003. *Le Temps en ruines*. Paris: Èditions Galilée.

Beckett, Samuel. 1983. *Disjecta: Miscellaneous Writings and a Dramatic Fragment*. London: John Calder.

——. 1996. *Nohow On: Company, Ill Seen Ill Said, and Worstward Ho*. New York: Grove Press.

Bethmann, Carla. 2013. *'Clean, Friendly, Profitable'? Tourism and the Tourism Industry in Varna, Bulgaria*. Berlin: LIT Verlag.

Buchli, Victor. 2007. 'Astana: Materiality and the City', in C. Alexander, V. Buchli and C. Humphrey (eds), *Urban Life in Post-Soviet Asia*. London: UCL Press, pp. 40–70.

Buchli, Victor, and Gavin Lucas. 2001. *Archeologies of the Contemporary Past*. London: Routledge.

Cairns, Stephen, and Jane M. Jacobs. 2014. *Buildings Must Die: A Perverse View of Architecture*. Cambridge, MA: MIT Press.

Carsten, Janet, and Stephen Hugh-Jones. 1995. *About the House: Lévi-Strauss and Beyond*. Cambridge: Cambridge University Press.

Creed, Gerald. 2011. *Masquerade and Postsocialism: Ritual and Cultural Dispossession in Bulgaria*. Bloomington: Indiana University Press.

Dalsgaard, Anne Line, and Martin Demant Frederiksen. 2013. 'Out of Conclusion: On Recurrence and Open-Endedness in Life and Analysis', *Social Analysis* 57(1): 50–63.

DeSilvey, Caitlin. 2017. *Curated Decay: Heritage beyond Saving*. Minneapolis: University of Minnesota Press.

Edensor, Tim. 2005. *Industrial Ruins*. London: Bloomsbury.

Frederiksen, Martin Demant. 2012. '"A Gate, but Leading Where?" In Search of Actually Existing Cosmopolitanism in Post-Soviet Tbilisi', in Caroline Humphrey and Vera Skvirskaja (eds), *Post-Cosmopolitan Cities*. Oxford: Berghahn Books, pp. 120–41.

——. 2016. 'Material Dys-Appearance: Decaying Futures and Contested Temporal Passage', in Peter Bjerregaard, Anders Emil Rasmussen and Tim Flohr Sørensen (eds), *Materialities of Passing: Explorations in Transformation, Transition and Transience*. London: Routledge, pp. 49–65.

——. 2017. 'Joyful Pessimism: Marginality Disengagement, and the Doing of Nothing', *Focaal* 78: 9–22.

——. 2018. *An Anthropology of Nothing in Particular*. Winchester: Zero.

Frederiksen, Martin Demant, and Anne Line Dalsgård. 2014. 'Introduction: Time Objectified', in Anne Line Dalsgård, Martin Demant Frederiksen, Lotte Meinert and Susanne Højlund (eds), *Ethnographies of Youth and Temporality: Time Objectified*. Philadelphia: Temple University Press, 1-21.

Ghodsee, Kristen. 2005. *The Red Riviera: Gender, Tourism, and Postsocialism on the Black Sea*. Durham, NC: Duke University Press.
Gordillo, Gastón. 2014. *Rubble: The Afterlife of Destruction*. Durham, NC: Duke University Press.
Hecht, Anat. 2001. 'Home Sweet Home: Tangible Memories of an Uprooted Childhood', in Daniel Miller (ed.), *Home Possessions: Material Culture behind Closed Doors*. Oxford: Berg, pp. 123–45.
Helliwell, Christine. 1996. 'Space and Sociality in a Dayak Longhouse', in Michael D. Jackson (ed.), *Things as They Are: New Directions in Phenomenological Anthropology*. Bloomington: Indiana University Press, pp. 128–48.
Kleinberg-Levin, David. 2015. *Beckett's Words: The Promise of Happiness in a Time of Mourning*. London: Bloomsbury.
Laviolette, Patrick. 2008. 'A Matter of Co-Opportunism: (In)Alienability in London Social Housing', *City & Society* 20(1): 130–49.
Leivestad, Hege Høyer. 2018. *Caravans: Lives on Wheels in Contemporary Europe*. London: Bloomsbury Academic.
Marcoux, Jean-Sébastian. 2001. 'The "Casser Maison" Ritual: Constructing the Self by Emptying the Home', *Journal of Material Culture* 6(2): 213–35.
Martínez, Francisco. 2018. *Remains of the Soviet Past in Estonia: An Anthropology of Forgetting, Repair and Urban Traces*. London: UCL Press.
Miller, Daniel. 2005. 'Materiality: An Introduction', in Daniel Miller (ed.), *Materiality*. Durham, NC: Duke University Press, 1-50.
Murawski, Michał. 2012. 'Cosmopolitan Architecture: "Deviations" from Stalinist Aesthetics and the Making of Twenty-First-Century Warsaw', in C. Humphrey and V. Skvirskaja (eds), *Post-Cosmopolitan Cities*. Oxford: Berghahn Books, pp. 141–70.
O'Neill, Bruce. 2017. 'The Ethnographic Negative', *Focaal* 78: 23–37.
Pamuk, Orhan. 2009. *The Museum of Innocence: A Novel*. London: Faber and Faber.
——. 2012. *The Innocence of Objects*. New York: Abrams.
Pehlivanova, Konstantina. 2015. 'Touristic Reconstruction in Plovdiv, Bulgaria, in the Run-up to Be a European Capital of Culture', in S. Doempke (ed.), *The UNESCO World Heritage and the Role of Civil Society*. Berlin: World Heritage Watch, pp. 103–6.
Pétursdóttir, Þóra, and Bjørnar Olsen. 2014. 'Imaging Modern Decay: The Aesthetics of Ruin Pornography', *Journal of Contemporary Archeology* 1(1): 7–23.
Ringel, Felix. 2018. *Back to the Postindustrial Future: An Ethnography of Germany's Fastest-Shrinking City*. Oxford: Berghahn Books.
Shevchenko, Olga. 2002. '"In Case of Fire Emergency": Consumption, Security and the Meaning of Durables in a Transforming Society', *Journal of Consumer Culture* 2(2): 147–70.
Skvirskaja, Vera. 2012. 'At the City's Social Margins: Selective Cosmopolitanism in Odessa', in C. Humphrey and V. Skvirskaja (eds), *Post-Cosmopolitan Cities*. Oxford: Berghahn Books, pp. 94–120.
Strandzhev, Ivan. 2004. 'The Landmarks of Plovdiv', in Nasko Nachev (ed.), *Plovdiv Guide Book*. Plovdiv: Business Agency JSC.
Taussig, Michael. 2004. *My Cocaine Museum*. Chicago, IL: University of Chicago Press.

Ulfstjerne, Michael. 2016. 'Unfinishing Buildings', in M. Bille and T.F. Sørensen (eds), *Elements of Architecture: Assembling Archeology, Atmosphere and the Performance of Building Spaces*. London: Routledge, pp. 387–405.
——. 2017. 'The Tower and the Tower: Excess and Vacancy in China's Ghost Cities', in S. Bregnbæk and M. Bunkenborg (eds), *Emptiness and Fullness: Ethnographies of Lack and Desire in Contemporary China*. Oxford: Berghahn Books, pp. 67–84.
Valiavicharska, Zhivka. 2014. 'History's Restless Ruins: On Socialist Public Monuments in Postsocialist Bulgaria', *Boundary 2* 41(1): 171–201.
Weller, Shane. 2010. 'Unwords', in D. Caselli (ed.), *Beckett and Nothing: Trying to Understand Beckett*. Manchester: Manchester University Press, pp. 107–25.
White, Kathryn. 2011. *Beckett and Decay*. London: Bloomsbury.
Yablon, Nick. 2010. *Untimely Ruins: An Archeology of American Urban Modernity, 1819–1919*. Chicago, IL: Chicago University Press.
Yukov, Nikolai. 2008. 'The "Unmemorable" and the "Unforgettable": "Museumizing" the Socialist Past in Post-1989 Bulgaria', in O. Sarkisova and P. Apor (eds), *Past for the Eyes: East European Representations of Communism in Cinema and Museums after 1989*. Budapest: Central European University Press, pp. 307–34.
Zlatkova, Meglena. 2012. *Etnosotsiologiya na Grada*. Plovdiv: Universitetsko izdatelstvo.

SNAPSHOT 4

Undisciplined Surfaces

Mateusz Laszczkowski

On 30 May 2006, residents of Kazakhstan's new capital Astana were alarmed by a plume of black smoke rising above the mid-construction government quarter. As it soon became clear, the 130-metre-high building of the Ministry of Transport and Communication was aflame. The fire had started on one of the top floors and quickly expanded, owing to the high flammability of the synthetic material used on the building's shiny facade. The bitter irony was that due to its cylindrical shape, the building had been nicknamed by the city's residents *Zazhigalka*, 'The Lighter'. The fire at the Transport Ministry was not an isolated incident. Several other prominent new buildings across Astana similarly caught fire. Elsewhere, heavy plates of imitation granite fell off buildings' facades and crashed on the sidewalks below, creating great danger to pedestrians and cars (Zhusupov 2008). At the time of my year-long fieldwork in Astana in 2008–09, everyday conversation was filled with numerous cases of pavements, roadways, curbs, elevators and pipes cracking or breaking, often before they were even put to use, or immediately thereafter.

The surfaces of new buildings in Astana were particularly charged with social and political meaning. Kazakhstan had achieved independence from the Soviet Union in 1991, and six years later the country's capital was relocated from Almaty to Aqmola, renamed Astana ('Capital' in Kazakh). From around the year 2000, a construction boom started, in an effort to transform this previously indistinct city into a worldly capital of a modern nation (Laszczkowski 2016). In the words of Victor Buchli, who visited Astana in the mid 2000s, it was 'at these surfaces that social life [was] made, specific subjectivities, ethnicities and nations [were] constituted and recognised . . . It [was] here that people [were] expected to know and recognise themselves and what it means to be Kazakhstani and modern' (2007: 42). But Astana's surfaces refused to serve as mere screens on which to project ideological visions and blueprints for social transformation. By catching fire, cracking and falling apart, they exercised their own tacit agency. They were undisciplined.

Cracks as Ontological Openings

Over the last two decades, social science and humanities have witnessed a massive 'turn to things' (Preda 1999), foregrounding and exploring material agency of non-living non-human actants (e.g. Bennett 2010; Henare, Holbraad and Wastell 2007). This neomaterialist paradigm has multiple origins. Actor-network theory (Latour 2005) and feminist studies of technoscience (Barad 2007) are among the most often cited. Within anthropology, the turn to things has more recently taken on a further twist. Engagements with ethnographic studies of non-Western cosmologies have generated an 'ontological turn' (Holbraad and Pedersen 2017; Viveiros de Castro 2012). Extremely simplified, its proponents argue that we should embrace radical ontological alterity and think in terms of *multiple worlds* generated by material agency (Law 2015). Critics, in turn, protest that such an ontological turn means disarming anthropology of conceptual tools necessary to critically analyse structures of inequality and domination in a shared human world (Bessire and Bond 2014; Martin 2014).

Here, I am following in the footsteps of Hannah Knox, who charts a 'clearing space' (2017a: 367) in which to bring these disjunct perspectives into dialogue. Attending to the embodied, affective relationships that people experience with material forms, she proposes, can be a productive way to de-essentialise received categories of political theory, such as the state or ideology. We may then be able to observe how material encounters structure and disrupt basic concepts through which humans make sense of the political and of their world(s).

Astana is a 'worlding' project in Aihwa Ong's (2011) sense of an 'art of being global' – rendering the city, and metonymically also the nation, 'world class' (Bissenova 2014). However, I also expand on Ong's original meaning of the term 'worlding' to mean *making worlds*. The new social and material cityscape in Astana implies a reconfiguration of geospatial and temporal relations on a world scale. It is staking a claim to create a holistic set of translocal social and geopolitical relations – in brief, *a world*. The construction of this cityscape is thus a geo-ontological act. This entails a particular geography, where Astana is 'the heart of Eurasia' (Nazarbaev 2005) – a geometric as well as political and economic centre of a mega-continent. It also entails a distinct temporality, a kind of fold in temporal continuity, where Astana – often dubbed the 'city of the future' – concretely materialises a future vision in the present. But the city's surfaces are also generative of other possible spacetimes and worlds.

One of my local interlocutors pointed to the provisional character of spectacular but poorly executed new buildings, bridges, monuments and roads. He quipped that these make-do forms amounted in Astana to a 'demo version of a city' (Laszczkowski 2015). 'Demo version' implies that beyond what immediately presents itself to the senses, there is also some other reality, truer than the demo. The demo is merely a simplified representation of the 'real'. It is perhaps an outline, a test or prototype (Knox 2017b) of a possible, desirable but as yet merely virtual world, supposedly to be developed. Perhaps the 'real thing' does not (yet) exist, but the demo covers up an imperfect reality from within which the demo itself is produced.

Another interlocutor narrated his 'discovery of the true face' of Astana. Upon noticing some particularly attractive new-looking buildings that he could not recall having seen before, he had come closer for a better look. His excitement soon turned into the bitter joy of unravelling an ugly truth: the buildings turned out to be old timeworn structures. They had been covered in shiny new siding on the front, but their dilapidation lay bare at the back. 'It takes merely walking round the corner to realise this is not a capital, not even a proper city at all, but some dusty little town!' my interlocutor concluded (Laszczkowski 2015: 158).

On some level, of course, these cracks and construction failures indexed corruption. This was the focus of anti-regime opposition media, such as the weekly *Svoboda Slova* ('Freedom of Speech'), though in contemporary Kazakhstan these groups are few and marginalised. However, the theme of corruption was conspicuously absent from most of my conversations with residents in Astana. 'Corruption' is a normative term that implies, and therefore affirms, the existence of a public order that is transparent and moral, and a clear divide between 'the state' and 'civil society' (Gupta 1995). In contrast, for my interlocutors, the cracks on the surfaces of new buildings upended fundamental categories that structured Kazakhstani politics and public life. Another world showed through the cracks on buildings' facades, and seemingly threatened to burst the ostensible world at the seams. In that other world, the meanings of city and village, centre and periphery, future and past, and progress and disintegration, were all unsettled and reversed.

The introduction to this volume invites us to reflect on the 'dialectic' of brokenness and repair. The emphasis, however, falls more towards repair, which is embraced as restoration of order and meaning. Brokenness is seen

Figure S4.1. Maintenance work underneath Astana's surfaces. Photograph by Mateusz Laszczkowski.

as rather negative, as 'failure', a problem to be solved. In contrast, here I have offered a rumination on a kind of brokenness that refuses repair – cracks that open before the surface is even complete. While certainly experienced as unwelcome elements in the sociomaterial environment, I suggest that in philosophical terms these cracks have a positive role. They are disturbing because they point to discrepancies and contradictions in our human world that cannot be easily glossed over. They provoke ongoing refiguring of the political and of relations connecting humans and 'things'.

Mateusz Laszczkowski is Assistant Professor at the Institute of Ethnology and Cultural Anthropology, at the University of Warsaw.

References

Barad, K. 2007. *Meeting the Universe Halfway: Quantum Physics and the Entanglement of Matter and Meaning*. Durham, NC: Duke University Press.

Bennett, J. 2010. *Vibrant Matter: A Political Ecology of Things*. Durham, NC: Duke University Press.

Bessire, L., and D. Bond. 2014. 'Ontological Anthropology and the Deferral of Critique', *American Ethnologist* 41(3): 440–56.

Bissenova, A. 2014. 'The Master Plan of Astana: Between the "Art of Government" and the "Art of Being Global"', in M. Reeves, J. Rasanayagam and J. Beyer (eds), *Ethnographies of the State in Central Asia: Performing Politics*. Bloomington: Indiana University Press, pp. 127–48.

Buchli, V. 2007. 'Astana: Materiality and the City', in C. Alexander, V. Buchli and C. Humphrey (eds), *Urban Life in Post-Soviet Asia*. London: UCL Press, pp. 40–69.

Gupta, A. 1995. 'Blurred Boundaries: The Discourse of Corruption, the Culture of Politics, and the Imagined State', *American Ethnologist* 22(2): 375–402.

Henare, A., M. Holbraad and S. Wastell (eds). 2007. *Thinking through Things: Theorising Artefacts Ethnographically*. London: Routledge.

Holbraad, M., and M.A. Pedersen. 2017. *The Ontological Turn*. Cambridge: Cambridge University Press.

Knox, H. 2017a. 'Affective Infrastructures and the Political Imagination', *Public Culture* 29(82): 363–84.

——. 2017b. 'The Problem of Action: Infrastructure, Planning and the Informational Environment', in P. Harvey, C.B. Jensen and A. Morita (eds), *Infrastructures and Social Complexity: A Companion*. London: Routledge, pp. 352–66.

Laszczkowski, M. 2015. '"Demo Version of a City": Buildings, Affects, and the State in Astana', *Journal of the Royal Anthropological Institute* 22: 148–65.

——. 2016. *'City of the Future': Built Space, Modernity and Urban Change in Astana*. Oxford: Berghahn Books.

Latour, B. 2005. *Reassembling the Social: An Introduction to Actor-Network Theory*. Oxford: Oxford University Press.

Law, J. 2015. 'What's Wrong with a One-World World?', *Distinktion: Scandinavian Journal of Social Theory* 16(1): 126–39.

Martin, K. 2014. 'Afterword: Knot-work not Networks, or Anti-anti-antifetishism and the ANTipolitics Machine', *HAU: Journal of Ethnographic Theory* 4(3): 99–115.

Nazarbaev, N. 2005. *V serdtse Evrazii*. Astana: Atamura.

Ong, A. 2011. 'Introduction: Worlding Cities, or the Art of Being Global', in A. Roy and A. Ong (eds), *Worlding Cities: Asian Experiments and the Art of Being Global*. Oxford: WileyBlackwell, pp. 1–26.

Preda, A. 1999. 'The Turn to Things: Arguments for a Sociological Theory of Things', *The Sociological Quarterly* 40(2): 347–66.

Viveiros de Castro, E. 2012. *Cosmological Perspectivism in Amazonia and Elsewhere*. Manchester: HAU Books.

Zhusupov, T. 2008. 'Gorod letayushchego keramogranita', *Vechernyaya Astana*, 2 October.

CHAPTER 4

A Ride on the Elevator

Infrastructures of Brokenness and Repair in Georgia

TAMTA KHALVASHI

When Nino finds out that she does not have a 10 tetri coin for the prepayment elevator to get to the ninth floor of her Soviet building apartment in Tbilisi, the first thing she does is curse. Then she calls her daughter and asks her to send a coin to her by elevator. Nino's daughter fetches the 10 tetri coin from a small wooden bowl standing on the shelf in the entrance hall of the apartment, walks out to the elevator and puts the coin on top of the prepayment box, a small iron machine fixed into the wall of the Soviet-era lift. Down on the ground floor, Nino then presses a button for the elevator. When the doors open again, the 10 tetri coin is waiting. Nino rides the lift home. 'When you come home after work or grocery shopping and you are absolutely tired, it is a nightmare to find out that you are out of 10 tetri coins', says Nino. 'Sometimes people are lucky to have family members at home to get coins quickly. But sometimes, you need to go back to a store and exchange money or wait for another neighbour who can give you a ride.'

Tbilisi has upward of ten thousand Soviet-era elevators, many of which long ago exceeded their recommended life-span and which are therefore in need of special maintenance. One stop-gap innovation has been the introduction of coin-operated lifts. Their goal is in part to raise funds for electricity bills and technical equipment repair for the elevators, but their immediate effect has been to discourage use of the elevator entirely for those who can walk, or for those (like most in Georgia) who have to watch their budget carefully. Users do not need to purchase or load up credit cards or tokens in advance, but ensure they have 5 or 10 tetri coins at their disposal, depending on the residential unit.[1] Inserting these coins into the sensor boxes installed inside the elevator directly mediates access to the flow of bodies and things, dividing rich from poor, healthy from weak, or mindful from unmindful, those who remember and those who forget to have coins

The increasing deployment of prepayment technologies within Georgian elevators reflects a larger political, temporal and semiotic shift in many parts of the world. Indeed, such technologies signal precarious times in which dependence on regular salaries and income has become increasingly problematic (Von Schnitzler 2016). They are therefore oriented to avoid the nonpayment of service charges, bypassing or illegal connection to services. While prepayment technologies, from mobile phones to electricity to water provision, are used ubiquitously in many parts of the world today, the prepayment elevators are not widespread phenomena and one can rarely encounter it today.[2] It was first introduced during the early 2000s to ensure the collection of fees for elevator maintenance and repair in a context of mass nonpayment and infrastructure breakdown. This was part of the larger political process in Georgia that implied the increasing decentralisation of state maintenance for common spaces in residential buildings, prompting people to critically reflect upon how to maintain crumbling spaces. As such, prepayment boxes emerged as additions to Soviet elevators to ensure money collection. In the past ten years, they have thus become a vivid and ready marker of transition from socialism to the brave new world of market economics. To be sure, the transition from socialism to neoliberal market economics created the problem of managing, caring for, and navigating urban spaces, and offered woefully insufficient solutions, that reveal the serious challenges to the very notion of common good not only on the level of state policies, but much smaller communities, such as Samezoblo or neighbourhood. Prepayment elevators therefore came to constitute the material domain through which the notions of space, community and the state are being retooled and reimagined. As such, they are part of the global trend of privatization and marketization that reproduce states of failure and unsustainability, especially when applied to outdated infrastructures. Prepayment boxes are markers of such trend, as they constitute a new urban order alongside the old one.

How, then, can we understand this breakdown of urban order in Georgia? One way is to think through Brian Larkin's idea that infrastructure breakdown is not simply failure but becomes a condition of existence for emergence (2008). As he argues, breakdown generates fixes and necessity for repair (Larkin 2016). Certainly, this seems to tap into what Larkin is getting at when arguing that infrastructures generate politics and poetics of space (2013). They thus create room to understand the role of breakdown and the forms of life to which breakdown gives rise. Indeed, broken Soviet elevators are objects that have created the conditions for the emergence of prepayment technologies to help repair and maintain outmoded elevators that had become increasingly dangerous. Yet, these new strategies of repair and maintenance have themselves become entrenched in free market logics and politics. Hence, while these technologies are essential for managing and caring for infrastructures, Soviet elevators nonetheless continue to break down. Small wonder, then, that prepayment boxes do not shape a new state of repair. Instead, they continue to reproduce states of failure. This shapes the part of urban order that I term *infrastructures of brokenness and repair*, creating both certainties and doubts about environments within which people move and experience space. This is to say that while I retain the idea that broken infrastructures have become grounds for certainty (Petersen and Carey 2017) to repair, I nonetheless stress the condition of their continuous breakdown to reproduce radical ambiguity.

Most prepayment elevators in Georgia are today operated by private companies rather than the centrally administered Soviet bureaucratic structures, which had previously provided elevator maintenance services. Despite their challenges, many choose prepayment machines over voluntary bill collections precisely because the latter are considered even more unreliable for providing elevator maintenance. Hence, the new urban order in Georgia is today predicated on the reciprocal exchange between humans and machines. Taking a ride on a paid elevator, with all the uncertainty about the availability of coins and regular breakdowns, has become a constant reminder to Georgians about their place in changing urban environments. Broken elevators in this way provide shifting experiential realities, often marked by affective relations (Brennan 2004) to space, state and community. Conceived of in this manner, what I refer to as infrastructures of brokenness and repair are also a series of techniques, strategies and skills by which people try to navigate uncertain urban environments. To be sure, residents, through their practices and strategies of cheating or bypassing, become infrastructures in their own right, as they continue to maintain uninterrupted mobility by using their bodily techniques and skills.

As Lauren Berlant in her study on infrastructure during transitional times argues, 'to attend to the terms of transition is to forge an imaginary for managing the meanwhile within damaged life's perdurance. . .' (2016: 394). Berlant provides a refreshing text for thinking about infrastructures as 'glitches', that involve local patching and mending, while not generating durable forms of repair. Drawing on Berlant, I argue that the terms of postsocialist transformation continue to be particularly troubled in Georgia precisely because obsolete infrastructures continue to create states of breakdown and repair. As I will demonstrate throughout this chapter, revitalising the broken elevators does not produce a reliable and enduring apparatus of repair and collective action. Instead, they continue to generate breakdowns and temporary fixes while reproducing provisional states of upkeep. So, if the infrastructural 'glitch' (Berlant 2016) makes apparent the conditions of disrupted movement or circulation, it also makes evident that collectivity stays bound to the ordinary failures that make up their immediate life and space. The prepayment elevators thus offer us a way of understanding the meanwhile – modes of breakdown and management, which are no longer seen as transitory. Hence, I propose infrastructures of brokenness and repair as an alternative to the neoliberal reform narratives that have dominated the postsocialist transition. There have been attempts to establish transition as a temporary process, leading to 'new states' and citizens based on market economy. Yet ambiguities or breakdowns have become embedded in everyday sociality and urban order. They are not merely the temporary legacies of socialism but part of the ordinary in their own right (Frederiksen and Knudsen 2015). Infrastructures of brokenness and repair in this way are a form of communication, affect and meaning. It is thus far from being a condition that applies only to the post-Soviet context.

Precarious Elevators

Anyone who has spent time in Georgian cities will have been struck by the disruptive presence of now derelict elevators in many Soviet building blocks. Using these elevators evokes associations with taking a ride on a rollercoaster, starting with the cracking noise of the rusting elevator chain and doors suddenly slammed shut. Most buildings have only one elevator, but some have two, one usually for freight and another for passengers. These elevators for carrying people and things up and down link Georgian cities to broader patterns of Soviet infrastructural modernity (Collier 2011). They also constantly resist the process of turning into the very scrap metal that they currently tend to produce.

Elevators were key architectural features of multistorey buildings as a result of vertical extension of building structures in Europe since the end of the nineteenth century. They have come to form the previously unknown semi-public material spaces within houses, making it possible to encounter strangers almost every day (Bernard 2014: 15). The progression of multistorey housing structures and elevators was therefore a crucial indicator of

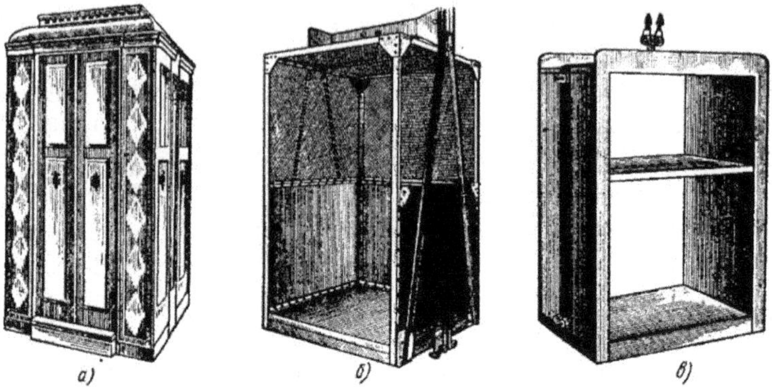

Figure 4.1. Soviet cabins for freight and passenger elevators, taken from *Elektricheskie Lifti: Ustroistvo i Montaj* [Electrical Elevators: Device and Instalment] published by the Soviet Scientific-Technical Press of Mechanical-Building Literature in 1952.

Soviet modernity, coinciding with other dimensions of a city's physical and social development.

Considered a key technical element in the Soviet city building, a book entitled *Electrical Elevators: Device and Instalment*, published by the Soviet Scientific-Technical Press of Mechanical-Building Literature in 1952, describes the significance of elevator machinery for the Soviet construction boom: 'Such grandiose construction requires the relevant extension of production and technical sophistication through installing in them passenger and freight hoists (elevators)' (Tushmalov 1952: 3).[3] In this way, the Soviet urban order depended on the improvement, operation and maintenance of electrical elevators.

The very qualities of elevators that made them crucial for modernity also accorded them affective significance. This affective significance hinged upon the elevator's very technical characteristics, and on the vertical transportation that it enables. In his book, *Lifted: A Cultural History of the Elevator*, Andreas Bernard touches on this in an account about elevators:

> That the staged prevention of a fall, the presentation of an automatic braking device, retrospectively became the primal scene of elevator history is inseparable from this deeply ingrained mistrust of the cable, reinforced by numerous mining accidents. The suspension of containers for vertical transport represented a latent danger, and for an invention such as the passenger elevator to become accepted above ground, it first had to explicitly guarantee the safety of the unstable principle of suspension. (Bernard 2014: 27)

Figure 4.2. Soviet guidelines for elevator chains. Taken from *Elektricheskie Lifti: Ustroistvo i Montaj* [Electrical Elevators: Device and Instalment] published by the Soviet Scientific-Technical Press of Mechanical-Building Literature in 1952.

Contingent on its fundamental technical traits, the elevator itself emerged as a precarious technical object. The possibility of an accident served recurrently as a catalyst for sophisticated technical guidelines on how to improve, install and maintain elevators. A glance at the numerous Soviet handbooks about vertical transport makes clear a notable focus on such technical details intended to avoid calamities and breakdowns. The Soviet architecture was articulated through the political use of infrastructure to promote a socialist order (Buchli 1999; Fehérváry 2013; Humphrey 2005) by making citizens subjects of state protection, rather than self-protection.

Elevators were centralised entities directly connected to the state-employed technicians or dispatchers through the elevator buttons in cases of emergency. Unlike the post-Soviet Georgian state that made citizens responsible for taking care of their own urban facilities and spaces, providing material structures was the perpetual preoccupation of the Soviet state. Any optimistic anticipation of an elevator's indestructibility by sophisticated technical guidelines, however, was frequently disappointed. Accidents in Soviet social life were in fact quite frequent and produced everyday fear, cynicism and feelings of uncertainty about the state. In other words, the fear of being stuck in the elevator was a source of politicisation. To be rescued from the elevator was not merely a technical operation but it mediated a specific relation with the state.

A memorable Soviet Georgian film, *Blue Mountains, or an Unbelievable Story* (1984), depicts this paradoxical working environment in a Tbilisi publishing house. An elevator is often out of order and employees often get trapped inside, forcing them to wait endlessly for the state elevator technician – both metaphorically and literally implicating the bureaucratic failures of the late Soviet state to maintain its infrastructural order. The

Figure 4.3. *Blue Mountain, or an Unbelievable Story*. Director Eldar Shengelaia, 1984. Screenshot taken by the author.

experience of being stuck in the elevator is thus presented as a normalised condition and omnipresent reality of that period.

When one employee gets trapped in the elevator, for instance, he continues editing his text with total indifference. As the man in charge of building maintenance informs him that the elevator technician is going to rescue him by the end of the day (hence, no reason to worry), the trapped passenger angrily replies, 'I am not afraid of anything'. Then with a smirk, he adds, 'whether you go up or down it does not really matter', indirectly hinting at the overall experience of uncertainty and nihilism generated by the late Soviet state crisis and failure.

'Disruptions and breakdowns', as Stephen Graham reminds us, 'allow us to excavate the usually hidden politics of flow and connection, of mobility and immobility' (2010: 3). Indeed, broken elevators mediate a puzzlement about the political – that is, they are sites through which technical and political concerns converge and produce uneasy affects. The question, then, is how a film made in a different political and technical system, addressing specific issues, continues to work in post-Soviet times, when we are said to live in a totally different system. In fact, contemporary Georgia represents the afterlife of Soviet modernity. It is a different temporality in which the Soviet ruins endure and shape an uncertain urban order. What joins the Soviet past and the present rests on infrastructural debris. It is not debris that is memorialised, romanticised or revered, but rather what people are simply left with (Edensor 2005).

Broken Infrastructures

'Before installing the [coin-operated] box, I was often stuck in the elevator because these elevators are so old and we did not manage to collect money to repair them', recalled Nino, the middle-aged woman living in the outskirts of Tbilisi, whom I introduced earlier. She was reflecting on the elevator's condition and its maintenance, which became a common issue in the early 1990s. 'If lucky, some buildings had an elevator technician as a fellow tenant who could rescue trapped people. But we did not. So, I had to wait until one of my neighbours would figure out how to rescue me.' What this experience left Nino feeling about her movement marks a remarkable segue, one that shows how broken elevators bridge uncertainty and technological predicament. She said, starting to laugh, 'When I entered these lifts, I started crossing myself, sometimes even praying'.

Nino was one of many residents in Tbilisi who had come to experience the constant breakdown of the Soviet-era elevators in the early 1990s. She recalled that during Soviet times, the maintenance of multifamily buildings, including cleaning and repairs for the common areas, was carried out by the state housing maintenance organisations. Residents paid for maintenance and utilities, but these costs were highly subsidised and fees were among the lowest in the world. Unlike the Soviet period, however, in the 1990s the state unplugged people from centralised systems of urban provisioning. The elevator breakdowns then became chronic in Georgia. As Nino pointed out, getting trapped in an elevator was not only due to the age of the elevators or lack of maintenance. Frequent power cuts and the theft of mechanical parts to sell on the scrap market, a ubiquitous practice in the early post-Soviet era, also contributed to the regular trapping of passengers.

The broken elevators emerged as objects of conflict, channelling political and material crisis and decay in early post-Soviet Georgia. Together with other infrastructures, elevators called into question established systems of state and space. This has been expressed in daily conversations as well as in media and literary works. One novel, *Hide*, by the Georgian writer Aleko Shugladze, ironically depicts this experience in 1990s Tbilisi:

> The theme of being stuck in an elevator is a very complicated one and requires deep analysis. Trapped people can be divided into two groups: those who fall silent and those who start screaming. This does not at all mean that the silent ones are fearless, they just lose their voice due to fear. The screamers perhaps are trying to encourage themselves . . . The silenced ones used the phrase: 'You'll rescue me, right?' while the screamers used the phrase, 'Rescue me, you motherfuckers!' (Shugladze 2016: 16)

Being repeatedly trapped in an elevator is indexical of uncertainty in 1990s Georgia. This actually resonates with many transitioning states across the world (Greenhouse 2002). It provides an opportunity to probe radical ambiguities brought by postsocialist transformations that became manifested in urban space of Georgia. To be trapped in the elevator did not merely emerge as a source of uncertainty about the political, however, but also came to define a particular relationship between space and community. It mobilised a feeling of mistrust connected to the unpredictability of being rescued by 'someone' (previously a dispatcher) and a sense of danger charged with the moral language of responsibility. In other words, language of responsibility, hinging upon the availability of caring publics to rescue trapped passengers, mediated the frustrations about the state that withered from many spheres of life.[4]

The broken elevators are embedded within wider political transitions and shifts, producing their own infrastructures of brokenness and repair. Geographers Steve Graham and Simon Marvin have demonstrated how the modern infrastructural ideal is severely fragile. They label this condition 'infrastructure crises' (2001: 94), indicating the breakdowns reflected in, among other things, electricity cuts, water shortages and potholed roads in many parts of the postcolonial and postsocialist world. In their account, Graham and Marvin outline the broad set of forces (re)producing such 'infrastructure crises'. In particular, they stress the role of liberalised models of infrastructural provision together with the obsolescent infrastructure networks that in the context of post-communist countries were incorporated unevenly into flows of privatisation, capital, information and technology.[5]

Indeed, the obsolescent legacies of Soviet elevators pose systematic challenges for the residents of Georgia. As old systems of maintenance disappear, new forms of urban provisioning do not provide equivalent services. Soviet infrastructures prove stubbornly 'intransigent', one reason being the lack of resources and institutional frameworks to upgrade crumbling infrastructures (Collier 2011). Infrastructural decay thus occupies multiple historical temporalities in Georgia. The broken elevators are the products of past defects that are permeated into the present. They are the ruins that serve as reminders of decay (Frederiksen 2016), as well as defiance against it (Manning 2008). Uncertainty and doubt in this way are also present in the invalidity of ruins (Pelkmans 2013), which are as much part of the former political system as they are the very manifestation of the current urban order. It is this uncertainty embedded in the urban environment that forces Georgians to develop practical techniques and solutions. These techniques, however, create their own states of brokenness and repair, and with them, affective worlds that are both distinct from and similar to those of the late Soviet state.

Fragile Maintenance

Like many other broken things, the elevators became a battlefield and a space of creative solutions to enable mobility in early post-Soviet Georgia. A crucial question that arose in the 1990s and that continues to linger today is who is actually going to repair or take care of outdated elevators? As I myself grew up in an eight-storey Soviet building block in Tbilisi and later moved to a fourteen-storey one (in both cases living on the top floor), I came to understand how this was achieved. The most active advocates of elevator maintenance were those living on upper floors, including my mother, who was actively involved in finding a way to make these rides possible and safe for us. Horrified by her own memories of walking the eight floors while carrying heavy grocery bags, she told me that a life of broken elevators had resulted in constant back pain. Yet even when the elevator would occasionally work due to a temporary repair of its parts, she was constantly afraid that one of us would be trapped if we chose to ride on it.

For many residential blocks, hence, there emerged a money collector, a resident of the building, usually living in a unit on the upper floors, who started to serve voluntarily as a housekeeper to provide technical maintenance or elevator repair. If the residents had formerly relied on the state to secure the mobility of elevators, in early postsocialist Georgia the elevator movement and maintenance in this way started to hinge upon individual collectors. In fact, the city municipalities revoked most of the state funding for maintaining residential buildings in the 1990s. It was only in the late 2000s that the state started to provide finances for major infrastructural breakdowns, but not for permanent maintenance. The money collectors thus came to be responsible for reaching out to an elevator technician or a private company to provide regular maintenance services, and to visit the neighbours in order to secure monthly payments, usually from 5 to 8 lari a month. In a way, the exhortation to pay for elevator maintenance came to be managed by the money collector, who replaced the moral obligation of the state to take care of common areas. The money collectors are thus still key in many residential buildings in Georgia. As well as collecting money for elevators, they sometimes also reach out to gather funds for cleaning or renovation purposes. In most cases, such payments are made in person, as most of the Soviet building blocks do not have bank accounts.

While the purpose of the money collector is to secure funds for elevator maintenance, the main goal of elevator technicians is to look after the derelict technical parts of elevators that need constant care. As Kote Mchedlishvili, a doctor of technical sciences, explained on a radio show about elevators, the way in which Soviet elevators are constantly maintained in Georgia hinges upon the recycling of their technical parts. He explained, 'When an old elevator is repaired, its extra elements are used for repairing other elevators', emphasising the expensive tariffs for installing new technical elements and the lack of funds to replace them.[6] The elevators thus depend on the existence of other broken elevators, whose technical parts are referred into circulation.

Let us return to the case of Nino, who in fact herself had served as a money collector since the 1990s, before installing the coin-operated paybox in her dilapidated Soviet building in 2016. At the time I met Nino in 2015, prepayment boxes had already replaced most of the human collectors in Georgia. Yet Nino still continued to gather payments in person and resisted installing the coin-operated box. Of all the money collectors whom I met during my visits in 2015 and 2016, it was Nino who seemed the most persistent in collecting money for elevator maintenance. Although Nino found it difficult to make neighbours pay, she insisted that it was cheaper to run the elevator by direct payments than by prepayment boxes. Nino noted, however, that many neighbours were unable to make payments. Identifying the causes of nonpayment was not a very difficult task for her. Careful to adopt a tone of voice that was not too angry, she said:

> This is one of the hardest and most stressful jobs I have ever done in my life. Most neighbours who live below the fifth floor often refuse to pay. Their explanation is that they are not using the elevator at all. But this is just an excuse. They are ashamed to say that they do not have the seven GEL a month to pay for elevator maintenance. Collecting money above the fifth floor is also problematic. But at least people on upper floors try to find a solution!

The nonpaying neighbours, as Nino continued, were not only the poor ones, however. There were also residents hiding behind those who could pay. 'In both cases, people were still using the elevator for free', added Nino, as she poured a cup of tea while slowly getting angry about her neighbours. Every effort made by her to urge neighbours from lower floors to help pay for the elevator failed. To avoid free rides, the technicians helped Nino fix the elevator so that it would not stop below the fifth floor. This was a common technique, especially in the 1990s. Another creative solution to limit unpaid rides reported to me across Georgian cities was to remove elevator buttons for the lower floors completely, as those living on lower floors were considered the most unreliable payers. These technical solutions to nonpayment, however, in turn birthed strategies of bypassing. The most common strategy, as Nino explained, was riding the elevator to one of the upper floors and then walking down – walking down being preferable to climbing. This left the elevator technicians the impossible task of controlling free transits.

When neighbours evaded payments, elevators lacked repairs and often broke down. This has evoked conflicts and unpleasant encounters between money collectors and neighbours. Elevator maintenance in this way generated a certain shift in the relations between neighbours, what in Georgian is called *mezobloba*, or the relations between neighbours based on solidarity and friendship.[7] While *mezobloba* is often revered and cherished in Georgia, the imperative to pay for elevators threatened to charge its meaning with new moral economy, generating a sense of mistrust. Nino's husband for more than twenty years often liked to recount nostalgically, 'We had much more amicable *mezobloba* before elevators broke down. Now neighbours do not even trust each other anymore'. Nino and her husband felt that the money collection generated a sense of mistrust that had previously not been part of their relations with their neighbours. 'It's not only about the difficulty of collecting money or bypassing but also about the mistrust that the neighbours express about such payments. Many of our neighbours think that we charge them more money to use it for personal reasons', concluded Nino.[8]

Nino's story opens the way for an understanding of people's capacity to imagine new strategies to take care of common areas in contexts of escalating socioeconomic inequalities. Yet it calls into question the collective forms of action or coordination, and reveals skills in finding provisional solutions to failures. Perhaps nowhere else is this more visible than in the fragile maintenance of elevators by money collectors in Georgia. I suggest that to some extent this is (re)produced because of insufficient funds for decayed elevators, and to some extent because they are not perceived as common things, that people start to capitalise on radical urban uncertainties. While the broken elevators generate strategies of repair and maintenance, these strategies are more often than not fragile. In fact, the lifting of bodies and things continues to reproduce breakdowns and generate doubts both in relation to space and among people. Like many other money collectors, Nino thus suffered from this spatial uncertainty, prompting her to finally give way to a prepayment apparatus that occurred as a moral technique to replace her.

Prepaid Spaces

Maintenance and repair entail moral relations to technologies (Jackson 2014), or, as pointed out by Bruno Latour, 'We have been able to delegate to nonhumans not only force as we have known it for centuries but also values, duties, and ethics' (1992: 232). In Georgia, to pay for the maintenance of common things, such as elevators, is indeed delegated less and less to humans, and more to non-humans, such as coin boxes. In other words, payment technologies substitute for the unreliable payers. Just like electricity meters that emerged as 'tools of moral improvement' in South Africa's townships after apartheid (Von Schnitzler 2016: 123), so did the coin boxes become moral devices to secure payments in post-Soviet Georgia. The coin boxes make the elevator ride not just an occasion of transportation, but an ethical experience. They are ineluctably embedded in prepaid motion and emotion and persist as apparatuses for maintenance.

The steady colonisation of Soviet elevators by prepayment boxes since the 2000s exemplifies this contention. In fact, the first elevator paybox was invented precisely because of this failure to pay for elevator repair and maintenance. Bacho Sharashenidze, a money collector and a skilled electrician who lived on the sixteenth floor of a Soviet residential building in the 1990s, devised the coin-operated box to finally end the moral battle of collecting payments.[9] By the late 2000s, and in a context of large-scale nonpayment, prepayment payboxes therefore began to be commercially produced by Georgian companies.[10] The coin-operated boxes were hailed as a major technological innovation that it was hoped could end nonpayment problems. It introduced market mechanisms of operation and maintenance into common areas that charged the residents on the basis of use. These iron boxes created the technical possibility for a kind of provisional moral unity of neighbours to share maintenance and repair costs. A ride on the elevator started to rely on a certainty in a prepayment apparatus that recognised the unreliability of collective responsibility.

While the political underpinnings of this major infrastructural change were not directly admitted, it was clear that this was part of larger efforts to officially decentralise urban provisioning in Georgia since 2007. The Rose Revolution reformers, who came into power in 2003 with the ambition to end the postsocialist transition and modernise the country, included housing repairs in their own neoliberal critique of state regulation. The reform implied moving away from a system of heavily subsidised, government-financed utility services to one in which housing is maintained and managed by the occupants. One exemplary document entitled 'Homeowners Associations in the Former Soviet Union: Stalled on the Road to Reform', produced as part of the World Bank's Cities in Eurasia project and reprinted by the International Housing Coalition in 2012, described this reform and its obstacles in various post-Soviet countries.[11] The author of the paper, Barbara J. Lipman, a consultant to the World Bank, observed: 'the legacy of Soviet times has left a mix of occupants of different incomes and ability to pay living under the same roof'. The paper continued: 'nor is public or private financing available for badly needed capital repairs and energy efficiency improvements. What can be done? Apartment owners should be given control of the common areas' (2012: 1).

A major purpose of that paper was to document the decrepit conditions of common areas in postsocialist residential building blocks and to underline the importance of the Home Owners Association (HOA) in their management and maintenance. The paper summarised the current state of thinking in Georgia among other countries in former Soviet Union: a turn from government intervention and regulation to its opposite, nonintervention, deregulation and privatisation of common areas. Despite adopting such views on urban provisioning, the market was still not seen as an absolute alternative mechanism for efficiently allocating infrastructures in Georgian cities. The local municipalities, hence, continued to provide some funds for major infrastructural renovations for common areas, precisely because of the lack of communal resource to repair and maintain the decayed residential buildings. Yet such state funds often proved insufficient. Broken roofs, cracked walls, shattered stairs and peeling hallways all mark the troubled afterlife of Soviet infrastructures in most residential buildings throughout Georgia.

The Georgian prepayment elevators emerged as a part of this much wider transformation of the postsocialist restructuring of the urban environment. They coincided with ambitious plans of the Rose Revolutionary government to form new urbanism by pursuing marketisation and privatization policies (Manning 2009; Rekhviashvili 2015). Common areas in residential buildings emerged as those few spaces that were subjected to the principles of common property by HOA, dubbed as Amkhanagoba in Georgian. Yet most of the common areas continue to be outside of any specific management structures or property law, which generates conditions of disrupted property regimes, responsibilities, recourses, moralities and circulation. The majority of residential buildings do not even have properly functioning HOAs. Instead, in many buildings, money collectors continue to play a crucial role in making things work.

Elevator stories hence powerfully transmit the common space tension and ambiguity. When I told him I was writing about elevators, Levan, an erudite former money collector and a doctor of technical sciences, plunged into a story about recycled elevator parts. Levan's friend, who had a spare elevator part, did not waste it, but gave it to Levan. Levan kept the gift in the shared attic to use in case of elevator breakdown. One day, the elevator part disappeared. It turned out that the new money collector, who was later elected as an HOA chief, had secretly sold the recycled part. This story helps us see that common spaces or things are not always used or seen as common. It is this ambiguous management of common areas and the social uncertainty about a ride on the elevator that plagued the rise of the prepayment boxes. In the constellation of elevator stories, the prepaid technologies are thus constantly evoked for resurrection and maintenance of common areas. Alexander, a retired biologist, told me how, despite the efforts of several neighbours to collect funds without machines, they were constantly lacking enough capital. Where the money collectors failed, the coin-operated boxes grew.

Shortchanged Lives

Technologies are unstable objects not only due to their malfunction but also in how people use them (Larkin 2008). While 'technical devices can define actors, the space in which they move, and the ways in which they interact' (Akrich 1992: 216), these devises can at the same time reiterate already existing social or cultural repertoires. For Hanna Knox (2017), although objects might have the capacity to affect and reframe actors as the grounds for new sociality, they may still reproduce conventionally framed forms of practices. Coin-operated elevators indeed illustrate such contentions as they both reframe and at the same time reproduce actions.

As a replacement for money collectors, the elevator coin boxes were cast to control the movement and to punish those who transgress them by denying them a ride. A great number of people living in urban Georgia thus came to be short of change, meaning that they do not have the loose change they need to pay for elevator transactions. While residents are shortchanged by life, as they lack the money they need, they shortchange coin boxes by using various strategies. These strategies are fostering the practices and ideas of thrift that are widespread in many postsocialist countries and beyond (Schlecker 2005). To be sure, thrift and cheating presume that a stream of wealth is limited. People in Georgian elevators thus use different bodily techniques and skills of bypassing, even though the intention of the coin-operated mechanisms is to control free rides. In this way, prepayment technologies continue to have tricky social lives in Georgia.

How the coin boxes are shortchanged and how apartments are reached by prepayment elevators diverges in each building. The practices of bypassing have a myriad of shapes and forms. The most common trick is the use of coins with a hole drilled through, which serves as a hanger for a thread. The user slides the coin into the box, which registers its disposal, and then through the help of the thread slides it back. The thread method does not fully deliver the change to the coin box. In this way, residents are always sure to have the necessary coin for the ride.

After installing the coin-operated boxes, Nino explained that she could not resist getting a drilled coin for herself. She made sure that her ride

Figure 4.4. A drilled 10 tetri coin for coin-operated elevator boxes. Creative Commons.

would be uninterrupted, even when she was out of coins. Using the coins every time someone had no change for the elevator ride, as many of her neighbours did, Nino said, was now a problem best avoided. Although Nino's neighbour, Eka, had a small family, consisting of a husband and her daughter, each of them had their own drilled coins at hand. One of them even used a Danish drilled Krones to save drilling a Georgian lari. 'Danish money is just what we need here in Georgia', Nino said.

Other physically more flexible residents produced even more complicated ways of bypassing the boxes. Because elevators without any weight in them can make unlimited rides, residents started to deploy this trick. In this strategy, it is crucial that a person holds their whole body up in the air by swinging on the ceiling or hanging on a rack of the elevator, until one gets to the designated floor. While this awkward form of movement resembles training in acrobatics, it is also about training in visceral and bodily adjustment to the elevators. If one suddenly falls down, the elevator gets stuck, hence this trick is mainly used by younger people who have more energy for such effects. The entrance of coin-operated boxes into

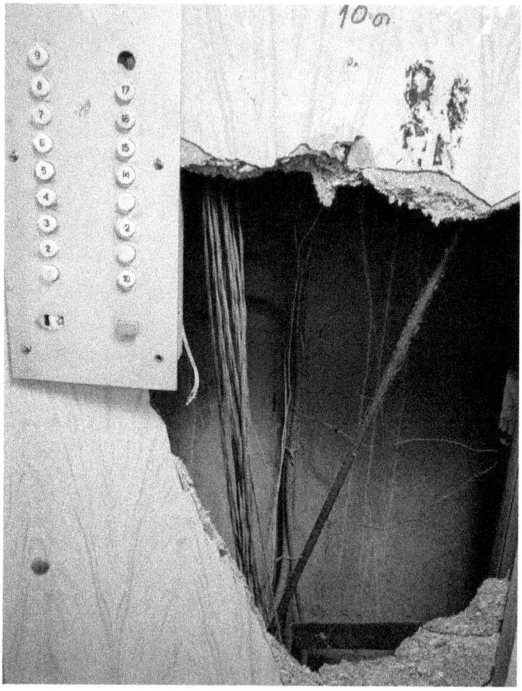

Figure 4.5. A hole in the elevator, marking the stolen coin-operated box. Photograph by Tamta Khalvashi.

the Soviet building blocks in this way makes residents dependent on how they can accommodate their bodies, skills and fantasies to the elevator and to new restrictions on elevator transportation. It should be clear by now why residents, through their practices and strategies of cheating, become infrastructures in their own right, as they continue to maintain incessant mobility by using their bodies.

While payment elevators were designed to produce funding for elevator maintenance and repair, such finances have often been difficult to achieve due to this myriad of bodily and social tricks. The payment boxes in this way did not produce morally charged publics; rather, they reproduced reluctance to pay. The iron boxes filled with thousands of 10 tetri coins, moreover, attracted thieves to the buildings. The breaking and stealing of these boxes became frequent. This form of payment thus came to hinge on a shift in embodied practices, not least of which is the transformation of bodily techniques and their insertion into technology.

Usually, it is the chief of the HOA or the money collector who is responsible for collecting the coins from the elevator boxes and exchanging

Figures 4.6 and 4.7. Coin-operated boxes with lockers and iron structures to avoid sliding drilled coins. Photographs by Tamta Khalvashi.

them in local shops to pay private companies for the service fees. Sometimes, this procedure is carried out by the elevator companies themselves. In any case, installation of payment boxes created new routines and rules of money collection in Soviet building blocks. Previously hazardous daily actions of payment collection now became an explicit object of securitisation and protection. In many instances, thus, the coin-operated boxes became shielded with extra technical elements to prevent the bypassing or stealing of coins. Lockers or convoluted sliding iron structures were among the numerous innovations that today try to secure elevator payments. With properly locked payment boxes, as one collector suggested, 'it becomes more difficult to break and steal these boxes'.

Coin-operated boxes are affective grounds (Thrift 2004) for learning new bodily techniques and tricks in order to manage constraints imposed by the technology. But there are also less visible bodily strategies that are brought about. For instance, because coins often get stuck, the elevators continue to be temporarily out of order. Indeed, coin traffic is one of the most ubiquitous complaints. Residents often use their own keys or sharp objects to make trapped coins flow through the slot and enable the sensory mechanism to work. If this technique fails, they call the chief of the HOA or a money collector who owns the key to the box to periodically liberate the coins. Given the height of Soviet building blocks, normally ranging from seven to fifteen floors, this means that people choose to wait until they make the box work. Thus, new technology is sometimes also sensed as time consuming. It is intimately linked to a 'political economy of waiting', not least because waiting is sensed as a waste of time and money (Hage 2009: 3). Hence, waiting time in these contexts is also seen as a measurement of the lack of efficiency of coin boxes. Elevator tricks and techniques therefore become a form of affective labour to make mobility possible.

Conclusion: Infrastructures of Brokenness and Repair

Breakdown is indicative of the state of ambiguity and a condition for constant certainty and repair. As many infrastructures in Georgia – water pipes, roofs, streets, sidewalks, squares and roads – are decayed or at the edge of breakdown, a sense of omnipresent traffic and immobility is taking hold around the urban environment. Yet people are reclaiming space to mend, fix and maintain at least bits of infrastructures through various strategies and techniques to enable flow and movement. However, these strategies and techniques are themselves entrenched in the logic of market economy rather than in alternative methods of organizing communities. In fact, private elevator companies compete to innovate in producing more sophisticated technologies of money collection. Hence, some buildings have introduced electronic payment cards that are intended to eliminate the problems of cost recovery. Yet, such practices of care cannot amend the systemic infrastructural problem. Instead, prepayment elevators continue to act as sites of ambiguity.

Throughout this chapter, I thus termed the urban environments and practices around them *infrastructures of brokenness and repair*, a placeholder for forms of endurance in times of crisis that have become constant. Hoping to contribute to the anthropology of infrastructure, the ethnographic case study of payment elevators provided a way to suggest that infrastructures may be conceived of as forming temporary practices of upkeep. They create techniques for taming the uncertain urban spaces in their immediacy. What I have dubbed infrastructures of brokenness and repair, thus, is not only governing logic of the state and strategies of navigating urban spaces, but also unsustainable states of repair and maintenance. The reason it is germane to speak about infrastructures of brokenness and repair then is that while neoliberal narratives promise sustainable states and permanent order, in reality they only endure the systemic crisis. This forms part of a 'loose convergence', making 'a collectivity stay bound to the ordinary even as some of its forms of life are fraying, wasting, and developing offshoots' (Berlant 2016: 394).

Forming temporary convergences through infrastructures in times of permanent crises resonates with many parts of the world today. In a documentary film, *Africa Shafted: Under One Roof*, for instance, an elevator in Africa's tallest apartment building in Johannesburg forces a unique interaction and conversation to take place between migrants from different countries.[12] The space of this communal vehicle triggers a series of interconnections that create temporary alignments and dialogues in the context of prevalent xenophobia. Similarly, a ride on the elevator in Georgia brings into being temporary states of repair in the context of a prevalent infrastructure crisis. Yet, while these machines register the ongoing techniques and strategies of mobility and transportation, they continue to create states of brokenness and repair around them.

Tamta Khalvashi is Associate Professor of Anthropology at the Ilia State University of Tbilisi.

Notes

1. Georgian currency, the lari, consists of 100 tetri.
2. There is a non-functioning coin-operated elevator in La Spenzia, Italy installed in the lift produced by Fiam (Fabbrica Italiana Ascensori Montacharichi) in 1950s.
3. All translations are by the author, unless otherwise indicated.
4. In Russia, for instance, where the government decided to take part of the state-owned Moscow Elevator Company, Moslift, and create a joint company with the American firm Otis, specially trained elevator mechanics rescue citizens trapped in elevators.
5. A famous documentary film, *Power Trip*, by director Paul Delvin, depicts how the American AES Corporation assumes control of the newly privatised electric company Telasi in Georgia but finds it difficult to renovate broken infrastructures and make the Georgian people pay for their electricity.
6. A radio programme on 'Elevators and Elevator Technicians', Radio Imedi, March 2015.
7. *Mezobloba* is a special form of social organisation, made up of neighbours who live in one building or in close vicinity to each other, who have known one another for many years, and rely on each other's help and solidarity. Foundational works that analyse the phenomenon of *mezobloba* with different spatial and temporal scales focusing mainly on rural environments in Georgia include those by Giorgi Chitaia and Tedo Sakhokia.

8. The collection of money became even more challenging when intense urbanisation created the grounds for housing mobility from the 1990s onwards. While the money collection requires a level of familiarity with the neighbours, creating a shared sense of responsibility and reciprocity, with the flow of new people it became more rigid.
9. An article published in the Georgian online journal *AT*, entitled *Liptis kutebis tsarmoshoba da evolutsia* [The Emergence and Evolution of Elevator Boxes], discusses how the prepayment boxes emerged in Georgia. Retrieved (2 September 2018) from: https://at.ge/2018/01/08/%E1%83%9A%E1%83%98%E1%83%A4%E1%83%A2%E1%83%98%E1%83%A1-%E1%83%A7%E1%83%A3%E1%83%97%E1%83%94%E1%83%91%E1%83%98%E1%83%A1-%E1%83%AC%E1%83%90%E1%83%A0%E1%83%9B%E1%83%9D%E1%83%A8%E1%83%9D%E1%83%91%E1%83%90/
10. One of the biggest producers of the coin-operated boxes in Georgia is Computer Land.
11. The project was carried out under the portion of that project directed by Christine F. Kessides of the World Bank, formerly in the bank's Europe and Central Asia office (ECSSD).
12. Information about this film, by Ingrid Martens (2016), can be found at https://www.imoriginal.co/africashafted.

References

Arkich, Madeleine. 1992. 'The De-scription of Technical Objects', in W. Bijker and J. Law (eds), *Shaping Technology/Building Society: Studies in Sociotechnical Change*. Cambridge, MA: MIT Press, pp. 205–24.

Berlant, Lauren. 2016. 'The Commons: Infrastructures for Troubling Times', *Environment and Planning D: Society and Space* 34(3): 393–419.

Bernard, Andreas. 2014. *Lifted: A Cultural History of the Elevator*. New York: NYU Press.

Brennan, Teresa. 2004. *The Transmission of Affect*. Ithaca, NY: Cornell University Press.

Buchli, Victor. 1999. *An Archaeology of Socialism*. Oxford: Berg.

Chitaia, Giorgi. 2001. *Sauniversiteto lektsiebis kursi etnograpiashi 'Svetebi'* [University Courses of Lectures on Ethnography 'Svetebi']. Tbilisi: Metsniereba.

Collier, J. Stephen. 2011. *Post-Soviet Social: Neoliberalism, Social Modernity, Biopolitics*. Princeton, NJ: Princeton University Press.

Edensor, Tim. 2005. *Industrial Ruins: Spaces, Aesthetics and Materiality*. Oxford: Berg.

Fehérváry, Krisztina. 2013. *Politics in Color and Concrete: Socialist Materialities and the Middle Class in Hungary*. Bloomington: Indiana University Press.

Frederiksen, Martin Demant. 2016. 'Material Dys-appearance: Decaying Futures and Contested Temporal Passage', in P. Bjerregaard, A.E. Rasmussen and T.F. Sorensen (eds), *Materialities of Passing*. London: Routledge, pp. 49–64.

Frederiksen, Martin Demant, and Ida Harboe Knudsen. 2015. 'An Introduction: What Is a Grey Zone and Why Is Eastern Europe One?', in M.D. Frederiksen and I.H. Knudsen (eds), *Ethnographies of Grey Zones in Eastern Europe*. London: Anthem, pp. 1–22.

Graham, Stephen, and Simon Marvin. 2001. *Splintering Urbanism: Networked Infrastructures, Technological Mobilities, and the Urban Condition*. London: Routledge.
——. 2010. *Disrupted Cities: When Infrastructures Fail*. London: Routledge.
Greenhouse, Carol J. 2002. 'Altered States, Altered Lives', in J.C. Greenhouse, E. Mertz and B.K. Warren (eds), *Ethnography in Unstable Places: Everyday Lives in Contexts of Dramatic Political Change*. Durham, NC: Duke University Press (1-37).
Hage, Ghassan. 2009. 'Introduction', in Ghassan Hage (ed.), *Waiting*. Melbourne: Melbourne University Press, pp. 1–12.
Humphrey, Caroline. 2005. 'Ideology in Infrastructure: Architecture and Soviet Imagination', *Journal of the Royal Anthropological Institute* 11(1): 39–58.
Jackson, J. Steven. 2014. 'Rethinking Repair', in Tarleton Gillepsie, Pablo J. Boczkowski and Kirsten A. Foot (eds), *Media Technologies: Essays in Communication, Materiality, and Society*. Cambridge, MA: MIT Press, pp. 221–39.
Knox, Hanna. 2017. 'Affective Infrastructures and the Political Imagination', *Public Culture* 29(2): 363–84.
Larkin, Brian. 2008. *Signal and Noise: Media, Infrastructure and Urban Culture in Nigeria*. Durham, NC: Duke University Press.
——. 2013. 'The Politics and Poetics of Infrastructure', *Annual Review of Anthropology* 42: 327–43.
——. 2016. 'Ambient Infrastructures: Generator Life in Nigeria', *Technosphere Magazine*. Retrieved 9 November 2018 from https://technosphere-magazine.hkw.de/article1/cd07bf50-921e-11e693417d6509c7f586/76704180-91e7-11e6-8d22-0bf4eeadcfb0.
Latour, Bruno. 1992. 'Where Are the Missing Masses, Sociology of a Few Mundane Artefacts', in Wiebe Bijker and John Law (eds), *Shaping Technology-Building Society: Studies in Sociotechnical Change*. Cambridge, MA: MIT Press, pp. 225–258.
Lipman, J. Barbara. 2012. Homeowners Associations in the Former Soviet Union: Stalled on the Road of Reform. International Housing Coalition Publication.
Manning, Paul. 2008. 'Materiality and Cosmology: Old Georgian Churches as Sacred, Sublime, and Secular Objects', *Ethnos* 73(3): 327–60.
Manning, Paul. 2009. 'The Hotel/Refugee Camp Iveria: Symptom, Monster, Fetish Home', in K. Van Assche, J. Salukvadze and N. Shavishvili (eds), *City Culture and City Planning in Tbilisi: Where Europe and Asia Meet*. Lewiston: Mellen, pp. 71–102.
Pedersen, Morten Axel, and Matthew Carey. 2017. 'Introduction: Infrastructures of Certainty and Doubt', *The Cambridge Journal of Anthropology* 35(2): 18–25.
Pelkmans, Mathijs. 2013. 'Ruins of Hope in Kyrgyz Post-Industrial Wasteland', *Anthropology Today* 29(5): 16–20.
Rekhviashvili, Lela. 2015. 'Marketization and Public-Private Divide: Contestations between the State and the Petty Traders over the Access in Tbilisi', *International Journal of Sociology and Social Policy* 35(7/8): 478–96.
Sakhokia, Tedo. 1950. *Mogzaurobani: guria, adjara, samurzakano, apkhazeti* [Travels: Guria, Adjara, Samurzakano, Abkhazia]. Tbilisi: Sakhelgami.
Schlecker, Markus. 2005. 'Going Back a Long Way: "Home Place," Thrift and Temporal Orientations in Northern Vietnam', *Journal of the Royal Anthropological Institute* 11: 509–26.

Shubladze, Aleko. 2016. *Gadamalva* [Hide]. Tbilisi: Diogene.
Thrift, Nigel. 2004. 'Intensities of Feeling: Toward a Spatial Politics of Affect', *Geografiska Annaler* 86 B(1): 57–78.
Tushmalov, V.A. 1952. *Elektricheskie Lifti: Ustroistvo i Montaj* [Electrical Elevators: Device and Instalment]. Moscow: Soviet Scientific-Technical Press of Mechanical-Building Literature.
Von Schnitzler, Antina. 2016. *Democracy's Infrastructure: Techno-Politics and Protest after Apartheid*. Princeton, NJ: Princeton University Press.

SNAPSHOT 5

Don't Fix the Puddle

A Puddle Archive as Ethnographic Account of Sidewalk Assemblages

Mirja Busch and Ignacio Farías

The puddle lives at the corner of Kingsland Road and Dunston Street close to the King's Canal in London. It has an oval form. It is approximately 130 × 50 centimetres and at its deepest, although this of course depends, is approximately 5 centimetres. It is one of those puddles that is almost always there, that stays almost unaltered even many days after the last rain. People don't seem to pay much attention to it. The sidewalk offers enough space to simply walk by. No conflicts of use on sight. The puddle seems to have created a spot of its own, earned a right to existence, a place from where to reflect on its surface the life of a London street.

We came to know this puddle in 2010, as we were living close by. Since then, puddles have become a shared matter of concern, a phenomenon to scout for and observe across every city we have visited ever since, an object at the core of a practice in between visual arts and anthropology, an artefact to collect, a thing to think with.

Puddles do not just proliferate in cities, but literally everywhere where humans create lines and surfaces in the environment. Just follow a path in the forest. Here is where the puddles are. The sidewalks of modern urbanism – imagined and designed as a tabula rasa for human displacement and sociality – are indeed the archetypical environment of puddles. Puddles thrive with modernism, in modernist environments. They are modern others. Not the other 'to' modernism, but the other 'of' modernism, similar in this regard to the modern monsters we are just learning to face in

Figure S5.1. Sampler from London. From *Puddle Archive*. Photograph by Mirja Busch.

Figure S5.2. Collecting puddles for the show *Puddle Archive*. Photograph by Mirja Busch.

the wake of the Anthropocene. But puddles are not monsters. Puddles are like modern shadows: a mostly overlooked, but omnipresent insinuation of darkness, pointing to the limits of modern design and control over environments given the overpowering excess of geological forces, the capacity of soil and rain, of earth and water, not to destroy the modern project, but to deform it, to render it strange.

We speak of puddle visions. Things appear on their surfaces upside down. Matter out of place. Sky on the ground. Trees on the pavement. Colours painting the grey pavement. Sometimes bright and shiny, sometimes transparent and timid, puddles offer us visions in the double sense of the word: the ability to see what is there and the experience of seeing things that are not there. Puddle visions reassemble the urban, stitching and mending entanglements among things that are to be kept separated according to modern urbanism. Urban natures and urban cultures, technical infrastructures and social practices, the city and the weather. Puddles transform supposedly human sidewalks into the life spaces of microbes, larvae, plants, or into the swimming pools of birds and other animals. They also transform a supposedly sober background for human practices into a cinematic experience with moving images changing with every step and

Figure S5.3. Sampler from Berlin. From *Puddle Archive*. Photograph by Mirja Busch.

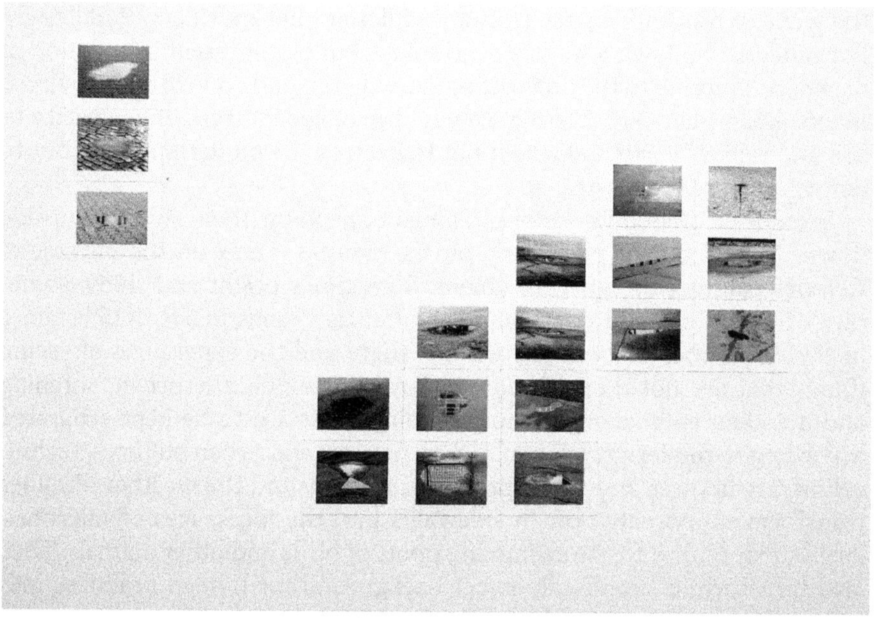

Figure S5.4. View of the show *Puddle Archive*. Photograph by Mirja Busch, Gallery cubus-m, Berlin, 2014.

every angle. Rather than signalling material decay, puddles bear witness to the situated hybridity of the urban.

Collecting puddles in cities thus becomes an archaeological practice into the variations of urban assemblages. Can you recognise a city through its puddles? Is there such a thing as the typical London puddle? How do they differ from other cities' puddles? The ones we saw in Buenos Aires? Brussels? Or any of the twenty cities from which we collected puddles? Suddenly the focus of attention is displaced and we start to pay attention to the materials and designs of sidewalks. I've surely walked on that kind of street, but where was it? Sidewalks are indeed anything but a tabula rasa. Bricks of different forms and tonalities, stone patterns, sandy joints, tile compositions, concrete ribbons with or without expansion joints, continuous slabs, curb and edge forms, trench drain systems, manhole covers: sidewalk materials, technologies and designs are significantly different from place to place, also depending on the historical periods and trends of sidewalk construction. And yet, by displaying them together grouped by cities, we are doing more than insinuating a comparative method for the elucidation of urban identities. If we look long enough at each of these urban compositions, we might start to discover urban difference, the radical

Figure S5.5. View of the show *Puddle Archive*. Photograph by Mirja Busch, Gallery cubus-m, Berlin, 2014.

multiplicity of cities, the irreducibility of each corner, each sidewalk, each puddle.

Water . . . at Last

An insight into how things are under the surface. Groups of bottles containing the water of single puddles. If the total water volume of a puddle was a conundrum, imagine colour. So here we are surrounded by 199 bottles containing eighty-three puddles from different places in Berlin – a parking lot, a street crossing, a backyard, a Catholic cemetery, a playground, a hospital entrance, a building site, a museum stairway, an airfield, a castle, a memorial, a bridge, a promenade, a tourist attraction, a train station, a park, a wasteland, a red-light district, a schoolyard, a truck stop and so on. The surprisingly wide chromatic spectrum of puddles invites or rather forces us to think about the specific materials that shape the practices unfolding in these places. Can we trace the particulate material floating within each bottle back to these uses? The materiality and colour of puddle water as a speculative device to reconstruct urban social practices, to activate knowing and speculative exercises. The puddle archive as an ethnographic experiment, that is, an experimental way of documenting and archiving urban materials, urban lives, urban worlds.

Mirja Busch is an artist working and researching on new forms of existence and experience of objects.

Ignacio Farías is Professor and Chair of Urban Anthropology at the Institute of European Ethnology, Humboldt-University of Berlin.

CHAPTER 5

What Is in a Hole?

Voids out of Place and Politics below the State in Georgia

FRANCISCO MARTÍNEZ

Thinking about Holes

This chapter is a journey through different types of holes in Georgia to understand the connection between social and material forms of order. Based on a material and discursive analysis of both holes and vertical powers, this research explores the way in which urban voids and material failures participate in the articulation of political discourses, coming to regulate public life, keeping people on hold, perpetuating or mediating a particular (subterranean) order. Hence, it puts the emphasis on what holes do to people, and how holes shape our political lives, instead of focusing on what holes are. In this light, I agree with Roberto Casati and Achille Varzi, who argued in *Holes and Other Superficialities* (1994) that there cannot be a single definition of holes, since these forms are rather the variation of an idea.

The research oscillates from the aesthetic to the political, and it combines ethnographic fieldwork with an exhibition, two workshops, thirteen semi-structured interviews with contemporary artists and curators, and a typology of holes. I make use of the representational qualities of holes to study the oscillation between lack and excess in Georgia, hence holes are here taken as devices to think with. Paraphrasing Mary Douglas (1966),[1] we can refer to holes as voids out of place – necessary to establish discourses of normality and order. In a similar way, a hole can be understood as what does not fit, an element excluded from the normative, rejected from the system and presented as potentially dangerous – elements moved off to the side, which contribute to our consciousness as an alien presence (Kristeva 1982; Leder 1990).

In their incompleteness, holes enable and defy human agency simultaneously, blending us into their gravity; hence the comprehension of holes requires an understanding of the relations around them. Often, material failures become a sign of the inability of the state to act or invest in maintenance, but they also convey 'voids' in the relationship between state and society, standing as a form of communication or separation, connecting people to the state in qualitative ways. The paradox, however, is that holes do not quite qualify as political, and do not respond to the criteria for widely recognised forms of political action. They are rather infrapolitical, de-centred and beneath the threshold of politics (Marche 2012). Yet they are infrapolitical not as counterpoints to the state's project (Scott 1990), but rather as the underpinning of more visible political actions and infrastructures, putting disrepair in action (Chu 2014), becoming part of the engineering of state affect and establishing particular modes of connection and disconnection (Laszczkowski 2016).

Systemic Excess

In Georgian language, 'hole' can be written in different forms, depending on contextual nuances: ორმო (*ormo*) is a word most likely used for broken infrastructures and potholes, while ხვრელი (*khvreli*) rather refers to dark corners and caves. The research puts the emphasis on how Georgian society perceives and experiences the state in daily life. Originally, it was inspired by Filip de Boeck's work on Kinshasa's *topoi* of power, in which he observes how holes 'may become infrastructural elements in themselves, because they create thickenings of publics, and offer the possibility of assembling people, or of slowing them down . . . As such they generate many shortcomings and impossibilities, but also different opportunities, different kinds of space' (de Boeck 2012). Yet my interest in holes started during my rides with Nikoloz Gambashidze, who had been acting as my driver in the country. I often hear laments such as 'that road has been repaired many times in the last years, and they never finish it for good', or 'look here, they built it a month ago and is already falling apart', noting that potholes might emerge when surfaces are not yet complete. Once, driving to the monastery of David Gareja, which has an especially difficult road leading up to it, Nikoloz began to imagine a future with better pavements in Georgia, with more comfortable rides and a multiplied number of tourists wishing to travel outside of Tbilisi. Also, he wondered how the increase in visitors would eventually change the auratic atmosphere of the monastery. I then started to think how holes serve as devices that visualise visions of the future and trigger new approaches towards the past. The bad state of these roads, as well as the abandoned state of infrastructures such as railroads, served as a trigger for a reassessment of the past by Nikoloz, admitting, for instance, that in the 1980s they did not sufficiently value certain infrastructures, which years later fell into disrepair or suffered from a lack of sustained maintenance.

Despite their relation to political discourses, the functioning of the state and the experience of cities, holes are an under-theorised part of urban materiality and assemblages. They are points where the political encounters the social world materially. But how can we represent and conceptualise these points of encounter? Already in my initial fieldwork, I noticed how holes are implicated in the human experience of Tbilisi and in shaping social identities, appearing as devices through which subjectivities and relationships to the state are formed. Also, several of my informants observed how Georgian society is organised around the oscillation between incompleteness and excess, 'caught between the unattainable and the inferior' (Frederiksen 2012: 131). For instance, in our interview, photographer Yuri Mechitov[2] explained:

> The system is not meant for helping people, but for using us ... the Georgian society is a system that works through excesses; and tourists come to see this excess, in food, hospitality, emotion ... but that very system is economically suicidal, and produces moral and physical trash.

Thinking of how to carry research on the topic of excess, material failures and existential repair, and how to reimagine the boundaries of the political sphere, I decided to organise several events with local artists, here taken as a community of experts, whose work is able to make social reality conceivable in a direct and visual way (Kosuth [1975] 1991). This was a rather explorative collaboration in the sense that artists were not my objects of enquiry, but rather active co-conceptualisers and co-reflectors of the political potential of holes, coproducing knowledge through experimental collaboration. The research has been an exercise of producing knowledge with others, who acted as interlocutors rather than as informants, demonstrating an ethnographic sensibility for analysing identity, memory and community in a similar way to anthropologists. Hence, in this project, artists and curators were not simply involved as the reality check for my interpretations, but also as my epistemic community in a 'joint problem-making' where aesthetics, knowledge production and participant observation intermingle (Holmes and Marcus 2012; Estalella and Criado 2018). Examples of our epistemic collaboration were two workshops and an exhibition concerning the ways in which a state of failure might be generated and sustained in the country. The show was called *Aesthetics of Repair in Contemporary Georgia*,[3] exploring the oscillation between a desire for wholeness and its impossibility since the results of repair works are fragile, always ongoing, defined by necessity, punctuated by paucity, by lack, by failure.[4]

We were curious to understand 'a situation in which quick, improvised solutions are deployed as a mode of governance, mostly bumbling about, acting on the basis of half-knowledge' (Dunn 2012: 15). In the first workshop organised in Tbilisi immediately after the show, I presented the results and impact of the exhibition in Estonia. In the second workshop, organised at the Free University of Tbilisi, I invited local art students to imagine an artwork on this topic, and to explain their view. For instance, Shotiko argued that failures are the negative material that generates the developing process of a system and can be discarded afterwards. Another student, Mako, considered how people tend to get used to disturbing elements by internalising breakdown and failure as normality. She asked then rhetorically: 'Does it turn you into a victim?' Further, Inga and Salome acknowledged that, for them, failure is related to the feeling of shame, and that one can be a piece in the assemblage of failure without being aware of it. Tika found it relevant to extend the borders of what a system is in our thinking, as well as to be able to introduce elements of transgression. Finally, Anastasia outlined several examples of how systemic errors are used in everyday life to attain something bigger, thereby reflecting on the way these failures might be socially operative in Georgia.

Errorjungle

Artist Levan Mindiashvili entitled his contribution to the *Aesthetics of Repair* exhibition *Unintended Archaeology*, in which he assembled remnants of what once might have been a home. Asked later about how he sees holes, Levan had a rather positive view of them: 'holes are first of all channels of communication and desire. They are also an escape from isolation, a way of leaking out, entering into a different temporal and spatial register', as if they were the beckoning gate of Alice in Wonderland. Artist Vajiko Chachkhiani shared a rather neutral view of holes, as 'always formless things that call for being filled, constructed or at least given a shape. They help us to understand what it means to be in or out'. In his view, incompleteness might open up interesting forms of experimentation and accentuate elements of artistic practice such as exploration, discovery, failure and historical shifts (see also Martins 2015). For sound artist Natalie Beridze, systemic failures are like holes, letting in streams of fresh air, preventing the system from becoming totalitarian. Another artist, Nika Kutateladze,[5] explains that holes refer to mobility and circulation, to the displacement of water and people. As he argues, the worst thing that can happen to a person is stagnation.

Holes are paradoxes that can serve as sites of both tragedy and resistance, of normality and transgression, of beauty and pain. They are experienced as zones of awkward engagement and cultural friction whereby knowledge, politics and nature come into contact (Tsing 2005). Holes can acquire a dynamic quality as well as materialise a troubled transmission, standing as a living mediation with the capacity of organising social life (Berlant 2016). For instance, artist Thea Gvetadze,[6] with many years' experience living in Germany and the Netherlands, acknowledged:

> I have a different approach towards society here than the one I had back in Germany. I am fascinated by how things keep working despite the errors everywhere! This is the magical and almost undesirable talent of this society – to be able to survive in an *errorjungle* . . . The errored system is still functioning because of the society, or more or less functioning. And there is something very dramatically beautiful in the whole thing.

Yet failure does not always motivate us to try again, harder or better; most often, it may also result in giving up and accepting our surrender because of the difficulty in understanding how power is organised or exercised (Dzenovska and De Genova 2018). As Lali Pertenava,[7] curator and art critic, argued:

> The situation in Georgia is not a dystopia; it is a totalitarian error because it keeps working, it is operative . . . this is a self-colonised society by how they treat their own people. As an example, we are now organising an exhibition about art in Georgia in the '80s and '90s, and the state had to appoint a foreign curator for it. Perhaps they wanted a neutral and distant view on the works, or the Ministry of Culture prefers someone that can be kind of controlled, not too political . . . but they are not that sophisticated. They just need a foreign master. But it is not only that; also, what they pay the artists, how they treat them, the means invested and the goals. They politicise the art, but then say that the artworks should not be political. Also, they try to avoid the term contemporary while referring to art because they wanted it to be folkloric and serve to attract tourists.

For the *Aesthetics of Repair* show, artist and gallerist Nino Sekhniashvili documented the building of a DIY house created by her father, a bricoleur architect who worked audaciously through approximations, despite limited professional skills. Nino explains:

> In the middle of all the sadness around, nobody thinks that the arts are important and can make a difference, especially those in power . . . Failure is related to personal expectations, and for me it can be also generational. When I think of failure

> and success, the fairy tale 'The Fox and the Grape' comes to mind. It tells how the bunch of tasty grapes are there in front of the fox but hanging higher than the animal could reach. No matter how hard the animal tries, the fox could not reach the grapes, so, in turn, the fox decides to despise the grapes and convince himself that they must be sour.

Nino's latest project is called 'Parks of Tbilisi'. Strolling around the city with her daughter Vera, Nino has discovered that many of the former parks have been constructed into something else in the last few years, also noticing how voids – resulting from the abandonment of past buildings and infrastructures – have emerged as the parks of the future (if permission for construction is not granted). For instance, in their documentation, they have listed the former factory Kombinat Megobroba, the former velodrome, the foundation of an unfinished 28-storey hotel on the embankment of the Mtkvari River, or the area of Mziuri, which changed due to flooding (in 2015, which freed the animals from the zoo) rather than dismantlement.

Archaeologist Colin Renfrew (2003) argues that his experience of excavating and interpreting past remains can be compared with those who visit a gallery of contemporary art for the first time: both try to make some sense out of an assemblage of artefacts. At this point, we can refer to Jacques Rancière's distinction (2006) between 'aesthetic politics' (distribution of the sensible and how aesthetics can be employed to make political

Figure 5.1. Foundations of the former 'Lechkombinat' complex, by Nino Sekhniashvili, 2017.

demands) and 'politics of aesthetics' (concerned with the political meanings inherent in works of art). Holes can be taken to far-reaching entanglements of elusive politics, not simply through making statecraft appear contingent, fragile and contestable, but also by reinforcing their power and preventing local people from thinking critically about the present. Holes become in this case an element of secrecy, pointing at what 'is generally known but cannot be articulated' (Taussig 1999: 5). Through holes, a particular mode of absence takes the stage, making explicit what not to know and displacing results to some point in the future (Frederiksen 2014). Holes can work as a closure, contributing to the reproduction of practices that reinforce the 'opacity and uncertainty of the political' (Gotfredsen 2015: 127), or as an opening, demanding compensatory efforts to shore up something that appears as ceasing to exist. Hence, they do not simply signify a rupture, they can be part of a continuum too, as a sustained suspension of knowledge, or as a pause in a longer temporal frame.

A Forensic Inventory of the City

Holes are materialisations of emptiness that upset social order and do not appear according to the established canons of modernity. They stop us and defy signification with a particular sensorial impact, drawing attention to themselves, simultaneously intimidating and attractive, thus emanating a pre-discursive affective force (Laviolette 2014). Here, holes are taken as an ethnographic and artistic object, and also as an epistemological vantage point from which to understand and to theorise politics in Georgia, foregrounding thus the materiality of political expression and mediation. Holes and material failures can be treated as both a sensor and an agent of politics (Weizman 2014).[8] They are also a mode of occupying the present (preventing people from being involved in what concerns them) and a display of work-in-progress through which the idea of the state is reified (Ssorin-Chaikov 2003).[9]

Hence, it is not as simple as to merely account for the erratic nature of the state's participation in society; holes, with their surplus of negativity, also manifest the impossibility of understanding politics and of self-realisation at large. They come to scar a surface, often emerging from deeper forms of breakdown and vulnerability, such as the inability to renovate, preserve and develop buildings and infrastructures. Martin Demant Frederiksen (2016) draws on this hypothesis in his study of the renovation of Aghmashenebely Avenue in Tbilisi. He correlates the speed of the construction works with the velocity of its material decay, describing the falling of the plaster ornamentation, the peeling of the paint and the scarring of buildings to conclude that the problem is their wrong way of being broken.[10] For Frederiksen, these remnants that did not decay properly came to animate something else, anchoring political critiques, reminding us of collapsed visions, evoking the constant interaction between force and form. These holes and urban failures are an epistemological part of the inventory and morphology of Tbilisi as a whole – forming a sort of *hole-ism* (Murawski 2013), since they impose their own spatial and temporal logic – disruptive, invasive, distractive, intervening – conditioning agency while contesting any utopian optimism of planning (de Boeck 2015).[11]

As the architect David Bostanashvili notes in the catalogue of our exhibition (2016), in the Georgian capital there is no sufficient urban planning, and several buildings of cultural heritage have been demolished in recent years. An example of this breaking gravitas was brought forth with the documentation of the Palace of Poetry (2001–2013), an ensemble of pavilions hand-carved by Shota Bostanashvili (David's father), which was destroyed just a few years after construction. The documentation shows Shota reciting poetry while the Palace is being destroyed, or more precisely, transformed into a monumental vacancy able to achieve attractive effects without trying (Smithson 1967). For David,

Figure 5.2. Palace of Poetry, by Shota Jojua, 2005.

> the topic of failure is really relevant to Georgia, since the distinction between system and error is indeed blurred . . . At first, I thought, *why are you asking me about how the system works? Why is this a question?* There is no system in Georgia! But reconsidering your question, it makes me see that maybe all the 'errors' and 'failures' are not accidental and constitute the system itself. . .

For Irena Popiashvili, Dean of the Arts Department of the Free University, director of the Tbilisi Kunsthalle, and with many years' experience of living in the USA,

> In order to understand the relation between system and error, we have to be mindful of what kind of resistances we will face, including absence . . . Also, one has to be aware that the system will keep working anyway, even if through failure . . . the need to build from scratch a new system for the contemporary art scene might be extended to the state too; that's why I say to my students that they are the 'generation ground zero'.

For the *Aesthetics of Repair* exhibition, Group Bouillon prepared a scatological performance: all six members cut off each other's hair during the opening as a way to get rid of bad energy, start from scratch and escape from civil pessimism.[12] As explained by Natuka Vacadze, member of the artist group:

> The Georgian system is based on individual shame; the government controls public affects by making people feel proud of some things and ashamed of some others. The state invites us to enjoy the past, but prevents us from thinking critically about the present, and failure plays a role in this . . . By shaving our heads, we wanted to purify ourselves against the system; yet the hair grows again and the depressive energy soon takes over you. In the meantime, the fight against negative energy takes all your energy, and the only thing left is hope, the hope that one day the hair won't come back.

The break-up of the Soviet Union and the following civil war in Georgia produced a deep economic crisis and a radical erosion of the formal state apparatus (with the subsequent incapability to provide basic services), a situation of state failure that not only increased informal survival strategies and created openings for economic benefit by different non-state actors, but also left a void with regards to political power. Likewise, infrastructural provisions of water and heat were, to a great extent, transformed from an affair of the state to an affair of households or private entrepreneurs, generating a way of living as logistics characterised by a constant recalibration of edges, boundaries and interfaces (Collier and Way 2004; Simone 2017). Reflecting back on this matter, Nanuka Zaalishvili, architect, photographer

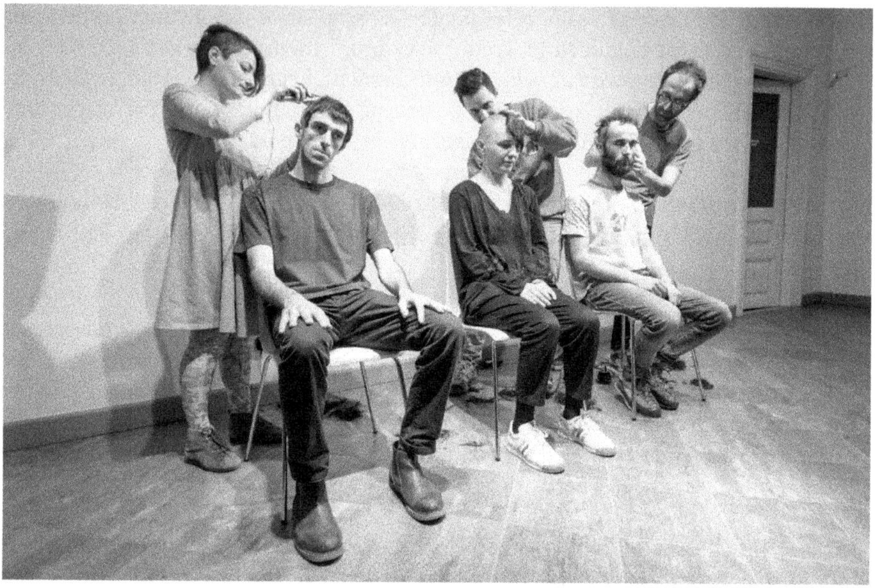

Figure 5.3. Bouillon's performance, by Johan Huimerind, 2016.

and author of the book *Soviet Bus Stops in Georgia*, takes the geological fissures of Tbilisi as a link between body and politics:

> In the dark 1990s, as we call it, we kids literally used to play in street holes and damaged infrastructures. Back then, we didn't have much choice, all the roads were full of potholes and no one cared to fix them. This didn't stop kids playing and using these holes as the source for new imaginations and experiences. Rainy days were not only the worst but also the funniest. Our city had everything broken: roads, buildings, citizens, generating very particular aesthetics, shapes and textures. We can talk of 'post-Soviet brokenness', epitomised by grey concrete buildings and weird balcony extensions, badly made, with owners that didn't care to fix material scars and holes in the walls.

Interpreting the Void

Analytically, the chapter describes examples of holes in order to study how the political is both mediated and expressed in different material forms. I encountered the following fourteen types of holes during my fieldwork, gazing, experiencing and identifying meaningful analytical *pigeonholes* in Georgia. The (*etic*) typology of holes relies on a rather discursive understanding of them and they are here organised thematically:

Infrastructural

- *Potholes* are entropic, the bigger they get, the faster they grow. Potholes generate driving hazards and risks, yet also slow cars down so people living in countryside areas can sell their wares along the road. They are not meant for helping people, but sometimes they make the speed of life slow and generate assemblages of relief around them.
- *Inverted holes*: non-underground structures meant to function as a hole yet standing. For instance, the municipality of Khoni had to build a concrete structure with pedestrian stairs in the middle of a road, hence going nowhere, just because the neighbours did not respect the prohibition of circulation on that road.[13] As in other cases in Georgia, fines and traffic regulations were ignored, and metal barriers on both sides of the road were broken, so cement and concrete appeared for the municipality as the proper solution.
- *Entangled holes*: failures mobilise a series of assemblages that are perceived as mismatching. For instance, walking around the city centre of Tbilisi we can meet with multiple metal bars, pillars and columns improvised to support a crumbling façade or building.
- *Hygienic holes*: in July 2015, I visited Dvani, a village located on the military border with South Ossetia. Five houses are still burned out from the war against Russia and the village is losing its population, especially the youth, who escape to Tbilisi in the hope of a better future. For Nodar, the mayor of Dvani, the current problems in the village were not the fault of the Ossetian people but the result of big politics being played in the region (Dvani's circumstance was an error of geopolitics). During the *Supra* (a traditional Georgian feast), I asked Nodar where the bathroom was, to which he apologised for not having a 'civilised' toilet, simply pointing at a wooden booth in the backyard with a hole in the ground.

Economic

- *Labour holes*: underground working areas where working activities such as baking bread take place. These places might have several working holes inside them, oven-like.
- *Global holes* such as the one created in 2011 by Hayastan Shakarian, a pensioner who, when digging for scrap metal in her garden, hacked into a fibre-optic cable and cut the internet in Georgia and Armenia for some hours. On the side roads, it is possible to see many signs displaying the handwritten word ჯართი ('scrap'), dealers, who pay 11 lari (2 euro) per kilo for various metal remnants.

Architectural

- *Vertical holes* demonstrate a relation between material incompletion, emergency housing and imaginative engagement. In Tbilisi, there is a long tradition of vernacular architecture, which makes use, tactically, of the existing structures and materials to negotiate quotidian needs and economic shortage. The outcome is a particular typology of performative architecture and self-organising urbanity, which expands the past in constant conversation with pre-existing structures, inhabiting what is disintegrating based on makeshift extensions and bricoleur-like reappropriations (Warsza 2013).
- *Furniture holes*: gaps in public spaces that are used for storage or to exhibit things.

Cultural

- *Cunicular holes*: the multiple passages and tunnels of Tbilisi give access to businesses, workshops and behind-the-curtains scenes of life, which might resemble a liminal experience (Turner 1969).

Figure 5.4. Inverted hole in the city centre of Tbilisi, January 2015, photograph by Francisco Martínez.

- *Traps*: to meander successfully through all holes, traps and barriers found on the streets of Tbilisi demands drifting skills and a particular sense of awareness. Such a challenge generates a particular enjoyment for the post-tourist who enjoys walking close by, as if holes would make our movements more pleasurable, unleashing a vital plurality or authenticity (Mäe and Nava 2016).
- *Public dark corners*: holes do not always signify a separation but they can also serve as grey public spaces where groups of males socialise, thereby generating counter-hegemonic narratives and informal practices of resistance. These areas are often referred to as *birzha* and might entail conflictual relations with top-down projects of urban renovation (Curro 2018).
- *Sporty holes* such as swimming pools. For instance, the children of a school in Kutaisi are learning to swim in a swimming pool without water. The teacher was promised by local authorities that the pool would be repaired at the end of the course; not simply does he believe the promise, but he also claims that 'we might be training the next Olympic champion' (see, e.g., Sarkisyan 2018).

Figure 5.5. An example of a furniture hole in Tbilisi, January 2015, photograph by Francisco Martínez.

Memorial

- *Bullet holes*: these holes appear as unintended memorials of the multiple wars this country has suffered in the last decades.
- *Anti-heritage holes*: this type refers to material legacies that fall into an active forgetting and disrepair (Martínez 2018), such as the cultural monuments built by the Armenians of Tbilisi that are being destroyed or rebuilt in a manner depriving them of their authentic look. In search of an example, I visited the Armenian Cathedral of St George (1251) once a month during 2015. This is a beautiful architectonic specimen, where excavation and renovation works continued simultaneously. This place caught my interest because there I discovered several skeletons uncovered, one of them of the popular *ashughi* poet Sayat Nova (1712–95). No worker or guard watched over the archaeological site (situated in the core of the Old Town). Anybody could have taken the bones of this great eighteenth-century poet, who wrote and sang songs in three languages. Also litter (i.e. Coca-Cola cans) and construction material would often fall into the holes where the skeletons were.

Figure 5.6. Another example of a furniture hole in Tbilisi, January 2015, photograph by Francisco Martínez.

Figure 5.7. Labour hole in Tbilisi, January 2016, photograph by Francisco Martínez.

Figure 5.8. Another labour hole, January 2016, photograph by Francisco Martínez.

Figure 5.9. Cunicular hole in Tbilisi, July 2017, photograph by Francisco Martínez.

Figure 5.10. Post-tourist trap in Tbilisi, May 2018, photograph by Francisco Martínez.

Figure 5.11. Another post-tourist trap in Tbilisi, May 2018, photograph by Francisco Martínez.

Figure 5.12. St George Cathedral during the renovation works, June 2015, photograph by Francisco Martínez.

Figure 5.13. An example of a hygienic hole in Dvani, July 2015, photograph by Francisco Martínez.

Vertical Dimensions of Power

The study of the varied forms of interaction between society and state through holes can be complemented with the use of its opposite, a vertical topological figure. As noted by de Boeck in the case of Kinshasa (2017; see also de Boeck and Baloji 2016), the hole stands in contrast to the mountain, being part of a vertical dimension of power that goes underground. In Tbilisi, old and new vertical powers materialise distinct temporalities, while skyscrapers and churches project a solid past and future, leaving the fragile, contested and contingent present for the holes. Also, vertical powers appear as static, fixed and well positioned, suppressing contestation, while current politics have to be constantly renegotiated and refigured through the holes. In Tbilisi, we can recognise three distinctive vertical landmarks, which come to represent different dimensions of power as well as temporal projections:

- *The religious.* In 2004, the Georgian Orthodox Church built the Sameba cathedral (87 metres high). The world's third largest church was built to symbolise the religious revival.

- *The executive.* Mtatsminda is a mountain plateau occupied by a television tower (276 metres); an amusement park; a funicular; Kartlis Deda (Mother of a Georgian, a 20-metre aluminium figure, erected in 1958, the year Tbilisi celebrated its 1500th year); the Pantheon of Georgian public figures (Alexander Griboedov, Ilia Chavchavadze, Zviad Gamsakhurdia and Stalin's mother are all buried in the Pantheon);[14] Narikala (the oldest fortress in Tbilisi); and the mansion of the richest and most powerful person in Georgia, oligarch and former prime minister Bidzina Ivanishvili, who is behind two polemical contemporary projects, the pharaonic Panorama Tbilisi real estate project and the transportation of ancient trees around the country to his botanical garden (see Lomsadze 2018).
- *The economic.* The Biltmore Hotel is a 138-metre tall, 32-storey building, self-categorised as a 'six star hotel' built between 2011 and 2017 by the Abu Dhabi United Group. The hotel occupies the historical Soviet-era building IMELI, constructed in the 1930s (by Russian architect Aleksei Shchusev, the designer of Lenin's mausoleum) to host the Institute of Marxism and Leninism, and which housed the Parliament of Georgia from 1992 to 1995. The building represents a new phallic power in the city, out of scale and imposed top-down, over and against 'the people' (Manning 2007), defying gravitational laws and urban zoning rules (Murawski 2016).

When compared with the Estonian case, holes are locally understood as residual from the Soviet era, politically toxic and belonging to the past, not the present, whereas the future is presented as flat, liquid and digital (Martínez 2018). There are hardly any distinctive vertical powers in Tallinn; we can find merely three small ones, but these are all foreign: the TV tower (Soviet), the Alexander Nevsky Cathedral (Russian) and the Toompea castle (German).

Conclusion: Parts, Wholes and Holes

In this chapter, holes have been proposed as a kind of meta-concept to reflect upon quotidian processes of social order, coming into focus as an enabling or disabling force in the course of everyday politics. Holes are not reducible to the political failures they presuppose; they might create new social possibilities and generate complex responses, gaining a performing capacity in relation to their actual context. A hole implies a bond and a relationship, yet it stands as a self-subsistent element in the social assemblage (DeLanda 2006), being productive of relations themselves, opening up the political, making it touch ground.

In holes, meaning is not evacuated but reinforced in turn. We might take actual holes as a fragment of a greater fragmentation, emerging from a correlation of weaknesses. Nonetheless, despite representing fragmentation, holes are perceived as forming an entanglement, entailing a mirroring relationship between a part and the whole, materialising public secrecy and the labour of the negative. By their potential effect, holes can be considered as 'political machines' due to their capacity to sustain order in excess, with social efficacy in shaping and constraining human agency (Smith 2015). They contribute to reproducing order through different ways of engaging with breakdown and material failure, turned into an infrapolitical medium, which organises ways of occupying time, makes visible or invisible, connects or disconnects. Holes are filled with politics because of their affectation of the relation between people, raising the question of audiences, meanings and mediums (Moreiras 2010; Marche 2012). They call for a response and also generate their own affects, stoppages and socio-material relations around it, appearing as a second nature in the organisation of everyday life.

Voids also have strong metaphysical implications, enacting a threshold to other ways of knowing, appearing as dark tropes of contagion and resistance. They transcend their very materiality, acquiring an ontological status, referring to that which is beyond representation, leading down into the underworld, nameless, primal, unknowable, dark, at once internal to the urban organism and external to reason, a place of the occult, of invisible forces, of awe, puzzlement, surprise, divergence, abyss, loss, guilt... an element of routine disorder, an Other of modernity and modernisation.

Francisco Martínez is a lecturer in the School of Museum Studies, University of Leicester.

Notes

I want to express my gratitude to Tamta Khalvashi and Patrick Laviolette for their comments on this chapter.

1. For Douglas, social systems are formed against dirt and waste, by defining and excluding that which is 'dirty', marking the order and boundaries of the system. The problem appears when these elements do not pass away properly or when the hole is out of place, challenging the system's channels of expelling and propelling. See also Clark (2012).
2. Mechitov also served as minister of culture for a month, until he expressed his disagreement in public about the creation of a 'Museum of Occupation' in Tbilisi.

3. Co-organised with curator Marika Agu, Tartu Art Museum, 2016.
4. To understand this, we drew on local terms such as *scrappiness* to describe those arrangements that constitute finality without being finished; *khaltura*, which expresses a state of unstable equilibria and low-key engagements; and *euroremont*, a practice that emerged out of the will to achieve social status by following what seemed to be Western standards and values. With these terms, we placed the emphasis on the radical processes of construction and rejection in which Georgia has been, and continues to be, immersed.
5. In May 2018, Nika presented his project, *Watermill on Former Pavlov Street*, as part of the Kunsthalle Tbilisi programme. For this site-specific installation in Tbilisi, the artist brought a watermill for corn grinding from the Guria district, now re-accommodated in a Soviet-style apartment block in the capital as a *Kabakovian* installation. As he explained, the watermill followed the same route as many migrants from rural areas, who generally look for homes in the modernist buildings of the suburbs of Tbilisi.
6. Thea contributed to our *Aesthetics of Repair* exhibition with *Esophageal Foreign Bodies* – a ready-made sculpture of her father, a doctor who collected coins, sticks, pins and other miscellanea from people's throats during his career and then framed these obscurities, offering them to his daughter as a present.
7. Lali also took part in the *Aesthetics of Repair* project by writing for the catalogue.
8. Agreeing with Eyal Weizman (2014), failed materiality can be taken as evidence of power relations – a proof to be used in courts to prosecute political abuses, as if it were a forensic testimony.
9. For instance, Nikolai Ssorin-Chaikov noted in his ethnography in Northern Siberia (2003) how the Soviet system also materialised in unfinished constructions, turning brokenness into an ingredient of transformations and an instrument of power. Also, we have to account for the affects and manufactured aspects of reality created by the state, which have potential consequences (Navaro-Yashin 2012).
10. These crumbling materialities were a materialisation of failure, showing that the manners of construction were hasty and that the reforms were only interested in the façade (producing hollow touristic shells), not the inside.
11. In Tbilisi, official discourses of success are related to attracting capital through investment and tourists, and not necessarily to improving the living conditions for those actually resident in the city. An example of how brokenness and repair reveal a hoard of significant meanings is the ongoing 'renovation' of Tbilisi's Old Town, in which very little remains of historic buildings. For many private owners, it is cheaper to remake old ornaments and façades (*ersatz*-like) than to fully renovate the buildings. Paradoxically, in 2000, UNESCO attempted to list Tbilisi's Old Town as a World Heritage Site, but soon suspended the project due to the lack of will from local authorities. Demolitions in the Old Town and the rebuilding of houses without supervision or planning have provoked the repeated protests of 'Tiflis Hamqari', an NGO protesting for the protection of the heritage of Tbilisi (https://www.facebook.com/TiflisHamkari?fref=ts, last accessed 30 April 2019).
12. Zurab Kikvadze, member of the Bouillon group, says they have no other choice than to persist and try again. As he puts it, 'In Georgia, we have a normality of

crisis; when you work 12 hours a day, or have several employments, and cannot make ends meet'.

13. See: ქუთაისში ცურვას უწყლოდ სწავლობენ ('How swimming is studied in Kutaisi'), retrieved March 2019, from http://www.myvideo.ge/v/521669.
14. In 1938, there were discussions about changing the name of the site to Stalin's Mountain. See კანდელაკი, ბ. [Kandelaki B.], (1955), მთაწმინდა [Mtatsminda]. Tbilisi: საქართველოს სსრ განათლების სამინისტრო საბავშვო და ახალგაზრდობის ლიტერატურის სახელმწიფო გამომცემლობა [Children and youth literature state publishing house of the Ministry of Education of Georgian SSR].

References

Berlant, Lauren. 2016. 'The Commons: Infrastructures for Troubling Times', *Environment and Planning D: Society and Space* 34(3): 393–419.

Bostanashvili, David. 2016. 'Red Letters', in F. Martínez and M. Agu (eds), *Aesthetics of Repair in Contemporary Georgia*. Tartu: Tartu Art Museum, pp. 192–97.

Casati, Roberto, and Achille Varzi. 1994. *Holes and Other Superficialities*. Boston, MA: MIT Press.

Chu, Julie. 2014. 'When Infrastructures Attack: The Workings of Disrepair in China'. *American Ethnologist* 14(2): 351–367.

Clark, Emily. 2012. 'Only the Darkness Knows Who I Am', Ph.D. dissertation. Wellington, NZ: Massey University.

Collier, Stephen J., and Lucan Way. 2004. 'Beyond the Deficit Model: Social Welfare in Post-Soviet Georgia', *Post-Soviet Affairs* 20(3): 258–84.

Curro, Costanza. 2018. 'Birzha', in A. Ledeneva (ed.), *The Global Encyclopaedia of Informality*. London: UCL Press, pp. 303–6.

de Boeck, Filip. 2012. 'Infrastructure', *Cultural Anthropology*, Special Issue: Urban Africa towards an Anthropology of Infrastructure. Retrieved 15 March 2019 from https://www.academia.edu/4670577/De_Boeck_F._2012_._Infrastructure_Commentary_from_Filip_De_Boeck._Contributions_from_Urban_Africa_towards_an_Anthropology_of_Infrastructure.

——. 2015. '"Poverty" and the Politics of Syncopation: Urban Examples from Kinshasa (DR Congo)', *Current Anthropology* 56(11): 146–58.

——. 2017. '"The Hole of the World": Designing Possibility through Topography in Congo's Urban Settings', *Forum: Resilience & Design* 6(1): 42–50.

de Boeck, Filip, and Sammy Baloji. 2016. *Suturing the City: Living Together in Congo's Urban Worlds*. London: Autograph ABP.

DeLanda, Manuel. 2006. *A New Philosophy of Society*. London: Continuum.

Douglas, Mary. 1966. *Purity and Danger: An Analysis of Concepts of Pollution and Taboo*. New York: Routledge and Kegan Paul.

Dunn, Elizabeth Cullen. 2012. 'The Chaos of Humanitarian Aid: Adhocracy in the Republic of Georgia', *Humanity* 3(1): 1–23.

Dunn, Elizabeth Cullen, and Martin Demant Frederiksen. 2014. 'Introduction: Ethnographies of Absence in Georgia', *Slavic Review* 73(2): 241–45.

Dzenovska, Dace, and Nicholas De Genova. 2018. 'Introduction: Desire for the Political in the Aftermath of the Cold War', *Focaal* 80: 1–15.

Estalella, Adolfo, and Tomás S. Criado (eds). 2018. *Experimental Collaborations: Ethnography through Fieldwork Devices*. Oxford: Berghahn Books.

Frederiksen, Martin Demant. 2012. '"A Gate; but Leading Where?" In Search of Actually Existing Cosmopolitanism in Post-Soviet Tbilisi', in C. Humphrey and V. Skvirskaja (eds), *Post-Cosmopolitan Cities*. Oxford: Berghahn Books, pp. 120–40.

——. 2014. 'The Would-Be State: Reforms, NGOs, and Absent Presents in Postrevolutionary Georgia', *Slavic Review* 73(2): 307–21.

——. 2016. 'Material Dys-Appearance: Decaying Futures and Contested Temporal Passage', in I.P. Bjerregaard, A.E. Rasmussen and T. Flohr Sørensen (eds), *Materialities of Passing*. London: Routledge, pp. 49–64.

Gotfredsen, Bendtsen Katrine. 2015. 'Invisible Connections: On Uncertainty and the (Re)production of Opaque Politics in the Republic of Georgia', in I.H. Knudsen and M.D. Frederiksen (eds), *Ethnographies of Grey Zones in Eastern Europe*. London: Anthem Press, 125-139.

Holmes, Douglas R., and George E. Marcus. 2012. 'Collaborative Imperatives: A Manifesto, of Sorts, for the Reimagination of the Classic Scene of Fieldwork Encounter', in Monica Konrad (ed.), *Collaborators Collaborating: Counterparts in Anthropological Knowledge and International Research Relations*. Oxford: Berghahn Books, pp. 127–43.

Kosuth, Joseph. (1975) 1991. *Art After Philosophy and After: Collected Writings, 1966–1990*. Cambridge, MA: MIT Press.

Kristeva, Julia. 1982. *Powers of Horror: An Essay on Abjection*. New York: Columbia University Press.

Laszczkowski, Mateusz. 2016. *'City of the Future': Built Space, Modernity and Urban Change in Astana*. Oxford: Berghahn Books.

Laviolette, Patrick. 2014. 'Excavating into the Dark Corner', in *I Looked into the Walls and Saw. . .* Exhibition by F. Martínez and M. Krivy, ISFAG gallery of Tallinn.

Leder, Drew. 1990. *The Absent Body*. Chicago, IL: University of Chicago Press.

Lomsadze, Giorgi. 2018. 'Georgia's Traveling Trees'. Eurasianet, 22 March. Retrieved 15 March 2019, from https://eurasianet.org/s/georgias-traveling-trees.

Mäe, Rene, and Juuli Nava. 2016. 'Exploring Tbilisi as a Post-Tourist', in F. Martínez and M. Agu (eds), *Aesthetics of Repair in Contemporary Georgia*. Tartu: Tartu Art Museum, pp. 184–90.

Manning, Paul. 2007. '"Our Beer": Ethnographic Brands in Postsocialist Georgia', *American Anthropologist* 109(4): 626–41.

Marche, Guillaume. 2012. 'Introduction: Why Infrapolitics Matters', *Revue française d'études américaines* 131: 3–18.

Martínez, Francisco, and Marika Agu. 2016. *Aesthetics of Repair in Contemporary Georgia*. Tartu: Tartu Art Museum.

Martínez, Francisco. 2018. *Remains of the Soviet Past in Estonia*. London: UCL Press.

Martins, Susana S. 2015. 'Failure as Art and Art History as Failure', *Third Text Online*. Retrieved 15 March 2019 from http://www.thirdtext.org/Failure-As-Art.

Moreiras, Alberto. 2010. 'Infrapolitical Literature: Hispanism and the Border', *CR: The New Centennial Review* 10(2): 183–204.

Murawski, Michał. 2013. 'Palaceology, or Palace-as-Methodology: Ethnographic Conceptualism, Total Urbanism, and a Stalin Skyscraper in Warsaw', *Laboratorium: Russian Review of Social Research* 2013(2): 56–83.

——. 2016. 'Big Affects: Size, Sex and Stalinist "Architecture Power" in Post-socialist Warsaw', in M. Bille and T. Flohr Sorensen (eds), *Elements of Architecture*. London: Routledge, pp. 63–83.
Navaro-Yashin, Yael. 2012. *The Make-Believe Space: Affective Geography in a Postwar Polity*. Durham, NC: Duke University Press.
Rancière, Jacques. 2006. *Politics and Aesthetics*. London: Continuum.
Renfrew, Colin. 2003. *Figuring It Out: What Are We? Where Do We Come From? The Parallel Visions of Artists and Archaeologists*. London: Thames and Hudson.
Sarkisyan, Anna. 2018. 'The Armenian Heritage of Tbilisi: Resisting Oblivion'. *Journal of Conflict Transformation*, 28 March. Retrieved March 2019, from http://caucasusedition.net/the-armenian-heritage-of-tbilisi-resisting-oblivion/.
Scott, James. 1990. *Domination and the Arts of Resistance: Hidden Transcripts*. New Haven, CT: Yale University Press.
Simone, AbdouMaliq. 2017. 'Living as Logistics: Tenuous Struggles in the Remaking of Collective Urban Life', in G. Bhan, S. Srinivas and V. Watson (eds), *Routledge Companion to Planning in the Global South*. London: Routledge, 399-418.
Smith, Adam T. 2015. *The Political Machine*. Princeton, NJ: Princeton University Press.
Smithson, Robert. 1967. 'A Tour of the Monuments of Passaic, New Jersey', *Artforum* VI(4): 48–51.
Ssorin-Chaikov, Nikolai. 2003. *The Social Life of the State in Subarctic Siberia*. Stanford, CA: Stanford University Press.
Taussig, Michael. 1999. *Defacement: Public Secrecy and the Labor of the Negative*. Stanford, CA: Stanford University Press.
Tsing, Anna L. 2005. *Friction: An Ethnography of Global Connection*. Princeton, NJ: Princeton University Press.
Turner, Victor. 1969. *The Ritual Process: Structure and Anti-Structure*. Chicago, IL: Aldine.
Warsza, Joanna (ed.). 2013. *Ministry of Highways: A Guide to the Performative Architecture of Tbilisi*. Berlin: Sternberg.
Weizman, Eyal. 2014. 'Introduction: Forensis', in Forensic Architecture (eds), *Forensis: The Architecture of Public Truth*. Berlin: Sternberg, pp. 9–32.

SNAPSHOT 6

Maintaining Whose Road?

Agnieszka Joniak-Lüthi

Imagine a road. Is there anything more associated with a sense of placelessness, of being in between, both not here anymore but also not there yet? At the same time, as iconic books and films such as Jack Kerouac's *On the Road*, Dennis Hopper's *Easy Rider* or, less well known to an Anglo-American audience, Andrzej Stasiuk's *Wschód* and other road stories make vividly clear, a road is also a place of experiencing, a place where ideas, things and relationships come into being and fall apart. In contrast to their representations on maps as seemingly smooth and straightforward lines, roads 'in experience' are in fact continuously transforming bundles of social relations between materials, humans, discourses, knowledge, environment, the state, capital and more – relations that stretch across place and time.

Julie Chu (2014: 353) argues that 'thinking infrastructurally ... demands an outward orientation to ... distributive forms of agency drawing efficacy from links to elsewhere and elsewhen'. In a similar line of inquiry, Brian Larkin (2013) notes that infrastructures, roads including, have a 'peculiar ontology', which is grounded in the fact that they are things but also relations between things, and that they are matter that enables the movement of other matter. It has been suggested that this 'peculiar' rhizomatic ontology supposedly emerges from its usual invisibility upon moments of 'breakdown' and 'malfunction' (Star and Ruhleder 1996; Graham and Thrift 2007). These moments reveal the complexity of relations out of which infrastructure is fashioned. Yet breakdown and malfunction, both negatively charged normative terms used to describe a situation of 'failure' (Ureta 2014), appear to imply a simple binary where an infrastructure can either be in a state of function, when things work 'properly' (i.e. in a way envisaged by the producer, engineer, designer or the state), or in a state of malfunction. The latter designates cases where infrastructures do not work as they are nominally expected to do, which is implicitly assumed to be to everyone's disadvantage. However, other studies demonstrate that the spectrum is broader and more ambiguous, necessitating a shift beyond the duality of function and malfunction (Campbell 2012; Kernaghan 2012; Barnes 2017). Thinking of the ways in which roads are frequently used in Central Asia as surfaces for drying grain and fruit in autumn, or how they feature globally as platforms for social protest – both resulting in their clear malfunction in the eyes of engineers – reveals the difficulty of differentiating where (and for whom) function ends and malfunction begins. Though I would like to distance myself from the normativity of malfunction and breakdown, the process of decay – the term I prefer – and the work of maintenance to patch it up are nonetheless ethnographically highly interesting as they lay bare the multiple and competing interests, projections, appropriations and asymmetric relations of which roads, similarly to other infrastructures, are always part and which are influenced by their dilapidating materiality.

Scholars have drawn attention to the inherent sociality of maintenance (Schwenkel 2015), and have also discussed maintenance as a source of technological innovation and maintenance as learning (Graham and Thrift 2007). On the other hand, maintenance work has been used as a lens through which to recast infrastructure as dynamic and mutable (Strebel 2011; Denis and Pontille 2014) among other things. In this snapshot, my aim is to focus on the politics of maintenance, and its social ambiguity. Jessica Barnes (2017: 148) points out that although the material object of maintenance appears in most situations to be quite clear (for example, a damaged road surface), the purpose of maintenance is much more complex and involves restoring 'the social and political relationships in which that object is embedded'. In regard to roads, the complexity of those relations reflects the fact that 'roads are sticky metaphors' (Campbell 2012: 483): they mean different things at different times to different people. They are platforms for projecting dreams, expectations, fears, claims to power and political agendas, which are all extremely dynamic. Because of this, their decay and maintenance are ambiguous processes around which tensions accumulate.

Roads in northern Xinjiang Uyghur Autonomous Region, and in particular the recently built expressways, are the locus of such tensions. Situated in northwest China at the border with Kyrgyzstan, Kazakhstan, Russia and Mongolia, extensive rocky deserts and expansive pastureland characterise the area. The latter has been used by, mainly, Kazakh pastoralists to graze their sheep and horses. Having in the past rotated seasonally between a few camps throughout the year, under government pressure transhumance has been reduced over recent decades to migration between, most often, just two sites: the summer pastures and the winter settlement. The section of expressway that comprises the main focus of this snapshot passes through the Tengri Tagh/Tian Shan mountains between the city of Ghulja/Yining and Sairam Lake, where some excellent pastures are located. It was completed in 2015, replacing the old, winding dirt road. This change in the materiality of the road – from a simple dirt/gravel track to a four-lane, asphalted and fenced-off highway – has had various effects on the Kazakh pastoralists in this region. For one, the expressway bisects and has thus blocked some of the seasonal migration routes. As funds for underpasses to enable the migration of wild and domestic animals appear to have often been 'repurposed' by local government and Communist Party officials, pastoralists and their herds find themselves incarcerated by highway fences and embankments.

While the purpose of the new highway is to facilitate faster travel, this acceleration is granted selectively only to those who can afford it, individuals who take advantage of the road to move between urban centres where the few access ramps are located. Numerous pastoralists, who moved from distant locations in the grasslands to the direct vicinity of the road with the aim of connecting to this new speedy world and profiting from its increased traffic flows, found themselves excluded by fences, dykes and embankments. Responding to this engineered exclusion, herding families have removed sections of fence from along the expressway and added some makeshift earth structures to bridge the dykes and establish access to the road. This has also made it possible for motorised tourists to reach the pastoralists' roadside yurts, where they offer food, entertainment and accommodation. At the same time, herders have obtained direct access to the expressway, which facilitates individual travel and has also become crucial in the transportation by truck of herds between summer and winter pastures.

Hence, by destroying parts of the expressway infrastructure, the herders have *maintained* their access to the new road. As the pastoralists remove parts of the fence and make changes to the hard shoulder, maintenance teams repeatedly repair those fences, remove the improvised additions and streamline the roadside, with the purpose of *maintaining* the road in the form designed by the engineers and representing the priorities of the central state. The road is meant to be convenient and smooth for those who pay for it at toll gates, not for the herders who live between them. Secondly, as the crucial link in the emerging Belt and Road Project, the expressway is intended to enable long-distance transport between China and Central Asia, in addition to spurring tourism and facilitating circulation of government, Party and military personnel in this border region. As the road 'travels' (Clifford 1992) through different spatial scales, being a local, translocal and also transnational connection, tensions arise around the question of which social-material relationships should or should not be prioritised and maintained. Further questions about who holds the power to decide what kind of maintenance work is needed, and who should conduct such work in a region as ethnically divided and riven by anti-state violence as Xinjiang, must also be considered as state-sponsored infrastructures and forms of mobility are in the process of appropriating and encroaching upon other material practices.

Agnieszka Joniak-Lüthi is Assistant Professor of Anthropology at the University of Zurich.

References

Barnes, Jessica. 2017. 'States of Maintenance: Power, Politics, and Egypt's Irrigation Infrastructure', *Environment and Planning D: Society and Space* 35(1): 146–64.

Campbell, Jeremy M. 2012. 'Between the Material and the Figural Road: The Incompleteness of Colonial Geographies in Amazonia', *Mobilities* 7(4): 481–500.

Chu, Julie Y. 2014. 'When Infrastructures Attack: The Workings of Disrepair in China', *American Ethnologist* 41(2): 351–67.

Clifford, James. 1992. 'Travelling Cultures', in Lawrence Grossberg, Cary Nelson and Paula Treichler (eds), *Travelling Cultures*. New York: Routledge, pp. 96–116.

Denis, Jerome, and David Pontille. 2014. 'Maintenance Work and the Performativity of Urban Inscriptions: The Case of Paris Subway Signs', *Environment and Planning D: Society and Space* 32: 404–16.

Graham, S., and N. Thrift. 2007. 'Out of Order: Understanding Repair and Maintenance', *Theory, Culture & Society* 24(3): 1–25.

Kernaghan, Richard. 2012. 'Furrows and Walls, or the Legal Topography of a Frontier Road in Peru', *Mobilities* 7(4): 501–20.

Larkin, Brian. 2013. 'The Politics and Poetics of Infrastructure', *Annual Review of Anthropology* 42: 327–43.

Schwenkel, Christina. 2015. 'Spectacular Infrastructure and Breakdown in Socialist Vietnam', *American Ethnologist* 42: 520–34.

Star, Susan Leigh, and Karen Ruhleder. 1996. 'Steps toward an Ecology of Infrastructure: Design and Access for Large Information Spaces', *Information Systems Research* 7 (1): 111–34.

Strebel, Ignaz. 2011. 'The Living Building: Towards a Geography of Maintenance Work', *Social and Cultural Geography* 12(3): 243–62.

Ureta, Sebastián. 2014. 'Normalizing Transantiago: On the Challenges (and Limits) of Repairing Infrastructures', *Social Studies of Science* 44: 368–92.

CHAPTER 6

Dirtscapes

Contest over Value, Garbage and Belonging in Istanbul

AYLIN YILDIRIM TSCHOEPE

A man in uniform kindly held the doors of the elevator of Şişhane Metro Station open for me so I could jump in. He had a trash bin with him, in which he gathered empty 500 ml water bottles. It was not one of the large grey bags that non-municipal garbage workers carried around, but one of the green bins the municipal recycling management service provided. 'People drink a lot of water these days', I said, to break the usual awkward elevator silence. He smiled: 'It is hot today [in Istanbul]. I have been picking up a lot of these in the metro'. Like other garbage workers I have met, Metin (all interlocutors' names changed) complained about how people threw their waste onto the street and expected him to pick it up; that people are too lazy to take two steps to the next trash can; that they drop their garbage in front of him; that they would not talk to him or look him in the eye; that they treat him like a second-class citizen; that he hoped the municipal contractor uniform could restore his dignity, that it would lift him above non-municipal garbage workers, especially above 'those Romani who do a lot of the informal work'.[1]

Metin mentioned that foreigners treated him differently than most Turkish people, and went on to tell me about a group of Japanese tourists he was impressed with because they not only brought the trash to his bin but also thanked him. He added that most locals would rarely do that and would instead drop the trash right in front of him. In all his disappointment he asked me: 'Why would you not thank someone who does that kind of [dirty] work for you?'

While Metin himself was by no means in a privileged social position, he still occupied a higher place on the social ladder than his non-municipal colleagues. Even if classism still worked against him in everyday encounters, officially he was established as a proper citizen with social security, healthcare and a safe work environment.

Municipal officials claimed they hired people in their recycling management workforce regardless of ethnicity. The unofficial truth, however, is that the selection process was a discriminatory practice along intersectional lines of ethnicity and gender: there was a strong preference for hiring Turkish men. In the Turkish conservative-religious imaginary, women are not supposed to carry out 'dirty' work outside of the domestic realm, while it is acceptable that they work as cleaners in their own and others' households. Therefore, Turkish female garbage workers were frowned upon. It was, however, tolerable – or, rather, consciously ignored and looked away from – that Romani women and children worked on the streets picking trash from morning to evening: '. . . You know, in our [Turkish] society, women cannot work in the streets', Metin told me, 'but their [Romani] women are a different case'. Towards the end of my fieldwork in 2016, no one among the Romani group I got to know in the non-municipal recycling sector had any chance to benefit from the safer work offered by the municipality, especially not the women and children among them, who were left with the most precarious and less valuable garbage.

In Turkey, as much as anywhere else, garbage arranges society, space and culture and organises corresponding knowledges, practices, performances and institutions. In a way, it is a 'total social fact', 'at once legal, economic, religious, aesthetic' (Mauss 1966) and intersectional. It also relates to the creation and destruction of value, and, therefore, changes of status, ideals and orders of value with circulation (Thompson 1979). Among various actors who produce, manage and recycle garbage in its various cultural and material forms, my research deals with the contest among groups and individuals who co-create landscapes of purity and pollution in a process of contest and constant negotiation. As these actors define and defy urban, material and bodily dichotomies between value and garbage, they complicate and question structural binaries: they perform their roles along and against them, depending on spatial and situational context; they renegotiate Self and Other as they self-/stereotype, stigmatise and reflect. They equally organise and empower each other within groups who are in conflict with each other. I will draw on the specific case of recycling management in Istanbul as part of my fieldwork over the years 2014–16, and focus on the conditions of non-municipal garbage workers in Istanbul, particularly the minority group of Romani Turks.[2] Situating non-municipal Romani garbage workers among other relevant actors, such as municipal services and recycling management authorities, my main questions are: What strategies exist to disable or enable non-municipal work with waste, and to accept or abject individuals and groups as part of a larger framework of social and spatial transformation in Turkey? What tactics and performances have developed to counter and complicate the situation?

It is striking how garbage workers go unnoticed by most of the population. I saw many passers-by dropping their empty cups from coffeehouse chains right in front of them. Some would even bump into garbage workers, as if they were invisible. Non-municipal workers would probably have preferred to remain in this invisible state and merge with the city, walking the streets they know better than anyone else. Their new visibility – not simply physically, but in front of the law – renders their practice illegal and leaves those who already carry out the least desirable work of the city in a desperate situation.

Multiple Abjections Devaluing Individuals

The forging of Turkishness and Turkish landscape through governmental strategies structures subjects into dichotomous categories that determine an individual as suitable (valuable) to be a citizen or not. This valorisation of proper versus improper citizens works most obviously against political and intellectual opponents of those in power. Concurrently, it takes less visible but more destructive paths among the urban poor such as Turkish internal labour migrants, many of them Kurds or Romani, and refugees – in short, those who do not belong to a 'hegemonic ethnoclass' (Wynter 2003). The process of devaluing individuals is intersectional in the form of a class-based, gendered and ethnic abjection.[3] Several governmental and municipal actors in Turkey, among other actors, used strategies to polarise civil society and create binary oppositions among its subjects and definitions of urban space: proper as opposed to improper citizens, and clean and healthy spaces, practices and bodies as opposed to dirty, dangerous and (culturally and physically) contaminated ones.[4]

The term 'White Turk' has been engaged differently by various authors during previous periods of history. I use it in reference to the hegemonically constructed ideal citizen: the nouveau riche, the neo-Islamic elite who have risen under the rule of the AKP (Adalet ve Kalkınma Partisi; Justice and Development Party), also referred to as AK Partisi, the White Party.[5] Hereby, whiteness needs to be contextualised and differentiated from a Western understanding of a racial epidermal scheme. It goes beyond colour and refers to ethnicity, class and different forms of capital. Many among the Turkish hegemonic ethnoclass have gained their position through prestige and privilege that came not through merit but through other channels such as inheritance, kinship, fictive kinship or clientelism. The subject is constituted through perceptual and conceptual boundaries (Kristeva 1982; Shimakawa 2002); the White Turk needs an Other in terms of class and ethnicity and abjects the 'not-I': Romani are exemplary Others to a Self that is constructed as a 'proper' Turkishness. The Romani garbage workers, although Turks by citizenship, often considered themselves treated as secondary citizens in their daily experience, performance and practice in the city. Older quarters and minority neighbourhoods were strategically selected and deemed structurally unsafe, which, in a risk-prone city like Istanbul, easily convinced better-off residents of the necessity to redevelop these areas. The ease and feeling of safety of the dominant Turkish Self in the face of cleansing urban space from unwanted bodies – that is, the urban transformation of settlements where minorities and migrants live – comes at a price: a prevailing culture of control not only subordinates the Other, but also contains the Self in gated communities through a 'politics of fear', by which I mean governmental strategies of a legal, spatial and biopolitical nature that create and then presumably target internal, external and ecological dangers, both real and imaginary. The performances of oppositional and non-hegemonic groups in response to such creations have been rendered dangerous, either because they do not mimic dominant identities and absorb state ideology (see Bhabha 1994), because these groups act autonomously, or because they criticise the state.[6] As stated, the individuals central to this research were particularly impacted. They were not simply workers of discard; their activity made them discarded in the eyes of Turkish authorities, as if they were wasted humans (Bauman 2004), as if their working material – trash – were turned discursively into an identity classification that always occupies the negative side in society discourses, namely Romani, woman, poor. Through their practice, the location of their homes in the city's ethnic, poor neighbourhoods, and their origins in the hinterlands and history as an ethnic group in Turkey, the Romani Turks as part of this research expressed their situation as Other to the rising 'white' Turkish Self.

From Tinkers to 'Trash Pickers'

The Self is constructed 'as a body in a spatial and temporal world' (Fanon 1952: 91). The inherent issue is not only that certain expectations are inscribed on the body as part of the individual's responsibility, but also that this body carries the burden of race, ethnicity, history and ancestors (ibid.: 92–93). The very means of establishing citizenship and belonging to a country, in the case of this research the Turkish ID card, also became a tool to localise citizens along the axes of gender, history, kinship, ethnicity. On blue cards for men and orange cards for women were inscribed the names of holders' parents, registration of birth place, current home location, as well as religious affiliation.[7] The black letters on this document, sometimes interspersed with handwriting from officials, also inscribed the identity of an individual onto their body; this allowed employers to immediately locate a person on an ethnicity and class map of Turkish society, for example through Romani-sounding names, typical places of Romani settlement throughout Turkey, and the stereotypically ethnic neighbourhoods in Istanbul. If an individual's past and future are already determined through the inscription of one's identity card, what powers are left to the individual to change their fate? Many conversations with interlocutors touched on the question of fate or destiny at one point or another. One of these conversations took place with Adnan Abi, whom I accompanied during his tours and breaks.[8]

Adnan Abi, a male garbage worker in his early forties, leaned against his garbage-picking cart. Two young women, Hande and Berna, squatted in front of their cart next to his. Their cart became heavy once it was filled up with old paper, plastic and metal, which is why these two women, possibly fifteen or sixteen years old, were usually found together on their tours, picking through the valuable garbage of upper-class neighbourhoods. Their sisterhood not only ensured safety from outside control and dangers (policing), it also empowered them against male garbage workers from other groups. I had seen them successfully fighting off young men from another garbage workers' kin group. In conversation with the three of them on questions of fate and identity inscription, Adnan Abi asked the following:

> Look at these two young women. Wouldn't it suit this one to be a teacher? Wouldn't it suit that one to be a secretary? Isn't she pretty? Don't her eyes speak of her intelligence and vivid mind? Could you not imagine her sitting and greeting the clients of a large company? Don't you think that is what she could be doing right now if she had been given the chance to go to school?

The bitter smiles of the women spoke to what Adnan said. Not only did dominant municipal and governmental actors do very little to foster upward mobility for these women, but they added further to their hardship with recent laws that not only forbade the practice of non-municipal garbage work, but also introduced excessively exaggerated fines[9] for those (non-municipally contracted) individuals who were caught collecting garbage as well as for those who supported them (by providing packaging materials, for example). Adnan continued:

> Like me, these two women haven't learned anything else but trash picking. My ancestors were tinkers in the southeast of the country. We would travel around and mend kitchen utensils, farming tools and repair machines. Then they didn't need us anymore, so we moved to the larger cities like Istanbul and were left with the work no one else wanted to do. My father was a trash picker, and I went with him on his tours, learning the tricks of the trade. My eldest sometimes accompanies me, he says he wants to contribute to the family income. I don't mind the work, it's honest work. . . . I don't even want to work for the municipality. I have heard that they don't pay on time and if they do, it is never the promised amount. What I pick and sell to the recycling facilities[10] is my money, earned with my sweat . . . Since the law has come out that forbids us to pick trash [in January 2016], I have lost about 30 per cent of my income. If they catch you, fines are high. If the supermarkets continue to help us by giving us their packaging material, they get fines as well. Some still do it to support us, others are afraid of having to pay 5,000 Turkish lira [fine].[11]

Romani interlocutors carried anger over the restriction of their mobility, as their agency was limited by lawfare (restriction of their practice and substitution with municipal services) and biopolitical othering (Foucault 1978; Fassin 2001). Romani resisted such governmental strategies, exactly by *not joining* the municipal recycling workforce and by *retaining authority* over their practice, time and earnings. This defence strategy spoke to their self-determination as Romani (Okely 1983) – a correlation between self-employment and self-identity that interlocutors emphasised in words and actions ('I am my own master', 'We are honest people'). By doing so, they evaded subjectification through the state and did not respond to interpellation, but circumvented it through collective efforts in their social networks. An example of this was the reorganisation of their mobility tactics after eviction from neighbourhoods near their work site. Authorities, however, did not consider this evasion as an empowering strategy by the Romani, but as evidence of their uncontrollability, their polluting or improper citizenhood – the performance they expected from the workers in the first place. Such a bias reinforced the Turkish nation-state's class-based and ethnic, even gendered, abjection of the Romani.

Most nation-states rely on a homogeneous definition of nationhood and citizenship, which is why those nations establish themselves by abjecting what is other, foreign – in the case of the Romani, not-Turkish. This is clearly stated through a double language of abjection: through alleged uncleanliness and by working with garbage. Practices of national abjection can reveal the politics of representation of society, specifically what is seen as Other, as a fundamental part of the everyday (Shimakawa 2002). In the context of non-municipal garbage workers in Istanbul, their crafting of networks, subdivision and contest over urban spaces of valuable garbage, their performance with and against societal expectations can be best understood through the connection and reciprocal influence on multiple scales from body to city in which they negotiated their coming into visibility.

The garbage workers, predominantly non-municipal ones, are subjected as dirty or improper. They carried out dirty practices through their everyday dealing and valuation of what dominant actors deemed invaluable (garbage). They occupied what many officials considered dirty places, the 'dangerous' self-built settlements, squats in historic neighbourhoods, and slums of the city. Ironically, it is the garbage workers – the 'dirty people doing dirty practices and living in dirty places' – who, through their very practice of recycling garbage, keep the city clean, safe, proper, healthy and sustainable. They do so in a much more efficient way than the municipal recycling service because of their intimate knowledge of the city, where garbage appears and how to immediately respond to it.[12]

Urban transformation works as a governmental tool to cleanse minority neighbourhoods and informal settlements to implement residential and commercial projects. Biopolitics, through politics and media, defines the new Turkish identity and bodies. Lawfare supports urban transformation and biopolitics by legalising the destruction of minority neighbourhoods and illegalising not only their practices such as garbage picking, but also the support for their practice by other groups and individuals in the city through high fines.

'Someone Else Will Pick It Up'

Historically, authorities have used the argument of infectiousness and danger emitted by undesirable subjects of the state as sufficient justification for legal and physical action against these presumably impure subjects (Douglas 1984). The 'performative danger' (Mitchell 2015) in the case of the Romani was described by various interlocutors in authorities and among dominant groups through the language of purity and pollution: one must get rid of the 'unhealthy, unhygienic, uncontrollable, those who pollute urban space'. Those who have engaged this language of abjection imagined that pollution spread most literally through the infected bodies of workers in contact with dirt and diseases, while ideological pollution spread through the dangerous performances of otherness. One such performance was considered to be the Romani group's autonomy from the system: through their mere presence, but also by their actions, the garbage workers could infect the thoughts of proper citizens, potentially leading them to act and think autonomously as well.

The avoidance of dirt as a matter of hygiene and aesthetics is a widespread notion in various countries, and, more generally, 'dirt [is a] matter out of place' (Douglas 1984: 36), an offence against order (ibid.: 2), and has to be eliminated for that reason. The littering culture in Turkey is a very particular one with regard to garbage practices and social implications. Both garbage workers and individuals who produce garbage have communicated the existence of a strong social hierarchy, in which littering – throwing garbage onto the streets, out of windows, into green areas and parks – became a performance of higher rank: the act of littering positioned one above those who will have to pick it up, those who were 'second-class citizens'. In Istanbul, therefore, dirt is paradoxical: on one hand, it is a matter that has to take place, because it was a means to establish a particular social order. 'Someone else will pick it up' were the exact words used by all of those I approached after observing them litter on the streets, in public spaces and in the most scenic spots of Istanbul – on the ferries, in parks that overlook the Bosporus, in playgrounds accompanied by their children. Most of those I asked also reported that they visited the respective spaces frequently, but had no concern regarding their littering; they were sure that someone took care of their garbage so they would be able to come back to a clean spot for their next visit. On the other hand, dirt is a matter out of place, in reference to its material object form but also the people who ensured that spaces in the city remained clean; their recycling practices and the locations of their homes were also matter out of place.[13]

Interestingly, some of those I asked why they threw their bottles onto the street were also convinced that they were creating work for someone else by leaving garbage. Among those, there was a shared cultural understanding of non-municipal garbage workers as part of a larger urban ecology, but also a social hierarchy. Through denial of social mobility and abjection as an ethnic group, Romani garbage workers have become a sort of 'caste', or hereditary class. This notion was broken, not in favour of the workers and their social mobility, but to dismantle and replace them as a group in the urban ecology. Municipal systems were one of the means to control the streets and to extract financial value from collected dirt. The value that garbage created for the non-municipal garbage workers was a value that authorities have laid their hands on, threatening the livelihoods of those who had no chance of becoming garbage workers in the municipal services. This results in a disregard for rising issues like child labour, discrimination, displacement. Therefore, affected groups often do not see themselves represented or included by other actors, which in turn is why they lack trust in actors who could potentially become their allies. Instead, they derive support and seek empowerment from within their kin groups and larger social networks.

Dirtscapes

Landscapes of purity and pollution emerge from the production of knowledge over value and garbage and the use of 'abjective', binary constructions. I refer to these constructs as the 'dirtscape'.[14] The dirtscape stands in context with a particular culture of value and garbage, it has flexible boundaries, and subsumes what different interlocutors referred to as 'the uncontrollable, unhygienic, dangerous' in terms of space, bodies and practices. It is populated mainly by the urban poor, and often localised in squats in historic neighbourhoods, migrant self-built settlements, and low-cost housing. It gives justification to local authorities for measures of *temizleme* (cleansing) of space and people. The language of the dirtscape is made up of – but not limited to – metaphors and terms used by several bureaucrats and authorities, such as *temizleme*, tumour, cancer, undeserving, threat, danger, dirt (also referring to people), and the repeatedly mentioned imaginary of the *kontrolsuz* (without control). In sum, the dirtscape is a multiscalar phenomenon comprised of spaces, material objects, bodies, practices and performances, of values and rituals around dirt and cleanliness. It deals with dirt in its material, social and symbolic form, it is in constant flux and is renegotiated between different actors who each promote their differing cultural constructions of purity and pollution. Since the dirtscape consists of tangible and intangible layers of interpretation, its study requires a multidisciplinary approach to its constituent elements.

In Turkey, the line between cleanliness and dirt appeared to be the threshold of one's home: residents and guests likewise took off their shoes before entering to leave the dirt outside. The streets of the city, public spaces and parks were locations where dirt is left. At the moment when an item is dropped, it transforms from something valuable into garbage. The act of dropping something on the floor instead of in a trash bin is a result of either carelessness or intention. There is an underlying assumption that someone else will have to pick it up, someone less valuable: 'they treat us like garbage, too', as one garbage worker put it. It comes as no surprise that the non-municipal garbage workers in Istanbul are comprised of the urban poor – (internal) migrants, refugees, ethnic minorities; men, women and children alike. The stigma of garbage was reified in the places where they live: poor neighbourhoods, self-built settlements, squats in historic neighbourhoods. Apart from the latter, informal settlements often emerged in precarious urban locations: on slopes, close to highways, on polluted ground near factories or garbage dumps. In 1993, a garbage hill exploded in the Ümraniye District of Istanbul, taking the lives of many who lived nearby and dealt with the garbage (Kocasoy and Curi 1995). While some squats and low-income settlements have grown into socio-culturally and economically diverse, strong communities who feel very much at home in their neighbourhood, others are the places of individuals and groups who have no choice but to live in the city's dirtscape. These are under constant threat of eviction from renewal projects that are part of an urban transformation.

Through 'trash talk', new avenues open up for an understanding of an architectural ideology, and architecture and urban planning as hegemonic tools to produce the 'clean' city (Argyrou 1997; Yiftachel 2009; McKee 2015; Martínez 2017). Ethnic cleansing is often disguised in spatial cleansing (Herzfeld 2006), that is, the act of getting rid of undesirable residents and users of a particular space through demolishment, redevelopment and exclusion of previous residents from the new development. Cultural constructions of dirty bodies, spaces and practices therefore implicate each other. People are treated as dirt, precisely those who live in the dirtscape, while, at the same time, they take care of transforming and recycling it.

A typical example of governmental strategies and lawfare that target the dirtscape can be found in the transformation of the historic neighbourhood of Tarlabaşı. Renewal Law No. 5366: Preservation by Renovation and Utilization by Revitalizing of Deteriorated Immovable Historical and Cultural Properties, often simply referred to as the 'Tarlabaşı Law', was approved on 16 June 2005. The law enables local authorities to expropriate property owners in presumably structurally unsafe areas (structural safety being determined by municipal experts) as a form of eminent domain. The developer claimed that it was indeed for the common good, because they were getting rid of 'the cancer of the city' (interview, Beyoglu Gap Inşaat, 2010). The tools of lawfare also empower local authorities to suspend and overrule the status of Historic Asset Protection assigned to specific areas by the Council for Preservation of Sites of Historic Interest. Thereby, Law No. 5366 is repurposed not to preserve and renovate Tarlabaşı, but to exchange residents and transform space. More needs to be said about resilience such as practices of (re)organisation.

What has become garbage for one person still has value for another. Non-municipal local networks of garbage workers precede municipal formal services and more recent, globally inspired social movements around dirt. Garbage workers, mainly *çekçekciler* ('pull-pullers', those who pull things from the garbage), earn their livelihood from collecting reusable and recyclable items such as paper, plastic, metal, appliances and other materials, often also hazardous waste, and delivering them in large carts or collection trucks to recycling stations distributed all over the city. Non-municipal garbage workers have different forms of organisation. I have observed two main organisational strategies in two areas that are preferred garbage sites, that is, areas that produce the most valuable garbage: the commercial concentrations on Istiklal Avenue in Beyoğlu and the upscale neighbourhood of Nisantaşı in Şişli.

In the first case, the area around Istiklal Avenue, the garbage workers used to live nearby in areas such as Tarlabaşı. They used to come with carts to the Istiklal Avenue area and took the sorted garbage to storage areas of a *hurdacı* (waste dealer) (see Figures 6.1 and 6.2). Many garbage workers in the Istiklal area were organised under a *hurdacı*, someone who owns or rents (or squats) a storage place, often old parking lots of empty historic buildings. These were located in the rundown quarters near the Golden Horn and Bosporus shore before the widespread urban transformation through the Galataport Project took its toll on them. The garbage workers could rent trash-picking carts for a rental fee of 20 TL (around $5.50) per day from their *hurdacı* (Şen et al. 2014) and earned around 10 TL per full cart delivered, leaving them with 40–50 TL (around $11–14) on a good day, which, at the end of the month, was still considerably below minimum income (around 1,645 TL gross/month), even when working weekdays and weekends. Once enough recyclable material had been collected, the *hurdacı* organised transport to larger recycling and transfer stations on his trucks and received payment accordingly. The transfer stations were a kind of neutral ground for municipal and non-municipal services, where the value of garbage is prioritised over questions of legitimacy of the collector.

In the second case, the Romani garbage workers in the Nisantaşı area of Şişli were organised differently. Many of them had previously lived in a

Figures 6.1 .and 6.2. Two types of carts could be rented from the waste dealer according to material. The pushcart is mainly used for old appliances or generally old used items with a potential for a second life. The white trash-bag carts carry plastic, paper and cardboard. Photographs by Aylin Yildirim Tschoepe.

nearby settlement west of Nisantaşı, but were evicted or forced out by gentrification. They had to move to Gaziosmanpaşa, further west across the Golden Horn, which was also already a target area for district-wide transformation.[15] Their constant (imposed) life on the move led them to adapt their mode of mobility and organisational structure in comparison with other groups of garbage workers. The Romani individuals who were part of this research were not organised under a *hurdacı* but carried out their practice mostly as part of a kinship group. As families, they have invested in their own garbage trucks, which brought them to the places with the most valuable garbage, and allowed them to use their trucks as stationary and mobile collection vehicles (Figure 6.3). Adnan, whom I mentioned earlier, was one of those who had to move further away, but returned to his previous work site using his truck. While some brought their own trucks and used them as a base while working on a site, other garbage workers, often in groups of two or more women, were dropped off in the morning and picked up in the evening by their families, as in the case of Hande and Berna. In many cases, three generations collected together: grandparents, parents and children. Roles were clearly defined between those who collected garbage, those who took care of younger children, and those who stayed close to the truck to alert the family in case of policing. Mobility was necessary to evade the exorbitant fines for non-municipal garbage work

Figure 6.3. Garbage collection trucks owned by a group. Photograph by Aylin Yildirim Tschoepe.

that had been introduced in 2016. At the time of writing these lines, the workers have already moved sites of practice.

Imposed Identity and Social Determinism

One might argue that garbage workers consist of a transient population. This may be true for refugees or internal migrants, who have brief stays and use trash picking as a temporary means to bridge a financially and personally precarious situation with the hopes to move on soon to another place. The Romani garbage workers, however, are not transient. They have settled in the city after being forced to migrate from their ancestral homelands. The social (and ethnic) hierarchy they have found in cities like Istanbul left them with the position of garbage workers, which they have been carrying out over generations.

Imposed identity becomes a burden as it is inscribed onto the body over time and space. Some officials have spoken clear words to the question of identity and origin; they deemed certain minorities 'unreliable and lazy'. Others have found more inclusive tropes: 'I don't care if the garbage picker is a Turk, Kurd, Romani or Syrian. I want to turn them into formal labour and avoid illegal practices [like child labour]' (environmental consultant, Marmara Association, 2015). While a potential solution to poor labour conditions and an encouraging prospect on the urban political agenda, there was a glitch in the implementation of this strategy: the reality of formalisation processes was that they favoured male Turkish individuals as garbage workers. None of the formalised municipal garbage workers among the pool of interlocutors in different neighbourhoods of Istanbul knew of female colleagues, or Romani workers regardless of gender.[16] Romani or other minority women have little prospect of formalisation for socio-cultural reasons. Instead of offering them safer, more lucrative options, women often end up having to deal with the more precarious waste, work more hours, are left without job security, and receive neither child support nor holidays. When the whole family had to work on the street, the lack of childcare as well as the lack of financial support or job security for the family forced them to bring their children along. Often, they did not have the option to forgo the need to use a young child as labour, so many children from the age of five years helped out as part of the garbage worker group.

Mücela, the grandmother of a family of Romani workers, sorted some garbage next to their truck in Nisantaşı. Four children accompanied the family: an older girl of around seven, two boys of around four and five, and a young girl of around two years played on the opposite side of the street in the entrance area of an abandoned building. Mücela was around forty-five years old and dressed with a colourful scarf wrapped around her head in traditional fashion, a dark blouse and a wide, long skirt with flower prints. She married when she was eighteen and had her first child at nineteen. Her son got married and had children around the same age as she did, which is not unusual in Turkey. Mücela, always with one eye on the children, explained that she would prefer to have them at school, but that they could not afford to have one person stay at home to take them and pick them up:

> If [officials] would care about us, we would receive [subsidies] so the children would be able to attend school. The children shouldn't have to come here and go trash picking in the streets . . . They don't care about us anyway: I get sick often from dealing with garbage and my back hurts from carrying it.

I was surprised to hear this and asked why she did not get access to basic healthcare, as she should be entitled to get help in public hospitals.

> Well, that is what they pride themselves on [providing healthcare for all]. Yes, I can go to a public hospital, they pay for that, but they do not pay for medication I need. So, the doctor tells me I have pain, but I cannot afford the remedy.

The costs of medication were low, yet too high for someone who earned around 50 TL ($14) a day. When I left the field in 2016, the situation was already precarious and unpredictable for various garbage worker families. In fact, I could not find Adnan Abi on his usual route towards the end of my stay in Turkey, but was able to reach him on his phone: 'Adnan Abi, how are you? I could not find you on your route and haven't seen you for days. A group of refugees is picking in your area with push carts'. 'Yes, well, it has been difficult to be around there recently. We have been working somewhere else, I don't know what it will be.' Fearing for his safety and that of his family getting caught recycling, Adnan had to change his location, and when we last spoke he was working temporarily in other jobs.

Once the Romani workers leave the valuable garbage areas, other garbage workers, who are already in competition with them, will take over their routes. Precariousness and poverty will be passed down to those who feel they have nothing to lose: the unskilled among the refugees, who shun begging on the streets and are unable to find any other work in the marginal economic sector but garbage work. These are the ones who are even more desperate, willing to work for even less pay under more miserable conditions. These newcomers have not yet gone through similar skill-building processes and lack the social and spatial experience of the 'established' garbage workers, who have some, if few, chances of job mobility.

Conclusion: Performance and Knowledge as Resistance

Purity and pollution are culturally constructed notions as part of both locally and globally shaped value systems, which are flexible and contestable. From body to urban space, these systems are influenced by the nation-state's imaginary, instrumentalised through lawfare and identity politics, and manifested in the construction of a *dirtscape*. People, places, practices, their identities, histories and memories can be dirt, depending on their position along the trajectory from desirable to undesirable subject under the dominant ideology. The hegemonic agenda foresees cleansing the dirtscape: certain groups, their practices and performances, and neighbourhoods are symbolically and physically deemed dangerous and dirty, because they do not fit ideological visions of proper citizens and urbanity, because these places, people and practices are 'uncontrollable', and because they bear the danger of 'infecting' proper subjects and spaces.

As a governmental practice, citizens and urban spaces are brought under control through urban transformation. First comes the raising of fear regarding the threatening Other against a hegemonic 'ethnoclass' by depicting them as dangerous or toxic in a public discourse that constructs the connection of poor, ethnic populations with crime, drugs and violence.[17] Next, their spaces are rendered physically dangerous, that is, unsafe in terms of hygiene, structural stability and vulnerability to disaster – for many a knockout argument in earthquake-prone Istanbul. Third, a healthy, safe urban solution is propagated through newly transformed neighbourhoods for proper citizens in place of the previous residents.

Dirt has a financial, political, environmental, social and cultural value, and it is along those lines that different actors contest each other. Those garbage workers I have met do not pursue a political purpose; their practice is a survival strategy: garbage is collected for its reuse value. They bring garbage back into the commodity cycle. This is different from neoliberal environmental practices, which seek not only to commodify garbage and nature, but to eliminate possibilities for non-municipal garbage workers. The abjection of garbage workers and the strategy of forbidding their practices and redeveloping their living spaces is paradoxical: urban transformation does not drive them out completely – gentrified neighbourhoods not only advertise themselves as clean and safe spaces, but also produce valuable garbage. Thereby, they create the necessity for garbage workers to keep the spaces orderly, and attract garbage workers back into the neighbourhood.

What should receive consideration are the skills and creative energy that are necessary for collecting garbage in places such as Istanbul. Gar-

Figures 6.4. and 6.5. A non-municipal garbage worker arrives earlier in the day in order to pick the most valuable items before the municipal services arrive. Photographs by Aylin Yildirim Tschoepe.

bage workers are wanderers with an intimate knowledge of the city, urban rhythms and the lives of other dwellers through their littering practices and the archaeology of their garbage. They need to strategise and schedule routes and districts in order to avoid conflict with other groups and families, and coordinate visits to garbage sites before the municipal services get there. Understanding the traffic and parking situation in the city is key in finding suitable spaces for interim storage of garbage and garbage trucks. They have built experience regarding the nature of and time when garbage is brought out, and keep developing and inventing tactics to avoid policing and fines. The garbage workers in Nisantaşı had also set up and frequented designated social spaces, which served the purpose of meetings, exchange of information on the daily work situation, gossip and quick meal breaks. These spaces could change flexibly in order to escape a controlling gaze. The knowledge, experience and skill that are acquired through these practices of resistance and resilience could be leveraged towards a viable future for the garbage workers by themselves and other actors, who could be their potential allies – a future that may or may not be in garbage work.

Aylin Yildirim Tschoepe is a postdoctoral researcher in the Department of Social Sciences at the University of Basel.

Notes

1. Many interlocutors used the term 'informal' or 'illegal' to refer to particular kinds of work in the marginal sector. I choose to avoid these terms, given that the form of non-municipal garbage work this chapter deals with comes out of a vernacular economy and practice. I have referred to the practitioners as non-municipal garbage workers instead of the terms one often finds or hears (or as workers use to refer to themselves), such as trash- or rag-picker.
2. Interlocutors have expressed a strong sense of identity as Romanlı, Romani (also referencing their belonging to a group with a network beyond the local), but they also stressed the fact that they are Turkish citizens. More will be explained in this chapter. They are referred to as Romani in this text as they preferred to reference themselves as such over other identity markers in the context of this fieldwork, but it is understood that identity constructions are complex and fluid.
3. I focus on the non-municipal garbage workers in order to raise awareness of those less visible in the current urban and social transformation. The cleansing of urban space from marginal groups such as Romani garbage workers goes largely unrecorded and unnoticed, but has gained a new momentum in the tumultuous post-attempted-coup period since July 2016.
4. My reading of governmental strategies in this context is influenced by Foucault (2000).

5. See Sandra and Ayşe Çavdar on neo-Islam and urban transformation, in the exhibition *Başakşehir: An Urban Model* (2014). Retrieved 20 November 2018 from https://www.stadt-koeln.de/leben-in-koeln/freizeit-natur-sport/veranstaltungskalender/sandra-schaefer-basaksehir-urban-model.
6. The category of 'thought crimes' describes the pen (of critical academics, journalists, intellectuals etc.) as another form of weapon. See Mustafa Akyol in *Al-monitor* (17 March 2016) on thought crimes (retrieved 5 December 2016 from http://www.al-monitor.com/pulse/originals/2016/03/turkey-erdogan-introduces-new-thoughtcrimes.html).
7. At the time of my research, interlocutors were in possession of the older cards, which I describe here. Since 2016, new credit-card-sized ID cards can be obtained that do not display all the information on the physical card, but store it digitally.
8. 'Abi' means 'older brother'. The use of kinship terms for non-relatives in Turkey (sister, brother, aunt, uncle) is a sign of respect, empathy and personal connection through creating fictive kinship. The women were younger, so they would call me 'Abla', 'older sister'.
9. 'Restriction of Paper Picking and Fines', Zete online news, 21 February 2016 (retrieved 28 February 2016 from https://zete.com/bakanlik-kagit-iscilerini-issiz-birakti-toplayicidan-kagit-alana-140-000-tl-ceza/); 'New Arrangement Upsets Paper Collectors', Milliyet.com, 24 January 2016 (retrieved 15 March 2017 from http://www.milliyet.com.tr/yeni-duzenleme-kagit-gundem-2183439/).
10. Recycling facilities such as garbage transfer stations became the space where municipal recycling management and non-municipal garbage recycling come together on some sort of indiscriminate terrain.
11. My interlocutors spoke of a fine of 5,000 TL (approximately $1,390), which could go up to 140,000 TL (approximately $38,990). This legislation goes back to earlier years, but was enforced in January 2016.
12. According to interlocutors, garbage workers more diligently separate garbage and make use of what is reusable, while municipal services incinerate a large share of the collected waste.
13. Among other subjects currently considered 'matters out of place' (certain intellectuals, journalists, professionals and the political opposition)
14. I chose the term 'dirt' because of its ambiguity as both valuable and invaluable, in contrast to words like trash, litter or garbage. The phenomenon I describe as dirtscape emerges as 'scape' according to the definition proposed by Appadurai: 'terms with the common suffix *-scape* . . . indicate that these are not objectively given relations that look the same from every angle of vision but, rather, that they are deeply perspectival constructs, inflected by the historical, linguistic, and political situatedness of different sorts of actors: nation-states, multinationals, diasporic communities, as well as subnational groupings and movements . . . and even face-to-face groups, such as villages, neighborhoods, and families' (Appadurai 1996: 33).
15. The information on locations at a district level is already widely known. I have left out specifications when they were necessary for interlocutors' privacy and where they were unnecessary to understand the general dynamic.
16. I conducted this part of the fieldwork in 2015; towards the end of my stay in 2016, I did encounter some female Turkish municipal garbage workers. They

were, however, not part of the motorised cleaning force that did their work across all shifts and in all areas. The few women were on daytime shifts and were restricted to sidewalk-cleaning, equipped with a small vehicle or with a broom.

17. 'Drug Operation in Kustepe' (a poor/minority/migrant neighbourhood with many garbage workers), Hurriyet, 28 November 2016 (retrieved 6 May 2017 from http://www.hurriyet.com.tr/kustepede-uyusturucu-operasyonu-40261 112).

References

Appadurai, Arjun. 1996. *Modernity at Large: Cultural Dimensions of Globalization*. Minneapolis: University of Minnesota Press.

Argyrou, Vassos. 1997. '"Keep Cyprus Clean": Littering, Pollution, and Otherness', *Cultural Anthropology* 12(2): 159–78.

Bauman, Zygmunt. 2004. *Wasted Lives: Modernity and Its Outcasts*. London: Polity.

Bhabha, Homi. 1994. *The Location of Culture*. London: Routledge.

Douglas, Mary. 1984. *Purity and Danger: An Analysis of Concepts of Pollution and Taboo*. London: Routledge.

Fanon, Frantz. 1952. *Black Skins, White Mask*. New York: Grove Press.

Fassin, Didier. 2001. 'The Biopolitics of Otherness: Undocumented Foreigners and Racial Discrimination in French Public Debate', *Anthropology Today* 17(1): 3–7.

Foucault, Michel. 1978. *The History of Sexuality Volume 1*. New York: Pantheon.

——. 2000. 'Governmentality', in James D. Faubion and Robert Hurley (eds), *Power. Volume 3 of Essential Works of Foucault: 1954–1984*. New York: The New Press, 201-22.

Herzfeld, Michael. 2006. 'Spatial Cleansing: Monumental Vacuity and the Idea of the West', *Journal of Material Culture* 11(1/2): 127–49.

Kocasoy, Gunay, and Kriton Curi. 1995. 'The Ümraniye-Hekimbaşi Open Dump Accident', *Waste Management & Research* 13: 305–14.

Kristeva, Julia. 1982. *Powers of Horror: An Essay on Abjection*. New York: Columbia University Press.

Martínez, Francisco. 2017. '"This Place Has Potential": Trash, Culture and Urban Regeneration in Tallinn, Estonia', *Suomen Antropologi* 42(3): 1–21.

Mauss, Marcel. 1966. *The Gift; Forms and Functions of Exchange in Archaic Societies*. London: Cohen & West.

McKee, Emily. 2015. 'Trash Talk: Interpreting Morality and Disorder in Negev/Naqab Landscapes', *Current Anthropology* 56(5): 733–52.

Mitchell, Gregory. 2015. *Tourist Attractions: Performing Race and Masculinity in Brazil's Sexual Economy*. Chicago, IL: University of Chicago Press.

Okely, Judith. 1983. *The Traveller-Gypsies*. Cambridge: Cambridge University Press.

Rademacher, Anna. 2009. 'When Is Housing an Environmental Problem? Reforming Informality in Kathmandu', *Current Anthropology* 50(4): 513–33.

Sen, Alper, Özge Çelikaslan and Pelin Tan. (eds). 2014. *Surplus of Istanbul*. Istanbul: Friedrich Ebert Stiftung.

Shimakawa, Karen. 2002. *National Abjection: The Asian American Body Onstage*. Durham, NC: Duke University Press.

Tekin, Latife. 1996. *Berji Kristin: Tales from the Garbage Hills*. New York: Marion Boyars.
Thompson, Michael. 1979. *Rubbish Theory: The Creation and Destruction of Value*. Oxford: Oxford University Press.
Wynter, Sylvia. 2003. 'Unsettling the Coloniality of Being/Power/Truth/Freedom: Towards the Human, After Man, Its Overrepresentation – An Argument', *The New Centennial Review* 3(3): 257–337.
Yiftachel, Oren. 2009. 'Theoretical Notes on "Gray Cities": The Coming of Urban Apartheid?' *Planning Theory* 5(3): 211–22.

SNAPSHOT 7

Repairing Russia

Michał Murawski

Moscow c. 2018: The Era of *Plitka*

At 11 p.m. on a hot August night, my friend Timur goes off in search of a taxi. We are standing on 1st Tverskaya Yamskaya Street, a major artery in central Moscow. He takes a wrong step and is immediately kettled by a circumambulating procession of yellow diggers and forklift trucks, lurching at high speed around what remains of Tverskaya Yamskaya's pavement surfaces. He emerges from the blockade, only to stumble over a pile of asphalt pavement chunks, freshly ripped out of the ground. The mountains of asphalt chunks are interspersed – here as more or less everywhere else in central Moscow – with even huger piles of brand new granite pavement stones, waiting to be laid into the ground by armies of jumpsuit-clad workers, the vast majority of them *gastarbeiters* from Central Asia. The whole scene is framed, here and everywhere else, by a never-ending sea of white and green striped banners, the official visual brand – designed by the graphic design team of Strelka KB – of 'My Street', or *Moya Ulitsa*. Strelka KB is the hip urban consultancy that has increasingly monopolised 'public improvement' (*blagoustroistvo*) projects in Moscow and Russia during the late Putin era.

Moya Ulitsa is the name of the most ambitious *blagoustroistvo* programme carried out in Moscow since the fall of the Soviet Union, currently being exported with ever-increasing zeal throughout the Russian regions, the former Soviet space and – if Strelka realises its ambitions – to the world at large.

Plitka – the Russian word for tile or paving stone – is one of the most important words in Moscow under the reign of the technocratic Mayor Sergey Sobyanin, who has ruled the city since the dismissal of the strongman populist Mayor Yuri Luzhkov in 2010. Journalist Sergey Medvedev (2015) has gone so far as to christen the Sobyanin years the 'era of *plitka*'.

Once they have been liberated from their packaging, but before coming to their final resting place in the ground, the piles of *plitka* are laid in a bewildering array of formations throughout the city. In the revolutionary centenary year of 2017, as the museums of Moscow (and the world) put on blockbuster shows celebrating the art of the Soviet avant-garde, the *plitka*

Figure S7.1. Abstract *plitka* assemblage. Photograph by Michał Murawski.

of Moscow were arranged into quite spectacular formations, which often bore an uncanny resemblance to the abstract art of the early twentieth century. In and around the Stalin-era high-rise (*vysotka*) on Kotelnicheskaya Naberezhnaya, the *plitka* were assembled in towering arrangements strikingly reminiscent of Kazimir Malevich's *architektons*, the suprematist artist's sculptural fantasies on the theme of architectural verticality (let us call them *plitkatektons*). Elsewhere, cut chunks of *plitka* were balanced against each other – sometimes accompanied by a concrete traffic cone, discarded stone cutter blade, uprooted manhole cover or wooden crate – in a manner more reminiscent of an abstract work by El Lissitzky or Popova.

Sometimes the vernacular constructivist mise-en-scènes acquire a formal and temporal complexity, which seems to leave Eisenstein far behind. Outside the *vysotka*, workers ripping out asphalt from the building's driveways were forced to work their way around an inconveniently parked black Volvo, left lingering on a tiny island of asphalt in the dust (flanked by a square flowerpot and a *plitkatekton*). By the following evening, the three principal elements (car, pot, *plitkatekton*) were still in place, although some meaningful changes to the form and composition had taken place: the square concrete flowerpot had been replaced by a circular concrete flowerpot; the *plitkatekton* had been reduced in height by about two-thirds and

Figure S7.2. A Volvo flanked by a square flowerpot and a *plitkatekton*. Photograph by Michał Murawski.

moved behind the flowerpot; the asphalt island was gone, and the black Volvo had been replaced by a battered old BMW with flat tyres (now standing on the opposite side of the flowerpot to where the Volvo had been). The BMW was maxed out and could not possibly have been driven to its spot; it could only have been dragged or dropped there – whether out of the back of a lorry, or from one of the *vysotka*'s windows.

Plitka is not the only material artefact of Moscow's *blagoustroistvo* whose deployment has achieved a remarkable level of poetic and semiotic depth. This is even more true, perhaps, for the white and green banners (or *falshfasady* – 'false façades', as they are sometimes non-derogatorily called in Moscow). The *falshfasady* have been a staple of the Moscow landscape since the second year of the *Moya Ulitsa* programme in 2016. The distinctiveness of their design and the sheer extent of their proliferation during the most intense summer/autumn phases of *blagoustroistvo* quickly endowed these banners with an iconic status – it was difficult to take a photograph in central Moscow during the warm months of 2016–17 without a *falshfasad* making its way into your shot. The *falshfasady* very quickly became objects of artistic, fashion and design inspiration. White-green striped 'Sobyanin socks' and 'Sobyanin dresses' became must-wear items – and Instagram staples – of 2017, while users of the encrypted messaging app Telegram

Figure S7.3. The BMW arrived to stay. Photograph by Michał Murawski.

(partially banned by the Russian government in April 2018) were able to spice up their chats with a set of satirical *Moya Ulitsa*/Sobyanin-themed stickers.

The total distribution of the stripes throughout Moscow's cityscape and popular culture was no doubt a function of the successful work done by KB Strelka's graphic design team, but it was also an index of the vast scale of the *Moya Ulitsa* programme, a scale it would have been impossible to achieve without KB Strelka's access to the power vertical, and to the mechanisms of Russia's ever-intensifying, ever-more sophisticated 'authoritarian modernisation' project – in which the consultancy bureau plays an increasingly integral part. It is this hypernormalised – but at the same time otherworldly and surreal – political aesthetic of *blagoustroistvo* that performance artist and actionist Ekaterina Nenasheva highlighted in her 2017 project *Between Here and There.* Nenasheva spent three weeks walking around Moscow, her eyesight replaced by a VR headset displaying scenes from closed mental health institutions in which Nenasheva had volunteered: 'existing on the boundary between two realities, I was always stumbling upon the wreckage of some kind of third *perestroechnoy* reality.[1] *Moya Ulitsa* functioned, in my action, to some extent as a new Russian futurism . . . the fences, gaping holes in the ground, piles of construction materials always found themselves on my path, and sometimes drew me into totally new worlds'.

Figure S7.4. *Between Here and There*. Photograph by Ekaterina Nenasheva.

As *Moya Ulitsa* drew on and on, the banners became swiftly grubbier and more haggard, and the manner of their inevitable appearance and instantaneous proliferation following the onset of spring soon became an object of ridicule. In September 2017, Strelka failed to secure the municipal contract to continue project-managing the *Moya Ulitsa* programme (this was, well-informed sources in Moscow say, not a surprise – Strelka had long since reoriented their work towards the federal level). Yet many of the old green and white banners remain, having been printed (and plagiarised) in such quantities that – notwithstanding their increasingly vagabond appearance – they are ineradicable from the streets of the city, continuing to stand their ground, whether camouflaging rolls of turf in Zaryadye Park or erected into strange tent-like formations on Red Square.

Possibly the most spectacular collection of past-sell-by-date *Moya Ulitsa* banners can be admired on Paveletskaya Square, outside the major railway station of southern Moscow. Here, a former public square – which last underwent *blagoustroistvo* in 2004 – lies in a spectacular state of dereliction, awaiting the long-delayed construction of a vast shopping centre, mired in legal disputes for the last decade. All sides of the puddle- and rubble-strewn wasteground are (barely) concealed from public view by a gargantuan *Moya Ulitsa falshfasad* scroll, erected in 2016, and displaying renderings of some of the programme's key sites. The contrast between the luscious vi-

Figure S7.5. Green and white Strelka banner. Photograph by Michał Murawski.

Figure S7.6. *Moya Ulitsa* banners on Paveletskaya Square. Photograph by Michał Murawski.

sualisations of the luxurious city immaculate and the actually-existing city abject is rendered all the starker by the fact that many of the renderings are themselves in various states of mangled dissolution. On Paveletskaya Square, and elsewhere in *plitka*-era Moscow, the material artefacts of repair themselves appear to take on affects and aesthetics of brokenness.

Yet it would be a mistake to see Paveletskaya Square's brokenness as a symptom of *Moya Ulitsa*'s 'failure'. In fact, as I have written elsewhere (Murawski 2018a), it may be more ethnographically interesting – and theoretically generative – to view this and other instances of apparent calamity or dilapidation through the lens of success rather than of failure. Almost all of the projects featured on the Paveletskaya *falshfasady* have, in fact, been successfully implemented, in remarkable time. By many accounts, indeed, *Moya Ulitsa* has so far been a roaring success. According to its own (methodologically more-or-less dubious) criteria, *blagoustroistvo* has led to 23 per cent more pedestrians on city centre streets, and a threefold increase in the number of Instagram photos taken on Tverskaya and in the number of children photographed on Novy Arbat. *Moya Ulitsa* has also led to a one-third growth of restaurants on Tverskaya, versus an 18 per cent decrease in the number of banks on streets that underwent *blagoustroistvo*.

Moya Ulitsa is also a success if measured by the effects on Strelka's own corporate growth (see Murawski 2018b). But it is even more of a triumph if measured by the rewards reaped by development and construction firms close to the municipality (Golunov 2017). Over the seven years of Sobyanin-era *blagoustroistvo*, according to the calculations of journalist Ivan Golunov, half of the programme's 200 billion rouble (£2.5 billion) budget was split between five companies: over twenty billion roubles went to companies tied to prominent Russian-Vietnamese businessman Pavel Të (also a major beneficiary of Moscow's ongoing housing renovation programme), while eleven billion roubles went to companies run by Alexander Biryukov, the younger brother of Moscow Deputy Mayor for Housing and Infrastructure Petr Biryukov. *Blagoustroistvo* falls within the portfolio of the older Biryukov, who – on renewing the *Moya Ulitsa* programme, scheduled to end in 2018, until 2020 – told journalists that the programme may in fact be extended indefinitely: 'Our work for the good of Muscovites will continue without end', Biryukov said.[2]

Repair itself may look like brokenness, but every apparent calamity has the capacity to turn into a triumph. Correspondingly, while it may not always be easy to identify linear causal chains or lay down blame (or praise), it is rarely impossible; (almost) every apparent failure is someone else's success.

Michał Murawski is an anthropologist of architecture and Lecturer in Critical Area Studies at the School of Slavonic and East European Studies, University College London.

Notes

1. Nenasheva's chosen word literally means 'under-reconstruction', but it also invokes the social absurdities and uncertainties of Gorbachev-era perestroika.
2. For more info about the press conference see https://www.rbc.ru/society/07/07/2017/595f945b9a7947172457fb1a?fbclid=IwAR12yo09EAwUiW8A6mG25A-aqcsPeiyHhJYXNO0m-voU1xIFNouHT9yiY3o (retrieved 22 April 2019).

References

Golunov, Ivan. 2017. '270 millionov rubley za gektar Kak izmenitsya Moskva letom 2017 goda i kto na etom zarabotayet'. *Meduza*, 24 May. Retrieved 3 August 2018 from https://meduza.io/feature/2017/05/24/270-millionov-rubley-za-gektar.

Medvedev, Sergey. 2015. 'Epokha plitki: v chem politicheskiy smysl blagoustroystva Moskvy'. *Forbes Russia*, 8 September. Retrieved 3 August 2018 from http://

www.forbes.ru/mneniya-column/tsennosti/298897-epokha-plitki-v-chem-pol iticheskii-smysl-blagoustroistva-moskvy.
Murawski, Michał. 2018a. 'Actually-Existing Success: Economics, Aesthetics and the Specificity of Still-Socialist Urbanism', *Comparative Studies in Society and History* 60(4): 907–937.
——. 2018b. 'My Street: Moscow Is Getting a Makeover, and the Rest of Russia is Next'. *Calvert Journal*, 29 May.

CHAPTER 7

Village Vintage in Southern Norway

Revitalisation and Vernacular Entrepreneurship in Culture Heritage Tourism

SARAH HOLST KJÆR

This chapter provides an analysis of how policy-based criteria on place revitalisation work in a rural setting. Moving away from cultural activities as instruments for social cohesion and identity, I discuss the case of a regional revitalisation project that I worked on as research manager from 2016 to 2018.[1] In this project, and according to the funding criteria, 'local culture heritage' was supposed to work as 'an engine' for the destination's success and prosperity. I analyse how culture heritage was transformed into culture heritage tourism by the local entrepreneurs, volunteers and residents. I argue that the community performed a 'vernacular entrepreneurship strategy' focusing on self-made and self-defined goals. Hence, they moved away from the expectations of standardised 'corporate', industry and business practices. Policy-induced revitalisation can be defined as a repair strategy aimed at reframing the place in order to produce attractiveness to money-strong consumer groups. Still, my results show that this repair strategy is contested by a local and vernacular way of making entrepreneurship which, instead, focuses on executing and engaging the community through cultural activities, ultimately making 'Us' instead of 'the consuming Other' happen.

As a researcher, I worked with a commercial top-down perspective, informed by a market and led by standardised corporate-like business training. For instance, I noted that culture activities in a rural setting more often are based on local volunteering, residential participation and the quest for social cohesion than on a professional producer–consumer exchange (see also Andersen et al. 2010; Frisvoll and Rye 2016). Yet what kind of implications does this social and geographical condition have for undertaking culture-led revitalisation and repair of a place? What happens when a community works with transforming culture heritage into tourism and how do local entrepreneurial practices negotiate and adapt to consumer criteria in a market-oriented project?

The results show that a vernacular form of entrepreneurship is focused on social cohesion, local routines and the mere execution of cultural activities more than on an external market guiding the entrepreneurial decision-making processes. The consequence of not meeting the market-oriented criteria is that the village community and its residents did not obtain the influx of capital that was necessary to professionalise and prepare for further investments and resources. These investments were important to secure the quality of the tourism experience, the repair of the village and the improvement of the infrastructure. In a larger perspective, the consequences are that the area would stay as it is simply because the requested 'corporate management principle' in the culture-led regeneration project could not translate into rural destination development practices. Hence the village would lose out on support from the official society.

The upcoming section examines how local tourism and business entrepreneurs implicitly and explicitly negotiated policy-based, 'corporate' or even 'elitist' definitions of the market-oriented revitalisation of rural destinations. It gives insight into how corporate entrepreneurship was replaced by a vernacular form of entrepreneurship. Specifically, I discuss the case of a coastal village named Vanse, located on the peninsular of Lista in southern Norway. Here I spent around one month over a two-year period aiming to map and understand how the entrepreneurs could establish a profit-oriented destination based on local culture heritage activities.

Norwegian-American Culture Heritage

The village of Vanse and the entire peninsular of Lista was by the time of my fieldwork characterised by the historical period (1910–70) during which Norwegians migrated back and forth several times over the Atlantic Ocean in order to do service work in America, especially in New York City (Ringdal 2002). The place was affected by this migration period and was home to large quantities of American mass-produced consumer items such as 119 fully functioning, well-maintained American vintage cars, several bathroom interiors in pastels set aside in basements and storage units, kitchen appliances in chrome and plastic and hundreds of polyester and nylon party dresses with matching shoes and purses from the 1950s. Hence, clothing, kitchen appliances, interior decor, furniture, cars and buildings, dating mainly from the 1930–60s, could be found everywhere.

At the same time, this image was not a 'pure' destination image. The rural and coastal landscape also consisted of traditional Norwegian white wooden houses, supermarkets and factories built in square-sized cement units, and 'ordinary' mass-produced family homes from the 1950–80s. A brutalistic architectural style from the 1960s had inspired the town centre, officially named Brooklyn Square, indicating the town's Norwegian-American heritage. Here, the shut-down bus station now contained an American diner and a department store with imported American specialities such as root beer, cupcake toppings and Halloween napkins. The store even specialised in Christmas decorations; most of its annual sales came from the large numbers of regional customers drawn to the village during the Christmas period. In the old bus station, a private museum containing a collection of American mass-produced items occupied the second floor.

Most of the town's total collection of vintage materiality could be considered useless and outdated. It could be perceived as waste, broken and unfit for late-modern living. But the local residents cherished their bright-coloured vintage cars, their art deco furniture ornamented with chrome and their slim-waisted polyester dresses with zippers often in need of repair. It was not unusual for a work-migrating family who returned to Vanse after months, years and decades in New York City to bring home ten to twenty tons of American mass-produced consumer goods. Local ethnologists had already estimated that Vanse might be the Norwegian town that had been most influenced by modern American consumer culture, artefacts and architecture. Statistics suggest that there were around sixty-three thousand Norwegians living and working in New York City, mostly in Brooklyn, between the years 1930 and 1970. Several Norwegian institutions, churches, businesses and organisations had been established by countrymen and women abroad. This migration process resulted in exceptionally close connections which, still at the time of undertaking this culture-led innovation project in 2016–18, were said to exist between Norway and America (Ringdal 2002).

Being influenced by the dream of the hard-working American, and at the same time experiencing a migrant life in small apartments in heavily populated areas in New York City, some of the returning Norwegians had saved up for a single family home. They wanted it to look exactly like those built in the new developments of American suburbia. Between 1940 and the 1960s, they had sent home, or even copied, prefabricated suburban American-style houses. Coming from rural and poor conditions, the Norwegians had also enjoyed the American kitchen appliances – blenders, toasters, mixers – so much that when they built their American-style houses on the peninsular, they installed two electricity standards, both the American 110 voltage and the Norwegian 230 voltage (Ringdal 2002).

The local tourism industry was strongly influenced by the theme of this Norwegian-American migration period. Some private initiatives of collecting and semi-organising the material culture heritage had already been undertaken. They were supported by the local municipality mainly as identity projects such as local school projects, ethnographic research projects, museological and documentary projects. Different intercultural connections, such as a friendship between the town of Vanse and a neighbourhood in Brooklyn, New York, had also been established (Ringdal 2002, 2014). Many local cultural institutions had hence been involved in the migration theme, but did not perceive themselves as business actors able to contribute to regional development, heritage tourism and entrepreneurship (Aas, Hjemdahl and Kjær 2016).

The rural Norwegian scenery had stone hedges, white sandy beaches and green fields. At the same time, the frequently seen American vintage car was cruising the landscape. There were old neon bowling alley signs. A 'half skyscraper' in the town's centre – an ambitious art deco building project from the 1930s – still stood half-finished, with a staircase pointing upwards on the rooftop. The story went that the local municipality had discovered what a skyscraper actually was and had put a stop to the project. The half skyscaper symbolised a conflict between the inhabitants coming home from 'Junaiten' (Norwegian lingo for the United States [Ringdal 2002]) and the locals who stayed behind, not really comprehending what the migrants had experienced in the big city. From others I heard that the building project had gone bankrupt and that this explained why the skyscraper was only half-built.

The existing cultural activities were, to a certain degree, commercialised for experience production, but without the establishment of a professional apparatus around them, such as a website with payment systems and systematic, quality-assessed experience-product deliverances with a supporting service infrastructure.

Methodology

Culture researchers and ethnologists, including myself, accustomed to working in the field of heritage tourism and with hands-on fieldwork methods, set out to pioneer the outskirts of the region, assisting local communities in defining and strengthening their self-identity and well-being, and assisting them in getting their voices heard. I also set out to observe 'cultural traditions in action' at the American Festival (2017) in Vanse. In contrast to other ethnographic researchers, I carried out a 'business ethnography' (Kjær 2012) aiming at commercialising and productifying local culture identity. I analysed local entrepreneurship practices and culture event executions from an external consumer perspective. Due to the funding criteria, I was obliged to make the residents evaluate their performances from an outside corporate- and market-oriented perspective. Therefore, I did not focus solely on the society's self-identity or social cohesion, but instead on whether or not the destination would be found attractive as a consumption product.

Since the project was market-oriented, my goal was to understand a possible future market of homecoming Americans who wanted to explore their Norwegian roots in this particular setting. In order to analyse this relationship-based market of Americans of Norwegian descent, I followed some local entrepreneurs, including the owner of the American department store, Bettina, aged thirty-six, who ran the shop as her day job with a small group of staff assisting her. Bettina visited her partners, relatives and mentors in New York once every year and often around fifteen entrepreneurs from the small town went on the trip with her.

In the United States, I followed a group of female entrepreneurs for two weeks in order to observe their meetings at, for example, the Norwegian Seaman's Church. On this trip, I also conducted fieldwork among professionals at Cornell University's School of Hospitality Management. Here, a Norwegian-American researcher, whose parents also came from Vanse, was eager to see the village thrive. She gave me important insight into what can be generalised as 'the American taste' in heritage tourism consumption, American experiencing strategies at destinations and sentiments about Scandinavian culture heritage belongings. This made my global-local 'market results' plentiful and concrete in regard to product and service development aimed at this outbound travel market. Many of the Norwegian-Americans we met had connections to southern Norway. Many had been to Vanse and had strong opinions about how the place should develop.

The American Festival was located in the town centre of Vanse, and the old bus station with its American-style shops was an obvious focal point. From my desk research, mainly based on media clippings and the festival's homepage, I had the preconception that the planning, organisation and sustainability of the event were strong: managerial routines for venue organisation, collaboration with the city regarding safety and infrastructure, the recruitment and training of volunteer staff, culture-content curation, contracts with artists, food and beverage offerings, shopping and pop-up shops, restaurants, bars, camping sites, hotels and other services around the town festival could be expected. Also, I had seen annual visitor figures of fifteen to twenty thousand participants for the three-day event.

The last e-mail I had received from the local destination management office, which was very interested in the commercialisation of the culture heritage, contained the encouraging words that the entrepreneurs were eager to show me how culture events were produced in the village. In the local community I had scheduled 'promenade interviews' with the busy entrepreneurs, keen to obtain information on how they executed their practices. I also focused on how 'close' these practices were to the policy criteria and national tourism strategies that governed, or 'should' govern, the tourism industry that had obtained public funding. Additionally, I interviewed guests and visitors in order to find out how the venue, products and services were experienced from a consumer perspective.

How did the festival manager and local shopkeepers plan the destination events in order to receive its guests? How was the event organised and scheduled; how was work organised and divided; how were volunteers trained and managed; how was the stage area set up and decorated; and how was the camping site, for example, supplied with maps, signs, water and electricity? These were just a few of the questions I had in my interview guide, which aimed at exemplifying how culture-led place innovation happens in practice. This can be characterised as a business ethnography framework for destination design, management and entrepreneurship (Kjær 2011). I will later discuss how regional tourism entrepreneurship was practised not as instructed by corporate standards, but rather was informed by a kind of vernacular, social-consensus seeking, focus on entrepreneurship. For this discussion, I include extracts from interviews I conducted with the festival manager, Rebecca. She was a trained nurse at the local hospital and was around thirty years old. She had been part of the festival committee for three years and was now the manager because no one else wanted the (voluntary) job.

I also interviewed and followed others, such as the estate owner of the old bus station, a woman named Karen who was around sixty years old, as well as her daughter Maria, aged thirty. Maria was, outside of her day job, working as the developer of the bus station, aiming to transform the building into a museum and a motel. In a storage space, Karen and Maria had a large collection of bathroom and bedroom décor in pastel colours. Following the Americanised theme of the village, they had a dream of creating a 'Heartbreak Motel' on the third floor, which was now empty. The rest of the building was rented out to the American diner, a smoothie bar and some small clinics and offices. Karen and Maria were both trained physiotherapists and had participated in the American Festival since it started in 2007. This family was thoroughly engaged in the festival's venue-making on Brooklyn Square, which was just outside the bus station. The family business had worked on several culture development projects over the years and was highly dedicated to revitalising the village according to the Norwegian-American migration theme.

Revitalisation

Culture-led revitalisation of places has almost become a mantra in culture policy (McGuigan 2009). 'Revitalisation' often points to a place that needs to be rejuvenated and refreshed (Florida 2005). Revitalising local culture heritage has been defined as the refinement of a society's 'raw products'. Cultural things, customs and traditions of a common social past are perceived as a raw material that can be upcycled into more customised, productified, themed and performed experience products (Olsen 1999; Sjöholm 2011; Sletvold 2001; Strömberg 2011). Revitalisation is thus a kind of repair strategy which, when it is 'culture-led', implies tools and metaphors such as place-making, makeover, culturalisation, theming and framing. Art historian Per Strömberg (2015) defines 'theming' as a way of restoring a place by 'pure-washing' a story or a theme out of the existing conditions. Theming can also work as an 'add on' to or a makeover of a place. Here theming means camouflaging elements that do not seem relevant to the entrepreneurs. In other words, theming involves the use of an overarching theme that can work as an added value in order for a destination to stand out and create a total experience. Strömberg (2015: 546) explains that 'pirates, the Wild West, Egypt, or a self-referential brand such as Nike, create a holistic and cohesive spatial, cultural, and social organization of a consumer venue'.

'The visual' is a strong component in tourism marketing. In place-making, though, all senses need to be blended into a perfect balance, containing the right mix and ideal combinations. Hence, entrepreneurs need to understand how their developmental practices should be carried out in order to stimulate the right type of tourist 'sensing' at a particular place.

In revitalisation projects, theming a place implies curating and packaging the experiential cultural content by engaging all 'the right' or positive sensing. In this sense, the goal is to improve the experience product. The value-creating potential of a place also lies in transforming intercultural and personal relationships, friendships and family ties, city-to-city and business-to-business relations into a new tourism market. Hence, the consumer experience should, according to the project's funding criteria, guide the village of Vanse in how it could become a 'thriving destination'. Ideas about a local 'unique' feeling, not possible to find anywhere else meant that this destination, through its Norwegian-American heritage, could or should 'stand out' and differentiate itself from other heritage destinations, while at the same time be profiting from a larger global market.

Ethnologist Robert Willim (Willim et al. 2006) has discussed how the concept or strategy of 'mixing' different, sometimes seemingly incompatible elements is used in place-making in order to find 'the right' or unique formula that will lead to a magic or extraordinary experience. Especially in heritage destinations, one will find 'weird mixes' or new combinations of local and migrating elements. Related to the context of Vanse, American tourism consumers, in contrast to Europeans, are accustomed to and appreciate the mixing of thematically different cultural elements (Kjær 2016).

'Culture heritage tourism' in a rural setting can be perceived as a form of counter-urbanism demanding the same living conditions as the metropolitans have (Hall, Roberts and Mitchell 2003). In order to obtain this, local identity can be transformed into a corporate-like business opportunity when profit is realised through a business model. In this perspective, a 'business model' is a concept that refers to the field of local culture heritage becoming a new experiential product and service through culture heritage tourism. A business model hence implies that a network of local entrepreneurs have strategised and decided upon how to conduct business together, dividing tasks among them in complementary ways, sharing a market and hence also sharing its potential risks and profits. In policy-induced culture projects, it has, in addition, become more common to expand the network of business collaborators to include non-profit and non-commercial organisations and groups of volunteers in the value creation of a place. These groups are often evident parts of the social community fabric and the obvious culture-content producers of heritage. In a policy-based culture project, an ideal, non-commercial volunteer base cannot 'invest' their work hours in the project and match the funding, since volunteer work is not 'real' (Lysgård 2016). This ultimately makes rural business models of collaborative ideal-commercial work impossible. This project condition makes it difficult for community-based initiatives to enter a 'real market' defined by professional corporations and entrepreneurs attractive to external consumers.

Moral and value-based connotations are also attached to market-based rural revitalisation. What is most often meant by revitalisation is, to start with, perceiving a place as a product (Falkheimer and Thelander 2007). 'Tailoring' experiences, 'branding' the destination and 'packaging' services and experiential products in order to facilitate consumers is a common terminology in culture and tourism business management (Mossberg 2007; Thufvesson 2009). The tourism business in general seeks the money-strong consumer; often Western, upper-middle class, experienced, and aware of high-quality, good designs and satisfactory service performances. In a consumer-oriented perspective, the customers – not the locals, other social groups or classes – make the overall judgement of a destination. In order to meet values of quality, comfort and relevance, the destination entrepreneurs have to view themselves from the outside and take a consumer perspective on their own performance. Success or failure are judged externally.

A Future Market?

The American retro materiality, which now was a rare experience in America, was possible to experience in abundance in Vanse. But the village destination was not well connected to the internet by way of a visible digital profile or connection to international payment systems; the packaging of experiences was not transparent or customer friendly; and the overall impression of the maintenance of the town and the running of cultural events did not live up to what can be expected in a high-cost country. On the positive side, this strange mix of vintage America appearing in the rural Norwegian countryside was something attractive to the homecoming American tourist.

During the market research in America, I, together with Bettina, the shop owner, met up with her mentor, a successful businessman of Norwegian descent, in the Norwegian Seaman's Church. He had been to Vanse several times. He explained to us:

> The town centre looks crappy. Sorry to say. You cannot have empty shops in a town centre. The place looks abandoned. As if no one wants to be there. You can easily get some huge American flags customised and designed to cover up the sad-looking façades. That is fun! It needs to be a little 'Harry'. I can mail you the link to the company who does these façade covers. That would help a lot. (Extract from fieldwork diary, November 2016)

In contrast to what one might think, the American flag in a Norwegian context was not controversial; however, making the place 'Harry' could be. Back in Norway, when I interviewed the children in the town of Vanse, they said, 'Please, don't make the place Harry'. 'Harry' is a man's name referring to a Norwegian 'hill-billy', simple-minded and unsophisticated. What was fun to the homecoming Americans was not fun for the local children and their sense of identity. On the contrary, they could be quite embarrassed when their parents dressed up in funny costumes for the festival. The right type of rural revitalisation was also important for future generations.

Bettina was more concerned that the town centre looked abandoned in the eyes of her mentor. 'Should we cover the windows with American flags?' she asked me. At this point, I didn't know what to do with the empty shop windows. It could be attractive in the eyes of the American homecoming consumer to experience a vintage America strangely located in a Norwegian traditional rural landscape. Still, this mix needed strengthening, theming and fixing, since the village in reality was run down. It needed mending and was infused with several other architectural trends and building techniques from different periods, creating a cluttered aesthetic.

On the American festival's website, the event was marketed as 'fun and cool'. The residents had worked in their own ways to transform culture heritage into culture heritage tourism. Thus, previous attempts to create experience products had already been made. A logo with the inscription 'American Festival Lista' symbolised both the American Festival and the local identity. A local graphic designer had created the logo for the first festival in 2007. It was used to market experience products such as vintage car taxi driving and a guided tour along 'Route 8', the road in the peninsular landscape that connected the American-style houses. From the American diner, one could pre-order a guided tour and some commercial travel companies arranged for Norwegians to have a package experience visiting the American Lista by bus. This trip included a meal, and the chef at the American diner made sure that the eating experience was authentic, using original recipes collected by the local museum. Most often, the dishes served were 'fun', based largely on industry-processed and tinned food mixed in homemade dishes to colour and spice up more basic food. The menu often included the Norwegians' favourite comfort foods from the migration period.

A destination logo, like the 'American Festival Lista', has influence and non-influence in framing what is already 'there'. The logo showed a happy and a sad theatre mask, some music notes and the American and Norwegian flags intertwined. But was the 'American Festival Lista' a self-referential brand (Strömberg 2015) framing the festival and destination? The intertwining flags could – on a concrete level – symbolise the cultural mix which the destination was made up of, and Bettina liked the logo very much. She also liked the fact that the designer who had created it was a part of the social community. How does one know when a destination logo is still in style? How can one argue that a certain type of symbolism is over-used, outdated or even unsophisticated? What made the intertwining Norwegian-American flags in the abandoned shop windows right or wrong? What about the logo's sad and happy masks? While these were referring to theatrical conventions, the flags were referring to migration conventions (Gradén 2003). Would *The Norwegian Tourism Strategy* (2012), which in a publicly funded innovation project it was mandatory to follow, give any advice on when a destination brand had gone out of style, or would the strategy instead assume that all entrepreneurs had the same perception of destination-design and market trends?

A revitalisation plan for the destination would take the point of departure in what was already there. But perhaps the intertwining flags needed reframing or a new way of mixing the existing components, an experiential mix of culture activities (Willim et al. 2006) containing both the 'traditional Norwegian' (e.g. arts and crafts, local food specialities and the experience of a pure coastal landscape) and the 'vintage American' (the classic cars, the American-style houses, the diner with its Norwegian-style hamburgers). This type of mix could, to American 'home-coming tourists', be a way to revitalise, improve and reframe the destination.

The American Festival

In a rural revitalisation project perspective, the American Festival could be perceived as an 'engine for place-making', referring to the organised event as a way to attract visitors through spectacle. An 'event' can be considered a low-cost, ad-hoc and pop-up experience product that can be changed and adjusted quite easily from year to year. In addition, an event can make use of non-commercial and non-profit value creators, such as volunteers who offer their time to fill the culture content and make the event happen (Kjær 2012).

I arrived in the run-up to the festival weekend. The whole town was busy putting up signs. Boxes of programmes were delivered, tents in the market were raised. A circus had occupied the town centre's parking lot and several pop-up shop owners were arriving from far away, getting their products ready for sale. Everything from stands with specially imported top-quality cowboy hats to home-made hamburgers, Norwegian handicrafts and plastic toys now transformed the town park into a market fair. On Saturday night the town centre's Brooklyn Square would transform into the heart of the festival, hosting a party with line dancing and the local, Las Vegas prize-winning Elvis impersonator 'Kjell-Elvis', who was the festival's top name.

Some local women, friends of Maria, the developer from the bus station, were preparing to get into their vintage dresses and narrow 1950s pumps. They had borrowed the outfits from the museum and were planning to throw a private party in some of the rooms in the museum. It was even possible to have one's hair and make-up done in a beauty parlour, by professionals Maria had recruited from Oslo who specialised in original styles from the 1950s. They were also using salon interiors and apparatuses from the museum.

Studying experience product development while doing a business ethnography, it is common to conduct 'action research', which implies suggesting improvements to the entrepreneurs during fieldwork. Quickly, I suggested to Maria that her idea could be developed from serving her personal friends into a business model, through which she could make a profit. Transforming an idea into a business would have demanded entrepreneurial elements such as pricing, marketing, collaborating with others, sharing sales, creating a stock of outfits and designing a venue. Maria, I suggested, could take this year's festival as an opportunity to observe how the market reacted to her idea. She could refine the idea through a business model perspective and hence launch it as a product at next year's festival. Maria did not think this was a good idea. The dresses were borrowed from the museum; to her they were delicate heritage objects that should be protected. To rent out dresses to strangers would risk damaging important museum artefacts. Ways to avoid this scenario were not further discussed or tested.

This last weekend in June, the Norwegian-American relationship was celebrated for the tenth time. Under the website motto 'Unique, Different and Lots of Fun', the festival and the parade this year were visualising the theme of American popular history. In my promenade interviews, the festival manager, Rebecca, explained to me that she herself had organised the content of the parade theme. Some elements had become tradition, for example opening with a woman dressed as the Statue of Liberty and ending with the cruising vintage cars. Somewhere at the front of the parade, the obligatory group of school children had, as their school projects, designed different Disney costumes. This year, in 2017, the snow queen Elsa of Arendal was the prime figure. The local line dancing group appeared, the women in vintage dresses and heavy make-up and 1950s hairstyles, and the local Kjell-Elvis was sitting in the back of a white Cadillac dressed in the iconic white beaded costume, together with bare-shouldered Honolulu girls draped in Hawaiian flower wreaths. The girls were actually the staff from the local Thai restaurant, and several of them were married to Norwegian men. In the parade, two black men, dressed in black and white tuxedos, were demonstrating for black power, symbolising the American civil rights movement from the 1950s to the 1960s. Rebecca had, in between her shifts at the hospital, also been able to involve the nearby refugee camp. She was pleased that some of the Syrian refugees had volunteered to participate as black civil rights fighters. To her, this festival was mainly about the local community's social cohesion, getting to know and becoming friends with the next-door neighbour, although on a larger scale she dreamt of the town becoming a certified heritage village protected by national culture heritage funding. During my fieldwork I realised that Rebecca did everything from guiding traffic to calling the city's renovation department when the public toilets broke down. She even participated in the parade and pointed out when signs to the campsite were pointing in the wrong direction.

Vernacular Entrepreneurs

The town of Vanse can be characterised as a small village. Just like many other coastal and rural communities, local residents live a secluded life far away from national interests and public investments (Lysgård 2016). The fact that this small community had a strong cross-Atlantic orientation to the hyper-urbanism of metropolitan New York (Ringdal 2002) had led to a specific 'community feeling'.

Culture heritage tourism is often perceived as an economic practice that can repair the rural periphery (Hall, Roberts and Mitchell 2003). In Norway, culture-led destination development projects are created through shared funding between regional stakeholders and the local businesses themselves. The criteria for obtaining funding mean that the entrepreneurs should pay for half of the project with their work hours. As I noted during my fieldwork, the local entrepreneurs did not show high regard for the national bureaucracy through which the local culture and tourism practices were assessed. These entrepreneurs considered policy-making and the project funding that came along with it elite, irrelevant and unnecessarily difficult to work with.

Still, the point of departure of this market-oriented project was to collaborate in creating totality in the destination design and the experience products. This would imply a new way of organising the local entrepreneurs, businesses and volunteers at the destination. For example, the entrepreneurs could work with business models on how to develop a system for sharing profits and improve the products in order to attract the needed investors. These place-making processes could hence be viewed as a way for the entrepreneurs to work successfully together, finding a model for shared profit and, through a joint concept such as the American-Norwegian mix, transform the already large collection of things, cars, houses, photos, furniture and clothing into experience- and service-product designs and ultimately American outbound travel products. Creating a novel market, distributing the themed experience products, channelled through personal and cultural Norwegian-American bonds and relations, would in addition transform personal visitors into consuming tourists.

The vernacular entrepreneurship at the American Lista was defined by geographical conditions and the social implications that come along with them. The local, place-bound managerial routines could in a corporate management perspective be considered semi-structured, half-finished and focused on local relationships instead of relating to a market. This volunteer-driven destination was, it seemed, more concerned with the mere execution of culture activities, engaging in and sustaining social cohesion and the sharing of a common past. The non-profit organisation was the entrepreneurial fabric of the American Lista. Most people, including Bettina, Karen, Maria and Rebecca, had volunteered to help. The characteristics of the destination's entrepreneurial work were improvisation or the process of being 'thrown into' developing a new work routine while, at the same time, being able to fit into routines already established or preferred by other volunteers.

The local entrepreneurs staged and organised the town and the experiential culture content of the festival in many different ways. Like in other small communities, based on voluntary work, the community was engaged throughout the year in costume-making, rehearsing music or organising volunteers as entrance, parking and camping assistants, applying for different services and permissions at the city council, such as permission to sell alcohol and food, and getting a working infrastructure in place to facilitate cases of emergency. Hence, the local culture presented a form of vernacular entrepreneurship that could be perceived as a way to repair, restore and make the identity of a local community (Gradén 2003). The power of engaging those already there meant accepting the destination entrepreneurship as vernacular.

The local community was interested in presenting a place identity guided by a combination of a past of personal migration and a broad theme of American popular culture. Rebecca, the festival manager, thought that anything American could be in the parade; Karen, the estate owner of the bus station, had also been very active in the festival over the years, would argue that 'everything after the assassination of President John F. Kennedy' should not be accepted. Ultimately, these perspectives on how the event should be performed or developed were guided by principles of contrasts in taste. In Karen's perception, the American Lista should present a migratory past that was 'correct', before the world went wrong. Rebecca, on the other hand, had an 'anything goes as long as it is fun and inclusive' way of managing the parade. These contesting viewpoints were hard to bridge,

Figure 7.1. Kjell-Elvis, photograph by Thomas Høyrup Christensen, 2017.

Figure 7.2. American parade, photograph by Thomas Høyrup Christensen, 2017.

Figure 7.3. Rundown building, photograph by Thomas Høyrup Christensen, 2017.

Figure 7.4. Bowling sign, photograph by Thomas Høyrup Christensen, 2017.

and redirected the focus from the external consumer perspective to local perspectives.

The promenade interviews shed light on how a local community in need of investments attempted to prolong the life of things by working in vernacular ways, combining habits, sentiments and self-learned skills in order to preserve the Norwegian-American migration heritage. By throwing the annual American Festival and by volunteering to preserve and fix cars, clothing, things and buildings, and by learning about the local history and taking tourists on a guided tour, 'the past' at first worked as a local identity project. The question was how ready the entrepreneurs were to view themselves from the outside, taking the point of departure in the demands of an American outbound tourism market.

Conclusion

One of my original research interests was to discuss how a local community's entrepreneurs within the tourism and experience industry made use of and comprehended the tons of colourful vintage consumer items as value-creating raw material. Regional destinations are often conditioned by their ability to single out one narrative, brand or main attraction that will be attractive from a consumer perspective. In order for a rural village to reach its ambition of becoming a global destination, making a profit and sustaining its residents, the mobilisation of local resources is vital. Commercially transforming cultural heritage into value-creating tourism and experience services had already been attempted at the destination. But the tastes and preferences of an American homecoming market were difficult to put into practice.

The touristic reuse of the American-Norwegian migration heritage could be an entrepreneurial strategy to professionalise, commoditise, refine and coordinate the destination in relation to an external, targeted market. Nonetheless, local entrepreneurs did not work along the lines of a corporate business-model like practice. As I have shown, these entrepreneurs analysed their performances not from an outside perspective, but rather they were absorbed in social dynamics and next-door neighbour collaborations. In addition, they took a 'volunteer approach' for which 'getting cultural activities executed' was of the most importance.

A great part of designing a heritage destination is created by ideals and norms about place identity, originating in self-perceptions about 'who we are' or who we want to be. In order to reach these ideals, repair, maintenance and fixing activities were organised, from which both frustration and pleasure emerged, depending on the result. These feelings, in turn, defined the vernacular entrepreneurship strategy performed by Karen, Maria, Bettina and Rebecca. In this context, I, as a representative of the public society, was not able to fill the gap between the policy ideals of corporate entrepreneurship and the vernacular business practices of the rural destination. Culture-led revitalisation projects have a policy whereby corporate entrepreneurship works as the formula for success. 'Failure' or 'what should not be done' is not defined, however, and these project conditions are often summed up in a business language far from local vernacular practices.

Sarah Holst Kjær is an assistant professor in European ethnology at the University of Stockholm.

Note

1. The title of the project was 'The American Lista: Culture- and Art-Based Place Development and Norwegian-American Travel Routes Products' (2016–19). The project was categorised as an 'industry research project' and was financed by the Regional Research Foundation Agder (RFF), Norway. The project was

aborted in 2018 because the funding criteria's 50-50 publicly and privately shared investments was not possible to meet by the local, volunteer-driven entrepreneurs.

References

Aas, Tor Helge, Kirsti Mattiesen Hjemdahl and Sarah Holst Kjær. 2016. 'Innovation Practices in Cultural Organisations: Implications for Innovation Policy', *International Journal of Tourism Policy* 6(3/4): 212–34.

Andersen, K.V., M.M. Bugge, H.K. Hansen, A. Isaksen and M. Raunio. 2010. 'One Size Fits All? Applying the Creative Class Thesis onto a Nordic Context', *European Planning Studies* 18: 1591–1609.

Falkheimer, Jesper, and Åsa Thelander. 2007. 'Att sätte en plats på kartan: Mediernas betydelse för platsmarknadsföring', in Rickard Ek and John Hultman (eds), *Plats som product*. Lund: Studentlitteratur, pp. 120–46.

Florida, Richard. 2005. *Cities and the Creative Class*. London: Routledge.

Frisvoll, Svein, and Johan Fredrik Rye. 2016. 'Elite Discourses of Regional Identity in a New Regionalism Development Scheme: The Case of the "Mountain Region" in Norway', *Norwegian Journal of Geography* 63: 175–90.

Gradén, Lizette. 2003. *On Parade: Making Heritage in Lindsborg, Kansas*. Uppsala: Acta Universitatis Upsaliensis.

Hall, Derek, Lesley Roberts and Morag Mitchell. 2003. *New Directions in Rural Tourism*. Aldershot: Ashgate.

Kjær, Sarah Holst. 2011. 'Meaningful Experience Design and Event Management: A Post Event Analysis of Copenhagen Carnival 2009', *Culture Unbound* 3: 243–67.

——. 2012. 'Museal stedsudvikling: Tordenskjold was here!' *Nordisk Museologi* 2: 64–82.

——. Frykman and Maja Povrzanović Frykman (eds), *Sensitive Objects: Affect and Material Culture*. Lund: Nordic Academic Press, pp. 237–55.

Lysgård, Hans Kjetill. 2016. 'The "Actually Existing" Cultural Policy and Culture-Led Strategies of Rural Places and Small Towns', *Journal of Rural Studies* 44: 1–11.

McGuigan, Jim. 2009. 'Doing a Florida Thing: The Creative Class Thesis and Cultural Policy', *International Journal of Cultural Policy* 15(3): 291–300.

Mossberg, Lena. 2007. 'At skabe oplevelser ved hjælp af storytelling', in Jørgen Ole Bærenholdt and John Sundbo (eds), *Oplevelsesøkonomi: Produktion, forbrug, kultur*. Frederiksberg: Samfundslitteratur, pp. 321–39.

Olsen, Kjell. 1999. 'Reiser til fortiden', in Arvid Viken (ed), *Turisme: Stedet i en bevegelig verden*. Oslo: Universitetsforlaget, pp. 132–42.

Ringdal, Siv. 2002. *Det amerikanske Lista: Med 110 volt i huset*. Oslo: Pax Forlag.

Ringdal, Siv. 2014. '110 Volts at Home: The American Lista', *Journal of Design History* 27(1): 79–96.

Sjöholm, Carina. 2011. *Litterära resor: Turism i spåren efter böcker, filmer och författere*. Stockholm: Makadam.

Sletvold, Ola. 2001. 'Vikingene i norsk turismeutvikling', in Arvid Viken (eds), *Turisme: Stedet i en bevegelig verden*. Oslo: Universitetsforlaget, pp. 126–50.

Strömberg, Per. 2011. 'Destinationsdesign – iscensatta fjällbyupplevelser', in Jahn Thon (ed.), *Hvem eier byen? Tekst, plan, historie*. Kristiansand: Universitetet i Agder, pp. 159–74.
——. 2015. 'Theming', in D.T. Cook and J.M. Ryan (eds), *The Wiley Blackwell Encyclopaedia of Consumption and Consumer Studies*. London: Wiley, pp. 545–49.
Thufvesson, Ola. 2009. *Platsutveckling*. Helsingborg: Plattformen.
Willim, Robert. 2006. 'It's in the Mix: Configuring Industrial Cool', in R. Willim, Robert and O. Löfgren (eds), *Magic, Culture and the New Economy*. Oxford: Berg, pp. 97–104.

SNAPSHOT 8

A Story of Time Keepers

Jérôme Denis and David Pontille

One day in 1965, at 10.49 a.m., in the heart of Paris, the Wagner clock, which has been standing over the Panthéon's mausoleum for national heroes since the middle of the nineteenth century, stopped. It would seem that it was sabotaged by the very person who was then in charge of winding it every week, and who, probably tired of this task, hit it with an iron bar until it passed away. The clock remained inert for forty years, its mechanism slowly oxidising, until September 2005, when members of a group of clandestine explorers (called *UX*, for 'Urban eXperiment') who had made a habit of wandering the Panthéon for years fell on it and decided to restore it. A confirmed watchmaker who co-founded the group convinced the members of Untergunther, the branch of UX dedicated to the restoration of what they call the 'invisible or abandoned cultural heritage sites' (Murray 2008), to embark on this adventure. This was hardly their first project. Among the few they agreed to make public, we know that they previously rebuilt an abandoned 100-year-old bunker and renovated a twelfth-century crypt (Sage 2000).

One year after they decided to take care of the Panthéon's clock, its mechanism was shining like on the first day, and the clock was working again. To achieve this spectacular result, the group built a secret workshop, hidden in the heights of the Panthéon, into which they brought the clock mechanism and subjected it to a series of delicate operations. They notably soaked it in a bath, polished all its surfaces, replaced a few cables and pulleys, repaired the mechanism's glass cabinet, and completely restored the sabotaged escapement (Lackman 2012). The intervention cost them four thousand euros in all.

What can be learnt from this repair story, this 'preservation without permission' as Steward Brand called it (2012), introducing the *Long Now* seminar dedicated to Untergunther? First, it reminds us that an object as visible as the clock of the Panthéon, a site emblematic of Paris and all France, can be neglected and wither away. It comes, after all, as no surprise: not all cultural heritage is preserved and, most importantly, there is no consensus on what is considered heritage and what therefore needs special attention.

Second, and consequently, this story highlights the crucial role of very particular protagonists. Indeed, one could easily imagine that repair is an activity that involves only two types of people: specialised professionals who deal with the objects for which they are responsible, and amateur tinkerers who repair their own things. In this case, however, it is a group of clandestine repairers who decided to take care of the clock. This shows that repair can involve a technical but also a moral distribution of work, which can be summarised in one simple question: *who cares?* Who wants, who can, who should, and even sometimes who is authorised to repair a given object? This is very clear from the various statements that Untergunther members made in the media at the time: it's all a matter of responsibility. They felt obliged to repair the Panthéon's clock because, at that time, no one considered themselves responsible for this piece of cultural heritage. Untergunther managed to 'replace the state where it was incompetent' (Boyer King 2007). Nowadays, many situations remind us how challenging this distribution of repair work can be, whether it reinforces inequalities between Northern and Southern countries, or results in controversial claims for the establishment of a 'right to repair' in various domains.

But let's go back to the Panthéon. If you come to visit the mausoleum today and raise your head, you will probably be disappointed to discover that the clock is not on time, and that its hands remain motionless. What happened? In fact, the clock did not work for long. Once their operation was over, the members of Untergunther were faced with a major problem: for the clock to continue to work, they had to find someone in the Panthéon who would agree to wind it up each week and take care of it. Someone who would be responsible for it. They had little choice but to notify Bernard Jeannot, the Panthéon's deputy administrator, with whom they arranged an informal meeting. He was enthusiastic and admiring of the group's efforts. Unfortunately, once informed, his hierarchy within the Centre des Monuments Nationaux did not share his euphoria; quite the contrary. Outraged at the repeated intrusion of the clandestine repairers into the public building, Mr Jeannot's superior fired him and brought a lawsuit against Untergunther. The court stated that clock fixing could not be considered a crime, and the case was dismissed. Yet Pascal Monnet, the new deputy administrator, did not stop here. He hired a clockmaker to bring the clock back to its previous condition: sabotaged. Refusing to break any parts, the clockmaster eventually agreed to remove the escapement, the very part that was rebuilt by Untergunther, consequently stopping the clock mechanism (Lackman 2012).

What does the conclusion of this story tell us? An important clarification, to begin with: repairing is not maintaining. The mere fact that the clock mechanism is restored does not mean that the clock can operate on a daily basis and keep time for the coming decades. The repair operation, however important it may be, does not replace the need to take care of the clock and to identify a responsible person who is engaged to maintain it. This simultaneously shows that breakdown itself is not a univocal phenomenon that would systematically call for repair. Objects may actually remain in intermediate states, in which they are neither properly broken nor fully functional.

Is the whole operation a failure for Untergunther then? Not necessarily. Among the sometimes contradictory and deliberately misleading statements of the group, one can find this one, made by Lazar Kunstmann (2009), its representative: 'The goal wasn't to make the clock work, but rather to make sure it didn't disappear'. If we agree to take this sentence seriously, we can better understand what has actually been repaired through the action of the clandestine restorers. As Kunstmann explains during his talk at Steward Brand's *Long Now* seminar, what is most important to Untergunther is to 'preserve traces of our past' and to 'conserve things as numerous as possible and as direct as possible in their testimony'. From this point of view, the mere existence of the Panthéon's clock, which the rust was gnawing away and threatening to disintegrate, is a success.

But perhaps we can go a little further by trying to understand more precisely what the new deputy administrator sought to do when he asked for the clock to be sabotaged again. Didn't he want to go back in time as well? Didn't he engage himself in some kind of restoration, as he attempted to recover the state in which the clock mechanism had been for forty years, before intruders came to disrupt its peaceful existence? Maybe that's why today the hands of the Panthéon's clock indicate 10.51, as if only two minutes had passed since 1965.

Jérôme Denis is Professor at the Centre for the Sociology of Innovation, Mines ParisTech.

David Pontille is Researcher at the Centre for the Sociology of Innovation, Mines ParisTech.

References

Boyer King, É. 2007. 'Undercover Restorers Fix Paris Landmark's Clock', *The Guardian*, 26 November.

Brand, S. 2012. 'Preservation without Permission: The Paris Urban eXperiment', *Introduction to the Long Now Seminar*, 13 November. Retrieved March 2019 from http://longnow.org/seminars/02012/nov/13/preservation-without-permission-paris-urban-experiment.

Kunstmann, L. 2009. Interview in *Article 11*, 1 December. Retrieved March 2019 from http://www.article11.info/?Lazar-Kunstmann-porte-parole-de-l-a_titre.

Lackman, J. 2012. 'The New French Hacker-Artist Underground', *Wired Magazine*, 20 January.

Murray, C. 2008. 'Clandestine Encounter: The AJ Speaks to Guerrilla Restoration Group, the Untergunther'. *The Architects' Journal*, 20 February.

Sage, A. 2009. 'Underground "Terrorists" with a Mission to Save City's Neglected Heritage', *The Times*, 27 September.

CHAPTER 8

Keeping Them 'Swiss'

The Transfer and Appropriation of Techniques for Luxury-Watch Repair in Hong Kong

HERVÉ MUNZ

Repair Matters Globally: The Case of the Swiss Watch Industry

In this industry, mainly located in the western, French-speaking part of Switzerland, the word 'repair' is rendered in French with the professional term 'rhabillage', which does not refer only to the process of fixing a watch that is out of order or broken. The word also has a broader meaning, referring to all technical actions that attempt to maintain the functioning and optimise the sustainability of a timepiece after it has been used. Consequently, repair practices encompass a wide spectrum of actions on watches and clocks. In other words, the notion of rhabillage, or repair, merges with the general business of servicing and maintaining a product.

We can better understand the current importance of repair practices in the watch industry in Switzerland by bringing together two observations. First, many Swiss brands have become big luxury businesses over the last thirty years. They are highly concerned with optimising the improvement of their reputation and controlling every stage in the chain of value (Munz 2016; Donzé and Fujioka 2017), including the after-sales stage which encompasses servicing and repair. In the last decades, the success of Swiss watches on the international scene has been structurally linked to the gradual repositioning of this industry within the market of luxury goods (Munz 2017b). Since the beginning of the 1980s, the categories of 'heritage' and 'transmission' have been progressively used as a means for industry leaders to update the value of their mechanical products and place them into the luxury market (Munz 2017b; Oakley 2015).

In this context, the term 'repair' is often used to evoke the unlimited lifetime of these watches, to define their luxury value and to justify their price. Brand managers argue that, unlike with common goods, including cheap or lower-end watches that are meant to be discarded after use, the value of Swiss luxury watches is linked to their timelessness and viability: they are made to last, which is why their price is so high, starting at several tens of thousands of dollars.

According to these brand managers, the luxury dimension of these watches rests on the fact that they are 'forever repairable'. Another, related, important source of the luxury value of these watches is their affiliation with Swiss technical culture and their rootedness in Swiss territory. Thus, repairability according to Swiss standards has become a strategic tool in the brand messaging that proclaims the sustainability of products and defines them as luxury goods.

Watchmaking is indeed, undoubtedly, one of the activities most commonly associated with Switzerland. For more than a century, within the country's borders and abroad, it has been a much-celebrated form of 'traditional Swiss craftsmanship', embodying the emblematic values of quality and precision that are claimed to define the country. Watchmaking in Switzerland is also much more than that. It currently employs nearly sixty thousand people[1] and reports exports valued at about 19.4 billion Swiss francs (CHF) per year,[2] making it the country's third largest export sector (after pharmaceuticals and machine tools).[3]

In addition, over the last thirty years, brand-name firms and organisations within the Swiss watchmaking industry have based their marketing strategies on the creation of an image of high-end mechanical watchmaking as an 'authentic Swiss' practice whose authenticity is reflected in the products themselves. These strategies have been supported by stereotypical views of this craft: Swiss watches have been presented as having been made and strongly anchored in Switzerland, for more than four centuries, in almost total national self-sufficiency.

However, what happens to the constitutive forms of knowledge and techniques of repair that underlie the 'authenticity' of such a national industry when its activities, sales and services occur worldwide? The apparently complete self-sufficiency of the Swiss watch industry is challenged by the fact that 95 per cent of the watches currently produced on Swiss territory are intended for export. Obviously, the 'authentic' dimension of Swiss watches is also presented outside of Switzerland. In interviews conducted with a variety of brand managers in Switzerland, for instance,

Figure 8.1. Cimier's advertising poster covering the brand's booth, displayed at the 2012 annual trade fair in Basel. Photograph by Hervé Munz.

they confessed that over the last decade, they had reinforced the tradition-oriented aspect of their storytelling to cater to their Asian customers' tastes.

The Global Construction of Craftspeople's Affiliation

In order to understand how the 'traditional' dimension of the Swiss watch industry and its reputation for quality are sociotechnically produced and maintained abroad, this chapter explores the international circulation of Swiss-made watches and the transfer of knowledge and techniques required for their maintenance in greater China[4] and particularly in Hong Kong. During the last decade, Hong Kong has indeed become the most important import market for high-end Swiss watches, where their repair has quickly come to be perceived as a problem for Swiss companies as well as for the Hong Kong and Chinese firms involved in the Swiss watch business.

This chapter is located where the anthropology of knowledge, materialities and craftwork (Marchand 2001, 2010, 2016; Ingold 2001a, 2001b, 2018; Harris 2007; Julien and Rosselin 2009) meets anthropotechnology, a francophone school of thought that is close to the anthropology of technology transfer, globalisation and design (Geslin 2002, 2017; Baudin 2012). My aim here is to reflect on the links between repair and servicing practices, and the value of luxury, highlighting the fact that the repair of luxury goods, as considered through the lenses of skills and transnational circulation, offers relevant insights into globalisation *in the making*. Within this theoretical framework, repair may be understood as a sociotechnical operation, a 'making' (Marchand 2010: 12) in which people engage with body, artefacts and materials. Repair knowledge is a 'process' (ibid.) or a set of 'skills' connected to 'fields of practice' (Ingold 2001a: 114). It is durational, not a fixed entity with definitive borders. It is, according to Harris (2007: 10), a 'way of knowing', rather than a 'form of knowledge'.

For the study of craftspeople and their links to national identity, there is also another set of studies that is particularly stimulating. Since the year 2000, there has been a significant number of publications renewing the paradigm of the 'invention of tradition', initiated by Eric Hobsbawm (1983), and questioning the apparent obviousness with which some cultural and technical practices are considered as folklore and as national traditions. These works, focused on various objects and contexts including cigar-making in Cuba (Simoni 2009), bread-making in Germany (Bendix 2014) and cheese-making in the Italian Alps (Grasseni 2016), have studied the ways in which the production or consumption of these goods is lived as an enactment of a certain affect linked to national belonging. In investigating the links between crafts and their transformation, these studies have mainly analysed processes at the national or regional scale. They have not really studied these links through the lenses of the transnational mobility of skills and craftspeople nor the global circulation of professional identities.

By focusing on the international diffusion of techniques, the recent developments in anthropotechnology make it clear that techniques never circulate unchanged from one group of users to another. To be transferred and acquired, professional knowledge (even when it is attached to materials or rigorously standardised) must necessarily be appropriated and transformed. These changes are what explains the adoption or rejection of such techniques among a new group of users, which is why it is important to pay attention to the potential forms of innovation, defined endogenously in dialogue with potential external norms and requirements, that result within the groups that receive these techniques.

Coming back to the servicing of Swiss watches in Hong Kong, therefore, my principal focus is not on the ways in which Swiss watchmakers have spread their luxury watches in Asia. Nor am I only interested in how the Swiss have tried to reproduce their technical culture there. This research is rather a window onto broader issues related to 'high-end' ambiguous globalisation, while exploring the worldwide construction of the identity of craftspeople and the transformations implied by the mobility of skills. It is an attempt to show that a technical transfer from Switzerland to Hong Kong simultaneously softens and reinforces, in the same ambivalent movement, the idea that the watch industry, Swiss identity and the national territory must go hand in hand and that there exists a typically Swiss watchmaker's craft.[5]

In Hong Kong, I carried out ten months of participant observation in a training centre, at trade fairs, and in stores and watch markets. I also visited the technical schools and customer service departments of Swiss firms, undertaking more than forty semi-structured interviews with a wide variety of stakeholders in both Swiss and Hong Kong organisations. Drawing from this fieldwork, the present chapter attempts to answer the four following questions:

- Why has the servicing of Swiss watches been identified as a problem by many firms in Hong Kong?
- How has this problem led to the transfer of technical knowledge from Switzerland to Hong Kong?
- How are Swiss techniques appropriated by Hong Kong workers?
- In what ways does the transnational circulation of these skills affect so-called Swiss standards?

This chapter also explores the links between repair and luxury. In the last few years, increasingly significant research has been conducted in the humanities and social sciences on repair and maintenance. Scholars have also focused on related phenomena such as brokenness, breakdown, damage and viability. In this research, the notion of repair is used both literally, to describe the action of fixing up, and as a metaphor. Underlining the variety of cultural significances assigned to the action of repair, these contributions emphasise different topics: the sociopolitical conditions for the emergence of repair practices (Henke 1999; Graham and Thrift 2007; Denis and Pontille 2015; Schulz 2015), the modes of valuation for such practices (Martínez 2017; 2019), and the techniques, materialities and bodily involvement they imply (Dant 2009; Houston 2014; Nova 2017). Yet while the topic of luxury has also become a prominent area of inquiry in the humanities (Sougy 2013; Donzé and Fujioka 2017; Abélès 2018), very few works have specifically questioned repair practices in intersection with the issue of range and the social categories of 'high-end' or 'luxury'.

Nonetheless, in spite of the relative lack of attention that has so far been paid to the question, it is remarkable, once one has begun noticing it, in how many various places and in connection with how many multiple industries (watches, jewels, leatherwork, textile/fashion, shoes, antiques, etc.) luxury worlds have become 'stages' on which the care of sustaining things over time and periodically servicing them is claimed by actors and organisations (Boltanski and Esquerre 2014; Munz 2016). This care for repair is explicitly displayed as a sign of quality in many companies' marketing strategies (Dematteo 2015; Donzé and Fujioka 2017). Consequently, it is worth conceiving of luxury as a relevant area in which to study repair practices and likewise to approach repair as a means of constructing, justifying and/or maintaining luxury value. In this regard, the Swiss watch industry offers a relevant case study. Indeed, this industry has occupied a dominant position in the market of high-added-value timepieces for more than twenty years now (Donzé 2014; Munz 2017b; Raffaelli 2018).

Coping Mechanisms, or the 'Swissification' of Greater China

Over the last fifteen years, mainly due to the market growth of Hong Kong, greater China has become the primary import market for Swiss timepieces. In fact, the statistics[6] show that over the last decade, the export value of Swiss watches to greater China has grown by around 350 per cent. Many observers believe that the fact that the Swiss watch industry did not collapse after the subprime crisis of 2008 was almost exclusively thanks to greater China. In this configuration, Hong Kong occupies a key role. The connections in the watch business between Hong Kong and Switzerland are not new, but today they are related to the importance of the Chinese market. On average, half of the purchases of Swiss watches by mainland Chinese take place in Hong Kong, mainly because luxury items are overtaxed in mainland China and because the Chinese do not trust their own watch market due to the problems of copying and fakes.

The economic success of Swiss watchmaking in greater China has been related to wristwatches that are perceived as luxury watches; this mostly means mechanical watches, which are usually far more expensive than electronic ones. The mechanisms of mechanical watches are also more complex than those of electronic ones.[7] Their production, maintenance and repair require a higher level of technical skill. In addition, due to their fragile mechanism, dust or a small shock may easily disturb their functioning, so that they need to be serviced more frequently. More generally, high-end mechanical timepieces are perceived by connoisseurs as being superior to quartz because they are more obviously 'technical' and are regarded as entities in motion that are almost alive and generate emotion.

The triumph of Swiss watchmaking in greater China has specifically concerned complicated and ultra-complicated mechanical wristwatches,[8] which are luxury items and remain more complex than simple watches. In the global hierarchy of the watch industry, complicated mechanical watches are the most luxurious and prestigious watches and considered to be the hardest to make, adjust, service and repair. In addition, the ownership of the craftsmanship related to such items is today appreciated by many Swiss actors and firms as 'national heritage'.

Since the year 2000, the repair of Swiss mechanical watches in Hong Kong has rapidly come to be perceived as a problem for many individuals and organisations. In fact, this issue is related not only to Swiss brands *per se* but also to non-Swiss brands using Swiss components and to Hong Kong and Chinese companies involved in the Swiss watch business – wholesalers, dealers or retail groups, independent stores or watchmakers, brands, trade associations, etc.

Until the second half of the 1990s, the greater Chinese market was not greatly attracted by Swiss mechanical watches. Swiss and Japanese quartz watches were more popular. The servicing of the few Swiss mechanical watches sold was easily manageable by brands and stores in Hong Kong. Firms only needed a few people in their service centres, to perform basic tasks, and when anything more was needed, mechanical watches were often sent back to Switzerland to be repaired. There was a sufficient number of qualified people in Switzerland and Hong Kong to meet the need. The standard of watch-repairing courses given by the vocational training council of Hong Kong was sufficient. Firms did not have to undertake the basic training themselves.

Since the year 2000, however, the meteoric increase in the sales of more technical watches has proportionally expanded the number of servicing requests. Moreover, Chinese authorities have raised the taxes that are levied on products leaving greater China for more than six months. As a result, many firms involved in the Swiss watch business now face new obstacles, including high maintenance costs, excessively long deadlines and a bad reputation due to dissatisfied customers who have sometimes had to wait months to get their watches back. To avoid these problems, these firms have reorganised their customer services and taken new measures to engage staff on site: they have extended their centres, increased their number of employees and organised more training sessions for their staff in Switzerland or with Swiss trainers.

Above all, they have committed to new knowledge-management policies for providing technical servicing according to Swiss standards and training local workforces to perform that servicing. Swiss groups such as Richemont or Swatch Group, for instance, have opened their own schools with Swiss training programmes in Shanghai and Hong Kong. Non-Swiss brands and Hong Kong dealers and retailers have also got in touch with Swiss watchmakers in order to implement training courses for their staff.

Figure 8.2. Doxa advertising poster, displayed in a mall in downtown Hong Kong in the summer of 2015. Photograph by Hervé Munz.

Various forms of craftsmanship transfer from Switzerland to mainland China and Hong Kong have been and are still being implemented in order to maintain the aura of Swiss timepieces in East Asia.

The Circulation of Swiss Standards in Hong Kong

This chapter points out how repair plays a key role in the international success of the Swiss watch industry, as much in the framing of its luxury image as in its logistical organisation and economic profitability. In order to study the transfers of skills and techniques organised by multiple companies in Hong Kong, I conducted ethnographic inquiries in vocational schools, training centres and occupational servicing workshops. The main thread of this research involved describing the ways in which Hong Kong and Chinese watchmakers were trained, through multiple transmission programmes in different organisations, in so-called 'Swiss standards'. I wondered how Swiss repair techniques were acquired by Hong Kong watchmakers and how the reputation and high prestige bound up with such practices were affected when they were passed on in translocal ways.

One of the locations of my fieldwork in Swiss watch customer service was a training centre belonging to the Hong Kong federation of watch trades. In the summer of 2015, I spent two months there as an apprentice, taking a part-time training course in watch repair taught by Leslie, a 63-year-old Swiss watchmaker, along with thirty Hong Kong in-service trainees who worked in firms the rest of the day.

I was allowed to sign up as an apprentice in return for my having hired Leslie in Switzerland two years earlier on behalf of the Hong Kong federation. That, in turn, happened because on my very first stay in Hong Kong, in 2012, I met a forty-year-old Hong Kong watchmaker named Robert who invited me to visit the school where he had been trained twenty years earlier. When we visited the school, we were welcomed by the main teacher, a sixty-something watchmaker named Barry, who explained that, in the early 1970s, at the beginning of his career, he had been trained in Hong Kong by the Swiss Watch Federation. Over the years, he had always respected what he called 'Swiss watch standards'. But he would soon be retiring and told me that he was afraid that this standard would not be maintained. He asked me to do whatever was necessary, once I was back in Switzerland, to find a master watchmaker who would agree to come to Hong Kong to teach Swiss watch-servicing techniques. The target group for these courses would be local watchmakers who worked in firms that were connected to the same professional association as Barry's school. These were not facto-

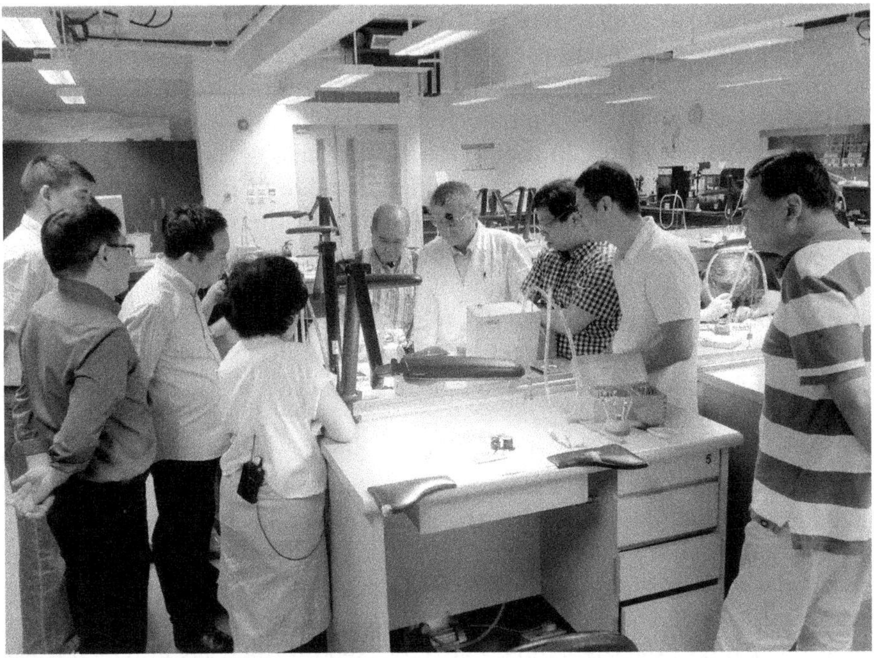

Figure 8.3. Leslie surrounded by his students during the training course. Photograph by Hervé Munz.

ries but rather stores, retail chains and even brands, mainly involved in the Swiss watches or components business.

I took Barry's request very seriously and, after returning home, I started to look for a watchmaker. Two months later, I met Leslie, a watchmaking teacher about to retire, who was very interested in teaching in Hong Kong in his retirement. A few months later, during the annual international watch trade fair in Switzerland, Leslie and I met the leaders of the association to which Barry's school was attached, who were impressed with Leslie's experience. Leslie and the Hong Kong association's leaders agreed to move forward together.

For a period of two years, because of Leslie's lack of English, I facilitated negotiations, taking care of the financial and logistical details of the collaboration. During the first meeting, I specified to the Hong Kong partners that I would not ask for any monetary payment, but that I would like to be permitted to accompany Leslie and enter the training school in Hong Kong to conduct ethnographic research there. I also asked to interview other representatives of their association. After several phases of negotiation, they refused to allow me to interview their colleagues. However, they eventually accepted me as 'Leslie's assistant' and allowed me to enter the school, while requiring me not to speak to any other trainees. At that point, Leslie suggested that he would prefer to consider me as another apprentice, and I was then allowed to work at the bench.

After a good first teaching experience in the Hong Kong training school, in 2014, Leslie was invited to come back on an annual basis. It was in July 2015 that I was able to accompany him for the first time and participate in his class in Hong Kong. In methodological terms, I followed Marchand's (2001) proposal to use apprenticeship as a mode of participant observation and a way to gain a closer understanding of the ways in which craft-based skill is acquired. Thus, I attended the daily classes with the other trainees, sitting at my bench and following the teacher's instructions. At the beginning, I was silent and discreet; over time, I was gradually invited by the other students to interact, to take part in discussions during breaks and to join them on the weekends for leisure activities such as hiking and sightseeing trips.

For two months, during the classes, I learnt some techniques of watch servicing while also carefully observing and noting the interactions among people in the workshops, mainly the Swiss trainer, his translator, the Hong Kong trainees and the school staff (director, teachers and assistants). I was particularly interested in the ways in which skills were passed on and how trainees learnt and appropriated techniques, gestures and problem-solving methods from Leslie's teaching. I also focused on the ways in which these forms of knowledge were identified, or not, by craftspeople as Swiss watch culture and how the so-called 'Swiss standards' were subject to permanent negotiation. Leslie gave the classes in French, because he spoke neither Cantonese nor English, and they were translated into Cantonese by a translator who had been engaged for the course by the school's leaders. For my part, because my Cantonese is poor and most of them spoke English, I interacted with trainees and staff in English.

Figures 8.4 and 8.5. At the workshop. Photographs by Hervé Munz.

More Swiss than the Swiss

Different findings drawn from my observations in the training centre show that the circulation of skills from Switzerland to Hong Kong redefines the ways in which belonging to Swiss watchmaking is expressed and lived. This kind of transnational mobility simultaneously nullifies and strengthens two ideas. First, that the Swiss watch industry is made up of Swiss citizens and contained on Swiss territory; and that there is such a thing as typical Swiss watch craftsmanship.

My first observation is that the 'Swissness' behind Swiss watches is not as strong as it seems. The Swiss watch industry today is a global system, made up of heterogeneous groups. It is represented by people of multiple national identities. For instance, over the last decade, Swiss brands have hired many Chinese and Hong Kong sales managers and even Chinese watchmaking teachers. In Hong Kong, the majority of the watchmakers who teach in the two Swiss schools are Chinese from Shanghai. Some of the Hong Kong managers who work for Swiss brands have been so successful that they have been invited to join the general boards of these brands and to become their decision-makers for Asian regions. Moreover, what I discovered in my fieldwork is that in the last twenty-five years, Swiss brands have also been taken over by Hong Kong and Chinese businessmen. When I first met the industry leaders in charge of the association that funded Leslie's class, I was expecting to meet executives of Hong Kong and Chinese brands. But what I learnt was that these managers were full members of Swiss brands, sometimes even the owners of those brands.

Second, so-called 'Swiss watch standards' are sometimes more strongly defended by Hong Kong watchmakers than they are by Swiss watchmakers. The normative categories that are valued by the Hong Kong watch industry are not always accepted by Swiss watchmakers. The industry includes many formalised norms linked to the processes of making and selling watches or teaching the watchmaker's craft (compendia of industrial norms, legal frameworks on the use of the labels 'Swiss' and 'Swiss made', training ordinances, etc.). During my inquiries in Switzerland, however, I noticed that Swiss watchmaking teachers and watchmakers rarely followed the formally codified standards in their practices. Those standards were highly controversial, if not contested. Instead, craftspeople adhered to diverse ways of proceeding and reminded me that technical norms varied greatly from one brand to another, mainly because of issues of competition and differentiation. I was led to the conclusion that Swiss standards were not definitively stabilised, despite the efforts of many stakeholders and organisations to achieve such a stabilisation and avoid excessive variability.

The transfer of skills from Switzerland to Hong Kong, by contrast, has served to reinforced Swiss watch standards. My observations in the school gave me a completely new view of the power of Swiss standards outside of Switzerland. A few anecdotes will illustrate this point. One day, Leslie announced to the director of the Hong Kong school that he would have to drop one of the exercises planned for the class because of a problem with the equipment. He assured him that this exercise was not central to his teaching and not necessary for the trainees. Nonetheless, he had to justify his decision for nearly an hour. In the eyes of the school manager, it was a huge problem for the class not to proceed as originally planned. When I tried to find out why, I understood that the aim of the course was to reproduce watchmaker training exactly as it was carried out in Switzerland, with no possible deviation, partly for the sake of prestige.

For the Hong Kong trainees, the standards to which they aspired were often associated with Leslie's opinions, technical gestures and practice rather than with any specific kind of material, metals or tools. The Hong Kong watchmakers taking the class were idolising Leslie as the master. The advice that he gave them was often perceived as a Swiss standard in itself, even when Leslie explained that sometimes he was only expressing his own point of view on watchmaking. More specifically, according to the trainees, this way of learning the servicing of watches according to Swiss standards transformed their connections to the materiality of work and their professional identity. Paul, forty-five, an engineer by training and self-educated watch repairman in charge of a family watch store, for example, asserted that:

> Even if we don't immediately use the techniques that we learn here in our business, they are not useless at all! By learning them, we acquire a methodology of work. This concerns, for example, the care we put into the visual control of watch mechanisms or even the thoroughness of the cleaning of components. All of that is really important, providing us with reference points that allow us to become more effective and save time.

During another informal discussion, Fanny, forty, a watch repairwoman working for a Swiss brand, noted:

> The fascinating thing about Leslie is his versatility! He masters many techniques and is able to cope on his own in many situations. For us, professionals, the key point is to practise the craft as completely as possible. We want to learn to make things with attention and care. And it is only the Swiss approach to the craft that allows that. Here in Hong Kong, everything is about money and profit. People don't respect the profession enough. Through Leslie's course, it is, first of all, a relationship to time that we are learning!

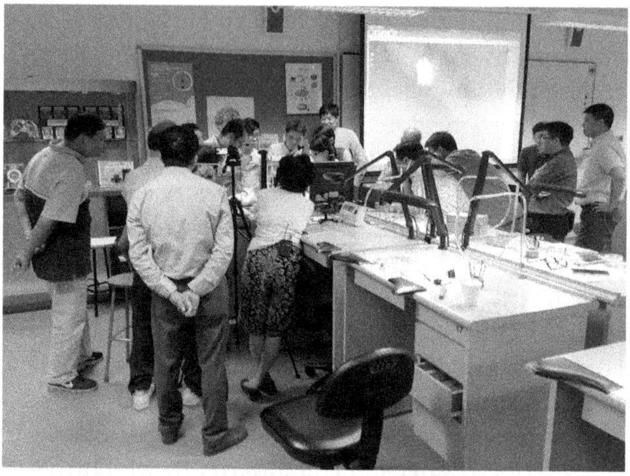

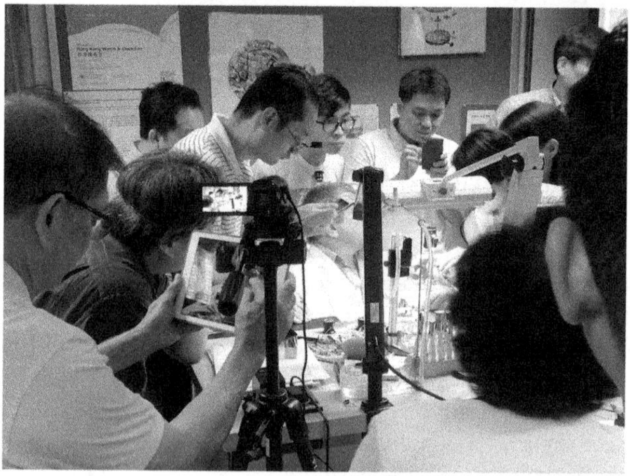

Figures 8.6, 8.7 and 8.8. At the workshop. Photographs by Hervé Munz.

At one point, an interesting misunderstanding emerged between Leslie and the trainees around the issue of the precision expected from the Swiss standards. It was during an exercise in which the students had to develop their professional observation, and they were wondering about relying so intensively on their senses; they were shocked when Leslie said: 'You should understand that the traditional watchmaker's or watch-repairer's craft is a skilled activity but not an accurate one. Most of the time, because of the smallness of the components we stare at and touch, we can only visually *estimate* their value, but we cannot *measure* it with our conventional tooling!'

The trainees were very unsettled: how could a Swiss watchmaker – a 'guardian of the temple of time', as Wu, a 42-year-old trainee, called Leslie – make such a statement? It was not that the Hong Kong apprentices were denigrating the expertise of their senses. But they were astonished that the Swiss practitioner dared to cast a shadow on the institution represented by Swiss watchmaking know-how, whose most important qualities they understood to be accuracy and reliability.

The time I spent with the Hong Kong trainees also helped me to understand how they trusted 'Swissness' as an assurance of quality (whether for end products, manufacturing methods or production monitoring) and how references to Swiss industry shaped their appreciation of fine work and craft-related identity. For instance, they used Swiss tools (files, pins, screwdrivers, tweezers, milling cutters, binocular microscopes, etc.) and machines (micro-lathes, drills, cleaning machines, etc.), claiming that Swiss components were unsurpassable and dreaming not only of working for Swiss brands but also of coming to Switzerland for an internship. This reification of Swiss standards by the trainees has to be understood in the light of the upgrade that the label of 'Swissness' provides in the broader context of their Hong Kong career. Indeed, after completing the course and achieving the certificate with a Swiss trainer's signature, some of the trainees were hired by other firms that used Swiss movements; quickly obtained better job conditions and salaries at their own companies; or were contacted by new customers (brands, shops) who wanted them to service, as subcontractors, the surplus watches that these companies were not able to handle in-house.

The third observation I made is that the craft of watch repair has been doubly revalorised by its transnational circulation through Leslie's teaching. I say 'doubly' because this transfer has helped to improve the perception that craftspeople have of their own trade not only in Hong Kong but also in Switzerland. At the same time, however, this 'revalorisation' and 'improvement' is in the context of the previous devalorisation of the craft in both countries.

In Hong Kong, the current tendency does not really promote the craft of watch repair. The official government training programme for this occupation was recently shortened and the skill level downgraded. When I met the Hong Kong trainer responsible for this programme, he explained to me that for the last thirty years in Hong Kong, before the success of Swiss watches in China, watch repair had not been considered a completely respectable job. He went on to explain the various reasons for this. Hong Kong had not

Figure 8.9. Mobile repair stall for electronic watches, tended by a local watch repairer on a Hong Kong street. Photograph by Hervé Munz.

been a watch-producing country since the end of the 1980s. Because of the arrival of quartz technologies, mainly from Japan in the 1980s, watches were considered cheap, low-end products. The craft of watch repair was therefore also perceived as requiring no specific skills. Moreover, watch repair was linked with the specific image of small trade: like shoemaking

Figure 8.10. The stall is located under an urban highway bridge. Photograph by Hervé Munz.

or key-making, watch repair was a craft practised in the street, in the dirt, and for little money. It had no prestige at all and was not attractive to young people. For these reasons, Hong Kong's vocational training school for watch repair had lost almost two-thirds of its numbers over the course of twenty years. This is why the government had decided to downgrade its training programme.

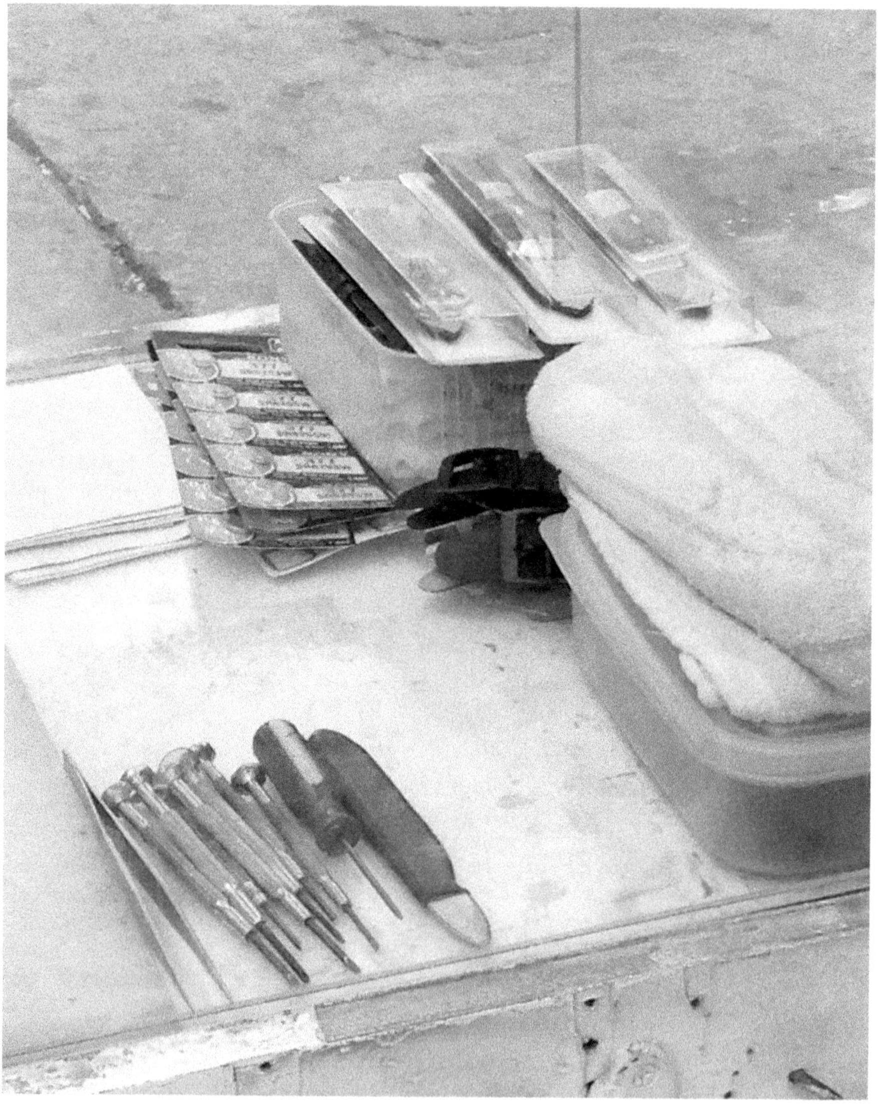

Figure 8.11. The equipment of a Hong Kong watch repairer: watch batteries, a case opener, hand tools (tweezers, screwdrivers) and a towel. Photograph by Hervé Munz.

In Switzerland, meanwhile, over the last ten years, watch-repairing skills and techniques have been marginalised by the mainstream industry, which is focused on production and sales, due to its worldwide success. Not much care is devoted to service or repair techniques. For many Swiss watchmakers like Leslie, who consider skills to be at the 'heart of the craft', this situation is considered a threat to the profession. I noted that, against the

Figure 8.12. All practical classes taught by Leslie to Hong Kong trainees were carefully recorded and preserved by the vocational training centre staff. Photograph by Hervé Munz.

background of the disrespect into which the craft has fallen in both Hong Kong and Switzerland, Leslie's knowledge transfer to Hong Kong was perceived, both by local watchmakers and by himself, as a way to increase and renew the value given to this specific trade.

Conclusion

Today, one of the most emblematic crafts and national myths of Switzerland is being at least partially performed, maintained and defended abroad, more specifically in greater China. The identity boundaries of the Swiss watch industry have changed considerably. There is no exact partnering between industry, technical culture and national territory. The Swiss watch industry is now not a cluster but a global, cross-cultural system in which Swiss territory has both a central and a marginalised role and in which Swissness is at the same time challenged and defended. More generally, the prestigious Swissness relating to watches and skills is the result of specific appropriations and operations of branding that happen worldwide but not everywhere. That is why Swiss references and national identities are being reinforced outside of Switzerland, in Hong Kong.

It is crucial to mention, echoing findings in anthropotechnology, that international transfers of watch-servicing skills and knowledge are more transformations than they are uniform reproductions. In the process of being transferred, they are translated and incorporated into new local configurations of knowledge, and in return they also transform their new environment of practice. This finding nourishes and extends Marchand's criticisms of the regular use in the social sciences of the notion of transmission, which often carries 'problematic connotations of mechanical reproduction and homogeneous transferral of facts or informations from one head (or body) to another' (Marchand 2010: 12). In other words, the imitation of others' ways of doing, in which all apprentices are involved, always implies a displacement and a shift from the original models (Tjitske Kalshoven and Whitehouse 2010). The mimetic principle that makes up a large number of training situations presupposes a transposition of gestures and an adaptive re-orchestration of these gestures. Through the lens of appropriation, the notion of transmission can be considered as a dynamic through which a field of new practices opens up, rather than as a form of repetition identical to the existing one. A transfer can only be the result of re-compositions that are equally metamorphoses. In other words, individuals never transmit what they receive. Transmission, passing on, is therefore equivalent to introducing a series of possible differences (Munz 2016: 354; 2017a).

Hervé Munz is a lecturer in anthropology, Department of Geography and Environment, Geneva School of Social Sciences, University of Geneva.

Notes

1. Website of the Convention patronale de l'industrie horlogère suisse, 'Census 2015 of Watchmaking and Microtechnology Personnel and Firms', La Chaux-de-Fonds, 2016. Retrieved 25 June 2017 from http://www.cpih.ch/fichiers/files/politique-patronale/Recensement%202015_FR_vmedia_def.pdf.
2. Website of the Federation of the Swiss Watch Industry (FH), 'The Swiss and World Watchmaking Industries in 2016'. Retrieved 25 June 2017 from http://www.fhs.swiss/file/59/Watchmaking_2016.pdf.
3. Since the second half of the nineteenth century, due to its centrality to Switzerland's economic growth, the production of watches has been a primary concern for national and regional authorities. This is why the gradual formation of watchmaking into a national symbol by economic, political, scientific and artistic elites cannot be dismissed as simply what some authors call 'banal nationalism' (Billig 1995) or 'everyday nationalism' (Edensor 2002).
4. Greater China includes mainland China, Hong Kong, Macao and Taïwan.
5. This chapter (as is also true for the rest of my work on the watch industry), even though it seems to be about the issues of time and time measurement, will not be an attempt to characterise the cultural dimension of the temporality at stake in the exercise or the global circulation of the watchmaker's or watch repairer's craft. I am aware of the anthropological tradition that has problematised the cultural variety of time conceptions (Fabian 1983; Gell 1992; Ingold 1993; and more recently Schulz 2012), and the works that have studied these conceptions in connection with watches and the watch industry (Balandier 1963; Landes 1983; Birth 2012). However, my work is not part of this tradition. Temporality and connections to time continue of course to be crucial issues in the making and servicing of watches; I have, however, chosen not to focus on watchmakers' temporal culture in my research, mainly because I have observed how so-called technical culture and its apparent values, including particular connections to time (including patience, perseverance, craftsmanship, traditions of know-how and intergenerational transmission) have been prominently used as promotional tools and monopolised by watch firms to distinguish their products on the global market. In these forms of dramatisation, Swiss craftspeople are represented as having surpassed other global competitors over the course of centuries of crafting timepieces thanks to their very specific cultural approach to time, materialised in their work of unmatchable quality.
6. Website of the Federation of the Swiss Watch Industry (FH) (see note 2).
7. On average, the 'motor' (called 'movement') of a simple mechanical watch is made up of two hundred components. A mechanical movement equipped with 'complications' (see note 8) is made up of six to twelve hundred components. A quartz watch movement, by contrast, consists of only a quarter as many components. A quartz movement is also easier and less expensive to produce.
8. In watchmaking, a 'complication mechanism' is a timing function that goes beyond just the hours, minutes and seconds. Distinctions are made between

'complicated' watches (with chronographs, annual calendars, moon phases and power reserve indications) and 'ultra-complicated' ones, which are even more technically complex and composed of a larger number of components (producing functions such as multiple time zones, perpetual or astronomical calendars and minute repeaters).

References

Abélès, M. 2018. *Un ethnologue au pays du luxe*. Paris: Odile Jacob.
Balandier, G. 1963. *Le temps et la montre en Afrique noire: Enquête économico-sociologique*. Bienne: Fédération horlogère suisse.
Baudin, C. 2012. 'Appropriation', *Laboreal* VIII(2), 111–14.
Bendix, R. 2014. 'Daily Bread, Global Distinction? The German Bakers' Crafts and Cultural Value-Enhancement Regimes', in R.L. Brulotte and M.A. Di Giovine (eds), *Edible Identities: Food as Cultural Heritage*. Burlington, VA: Ashgate, pp. 185–99.
Billig, M. 1995. *Banal Nationalism*. London: Sage.
Birth, K. 2012. *Objects of Time: How Things Shape Temporality*. New York: Palgrave Macmillan.
Boltanski, L., and A. Esquerre. 2014. 'La "collection", une forme neuve du capitalisme: La mise en valeur économique du passé et ses effets', *Les Temps Modernes* 3(679): 5–72.
Dant, T. 2009. *The Work of Repair: Gesture, Emotion and Sensual Knowledge*. Lancaster: Lancaster University Press.
Dematteo, L. 2015. 'Political Significance of the Timeless in the Promotion of Luxury Brands', paper given at the workshop *Routes of Luxury*, Collège d'études mondiales, 8–9 January 2015, Paris [unpublished].
Denis, J., and D. Pontille. 2015. 'Beyond Breakdown: Two Horizons of Maintenance Work', *i3 Working Papers Series*, 15-SES-08.
Donzé, P.-Y. 2014. *A Business History of the Swatch Group: The Rebirth of Swiss Watchmaking and the Globalization of the Luxury Industry*. New York: Palgrave Macmillan.
Donzé, P.-Y., and R. Fujioka. 2017. 'Introduction', in P.-Y. Donzé and R. Fujioka (eds), *Global Luxury: Organizational Change and Emerging Markets in the Luxury Industry since the 1970s*. New York: Palgrave Macmillan, pp. 1–15.
Edensor, T. 2002. *National Identity, Popular Culture and Everyday Life*. Oxford: Berg.
Fabian, J. 1983. *Time and the Other: How Anthropology Makes Its Object*. New York: Columbia University Press.
Gell, A. 1992. *The Anthropology of Time: Cultural Constructions of Temporal Maps and Images*. Oxford: Berg.
Geslin, P. 2002. *L'apprentissage des mondes, une anthropologie appliquée aux transferts de technologies*. Toulouse: Editions de la Maison des Sciences de l'Homme/Octarès.
—— (ed.). 2017. *Inside Anthropotechnology*. London: Wiley.
Graham, S., and N. Thrift. 2007. 'Out of Order: Understanding Repair and Maintenance', *Theory, Culture & Society* 24(3): 1–25.

Grasseni, C. 2016. *The Heritage Arena: Reinventing Cheese in the Italian Alps*. Oxford: Berghahn Books.
Harris, M. (ed.). 2007. *Ways of Knowing: Anthropological Approaches to Crafting Experience and Knowledge*. Oxford: Berghahn Books.
Henke, C.R. 1999. 'The Mechanics of Workplace Order: Toward a Sociology of Repair'. *Berkeley Journal of Sociology* 44: 55–81.
Hobsbawm, E. 1983. 'Introduction: Inventing Traditions', in E. Hobsbawm and T. Ranger (eds), *The Invention of Tradition*. Cambridge: Cambridge University Press, pp. 1–14.
Houston, L. 2014. 'Inventive Infrastructure: An Exploration of Mobile Phone Repair Practices in Downtown Kampala, Uganda', Ph.D. dissertation. Lancaster University.
Ingold, T. 1993. 'The Temporality of the Landscape', *World Archaeology* 25(2): 152–74.
——. 2001a. 'From the Transmission of Representations to the Education of Attention', in H. Whitehouse (ed.), *The Debated Mind: Evolutionary Psychology versus Ethnography*. Oxford: Berg, pp. 113–53.
——. 2001b. 'Beyond Art and Technology: The Anthropology of Skill', in M.B. Schiffer (ed.), *Anthropological Perspectives on Technology*. Albuquerque: University of New Mexico Press, pp. 17–31.
——. 2018. 'Five Questions of Skill', *Cultural Geographies* 25(1): 159–63.
Jackson, S.J. 2014. 'Rethinking Repair', in T. Gillespie, T., P. J. Boczkowski, and K. A. Foot (eds), *Media Technologies*. Cambridge, MA: MIT Press, pp. 221–39.
Julien, M.-P., and C. Rosselin. 2009. *Le sujet contre les objets, tout contre: ethnographies de cultures matérielles*. Paris: Editions du CTHS.
Landes, D.S. 1983. *Revolution in Time: Clocks and the Making of the Modern World*. Cambridge, MA: Harvard University Press.
Marchand, T.H. 2001. *Minaret Building and Apprenticeship in Yemen*. Richmond: Curzon.
——. 2010. 'Preface and Introduction: Making Knowledge', *Journal of the Royal Anthropological Institute* 16(1): 1–21.
—— (ed.). 2016. *Craftwork as Problem Solving: Ethnographic Studies of Design and Making*. Farnham: Ashgate.
Martínez, F. 2017. 'Waste Is Not the End: For an Anthropology of Care, Maintenance and Repair', *Social Anthropology* 25(3): 346–50.
——. 2019. 'Politics of Recuperation: An Introduction', in F. Martínez (ed.), *Politics of Recuperation: Repair and Recovery in Post-crisis Portugal*. London: Bloomsbury, in press.
Munz, H. 2016. *La transmission en jeu: apprendre, pratiquer, patrimonialiser l'horlogerie en Suisse*. Neuchâtel: Alphil.
——. 2017a. 'The Appropriation of Knowledge: An Anthropology of Transmission in the Context of Professional Training', in Ph. Geslin (ed.), *Inside Anthropotechnology: User and Culture Centered Experience*. London: Wiley, pp. 27–49.
——. 2017b. 'Crafting Time, Making Luxury: Heritage Regime and Artisan Revival in the Swiss Watches Industry (1975–2015)', in P.-Y. Donzé and F. Rika (eds), *Global Luxury: Organizational Change and Emerging Markets in the Luxury Industry since the 1970s*. New York: Palgrave Macmillan, pp. 197–218.

Nova, N. 2017. 'Démonter, extraire, combiner, remonter: Commodore 64 et créolisation technique', *Techniques & Culture* 67: 116–33.
Oakley, P. 2015. 'Ticking Boxes: (Re)constructing the Wristwatch as a Luxury Object', *Luxury: History, Culture, Consumption* 1(2): 41–60.
Raffaelli, R. 2018. 'Technology Reemergence: Creating New Value for Old Technologies in Swiss Mechanical Watchmaking (1970–2008)', *Administrative Science Quarterly* (online first), https://journals.sagepub.com/doi/full/10.1177/0001839218778505.
Schulz, Y. 2012. 'Time Representations in Social Science', *Dialogues in Clinical Neuroscience* 14(4): 381–87.
——. 2015. 'Towards a New Waste Regime? Critical Reflections on China's Shifting Market for High-Tech Discards', *China Perspectives* 3: 43–50.
Simoni, V. 2009. 'Scaling Cigars in the Cuban Tourism Economy', *Etnográfica* 13(2): 417–38.
Sougy, N. 2003. *Luxes et internationalisation (XVIe-XIXe siècles)*. Neuchâtel: Editions Alphil – Presses Universitaires Suisses,
Tjitske Kalshoven, P., and A. Whitehouse. 2010. 'Something Borrowed, Something New? Practices and Politics of Imitation: An Introduction', *Etnofoor* 22(1): 7–10.

SNAPSHOT 9

Lost Battles of De-bobbling

Magdalena Crăciun

In a small provincial Romanian town, Bianca, a young married woman in her late twenties, often feels annoyed with her relatives' opinions about clothes. Her mother and mother-in-law nag her to stop stuffing the wardrobe with things that the couple, especially Bianca, wear for short periods of time, far shorter than they would expect clothes to be worn. They keep telling her: 'I don't have to tell you why you'll wear this blouse only a few times, you know it very well!', 'You don't buy clothes, you're simply throwing away your money!', 'It's twice its initial size after three washes, of course you cannot wear it anymore!', 'Can't you buy something more durable than these disposable Chinese things?', 'Of a better quality, like something made in Romania?' Usually, out of politeness, Bianca shrugs her shoulders, refraining from commenting on her mother's durable – but drab – garments.

Her mother-in-law urges her to buy branded garments from the malls in Bucharest, reasoning that, if both she and her husband really like to dress smartly and have the money to spend on clothes, they should buy quality garments instead of not-such-high-quality clothes from the local shops, even if this means buying less and, thus, having a smaller wardrobe. Bianca's other relatives and friends also believe that branding guarantees quality. She, of the opposite opinion, does not hesitate to voice it whenever she has the opportunity. Especially when she meets some of her former schoolmates, who make an effort to dress themselves from the malls, but also endlessly complain about the bobbles, fading colours, weak seams and falling buttons of their branded garments.

On the positive side, when it comes to Bianca's cleaning and maintenance of their clothes, her mother and mother-in-law have only praise. They know that she invested in a good washing machine, only buys expensive laundry detergents and fabric conditioners, as well as hand-washing delicate pieces. They see her skills and patience in sewing buttons, mending holes, repairing hems and removing stains.

In response to these critiques, Bianca argues that she and her husband see things differently: for them, style is more important than the brand, as the latter offers no guarantee of quality. And more, for them, clothes become redundant when they are no longer fashionable, whereas, for their mothers, garments become redundant when they can no longer be repaired and, thus, are no longer usable.

This is what Bianca argues in public. Privately, in her conversations with this anthropologist, she is not so sure of herself. Many of her fashionable garments quickly lose their beauty: threads unravel, hems fray, seams come out; the tight-fit turns into the loose-fit, thick fabric becomes threadbare, smooth surfaces go bobbly. Displeased with the outdated look of the garments manufactured in Romania, convinced that the branded garments from the malls represent expense rather than quality, and preoccupied with the difficult maintenance and limited repairability of their garments, she is yet to fix this dilemma.

Her biggest fight is with bobbles – the small balls of fibre that form on the surface of clothes through friction and abrasion during wearing and washing. On the one hand, the 'bobbled look' is widely considered a socially unacceptable form of self-presentation. On the other hand, this repair process is particularly demanding. She strives to evaluate the materials more carefully, but often fails to determine the propensity of fabrics to bobble. Besides, she sometimes cannot resist buying flimsy, yet fashionable clothes. To prevent the development of bobbles, she washes everything inside out and doubles the recommended quantity of fabric conditioner. She even bought a professional bobble remover, but never showed it to her mother or mother-in-law. Whenever she is alone at home, she brushes, cuts or picks bobbles off their garments. This is her domestic secret.

She wins some battles. But in most cases, the fight is short. Much to her dismay, there comes a day when she has to admit that the bobbles are simply too many and de-bobbling is no longer possible. The bobbled clothes need to be discarded. However, for the worst affected clothes, the ones disgracefully bobbled all over that she would be ashamed to wear in public, she can neither wear indoors nor throw away. She fears that her attentive critics will notice either the clothes' compromised appearance or their sudden disappearance, and use this against her in their debates. Instead, she skilfully folds them and stuffs them at the back of the wardrobe.

In the terms of this volume, Bianca's secret, that is, de-bobbling, is part of a maintenance process that clothes constantly require. This process becomes more intense when the propensity to decay is enhanced through the planned obsolescence of garments. However, de-bobbling has to remain a hidden process. Bobbles index a faulty materiality and Bianca cannot tell her mother and mother-in-law that she de-bobbles garments. To confess this would mean to admit that they are right and that their garments are indeed prone to brokenness. Moreover, this particular repair process generates affects, not the contagious affects that sustain life together, but the kind of affects that one keeps for herself, that consume her, distance her from the others.

For Bianca, bobbling is different from other forms of material degradation. In most cases, she knows what to do and the results of her actions are predictable: a hole is mended, a frayed edge repaired, a stained fabric cleaned, a torn piece thrown away. She also knows what she can do about bobbling, but the results of her actions are unpredictable and only temporary. While she hopes to prolong the public life of garments and exasperatedly works to remove bobbles, they keep multiplying no matter how much she picks, brushes or cuts. In the end, there is nothing she can do to prevent the disgraceful appearance the garments take on. This always unfinished and unfinishable repair process gives her false hope and then lets her down. She feels ashamed, betrayed, defeated. Such negative feelings are stronger in a postsocialist context, which is not characterised by affluence and where the possibility for many people, including this couple, to dress to their hearts' desire is rather limited. This micro-ethnography demonstrates that repair can be not only an ethical answer to the dilemmas of overconsumption, as pointed out in the introduction of the volume, but also an aesthetic response to the dilemmas of consumption.

Magdalena Crăciun is Lecturer in the Department of Sociology, University of Bucharest.

CHAPTER 9

Small Mutinies in the Comfortable Slot

The New Environmentalism as Repair

EEVA BERGLUND

Introduction: Modernity Disconnected

> For the future, the most important thing is to construct lasting collaborations. It's about recycling structures, not wasting money on building new things when we can use the old and build on those valuable things that we have.
>
> —Pixelache festival open debate, speaker from the floor, August 2017 (from handwritten notes)

> Yes, these different urban initiatives do have a lot in common. They don't want to be on this treadmill, racing to the bottom.
>
> —Ruby van der Wekken, Finnish Urban Studies Conference, 4 May 2018, round table on self-organising in the city (from handwritten notes)

Not many decades ago anthropologists were able to write, without too much self-consciousness, about the SAE, the Standard Average European. I propose here a similarly abstracted ethnographic object – 'MN', the 'Modern Normal'. Such a construct allows me to essay and expand on why environmental activism, something I have been observing through anthropological lenses for a quarter of a century now, might be helpfully conceptualised as repair. In the 1990s, I worked on something that at the time was rarely a focus of such study: ordinary people in an ordinary town protesting ordinary threats to their environment and quality of life. I detailed these observations in my doctoral work, subsequently published (Berglund 1998).

Sympathising with my activist interlocutors, I agreed that if there was a problem in the situation, it was the growth-oriented, resource hungry politics of a recently reunified Germany, and the fact that it appeared standard and unremarkable. In critiquing that bundle of 'normal' goals, activists were being typically European. For critique is, as Bruno Latour has noted (2004), a core virtue of our era. It also has a tendency to run out of steam. Further, it can get detached from concrete troubles. What resonated in Germany then, and what one can encounter in Finland and elsewhere in Europe today, is a preoccupation with material change that alerts us to fragility and brokenness, provoking feelings of loss and frustration. Put differently, the bundle I am calling the Modern Normal is itself falling apart. Moreover, it is also blamed for having broken and spoiled valued environments, as well as provoking existential fears. Such a situation fuels an impulse to repair. This often means making good things that are wrong in the most practical, hands-on ways. It often means alleviating negative or uncomfortable feelings, particularly those arising from the paradoxes of European modernity.

I use the term modern because in everyday usage it appears as an unmarked condition, less tainted politically and more vague historically than 'industrialism' or 'capitalism'. The larger point is that as more and more people and places are devastated and/or abandoned while the health of the 'market environment' and 'innovation ecosystems' are prioritised, the great confidence once associated with modernity has receded. But materially, the modern way has left a huge range of things needing repair, an unholy modern mess where exploitation and destruction are totally normal (Berlant 2007; Fortun 2014).

Anticipations of some future apocalypse have already contributed to militantly defensive politics and anti-intellectual public discourse, in a way that surely links to personal disappointments, crumbling institutions and creaking or abandoned infrastructures bequeathed by the MN. But there are also heterogeneous, variously activist, countercultures that sometimes literally mend, fix and care for what we now have: the hugely growing phenomenon of pragmatic and surprisingly joyful – sometimes – activism that can profitably be thought of as repair. In conversation with anthropological, STS and other literature on repair and maintenance, and drawing from recent research and on personal experience, as well as on co-authoring with other activist-oriented scholars, notably sustainable design researcher Cindy Kohtala, I reflect on how activism as a form of repair responds to the unravelling of the promises of modernity. The grassroots repertoires I refer to are diffuse and emergent, but familiar by now: initiatives for improving the public realm or public services (Do-It-Yourself or guerrilla-type environmental improvements), averting or coping with vulnerable infrastructures (urban gardens), craft-oriented, hands-on making and repair, experiments with alternative economies and radically sustainable lifeways. The impulse to repair may also be part of a growth in activist pedagogy and of design and innovation for radical sociotechnical change from within professional contexts (Lenskjold, Sissel and Halse 2015; Escobar 2018).

In politics as in scholarship, we easily classify and assess such initiatives using familiar categories of political thought such as 'revolution' or 'reform', perhaps inadvertently delegitimising such initiatives as superficial. Yet whatever labels or analytical frameworks we use, S. Ravi Rajan and Colin Duncan surely capture something important about small-scale efforts to better human lives when they write that the 'world is rife with a million mutinies now' (2013: 70). Insisting on context-specificity, their ecological history approach defies the idea of some worldwide movement of resistance to an overarching force. They focus instead on seemingly unremarkable, even 'middling' cases. In their discussion of community initiatives North and South, rural and urban, Rajan and Duncan dub them 'ecologies of hope'. Rather than principled resistance or heroic social protest, these self-organised self-help initiatives arise from a need to secure a 'slightly more livable world' (2013: 75). They argue that their proliferation offers modest hopes for small but significant difference. Indeed, there is something striking about the similarities reported in the literature between initiatives from extremely different social, geographical and political contexts (see reference list). All arise from perceptions of threats to the local environment, but ones where the definition of the 'environment' is wider than bourgeois European notions of nature, and closer to what discourses of environmental justice have proposed. At stake is the world within which everyday life unfolds and flourishes, or fails to, where artefacts like built structures, invisible toxins or access to services are as important as biodiversity or climate.

MN and the Materialist Environmentalisms of Everyday Life

These reflections are based on observant participation in activism (unpaid and haphazardly recorded but informed by the academic literature cited) in a wealthy part of the world, Helsinki, Finland, where I was born and where I have been living for the past decade. People I describe may benefit personally and immediately from their activism, but they are doing it on a voluntary basis, as one way of coping with the messy legacies of globalisation, capitalism, growth economics and so on. As they intervene in the circulation of things, information and people in small-scale and generally ad hoc ways, activist practices alter material relationships and thus change society from the ground up. Following David Schlosberg and Romand Coles (2016), their endeavours can be usefully dubbed a materialist environmentalism of everyday life. They parallel and intersect – as this book does – with a dynamic growth in academic and artistic preoccupation with matter and its effects on the one hand (e.g. Graham and Thrift 2007; Connolly 2013), and with the design of things and processes on the other (e.g. Escobar 2018). This echoes Steven J. Jackson's idea (2014) of 'broken world thinking' and the implications thereof – that stability in human society is maintained through ongoing but usually overlooked work of maintenance, which is remarkably resilient, creative and widespread.

What follows is also informed by engaging with activism elsewhere in Finland, as well as the UK, Germany and the USA, over thirty years. My premise is that activism is an imperative that emerges out of a sense of duty as well as rebellion. Yet it is often hesitant and generally unfolds at different intensities through a person's life. And so there are many paradoxes involved when activists are, as Paul Chatterton and Jenny Pickerill (2010) put it a decade ago, 'against, within and after capitalism' or, indeed, against, within and after any aspects of the multiple historically shaped dependencies put in place as part of the Modern Normal over the last five hundred-plus years.

This raises questions about time and social order in modernity. Promises of improvements to come – always – were core to the MN, but these now ring hollow. There is even a growth industry of anxiously anticipating futures in think tanks and governments as well as business (Granjou, Walker and Salazar 2017). In such exercises, time is imagined as linear, a 'progression' of producing, acquiring and discarding things. Corporate and state actors habitually proclaim in a kind of declamatory future tense that such and such a future *will* come, whereas activists are self-conscious about choosing between alternative pathways and yet apprehensive about uncontrollable non-human powers. They proceed on the basis of many possible futures and their reluctance to proclaim very much at all about the future is striking. They practise normality differently, more humbly, perhaps enabling 'spaces of otherwise' (Martínez 2019). Mindfully – and sometimes with great effort – they are constructing less uncomfortable subjectivities or identities than those offered within the MN. In responding to and critiquing 'a range of problems with the production, supply, and circulation of everyday material needs' (Schlosberg and Coles 2016: 161), activism reconnects what modernity disconnected, frictionless comforts here and now with forms of violence sometimes very distant in time and space.

The picture has shifted considerably since the 1990s, when for me as a budding social researcher it was somewhat of a strain to present environmentalism as anything but a sociological problem, a cultural puzzle to be solved. Just a decade later, things were very different. And since then it has become ever easier to establish the MN as a massive problem. By 2007, Lauren Berlant for instance was able to write about a world system totally unremarkably destroying environments and exhausting people. But she also noted that the world was already '[pulsating] with counter-exploitative activity . . . in a variety of anarchist, cooperative, anticapitalist, and radical antiwork experiments' (Berlant 2007: 780; see also Krøijer 2015). The two examples I sketch out below are testament to such pulsating: Helsinki's first vegan junk-food kiosk, Jänö, a world-improving business; and Trashlab, an exemplary repair club.

Such initiatives grasp matter above all, but they are also repairing conceptually, culturally and in terms of behaviour the damage wrought over the past half a millennium. Their hesitations and heterogeneity make it foolhardy to attempt to classify groups or individuals as more or less activist or radical. However, in Finland where citizens' involvement in voluntary local associations has a long, broad and often remarked-upon history, my argument applies specifically to newer initiatives identified as self-organising or bottom-up (cf. Rantanen and Faehnle 2017). In many of these, as well as in the discourses that have emerged around them in the last decade or two, there is at least some impulse to be critical of capitalism and finance-driven globalisation, and to link local exhaustion – of people, environments and ideas alike – with translocal processes.

Such activity abounds around us if we only know to look for it. It is unfolding within the 'shell of the old', enacting different 'normals' while refusing to be subjected to some overwhelming external power such as globalisation or capitalism (Massey 2004). As pragmatic as this all appears, I also want to highlight how much emerging repertoires of activism rely on intellectual work. These new, more materialist forms of environmentalism require considerable trust in science (e.g. Berglund and Kohtala in press). However, those involved understand modern science as historically constructed and politically consequential, something that I observed already in the 1990s among the most confident environmentalists (e.g. Berglund 1998). As it seeks to reshape surroundings experienced as out of joint in some way, activism today unpacks the 'black boxes' that commercial production presents to 'users' or 'consumers' as inevitable, but also as the most developed. Activism as repair deconstructs technology made for profit, whether pursued through in-built obsolescence or data traceability. Additionally, activism is critical of intellectual property arrangements that only the most expensive lawyers can penetrate. But as alternative innovators, and thus as people who reconstruct as well as deconstruct society, activists hack the logic of proprietary capture and of passive, waste-producing consumerism. Whatever labels are used, this type of work fosters confidence in the critique of a vague everything, what I call the Modern Normal, at the same time as repairing its damage or at least alleviating its hurt.

The Comfortable Slot

Who are the people involved in this repair? They certainly are not the 'social wildlife' of the early anti-globalisation protests that observers from 'respectable society' complained about in the 1990s. More likely they are those with 'post-material values' more focused on quality of life than quantity of stuff (Schlosberg and Coles 2016, based on Ronald Inglehart's work). Also, they are among the most comfortable people: they may grumble about overtime and even useless landlords, but they are unlikely to go hungry or to live in nasty parts of town. In fact, as so-called creative talent, they often contribute to the marketable vibe of a city, so can be counted among the beneficiaries of the structures and funds set up also in Helsinki to make it internationally attractive and competitive. It was the city that made possible many early examples of the new urban activism. In the year 2000, Helsinki was namely one of ten European Capitals of Culture, which fed directly into an ecologically framed temporary pavilion for showcasing sustainable design and alternative culture (Kohtala and Paterson 2015). In 2012, World Design Capital funds fed into numerous activist projects in visible ways. What was compelling to the city and its corporate friends was that grassroots initiatives showed radicalism and heralded change but did not threaten socioeconomic order or, importantly, business (Berglund 2016). Nevertheless, campaign histories and activists' personal journeys do hark back to earlier waves of protest. Mobilisations against the World Trade Organization's growing power have been important, as has the altered socioeconomic situation left by the financial crisis that began in 2007.

Futures feel more precarious now, even for the wealthier, more academically inclined. The ever-young and beautiful people of lifestyle magazines and political programmes, who stood for the pinnacle of global progress in the twentieth century and still populate much public culture, are viewed less as exemplars now than as problems or fantasies. With shifts in work, the idea of a 'white collar' class is totally out of date, and 'middle class' is also a concept to use with caution (Carrier and Kalb 2015). Nevertheless, these traces of the twentieth century inform how futures are imagined – at least in advertising and policy rhetoric. If it ever existed as such, middle-class culture was a consumer culture, where 'goods' as material stuff were supposed to unlock progress. These images were the legitimation for rebuilding the entire world to service and serve the technico-politico-economic requirements of this cultural tradition. Though one should not overstate their significance, the events of 2007/8 nevertheless heralded a new phase in, if not the demise of, the social contract, and a discernible turning away from the political cultures that dominated before the crisis.

The genealogies of activism are not the issue here, however. Rather, the focus is on modes of materialist environmentalism of everyday life and their possible impacts on political and intellectual life. As Schlosberg and Coles (2016: 161) present it, the new environmentalism is not just beyond individualistic post-material values, it is acutely conscious of how everybody is embedded within 'collective institutions of material flows'. It is not just a form of resistance but of reconstruction, a prefigurative politics of constructing the hoped-for future now. It rethinks and redesigns ways of furnishing basic human needs in a way that 'acknowledges the human immersion in . . . the flows of the non-human realm' (ibid.: 161). What is noteworthy is how many people who could find a more conventionally valued place in business-friendly creative industries as analysts, designers, architects, researchers and artists of many kinds are engaged in it. In that respect then, 'they' are often 'us', hybrids of activist and academic. Not only do they enjoy social capital via professional competencies, they are – often – comfortable enough that they can afford to take on, temporarily at least, poorly remunerated work that leaves them 'out of pocket'. They are, as one audience member at a discussion on the future of Helsinki put it (with admiration), 'crazy activists who spend their time doing all this stuff' (event organised by Dodo at Pasila's *Turntable* urban garden, 12 June 2018). They are part of what could usefully be dubbed a 'comfortable slot'. Unsurprisingly, this group is also often seen, in both media and scholarship, as simply interested in assuaging 'middle-class guilt' (Fredericks 2014).

Indeed, middle-class life and 'ordinary' aspirations do incur vast environmental and social costs, and meanwhile cultural prohibitions against hopelessness have meant that it is not polite to point out what a pleasant dinner or fun holiday might cost in socio-environmental terms. The middle classes and their habits have also long been taken for granted as a Western European constant, unreflectively imagined and mobilised as the 'everybody' of management and marketing literature, as good consumers and thus virtuous members of society. Sociologically they have been less interesting than the destitute or the super-rich. They show up in recent research mostly as a vague force behind gentrification easily elided with 'market demand'. Until a recent apprehension that the middle classes – and their stabilising function as guardians of the 'social order' – might be under threat themselves, they have invited relatively little commentary or critique, academic or otherwise (exceptions include Carrier and Kalb 2015).

Ordinary life in ordinary places has been studied by sociologists, cultural studies scholars and others largely as 'consumer culture', if it has been studied at all. Anthropology has been more comfortable with subcultures or, when dealing with social power, with networks of tightly knit or occupationally specialist groups. In studies of middle-class activism, such as Kim Fortun's work in India or Stine Krøijer's in Denmark, anthropologists have often taken a sympathetic and nuanced approach. They show the articulation of material, conceptual and affective resonances, and point out similarities and connections between places, times and groups of people, without pre-judging the role of the lucky middle classes involved. They underscore that the life-sapping effects of complex and often intensely finance-intensive planetary processes are subject to resistance and challenge anywhere and by anyone.

For Rajan and Duncan (2013), ecologies of hope arise in what they call 'middling' spaces, where people 'simply and normally do what they can unless prevented', subsequently feeling neither like failures nor world-changing heroes (2013: 75). Living in Finland, a wealthy country by any account, puts burdens on nature and on other social groups that goes far beyond anything approximating sustainable, even if one is an environmentalist (e.g. Lettenmeier, Liedtke and Rohn 2014). Yet ethnographic principles require activist efforts to be taken seriously as genuine. Perhaps activist experiences in the comfortable slot are also significant in that they help shape 'public opinion'.

The idea of a 'comfortable slot' derives, in a roundabout way, from Michel-Rolph Trouillot's famous (1991) critique of anthropology as preoccupied with the 'savage slot'. In 2013, Joel Robbins observed that something like a 'suffering slot' had been shaping the discipline, and more recently still, Sherry B. Ortner (2016) discusses Robbins' own call for an 'anthropology of the good . . . focussed on such topics as value, morality, well-being, imagination, empathy, care, the gift, hope, time, and change' (Robbins, quoted in Ortner 2016: 58). Indeed, much of what is on that list is now firmly on the research agenda. However, and this is a concern shared by both Robbins and Ortner, in training its lens on such social institutions, anthropology has settled into an un-academic kind of security about what good and evil actually are. This also, as Robbins notes, allowed anthropology to de-emphasise what is so special about it, its attention to the specificities of living in particular places at particular times.

All of the things on Robbins' list are part of alternative world-making anywhere. In the comfortable slot, however, the focus on needing to repair and to assuage some deep hurt or existential fear comes into better focus, perhaps even a sense – voiced most easily in jest or private – that our problems don't have cultural fixes, they require wholesale change in the social, the economic, in everything. However, changing everything is beyond the possible. In fact, in Finland, which is easily imagined abroad as exemplary, a society as equal and stable as they come, many features of normality are considered worth conserving. Although here too consensus and sameness captured in a rhetoric of 'everyone' has long obscured structural inequality (Mustranta and Luhtakallio 2017), Finland's activist initiatives are rarely based in survival and more aimed at dysfunctions and fragilities mild by international comparison. This is not to say their calls for urgent change are disingenuous in any way, but rather to highlight the ease with which people here could – and do – avoid thinking about the extremity and riskiness of business-as-usual.

Robbins' interest was in how 'people live their personal and collective lives . . . pitched forward toward what they take to be better worlds' (2013: 459). Certainly, Helsinki activists are likely to be motivated or make sense of their own 'craziness' with reference to the good life. They are also pitching forward to engage in repair, of the small and near to hand, but also of something not clearly definable and yet calling them almost as a duty. As others studying repair and care have noted, there is here 'an ethical repertoire different to the liberal and modern conception of subjects as autonomous and free individuals' (Callén and Criado 2015: 21–22). This situates active citizens in relation to those around, who have expectations of them as members of the same moral community. It also puts them in relation to coordinates that resemble an older globalisation talk, not least in imputing a total lack of alternatives, since 'the global' (imagined as somewhere else) impinges upon the here and now. Indeed it does, but not as the MN narrative would have it.

Here and Now, There and Then

There is an interesting but nebulous similarity between materialist activists and political culture in Finland, namely a reluctance (or at least a reputation for such) to shout about one's doings, let alone achievements. When activists hesitate to shout about the value of their small-scale, poorly funded initiatives, they are in a sense acting rather typically. There is also a reluctance to appear political, not only for strategic reasons familiar from profit-driven post-political styles of environmentalism, but for historical reasons that have inculcated a still strong politics of consensus in Finland. (I discuss this in relation to Helsinki activism elsewhere [Berglund 2017]). Furthermore, activists are constantly drawn into situations of compromise and collaboration with institutions, through business sponsorship or co-optation by municipal agendas, for instance. Pragmatically accepting a range of collaborators supports the idea that the impulse of activism is less reform or revolution than repair. To illustrate, I sketch out – from ad hoc encounters and publicly available documents, and informed by long-term engagements with Helsinki's activist networks – two very different examples of material environmentalism of the everyday supported by sometimes but not always explicit environmental, economic and political arguments. Whether they are gardening or setting up alternative currencies or art-based urbanism, these groupings have no impulse to produce a 'blueprint', as in the case of so many utopian and intentional initiatives or policies. Instead, they have a pragmatic urge to keep as much space open as possible for adaptation, repurposing, reconfiguration and changeability (Callén and Criado 2015: 30), even for 'confusion' (Berglund and Kohtala in press).

The first illustration is a vegan junk-food kiosk near several popular night-time venues. It is right next door to a late-night snack kiosk that has long been a staple for late-night-early-morning Helsinkians hungry for something salty and greasy. The joke was that in purveying unhealthy vegan food, the kiosk punctured expectations that vegans would be self-righteous about their health as much as they are (apparently) about their world-saving. More seriously, it reuses an existing building, putting into practice at a small scale but in a symbolically significant way the principle of renovating and reusing existing building stock. In addition, its business model is a mix of crowd-funding through social media channels and conventional

Figure 9.1. Jänö vegan kiosk, Helsinki, May 2018. Photograph by Guy Julier.

bank loans, involving some considerable expertise in the legal structures of cooperative enterprise.

This is one of several initiatives highlighting the contrast between city-sponsored development at a massive scale and 'city-making' at the grassroots level, even in the realm of architecture and planning. For Helsinki has been in the grip of a massive construction boom for a decade. Building and construction sites are a new normal, causing disruption to travel and disturbing skylines and street layouts, even as some environmentally motivated people celebrate their promise of efficient city living.[1] All this is inciting shrill debate about what the city is and what it is good for. In this context, the reuse of the small wooden kiosks still owned by the city and which are an icon of summer in Helsinki has been one easy way for the city to present itself as sustainable as well as open to quirky initiatives. Alas, for decades, the city has not upgraded these early twentieth-century constructions. Tenants are thus expected to bring them to twenty-first-century health and safety regulation standards. Some, like this one, have been sold, so that a large part of the enterprise from the perspective of the activists was about documenting the renovations, recounting the story of the kiosk.

The kiosk was renovated, fitted with running water and a grease separation system to cope with the kitchen oils left over as residues of portions of 'Vöners with French Fries'. Clearly this was a case of repair. But in the process the work around the physical repair was a response to the dysfunctions of the Modern Normal. Solar panels on the roof deepen the vegan's interest in climate politics. Crowd-funding and the cooperative business model enact sharing economies' prevailing politics that support profit-driven start-ups and a technologically oriented innovation culture. And finally, for those content with being political consumers (or who are too exhausted for anything else), the kiosk has become a statement about how veganism can also be 'normal', no longer just for hair-shirted preachers of sustainability, or even 'hipsters' and 'eco-chic' new consumers. Indeed, the opening of the kiosk coincided with the coming out of a subculture and into the mainstream of a new diet: beer-and-fries veganism.

Both in the repair of an old building and in the repair of a destructive (to the planet!) diet, activism here addresses harms produced in the equally mundane activities of pursuing the good life's older version. The kiosk also enacts an ethic that tries to give future generations the right to live, perhaps even to live well. Beyond training its view on the distant past and the future, Jänö's builders are positioned in relation to distant geographies, where changing climate already endangers lives. For some punters, the causal links from the comfortable here-and-now to frightening times and places far away extend to the politically live question of immigration, with climate change considered a key driver of international migration patterns. My analysis of the kiosk, then, is that it is an instance of repairing the damages bequeathed by a temporally and spatially diffuse assemblage: the Modern Normal. Working out more precise motivations or reasons is not necessary. It is enough to act and even to enjoy, or to indulge a non-representational, affective politics.

Another type of repair enacted in Helsinki has been the work of Trashlab, an artist-activist-academic process under the aegis of the artist collective Pixelache. The aim of Trashlab has been to pursue collaborative, multidisciplinary explorations on waste streams, e-waste, overconsumption and sustainable solutions involving experimental electronics artists, designers, design researchers, media researchers and waste management experts. Institutionally somewhat precarious, it has been an important part of a longstanding and wide ecosystem of activist initiatives in Helsinki, as a blog post by Saša Nemec (2018) indicates. For instance in 2014, together with other experts in avoiding waste, it collaborated with the city, turning part of a municipal library once a month into a hands-on workshop. Library users came to tinker with broken mobile phones, laptops and music players or learn about household cleaning with past generations' technology. From these convivial settings, people were also drawn into the Recycling Olympic Games (or ROG) to seek the title of UpCycling Champion.

Environmentalism focused on e-waste particularly clearly links places of consumption with places where the produced waste and damage are 'dealt with' in variously dangerous ways (Brulle and Pellow 2006; Callén and Criado 2015). In that sense, Trashlab has encouraged discussion and culture change, and been remarkably principled in pursuing discussions that go beyond black versus white, as well as in exploring their dependency on others. As Nemec (2018: n.p.) writes, informal and open learning is to the fore, with a 'wider objective of the events [being] to think critically about the relationship with our belongings and their (non)disposability'. In practice, however, this is never straightforward, and it is impressive how tenaciously those involved have pursued their questioning: Who should be involved? How can they animate others in this ongoing conversation? How to rethink what seems normal?

Disconnecting as a Cultural Tradition

Activism in the comfortable slot, as I have described it, is a multifunctional practice. In fact, multifunctionality is something of a virtue in new forms of environmentalism, where it is often argued that business-as-usual is plagued by inefficiencies and alienating disconnections from the things, people and processes shaping our lives. Activism draws together or assembles multiple participants into stories that reconnect what has been forgotten and disavowed in the Modern Normal and attends above all to its built-in unsustainability. Like sustainability, activism in the comfortable slot is a vague concept, but it is suggestive and sufficient enough, I hope, to help mark out an international phenomenon, a new type of environmentalism related to but perhaps narrower in scope than Schlosberg and Coles' (2016) environmentalism of everyday life.

In both global South and North, among the comfortable and the less comfortable, activism is addressing the multiple problems of waste and built-in obsolescence, and challenging modern innovation and its inducements to consume. Parallel attention to the problems has been growing among designers (Tonkinwise 2014; Schultz 2016; Walker 2016) and indeed, my concept of the Modern Normal does align with how the design field has developed alongside industrialism. Social researchers such as geographers (Graham and Thrift 2007) and anthropologists (Martínez 2017, 2018; Schober and Eriksen 2017) have also increasingly contributed to the debate, helping to counter the technology-fetishism of the MN and arguing for the cultural nature of the problems. Thus, like this book, they support activist work. For instance, just to think about e-waste is to think about a multitude of networks and entailments that become concrete in everyday products designed for consumer comfort (Parikka 2016). Normally they are black-boxed and thus obscure and disavow links to anyone, anything or anywhere experiencing *dis*comfort. In reflecting on how things and values, material effect and cultural affect located here have consequences on lives far away, activists and academic researchers are often doing similar work. They are often the same people, but this overlap should not be overplayed.

Those of us still enjoying the privilege of research and educational jobs can contribute to the understanding as well as the practice of new forms of activism, particularly in the comfortable slot. But we need to take heed of our critics and ensure we are not just hanging out with people we like, or ignoring, or worse still judging, other modes of protest as populist. From my current engagement with design pedagogy and scholarship (as adjunct professor in a design department), and its impulse for world-improving projects, I sense potential for repurposing anthropology. The discipline's capacity to expand the imagination through ethnographic attentiveness might be even more valuable than we realise. Reaching outwards, it could go beyond offering anthropology as expertise on all that is exotic, something that designers and architects have been familiar with for over a century, since 'alternative' paths to dominant forms of industrialism were inspired by Europe's and North America's Others particularly. Anthropology could help to identify, assess and intervene in the extreme destructiveness of the cultural repertoire I have dubbed the Modern Normal, insisting on its oddity much like the new environmentalism alerts us to its destructiveness.

For repairing its damages will be far from straightforward. Anthropologists, educated in planet-embracing yet experience-near and historically situated analysis, may find it obvious that the idea (if not the reality) of modernity has always been rooted in concrete, often very comfortable and well-remunerated conditions. As Ortner's (2016) overview of recent anthropology shows, these days our discipline is particularly focused on counterbalancing an image of planetary reality where a 'Western' 'normal' prevails. Such anthropology re-establishes the links that others have cut, for instance from the extractive practices that produce harms, hopelessness and distresses and, as we are beginning to see, redundant or non-useful people or devastated, toxic landscapes. Always inventive and context-specific, resistance to this side of globalisation is inspiring to anthropologists who are putting it to use to develop both theoretical and real-world issues. One such real-world issue is the legitimacy or otherwise of protest by the overconsuming urban middle classes, the 'comfortable slot'.

Certainly that slot, in its unremarkable way, has produced unsustainability, created a mess (Fortun 2014), leaving in its wake breakage and endless combinations and recombinations of stuff that may or may not ever again be available for productive uses. No wonder many of us want to contribute to what Cameron Tonkinwise calls 'the project of transitioning our societies to less stuffed futures' (2014: 200). Following the editors and others who seek to highlight how the confidence, as well as the tangible experience, of modernity is coming apart, what I have argued is that this ethos is a response to inhabiting complex and overwhelming sociotechnical systems that 'creak, flex, and bend their way through time' (Jackson 2014: 223). It is a way of coping with an unholy mess that seeps across ontological categories into matter and affect.

Finally, let me defend the apparent vagueness of it all. The kinds of initiatives I have described, that connect ecologies, matter, politics and cultural preferences, could be framed as instances of environmentalism, alternative technology or social innovation, or even of design more generally, that show both great exuberance and lack of clear impact. If we frame it as a response to something like a cultural tradition – which would be implied in identifying modernity as the unmarked standard against which others have been measured – we can begin to see the 'modern normal' is utterly peculiar. As noted in the volume's introduction, brokenness is 'an offence against the neat and tidy . . . [it] foregrounds a misbehaviour, an error in the system, a defective piece in the gears'. By my model, that defect is now being identified as something – we don't know exactly what – in a whole package long taken to be unremarkable. It has been anything but.

Eeva Berglund is an Adjunct Professor of Environmental Policy at the Aalto School of Arts, Design and Architecture.

Notes

My sincere thanks to Francisco Martinez, Patrick Laviolette, Guy Julier and Cindy Kohtala and the many people in Helsinki whose ideas inform the ideas presented above, whether they are mentioned by name or not.

1. A Facebook group, 'More City for Helsinki' or 'Yimby Helsinki' has become quite an influential voice (https://www.facebook.com/groups/184085073617/, accessed 19 June 2019).

References

Berglund, Eeva. 1998. *Knowing Nature, Knowing Science: An Ethnography of Local Environmental Activism*. Cambridge: White Horse Press.

——. 2016. 'Impossible Maybe, Perhaps Quite Likely: Activist Design in Helsinki's Urban Wastelands', in P. Sparke and F. Fisher (eds), *The Routledge Companion to Design Studies*. London: Routledge, pp. 383–94.

——. 2017. 'Steering Clear of Politics: Local Virtues in Helsinki's Design Activism', *Journal of Political Ecology* 24: 566–80.

Berglund, E., and C. Kohtala. In press. 'Collaborative Confusion among Makers: Ethnography and Expertise in Creating Knowledge for Environmental Sustainability'. *Science & Technology Studies*, forthcoming.

Berlant, Lauren. 2007. 'Slow Death (Sovereignty, Obesity, Lateral Agency)', *Critical Inquiry* 33(4): 754–80.

Brulle, Robert J. and David N. Pellow. 2006. 'Environmental Justice: Human Health and Environmental Inequalities'. *Annual Review of Public Health* 27: 103–24.

Callén, Blanca, and Tomás Sánchez Criado. 2015. 'Vulnerability Tests: Matters of "Care for Matter" in E-Waste Practices', *Tecnoscienza* 6(2): 17–40.

Carrier, James G., and Don Kalb (eds). 2015. *Anthropologies of Class: Power, Practice, and Inequality*. Cambridge: Cambridge University Press.

Chatterton, Paul and Jenny Pickerill. 2010. 'Everyday Activism and Transitions Towards PostCapitalist Worlds'. *Transactions of the Institute of British Geographers* 35(4): 475-505.

Connolly, William. 2013. 'The "New Materialism" and the Fragility of Things', *Millennium: Journal of International Studies* 41(3): 399–412.

Escobar, Arturo. 2018. *Designs for the Pluriverse: Radical Interdependence, Autonomy, and the Making of Worlds*. Durham, NC: Duke University Press.

Fortun, Kim. 2014. 'From Latour to Late Industrialism', *HAU: Journal of Ethnographic Theory* 4(1): 309–29.

Fredericks, S.E. 2014. 'Online Confessions of Eco-Guilt', *Journal for the Study of Religion, Nature and Culture* 8(1): 64–84.

Graham, S., and N. Thrift. 2007. 'Out of Order: Understanding Repair and Maintenance', *Theory, Culture & Society* 24(3): 1–25.

Granjou, C., J. Walker, and J. Salazar. 2017. 'The Politics of Anticipation: On Knowing and Governing Environmental Futures', *Futures* 92: 5–11.
Jackson, Steven J. 2014. 'Rethinking Repair', in T. Gillespie, P.J. Boczkowski and K.A. Foot (eds), *Media Technologies*. Cambridge, MA: MIT Press, pp. 221–39.
Kohtala, C., and A. Paterson. 2015. 'Oxygen for Töölönlahti', in E. Berglund and C. Kohtala (eds), *Changing Helsinki? 11 Views on a City Unfolding*. Helsinki: Nemo, pp. 64–71.
Krøijer, Stine. 2015. 'Revolution Is the Way You Eat: Exemplification among Left Radical Activists in Denmark and in Anthropology', *Journal of the Royal Anthropological Institute* 21(S1): 78–95.
Latour, Bruno. 2004. 'Why Has Critique Run Out of Steam? From Matters of Fact to Matters of Concern', *Critical Inquiry* 30: 225–48.
Lenskjold, Tau Ulv, Olander Sissel and Joachim Halse. 2015. 'Minor Design Activism: Prompting Change from Within', *Design Issues* 31(4): 67–78.
Lettenmeier, M., C. Liedtke and H. Rohn. 2014. 'Eight Tonnes of Material Footprint: Suggestion for a Resource Cap for Household Consumption in Finland', *Resources* 3: 488–515.
Mustranta, Maria and Eeva Luhtakallio. 2017 *Demokratia Suomalaisessa Lähiössä*. Tampere: University of Tampere.
Martínez, Francisco. 2017. 'Waste Is Not the End: For an Anthropology of Care, Maintenance and Repair', *Social Anthropology* 25(3): 346–50.
——. 2019. 'Politics of Recuperation: An Introduction', in *Politics of Recuperation: Repair and Recovery in Post-Crisis Portugal*. London: Bloomsbury, in press.
Massey, Doreen. 2004. 'Geographies of Responsibility', *Geografiska Annaler: Series B, Human Geography* 86(1): 5–18.
Nemec, Saša. 2018. 'Trashlab and Its History'. Retrieved November 2018 from https://www.pixelache.org/posts/trashlab-and-its-history.
Ortner, Sherry B. 2016. 'Dark Anthropology and Its Others: Theory since the Eighties', *HAU: Journal of Ethnographic Theory* 6(1): 47–73.
Parikka, Jussi. 2016. 'Deep Times of Planetary Trouble'. *Cultural Politics* 12(3): 279-92.
Rajan, S. Ravi and Colin A.M. Duncan. 2013. 'Ecologies of Hope: Environment, Technology and Habitation – Case Studies from the Intervenient Middle', *Journal of Political Ecology* 20(1): 70–79.
Rantanen, Annuska and Maija Faehnle. 2017. 'Self-Organisation Challenging Institutional Planning: Towards a New Urban Research and Planning Paradigm – a Finnish Review', *Finnish Journal of Urban Studies* 55(3). Retrieved 15 March 2019 from http://www.yss.fi/yhdyskuntasuunnittelu-lehti/lehden-numerot/2017-3-vol-55/.
Robbins, Joel. 2013. 'Beyond the Suffering Subject: Toward an Anthropology of the Good Life', *Journal of the Royal Anthropological Institute* 19(3): 447–62.
Schlosberg, David and Romand Coles. 2016. 'The New Environmentalism of Everyday Life: Sustainability, Material Flows and Movements', *Contemporary Political Theory* 15(2): 160–81.
Schober, Elisabeth and Thomas Hylland Eriksen. 2017. 'Waste and the Superfluous: An Introduction', *Social Anthropology* 25(3): 282–87.
Schultz, Tristan. 2017. 'Design's Role in Transitioning to Futures of Cultures of Repair', in A. Chakrabarti and D. Chakrabarti (eds), *Research into Design for*

Communities, Volume 2: Proceedings of ICoRD 2017. Singapore: Springer, pp. 25–34.

Tonkinwise, Cameron. 2014. 'Design Away', in S. Yelavich and B. Adams (eds), *Design as Future Making*. London: Bloomsbury, pp. 198–213.

Trouillot, M.R. 1991. 'Anthropology and the Savage Slot: The Poetics and Politics of Otherness', in R. Fox (ed.), *Recapturing Anthropology: Working in the Present*. Santa Fe: School of American Research Press, 17–44.

Walker, Stuart. 2016. 'Design for Meaningful Innovation', in P. Sparke and F. Fisher (eds), *The Routledge Companion to Design Studies*. London: Routledge, pp. 395–408.

SNAPSHOT 10

Why Stories about Broken-Down Snowmobiles Can Teach You a Lot about Life in the Arctic Tundra

Aimar Ventsel

It was the end of October 2016, and for the first time in fifteen years I was in the Anabarskii district, located in the northwestern corner of the Republic of Sakha (Yakutia), the biggest territorial unit of the Russian Federation. In 2000–2001, I had spent almost a year in the district collecting data for my dissertation (Ventsel 2005, 2007). The district is located in the Arctic tundra zone and borders the Arctic Ocean in the north. The indigenous population lives in two villages, and are mainly reindeer herders and Dolgan and Evenki hunters. A few incoming Sakha work in village administration whereas the small Russian population usually works in the district's airport or in the diamond mines. All together, the district has approximately four thousand inhabitants and the majority of them (circa 2,500 people) live in the district's centre, in a village called Saskylakh. This time I was accompanied by a local scholar, an indigenous Evenki who comes from a reindeer herding family. Our goal was to visit different reindeer brigades in the tundra, spend some time in a small village called Popigai and return to Saskylakh and observe what has changed since new laws for reindeer herding and hunting were introduced in the Republic of Sakha.

In order to follow our plan, my colleague hired two local hunters, brothers, called Afonia and Valeri. On the first evening, we went to visit them. The hunters lived in a three-storey building, in a typical bachelor apartment – it was minimally furnished, the floor was covered with spare parts of a snowmobile, and hunting clothes and rifles hung on the walls. As it turned out, it was Afonia's flat and his brother, who permanently lived in another district, was visiting him to help out in the hunting season.

When we arrived, both hunters were cutting reindeer intestines and preparing a meal from them. After a while we sat down to eat and Afonia told us that we would have to wait a few days because he must repair his snowmobile. He had recently returned from a hunting trip and had to sell his hunting kill of a few reindeer and trade some Arctic fox furs. We were discussing the new hunting laws and how people worked around them and I noticed that the hunting economy had changed since I last visited the village. Most of the men who used to hunt were now engaged with fishing, and only occasionally hunted. The reasons are manifold: the new strict laws, falling meat prices, and increasing salaries in the village for the women, who had a steady income compared to the men.

Suddenly Afonia announced his problem with snowmobiles. 'When I was on a hunting trip in April, the snowmobile broke down in a snowstorm. I had to walk around the snowmobile for five days in order not to freeze, and when the snowstorm was over I went to the road, found a truck that brought me to the village.' When I asked how he managed to walk around his snowmobile for so many days, he chuckled and said: 'You don't want to freeze to death, do you?' He told us that it was not for the first time – last year the lights of his snowmobile broke during a snowstorm, so he had to wait for six days until the storm was over. By walking around his vehicle, of course.

Later, when visiting old friends, I discovered that the 'snowmobile revolution' (Pelto and Müller-Wille 1987) was in full sway in the district. While earlier most men had one or two snowmobiles, it was now common to have three or more, with at least one for the summer period. Riding the snowmobile during the summer months was something new for me because I knew that summer riding breaks the vehicles quickly due to the sand that can get into the machinery. Also, the local men now preferred imported Yamaha snowmobiles to the Russian Buran ones. Again, I heard stories of how snowmobiles break down and how expensive it is to maintain or repair them.

Currently Russia is the only Arctic country where one can encounter professional hunters who earn their main income from hunting wild animals. Stories of broken snowmobiles reflect some aspects of life in the country. First of all, indigenous people – as demonstrated by David Anderson (2006) – are eager to reach a level of comfortability offered by the modern world, and adopt, without hesitation, new tools and practices that make their life easier. This is the reason for owning several snowmobiles and driving them all year round. When commercial hunting and fishing are regarded as 'wage gathering' (Bird 1983), the fact that a big part of the hunter's income goes on spare parts and fuel impacts on the subsistence hunting life. According to my sources, the main financial supporters are in Saskylakh, and in fact are the women who work in schools, local administration, kindergartens or the village hospital. The men are hunting or fishing in order pay for snowmobiles, fuel and spare parts, which they now rely on in order to hunt and fish. Owning a snowmobile produces negligible extra value, yet even this small additional income is needed to feed a family in a remote village with high unemployment.

The existence of the hunting economy in the Russian North shows that the state is unable to create other work in its remote Arctic settlements. As my Evenki colleague from Yakutsk commented on the lifestyle in Saskylakh: 'Life here is like in the 1950s!' Saskylakh is a village without running water and canalisation, where most men need to go to the tundra in order to provide fish and meat for their families. In Russia, there has been a discussion about modernising the Arctic villages and establishing better connections to the 'outside world' but currently these villages seem to be more remote than fifteen years ago. Owning several snowmobiles is a necessity and paradoxically a luxury. On the one hand, snowmobiles make the subsistence economy more efficient; on the other hand, this form of economy is very costly, because snowmobiles must be replaced relatively quickly and broken ones can be used as sources for spare parts.

Figure S10.1. Snowmobile on the tundra. Photograph by Aimar Ventsel.

When an old friend borrowed a snowmobile from one of his brothers and fuel from another to show me around, I wrote in my diary that the snowmobile is not just private property but also provides security and income for the whole extended family. Snowmobiles can be a fragile instrument in a harsh climate where human life is precarious. I understood it again when I took off for the tundra with my colleague, Afonia and Valeri. On the first night a snowmobile broke down and we had to repair it in the freezing cold with a rising snowstorm. I observed how skilfully the hunters repaired the broken engine with the tools they had at hand. Due to the snowstorm and the repair time we lost our way, had to spend a night in the tundra and borrow spare parts from a reindeer herders' camp. The reindeer herders were relatives of our hunters, so the circle of people responsible for keeping vehicles intact was extended. Now I have my own story of a breakage, and I am also aware that repair is not that far from survival.

Aimar Ventsel is Senior Researcher in the Department of Ethnology, University of Tartu.

Note

This research was supported by the institutional research funding IUT34-32 ('Cultural heritage as a socio-cultural resource and contested field') of the Estonian Ministry of Education and Research.

References

Anderson, David. 2006. 'Dwellings, Storage and Summer Site Structures among Siberian Orochen Evenkis: Hunter-Gatherer Vernacular Architecture under Post-Socialist Conditions', *Norwegian Archaeological Review* 39(1): 1–26.

Bird, Nurit H. 1983. 'Wage-Gathering: Socio-economic Changes and the Case of the Naikens of South India', in P. Robb (ed.), *Rural South Asia: Linkages, Change and Development*. London: Curzon, pp. 75–87.

Pelto, Pertti J., and L. Müller-Wille. 1987. 'Snowmobiles: Technological Revolution in the Arctic', in R. Bernard and P. Pelto (eds), *Technology and Social Change*. Prospect Heights, NY: Waveland, pp. 208–41.

Ventsel, Aimar. 2005. *Reindeer, Rodina and Reciprocity: Kinship and Property Relations in a Siberian Village*. Berlin: LIT Verlag.

——. 2007. 'Pride, Honour, Individual and Collective Violence: Order in a "Lawless" Village', in K.V. Benda-Beckmann and F. Pirie (eds), *Order and Disorder: Anthropological Perspectives*. Oxford: Berghahn Books, 34–53.

CHAPTER 10

The Imperative of Repair

Fixing Bikes – for Free

SIMON BATTERBURY AND TIM DANT

Introduction

This chapter discusses how we can interrupt the cycle of consumption and disposal to reuse a relatively simple and ubiquitous item – the bicycle. We compare two projects that are non-commercial, community-based and involve volunteers who recycle, redistribute and assist with the repair of bicycles. The first is a project that repairs donated bikes and gives them to asylum seekers and refugees who have moved into an urban area. The repair of lives broken by the disruption of seeking refuge in another country is being helped with the life-enhancing mobility of a bicycle. The second is a network of community bike workshops open to anybody, which help owners to keep their bikes on the road by teaching maintenance skills (Batterbury and Vandermeersch 2016). Being able to repair their bike frees the user from having to pay and wait for a professional service to recover their velomobility. Both types of project operate at the margins of the system of capitalist production and consumption in which bicycles are originally manufactured. Both counter the tendency of advanced industrialised societies towards consuming new replacement goods rather than repairing the broken.

The bicycle is a cheap and uncomplicated means of transport that when in working order needs nothing other than the application of human energy to enable the seated rider to travel much faster over longer distances than the upright pedestrian. For more than a century this basic machine has enabled individual people to move about their environment as and when they wish. There has, however, been a significant decline in cycling as car ownership has increased all over the world (Parkin, Ryley and Jones 2007). In the UK, the proportion of all journeys by bicycle fell from 37 per cent in 1949 to 1 per cent in 2000, despite sales of bicycles continuing to be two and a half times those of cars (Horton, Rosen and Cox 2007). Whether or not to cycle for transport utility is linked to personal identity, the roads one has to ride on and the distances to work and shops (Skinner and Rosen 2007). There is also a suggestion that, in the US at least, cycling is an inverse marker of social status. As Gilroy points out, a car culture can distinguish a minority group from less fortunate groups living 'within the veil of scarcity defined ... by the alternative transit order of the bicycle' (2001: 102).

One aspect of taking responsibility is to repair and reuse the things we have. In doing so, we learn how they are made, what materials they use and how their useful life can be extended (Graham and Thrift 2007; Gregson, Metcalfe and Crewe 2009; Houston 2013). Bicycles, while simple machines, require maintenance and occasional repair. Cycling is a sustainable, non-carbon-generating mode of transport. Repairing a bicycle enhances the mobility of the user, engages her or him with how and what it is made from and how its useful life can be extended to save the energy and raw materials needed to replace it. When someone voluntarily helps to overcome its brokenness, it is an act of kindness and care between those with skills and the bicycle user. The material interaction between the experienced repairer and the bicycle mediates a social relationship of care with the user of the bike, responding to both the material disorder of the machine and the practical disorder in the life of the cyclist.

We will explore the role of people who voluntarily undertake or assist in bike repair and respond to what philosopher Hans Jonas calls the 'imperative of responsibility' to care both for people and the consequences of technological progress. Jonas recognised that the costs of technological progress are not primarily felt by the individual user or consumer but as risks to the future of humanity. The depletion of natural resources – energy and raw materials – along with environmental degradation are consequences that threaten all humanity. In response to the trajectory of technological innovation in the twentieth century, Jonas revised Kant's categorical imperative to give a new moral imperative of taking responsibility for our material lives: 'Act so that the effects of your action are compatible with the permanence of genuine human life' (Jonas 1984: 11). Jonas argues that our first responsibility is to other human beings, including those not yet born, but his 'imperative of responsibility' is also directed at technological progress. The development of technology cannot be reversed, and indeed we need it to manage the environmental effects of existing technologies, but we can take responsibility for it, understanding its consequences, accounting for our use of it.

Two Cases

The first example of taking responsibility, the 'refugee bike project', is based in a northern city in the United Kingdom where both authors have been repairers and have been able to undertake autoethnography and participant observation. The project repairs and maintains donated bikes for use by asylum seekers and refugees. The second example comes from Brussels, where one author (SB) was based in 2015, researching 'community bike workshops' (CBWs). In the workshops, volunteers help members to repair their bikes using components recovered from bikes broken beyond repair, discarded from local bike shops or bought in bulk. Their focus is on promoting *vélonomie* ('becoming an autonomous cyclist'), confidence and pride in doing one's own bike maintenance, as well as cycling confidently on the urban streets. A loose network of repair workshops also forms part of the urban non-profit sector, promoting grassroots actions to address severe pollution and promoting sustainable transport.

These non-commercial approaches to recycling bicycles share a number of features that we will draw attention to: donations, socio-material networks, cross-cultural engagements, and material practices including hand tool work and material cannibalism. Volunteers are motivated by a caring ethic to provide working bicycles to those who need them, through minimal use of 'new' materials and consumed objects. They participate in networks that donate bicycles, scavenge spare parts, work in free or cheap temporary premises, link with other supporting networks and support those who lack resources and skills themselves.

The Mechanics of the Bicycle

In advanced industrialised societies, we are less likely than people in the past to make or maintain the things we use. Production and consumption have been separated by de-industrialisation, and manufacturing now takes place closer to raw materials or where labour is cheap. In a global process of social stratification, those who consume are seldom those who produce. The advancing technical sophistication of domestic objects, vehicles and information technology has created many everyday material goods that are less amenable to repair and maintenance. The consumer culture driving their distribution has meant that replacement appears cheaper than repair; it brings a 'new' object, with the most recent technological innovations, the latest styling and a manufacturer's guarantee against short-term failure.

The bicycle as a machine resists this tendency. It has been around for well over a century. Its form is of two equally sized wheels, a chain driving the rear wheel from pedals rotating a gear wheel through cranks, with the front wheel being steerable via handlebars.[1] The position of the rider in relation to the wheels and pedals is fundamentally determined by the standard shape of the adult human body, which is why the mechanical form has remained so consistent.[2] The bicycle is a fundamentally straightforward machine; the operation of the mechanical components and how they relate to each other can be studied in use (although it is easiest if the bike is suspended on a stand and not actually moving). Most of the machine is visible and its workings available for scrutiny – a very few components, such as wheels, steering and bottom bracket bearings, are hidden from view (Dant forthcoming). The bicycle is uncomplicated compared to the motor car, which has gears hidden inside a gearbox, suspension underneath the bodywork, brakes hidden behind or even inside the wheels, engines enclosed in metal casing and nowadays a host of electrical and electronic controls interacting with all the mechanical components. The bicycle is straightforward to work on and its components very light. Replacing a gearbox in a car requires the vehicle to be jacked up high enough to be wheeled underneath and then jacked up itself until it can be attached with difficult-to-get-at bolts (Dant 2010). The bicycle's gear cassette fits easily within a hand and is slid onto the freewheel hub with one threaded fixing – albeit one that requires a special tool.

The simplicity, consistency of mechanical design, visibility of operations and accessibility of components makes the bicycle a relatively easy machine to maintain and repair. It requires little skill, few tools and minimal space or time. And yet many bicycle riders shy away from engaging with the workings of the machine that gets them to work, to the shops or to a day in the countryside. Repair still has a gendered quality; men are more likely to feel they should have a go, women much less so. But plenty of men don't want to get their hands dirty mending a puncture or cleaning the accumulated grease and dirt off a drivetrain (Dant and Bowles 2003). The machinery of bicycles does have a limited life, and cheap components last for a shorter time than good-quality ones. The most expensive components (gears, brakes, wheels and so on) are made to be light as well as strong, but mid-priced components are adequate for all but the aspiring racer. The cheapest, poor-quality components are usually unbranded, heavier and produced for new budget-priced bicycles. These look much the same as more expensive ones, but they are harder to ride, will wear more quickly and are more difficult to adjust and to maintain. And because the cheap unbranded componentry is often made to be sold directly to the bicycle manufacturer, it can be difficult to replace and standard components may not fit so easily.

The reluctance of many bike owners to maintain their bicycles, combined with the purchase of cheap bikes, mean that many are not used once they begin to require attention. They are left in cellars, garages and sheds and sometimes outside in a yard. The owners may buy a new bike, or they may just find other ways to get about. They may promise themselves that they will 'do up' that bike in the shed and get it back to the condition it was in when they bought it. But it is a daunting and unappealing task, so eventually they dispose of the bike. Some bikes will be given to friends or family members, but in any local council recycling centre you will see discarded bicycles. In 2018, the media reported how Chinese cities were impounding thousands of abandoned bikes that were clogging city streets, having been supplied by bike share schemes in excess of demand (Taylor 2018). Bicycles with visible signs of rust and with major bits missing are thrown into skips, but some – usually the better-quality bikes – will have been picked out by the recyclers at the centre as worth something. Another way of disposing of a bike is to give it to a recycling project. Some of these projects are commercial, acquiring bikes for free (e.g. through police authorities, universities, train stations) that have been abandoned, and then repairing them before selling them on. Such businesses may be 'not-for-profit' but use the income to pay workers and cover expenses.[3]

The Refugee Project

City of Sanctuary is a British NGO that offers help to people fleeing violence and persecution. They welcome and support asylum seekers and refugees who are temporarily rehoused in the area. Asylum seekers and refugees are distributed throughout the country and throughout the city; the policy is not to establish concentrations that might attract attention from those who do not approve of them being supported and allowed to live in the UK. However, having the use of a bicycle allows these precariously positioned people, who have very little money, to visit shops, attend English classes and visit each other. In some cases, bicycles are how their children get to school.[4]

The Bicycles

The project lends donated and repaired bicycles to these household groups of asylum seekers and refugees. At the time of writing, around 150 bicycles have been distributed, with more in preparation. Bicycles are usually shared within a household of four or five people and are difficult to keep track of as they are lent between groups and sometimes taken away from the city. The project began with bicycles donated by volunteers and friends linked to the City of Sanctuary. The word circulated through voluntary and religious groups that there was a need for more, and this has maintained a flow of bicycles into the project of different types: road bikes, mountain bikes, hybrids, shopping bikes and children's bikes. Early on, there were a large number of single men who needed bikes and fewer single women, many of whom were inexperienced riders. Later, a project linked to the arrival of families led to a need for bicycles for teenagers and young children.

The bikes being worked on were mainly between ten and twenty years old, with componentry that had been standard for the time of production. Most bikes that were donated were dirty and had flat tyres. Many of the bikes were originally quite cheap and had not been maintained well – or at least not recently. Bikes also came with worn brakes, frayed brake cable ends, poorly adjusted gears, loose bearings and attachments for no-longer-working components (e.g. bike lights, computers, reflectors, racks etc.). The dirt was sometimes covering up rust and sometimes was mixed with grease and oil, especially on chains and gear cogs. Some bicycles had damaged or missing essential components such as saddles, brake levers, pedals and so on. An online spreadsheet was used to keep track of the bikes – where they were, the type of bike, colour, frame number and notes on the work undertaken on them. Photos of the bikes were kept in a shared file. The spreadsheet was also used to keep notes on repairs that needed doing and expenditure on parts.

The Repairers

The team of active repairers began with just a couple of people but grew a little to a core of five, with three or four others joining in or providing particular support (e.g. locating used parts) on the periphery. The material interaction (Dant 2005) between individual repairers and their own bicycles meant they had self-taught to a certain level of skill and confidence, sometimes over many years. Most had learnt techniques and procedures from family members, friends, repair books and more recently from videos and articles on the internet; much of such learning was on a trial-and-error basis. Coming together in a group repair session to work on unfamiliar bikes that would be used by other people provided new opportunities for developing skills through sharing experiences and advice. In a convivial social atmosphere, repairers asked each other about techniques, tools and materials. Group members would, for example, discuss with others whether a brake cable that had begun to corrode and so not move freely in its 'outer' sleeve could be cleaned and greased or whether it needed to be replaced. Tools, hand creams and lubricants were shared along with techniques and informal checking of work. One member of the group had experience of teaching bike maintenance and earning money from maintaining and repairing bikes, but the others were 'amateurs'. Ages of group members varied from teens to late sixties and this gave a breadth of experience of different eras of bike engineering. Most of the core repairers were male, but one consistent repairer was a woman and a couple of other women joined in repairing from time to time. Decisions about when to repair or when to scavenge useable parts and dispose of the remainder were usually made by two or three repairers.

One technology enabled another. A Facebook site was set up early on that linked the repairers and some of the City of Sanctuary volunteers supporting asylum seekers and refugees. This network of more than thirty people not only identified a particular need for bicycles, it also organised donations. The Facebook site was used to arrange repair sessions where two or more repairers got together to undertake repairs. The communication through Facebook was supplemented with emails, instant messaging and occasional phone calls. There was no hierarchy among the project workers and no special roles, although one person who had been a volunteer in the parent support organisation tended to act as a 'go-between' with the households of asylum seekers and refugees.

Social Networks

There were three overlapping social networks: volunteers in the City of Sanctuary; bike repairers; and asylum seekers and refugees. The networks overlapped as individuals from one group interacted with individuals from another, but there were no occasions when the networks were formally connected. The bicycles provided the principal link between them. City of Sanctuary volunteers offered donations of bikes, passed on requests for bikes or reported repairs that were needed. Repairers sometimes visited households to deliver or repair bikes, but often the bikes moved between repairers and users via a store where users could also collect bike locks, helmets and lights. A feature of this project was that the users were from overseas and many came from cultures that did not routinely use bikes. A number of the users had to learn to ride a bicycle for the first time and few had any experience of maintaining bikes. As the refugee project progressed, it accessed some local authority funds to run sessions for small groups to learn riding skills and bike maintenance.

Locations

Early repair sessions were held in a backyard where some bikes and bike parts had been collected. Repairers also worked in spaces adjacent to their homes (garages, yards, cellars). The advantage of this was that repairing bikes could be fitted around paid, domestic and other work, and personal tool sets were ready to hand. The cellar of a cooperative food shop was made available for storing donated bikes waiting for repair and repaired bikes waiting to be collected by users. Two members of the cooperative helped with handing over bikes and distributing helmets, locks and lights. Later, an old boat-building shed, repaired by another community group, was used for repair sessions and for storing bikes and used parts. This shed had other uses, some of which required the removal of all the bikes, parts and tools. A second space became available in a covered yard with a lockable cupboard and permanent bike stand, but here space, especially for storing bikes, was limited.

Material Practices

The main focus was on getting bikes rideable and roadworthy and much of the repair work undertaken in the project was routine and mundane: mending punctures, replacing brake shoes, adjusting brakes, adjusting gears, lubricating moving parts and removing redundant fittings. Tyres and tubes were often a source of problems because where a bike had been left resting on flat tyres, the tyre walls were often damaged and the inner tubes were perishing. Although inner tubes could be repaired and tyres pumped up, worn tyres and tubes that were vulnerable to puncture meant they failed soon after. Replacing spokes, truing wheels and repacking bearings were tasks that came up occasionally but were not routine.

The repairers tended to use their own tools at home and bring them to joint sessions. Many bike tools are specific (e.g. cone spanners, removal tools for cranks, freewheels, cassettes, chain links) and using a bike stand makes working on a bike much easier. As the project progressed, a bike stand and various tools, including specialist bike tools, were donated. Early in the project, components such as inner tubes, spokes and brake pads were purchased as they were needed. The parent project had some funding and was able to reimburse expenditure on spare parts and on helmets, lights and locks for the riders. As the repair project developed, it built up a stock of recycled components from donated bikes that were no longer useable: brakes, cranks, chainsets, handlebars, saddles and seatposts, cables, nuts, bolts, pedals and so forth. These scavenged items were stored in plastic boxes so they could be used on other bikes. The discarded frames – rusty beyond use, bent or broken – were taken to the recycling centre, as were any discarded metal components.

Community Bike Workshops in Brussels

The collective repair of bicycles has seen a significant upsurge in Western countries since the 1990s, when a new phenomenon, the 'community bike workshop', emerged. CBWs are a self-help alternative to bike shops. Their origins included the 'Bikes not Bombs' movement in 1970s USA, and various community ventures in Europe that had a strong social support focus or an activist basis (Carlsson 2007). They are 'do it yourself' responses, a form of 'urban commons' where people come to repair their bikes, source second-hand and scavenged parts, and learn maintenance skills (Nixon and Schwanen 2019). Almost all are not-for-profits relying on volunteers to assist the visitors to learn repair skills, though a few have paid staff, and they are based in cheap or free premises. All try to contribute to sustainable transport through the transmission of bike repair skills, although they have diverse political leanings. In France, this type of skill acquisition is termed *vélonomie*, or the creation of a self-sufficient or autonomous bicycle citizen capable of riding safely and keeping their own bike maintained. Workshops are generally open to all, many having a fee structure (perhaps 10–20 euros a year membership or pay-per-visit). Workshops are 'demand side' operations – increasing demand for cheap and low-carbon-emitting transportation regardless of the participants' social status or identity, rather than 'supplying' new urban cycle lanes and infrastructure. They are therefore outside the state, or sometimes against the state.

Interviews were conducted in Brussels, Belgium in community bike workshops and among transport organisations for ten weeks in 2014–15, posing questions about their mission, participation, premises and links to mainstream organisations (Batterbury and Vandermeersch 2016). Simon Batterbury researched and participated in workshops, as an outsider but as part of the first academic exploration of the operation and socioeconomic contributions of community bike workshops worldwide.[5] Brussels had thirteen workshops operating in 2015; one closed, but the number had expanded to nineteen by 2018. Workshops are not only a site for repair, they also house discussion and networking around cycling and bicycle use. The city's bike enthusiasts fight against pervasive automobility, in a city where cycling forms only 4 per cent of the daily traffic.

Brussels' economic success coexists with social polarisation (Oosterlynck 2012). Some neighbourhoods and households suffer a considerable level of disadvantage. The city is also a refuge for many asylum seekers and immigrants without legal status, who frequent bike workshops. Aside from skilled and often temporary expatriate workers, the city has substantial populations of Italians, Spanish, Turkish, Moroccans and Congolese, some being descendants of guest workers in manufacturing who came to Belgium in earlier decades. Bikes are an affordable form of transport for many individuals across society.

Bikes and Parts

In Brussels, bike workshops are relatively popular. The 'stock' bike circulating in the city is a functional commuter bike, quite heavy and usually with gears to help with hilly terrain. Some bikes were sourced from local councils or donated by people in the vicinity, some from the transient international population of Brussels. A particular feature was that several bike shops were on good terms with the workshops and offered them crashed bikes, part-worn tyres and other components that they did not need. But there were occasionally shortages of spare parts in workshops. New items like brake cables were purchased from the (usually limited) workshop funds. Used bikes were sometimes broken down and the parts classified and sorted into receptacles. This is an essential feature of a workshop where members of the public are present during repair sessions, and there is a high turnover of parts and a potential for confusion. Classification of parts certainly aids repair work, although some workshops were neater than others. Another reason to strip down and classify parts is because the workshops often have uncertain tenure in their premises and could be forced to move. Tools stayed in the workshop and were sourced second-hand, occasionally new, and sometimes from the numerous small community grants available in the city.

The Repairers

Workshops tend to be staffed by people who are – largely – cycling enthusiasts and community development practitioners, similar to the 'refugee project' in the UK. They, and the workshop customers and their bikes, are all 'participants' in the unique social field/task group of the workshop, which combines camaraderie with practical actions and pedagogy. As one organiser says of their workshop, 'It's a tiny village in the middle of the city'. Because most workshop volunteers make their living in paid work or are students, hours of operation can be limited, often to evenings and weekends.

Even in the world of volunteer-run community enterprises, a desire to tinker around with bikes must be accompanied by basic management skills to connect the workshop to utilities, manage keys, pay bills, order a few new spare parts at bulk prices, check that rosters have volunteers (without which the workshop cannot open) and complete annual accounts if they are registered as non-profit organisations. This falls to the major workshop organisers and requires innovation on the job, since few have prior administrative experience (just one had this training). There were also two semi-professionalised workshops with paid staff, one with a subsidy from a university, and both had 'stand fees' and higher costs for parts (Vandermeersch 2015). Volunteers, largely but not exclusively male, are key for directing citizen and community engagement and the division of essential tasks like stripping down bikes to create a stock of parts. Four workshops had written rules to which volunteers must adhere when on the premises, concerning the handling of tools and dealing with clients. Formalised internal policies are more common in North American bike workshops.

Among the forty-four mechanics known to be volunteering in the thirteen workshops in mid 2015, only one was a paid bike shop mechanic beyond his workshop participation and five in total had full training in bike repair. Some learned their mechanical skills in Points Vélos (repair stations in major train stations, run by the Belgian NGO, CyCLO). Some volunteers work across more than one workshop. Even when they are worn thin, interviewees expressed a passion for being a part of the workshop project: 'I love working here, I'm in love with this workshop', said one ('j'adore faire *ça* ici, cet atelier, je suis amoureux de cet atelier').

Those mechanics who regard the bike as an education tool operate rather like teachers. They are patient with the customers, showing them how to do mechanical tasks, but they also expect punctuality and confidence among the other volunteers. The idea is to teach, not to take over. This skill is hard-won and one training exercise we heard about tied the volunteer mechanics' hands lightly behind their backs, to force them to explain maintenance to customers rather than taking it over. In the community sector, the skills and knowledge of those moved to participate can be variable. Professionalism can be uneven among volunteers – sticking with a tricky repair (like assisting with rebuilding a wheel) or seeing a repair task through to completion can be demanding. Brussels has a long tradition of countercultural protest and alternative politics, and urban radicals – particularly those opposing car culture – congregate in bike workshops. Because of this image, and despite the diversity of reasons why workshop users visit them, members of the public without much knowledge of transport politics may consider a workshop to be an unwelcoming space. Social media can reinforce, or dispel, a radical image.

Very few women in Belgium are trained bike mechanics and Brussels is no exception. Women are present in bike shops and Belgium's many competitive cycling teams, but workshops are not equally staffed or patronised. There were three women mechanics in Brussels among forty-four surveyed by Inès Vandermeersch (2015). These three felt welcomed in their workshops, developing mechanical skills among a male-dominated fraternity. Among the workshop clients, women are a minority too.[6]

Social Networks

There was talk in Brussels of 'scaling up' and 'federating' workshop activity. A broader coalition of organisations aiming to get more people mechanically competent and onto bikes would seem sensible. Workshop organisers are already active in broader pro-cycling initiatives. These include the monthly Critical Mass rides (Masse Critique or Vélorution), the Clean Air BXL anti-air pollution campaign,[7] and Cyclehack BXL, which is part of a global movement to enable grassroots design solutions for problems facing urban cyclists.[8] Bike workshops are seen as practical spaces for addressing social problems too. They partner other community-minded individuals and organisations. Nurturing key local contacts strengthens the capacity of each workshop to temper disagreements stemming from socio-cultural and age differences among participants and users. In terms of wider links, the Cycloperativa workshop, in an Arab neighbourhood, best illustrates the importance of developing and maintaining good relations with the community and its own social organisations.[9] While the mechanics enjoy their participation in the workshop, it has a particular aim to act 'for and with' (*pour et avec*) local people.[10]

Locations

As community-based non-profits, true community workshops have very little money for premises. A few workshops globally, such as Working Bikes in Chicago and the Bicycle Kitchen/Bicicocina in Los Angeles, own their building, but this is rare. Across Europe, workshops find space in squatted or borrowed premises, in buildings awaiting planning permits for redevelopment, or in spaces offered or subsidised by local or regional government. If there are genuine commercial rents to meet, this means earning enough revenue to cover these costs, and the only place to do this is through refurbishing and selling bikes, or charging for services. This can conflict with the 'repair' mission of serving the local population in a particular neighbourhood if that population is very low-income.

Brussels workshops have major difficulties in securing premises on anything other than precarious terms. Several, like Cycloperativa in Annessens, have an attachment to places (the *quartier*) and people. However, they were forced to move in 2015 and again in 2017. The stock of tools, bikes, and work benches and stands were relocated each time by volunteers with cargo bikes, first to a derelict shop and later to a unit with a local government subsidy. Such relocations are seen as part of the life of a workshop that serves a community while keeping costs very low. One mechanic said that 'to begin, and to maintain continuity, you must have a workshop, a place to work, in the neighbourhood. Without that it just isn't possible' (quoted in Vandermeersch 2015: 40). One of the most spacious workshops in Brussels is 123Velo, which is situated on the ground floor of a squatted former government building with an intentional community above it that supports and uses the workshop. It began as the effort of one individual in 2008 but has grown significantly over the last ten years. Its customers come from many countries, with different racial backgrounds, and speak several languages.

A respondent whose workshop had been forced to move twice listed the negative repercussions of working in temporary spaces: the chaos of moving, the loss of some local supporters and visitors from the immediate locality and even some volunteers. But workshops operate very differently from bike shops in this regard; they can get by with out-of-the-way locations and unattractive premises, as long as there is sufficient room to stage repair sessions and store a stock of bikes and parts securely. Interviewees made it clear that to contribute to community development and social cohesion, 'you must stay there, in the neighbourhood, or you lose support' ('Il faut rester à la, à la mesure du quartier, aussi non on le perd'). None of the workshops sought better premises just to expand; the quest was for stability, not profile or position. Above all, workshops want to remain accessible to the general public and in a building that makes this possible.

Each workshop has its own feel, though there are common spatial elements across them. Aside from stacks of junk bikes and some repaired for sale, there are working spaces and collections of stripped-down parts in tins, drawers and diverse receptacles. Tools are accessible and usually available to visitors rather than jealously managed. The more established workshops have sofas, a fridge and a place to make hot drinks. Electricity is necessary for evening activities. Running water and some heating is desirable, but a full set of utilities is not required for the limited opening hours that some workshops maintain. Several are wired for sound and internet.

Discussion

The two types of projects discussed in this chapter have key differences. In the refugee project, the bikes were repaired by volunteers and were effectively owned by the project. In the community bike workshops, in contrast, the bikes were owned by individuals who undertook their repair with the help of volunteers. Social interaction differed between repairers and users. Nonetheless, there were similarities between the projects.

Premises. Appropriate buildings and their accessibility haunt the voluntary sector and bike workshop activity in particular. Repair is materially located somewhere; while it can happen in private locations, this is isolating, and in Brussels almost impossible in a city of small living spaces and apartments. The workshops are a social space, sometimes with luxuries like armchairs and stereos. In both projects everything had to be moved from place to place when one premises had to be exchanged for another. Also, access to water, light, heat and electricity were limited and sometimes absent.

Social networks. Communication and socialisation during the shared practice of repair lead to new social bonds, friendship and mutual respect, as people get to know each other. In the contexts we have described, there were few skilled and trained individuals, so technique is learned, and certainly improved, not through formal training or instruction but on the job, in what Paul Richards (2010) calls the 'task group'. The task group is the loose network of volunteers bringing their accumulated repair skills to the workshop and then sharing and developing them as a group, around repair. Once established, the network of repairers developed into a new social group with its own shared interests and means of communication that then connected with other groups and activities (bicycle users, other volunteer organisations, political interests, leisure interests and so on) through the medium of the bicycle. Connections with outside groups are sustained by the efforts of individuals and there are stratifications within the repair group if decision-making is done by an 'inner' group rather than the occasional volunteers. And, of course, there can be occasional unpleasant behaviour, such as sexism, which contradicts the shared ethos of helping others through bicycles.

Value. A common feature of both projects was the absence of commercial valuation of the work and the artefacts. Neither the work nor the material of the bicycle is paid for; exchange of things and human effort is 'free', in the monetary sense. While spare parts were 'scavenged' wherever possible from bikes deemed unrepairable and available for cannibalisation, some parts do have to be purchased from ordinary outlets. The repairers in the refugee project used contacts to get discounts from local shops and consumer skills in purchasing parts online for the best price. The community bike workshops collaborated in acquiring and sharing some spare parts. In the refugee project, a small number of donated bicycles were sold on the second-hand market when it was agreed by the team (with the consent of the previous owner) that the bike was not suitable for use by refugees or asylum seekers. The money made from these transactions was recycled into the purchase of spare parts (e.g. brake shoes, cables, inner tubes). The repairers were keenly aware that selling bicycles was a deviation from the core aims and values of their group. Hence, the social activity and the material exchange of this type of repair activity largely took place outside the circuits of the conventional capitalist economy. The work and the material performance of the repaired bicycle is valued by individuals in terms of pleasure in riding and in being able to use the bicycle for transport. This valuation is expressed back into the repair network in terms of thanks and appreciation.

Skills. The repairers in both projects enjoyed the deployment of their repair skills; demonstrating know-how and applying it to achieve 'rideability' was a satisfaction in itself. The material interaction – the meaningful interaction between the repairer and the material stuff of the bicycle, tools and components – provides this satisfaction and pleasure to varying degrees. But the social interaction in both projects enhanced the experience of volunteers as well as their skills and capacity, working together, sharing skills and techniques, demonstrating, discussing and comparing enhanced learning, and getting pleasure from the experience (Richards 2010). In the refugee project, the amateurs enjoyed coming together in repair sessions and the community bike workshops brought novices and experienced volunteers together. Coming across difficult or unusual repairs provided a challenge and an opportunity for sharing skills. For example, in the refugee project, a bike with a missing seatpost had been damaged by a previous owner trying to insert one of the wrong size. A collaborative effort by three repairers using different techniques and 'bricolage' with adapted tools succeeded in reshaping the downtube enough to enable a correct-sized seatpost and collar to be fitted.

Conclusions

Our autoethnography and participant observation of bicycle repair reveals some new and some well-worn insights about social engagement with technology. While technology involves artefacts (tools, machines and processes), it also involves technique – 'knowing how to do something' (Richards 2010: 1). This is knowledge of a process or thing, applied in practice rather than as abstract or systematic knowledge. None of the repairers we encountered had been formally taught how to undertake repair work on bicycles, except for a tiny number of trained mechanics volunteering their time in Brussels. Rather, individuals were self-taught through pragmatic interaction and experimentation with bicycles that needed attention (Dant

2008). In Belgium, the workshop volunteers promote *vélonomie*, while also socialising among, and on, a bicycle as an artefact – participating in festivals, operating drop-in sessions, mobile fixing workshops and fundraisers. The volunteers aim to enlarge the social field, to grow the number of bike riders through gaining skills and enthusiasm, thereby creating a cleaner and less polluted city. The bicycle also has symbolic value; one wedding took place on bikes and there is participation in Critical Mass, selling posters and t-shirts, and occasional media work. The intention of repair differs in the refugee project and is lower-key; there is (as yet) little training of 'users' (or riders) in bike repair. But for the participants, there is the same sharing and learning of skills – a similar relation between user and artefact.

What was characteristic of the repair work undertaken in both the refugee project and the community bike workshops was the 'imperative of responsibility'. Accounting for our material lives and taking responsibility for the things we possess and use is part of Jonas's revision of Kant's categorical imperative to give a new moral injunction that underlies being human. All the repairers we talked with or worked with were motivated not by financial reward but by a feeling of responsibility towards those who were less fortunate than themselves, perhaps through being displaced from their home country, perhaps through poverty or social exclusion. The work of repair enabled the repairers to help sustain those other lives through a technology, the bicycle, that itself is a mechanised, sustainable means of transport.

Simon Batterbury is Honorary Professor at Lancaster University and Associate Professor at the University of Melbourne.

Tim Dant is Emeritus Professor of Sociology at Lancaster University.

Notes

Simon would like to thank the Brussels Centre for Urban Studies at Vrije Universiteit Brussel (VUB) for a visiting fellowship in 2015, and we thank all the participants in the projects studied in this chapter.

1. The safety bicycle, which originated in a number of designs around the 1880s, was able to compete with high wheel bikes (which were fast, but not so safe) because of John Dunlop's invention of the pneumatic tyre. We can easily think of ways in which the safety bicycle has developed over these 140-plus years: gears have taken on different forms (in the hub, in the bottom bracket, with a cassette and derailleur), handlebars have taken a variety of shapes, and although the diamond frame has remained dominant, other shapes exist. Perhaps most importantly, the materials of manufacture have changed, with steel alloys,

aluminium and carbon fibre bringing down the overall weight of many bicycles quite significantly. But as a machine, the bicycle has remained remarkably consistent in being a two-wheeled vehicle, propelled by human energy through a drivetrain linked through a chain.

2. There are of course variations: small-wheeled bicycles, recumbent bicycles and tricycles, cargo bikes and most recently the e-bike, using battery power to supplement human energy. Nonetheless, the vast majority of bicycles ridden take the same safety bicycle form and are very similar in the way they work.
3. There are a variety of different arrangements for recycling unwanted bikes. Another model is Re-Cycle in the UK and similar organisations that ship used and repaired bikes from the UK to African countries.
4. The bike project was set up to assist, and local volunteers sympathise with the plight of refugees relocated to their communities and support the aims of the City of Sanctuary. There are similar schemes that have made what they do public, operating in London (https://thebikeproject.co.uk/pages/about-us), Norwich (https://www.bbc.co.uk/news/uk-england-norfolk-43058874) and Scotland (https://www.facebook.com/BikesforRefugeesScotland/).
5. See www.bikeworkshopsresearch.wordpress.com (retrieved 30 April 2019).
6. Thirty-two per cent of workshop visitors were women in a 2013 survey in French-speaking Belgium outside Brussels, where there were around twenty-five workshops, and this figure was 40 per cent across French workshops in 2017 (Meixner 2017: 10).
7. http://www.cleanairbxl.be (retrieved 15 March 2019).
8. http://CyclehackBXL.be (retrieved 15 March 2019).
9. http://cycloperativa.org (retrieved 15 March 2019).
10. There are a number of directions in which these partnerships could expand, for example linking with the twenty-seven Brussels Repair Cafés (http://www.repairtogether.be), workshops to fix household items.

References

Batterbury Simon, and Inès Vandermeersch. 2016. 'Bicycle Justice: Community Bicycle Workshops and "Invisible Cyclists" in Brussels', in A. Golub, M.L. Hoffmann, A.E. Lugo and G.F. Sandoval (eds), *Bicycle Justice and Urban Transformation: Biking For All?* London: Routledge, pp. 189–202.

Carlsson, Chris. 2007. '"Outlaw" Bicycling', *Affinities: A Journal of Radical Theory, Culture, and Action* 1(1): 21–32.

Dant, Tim. 2005. *Materiality and Society*. Maidenhead: Open University Press.

——. 2008. 'The "Pragmatics" of Material Interaction', *Journal of Consumer Culture* 8(1): 11–33.

——. 2010. 'The Work of Repair: Gesture, Emotion and Sensual Knowledge', *Sociological Research Online* 15(3): 7. Retrieved 15 March 2019 from http://www.socresonline.org.uk/15/3/7.html.

——. 2019. 'Inside the Bicycle: Repair Knowledge For All', in I. Strebel, A. Bovet and P. Sormani (eds), *Repair Work Ethnographies: Revisiting Breakdown, Relocation Materiality*. London: Palgrave Macmillan.

Dant, Tim, and David Bowles. 2003. 'Dealing with Dirt: Servicing and Repairing Cars', *Sociological Research Online* 8(2). Retrieved 15 March 2019 from http://www.socresonline.org.uk/8/2/dant.html.

Gilroy, Paul. 2001. 'Driving While Black', in D. Miller (ed.), *Car Cultures*. Oxford: Berg, 133–152.

Graham, Stephen, and Nigel Thrift. 2007. 'Out of Order: Understanding Repair and Maintenance', *Theory, Culture and Society* 24(3): 1–25.

Gregson, Nicky, Alan Metcalfe and Louise Crewe. 2009. 'Practices of Object Maintenance and Repair: How Consumers Attend to Consumer Objects within the Home', *Journal of Consumer Culture* 9(2): 248–72.

Horton, Dave, Paul Rosen and Peter Cox (eds). 2007. *Cycling and Society*. Aldershot: Ashgate.

Houston, Lara. 2013. 'Inventive Infrastructures: An Exploration of Mobile Phone 'Repair' Cultures in Kampala, Uganda', Ph.D. dissertation. Lancaster: Lancaster University.

Jonas, Hans. 1984. *The Imperative of Responsibility: In Search of an Ethics for the Technological Age*. Chicago, IL: University of Chicago Press.

Meixner, Evan. 2017. *Etude d'évaluation sur les services vélos: enquête sur les ateliers d'autoréparation de vélos*. Angers: ADEME.

Nixon, Denver V., and Tim Schwanen. 2019. 'Emergent and Integrated Justice: Lessons from Community Initiatives to Improve Infrastructures for Walking and Cycling', in N. Cook and D. Butz (eds), *Mobilities, Mobility Justice and Social Justice*. London: Routledge.

Oosterlynck, Stijn. 2012. 'From National Capital to Dismal Political World City: The Politics of Scalar Disarticulation in Brussels', in B. Derudder M. Hoyler, P.J. Taylor and F. Witlox (eds), *International Handbook of Globalization and World Cities*. London: Edward Elgar, pp. 487–96.

Parkin, John, Tim Ryley and Tim Jones. 2007. 'Barriers to Cycling: An Exploration of Quantitative Analyses', in D. Horton, P. Rosen and P. Cox (eds), *Cycling and Society*. Aldershot: Ashgate, 67–82.

Richards, Paul. 2010. 'A Green Revolution from Below? Science and Technology for Global Food Security and Poverty Alleviation', retirement address, Wageningen University, 18 November. Retrieved 15 March 2019 from http://edepot.wur.nl/165231.

Skinner, D., and P. Rosen. 2007. 'Hell Is Other Cyclists: Rethinking Transport and Identity', in D. Horton, P. Rosen and P. Cox (eds), *Cycling and Society*. Aldershot: Ashgate, 83–96.

Taylor, Alan. 2018. 'The Bike-Share Oversupply in China: Huge Piles of Abandoned and Broken Bicycles', *The Atlantic*, 22 March.

Vandermeersch, Inès. 2015. 'Évaluation de l'impact social d'une initiative citoyenne: le cas des ateliers collectifs de vélos à Bruxelles', MA thesis. Luxembourg: Haute École de Namur-Liège-Luxembourg/Haute École Louvain en Hainaut.

SNAPSHOT 11

Repair and Responsibility

The Art of Doris Salcedo

Siobhan Kattago

The word 'repair' contains the hope that something can be fixed and restored. It also contains the idea that someone is responsible for repairing that which is broken. In theology and philosophy, the theme of spiritual repair is present in the Judaic idea of *tikkun olam* as repairing the world. For the observant, *tikkun olam* complements the mitzvah or anonymous good deed that one should do every day. Moreover, it encompasses love for the world as God's creation, whereby each person is its caretaker for the next generation. *Tikkun olam* offers a profound sense of social justice beyond individual redemption because the focus is on a broken world that can only be repaired by the words and actions of individuals. The Christian ideal to love one's neighbour as oneself suggests yet another aspect of repair. The Good Samaritan feels responsible for taking care of the beaten stranger at the side of the road, while the priest and villagers ignore him. If *tikkun olam* is directed towards the world, the Good Samaritan restores a broken life to health. Finally, the Christian tenet of forgiveness is perhaps the most difficult act to free individuals from past deeds and restore their broken souls. Immortalised in Dostoyevsky's *Crime and Punishment*, it is Sonja who helps to redeem Raskolnikov.

For Columbian artist Doris Salcedo, Dostoyevsky's stories of broken souls and redemption are central to her work. Salcedo, like Levinas, tries to stay true to Alyosha's words in *The Brothers Karamazov* (Salcedo 2000: 145): 'We are all responsible for everyone else – but I am more responsible than all the others'. It is the other person who calls me into existence. It is the other person to whom I am infinitely responsible.

Acknowledging that it is perverse to turn pain into beauty, Salcedo tries to dignify the lives of those affected by political violence. She begins each project by listening to the testimony and stories of 'a victim of political violence' (Salcedo 2015). It is from this process of listening that her choice of material and artistic form emerges. Moreover, Salcedo tries to 'honour the singularity of the victims' experience'. Eschewing figurative representation and photography, she works with everyday items such as chairs, shirts, shoes, tables, wardrobes, cribs, beds, bricks, wire, candles and flowers in order to portray the everyday life of those silenced by violence. Evoking absence, Salcedo tries to restore the unique story of the victim in public spaces and museums. Although a life cannot be restored, she nonetheless believes that art is uniquely suited to small steps of reparation.

Mindful of the limits of representation, she tries not to aestheticise the very violence that she depicts. Instead, each work of art evokes absence and its aftermath. In the spirit of Walter Benjamin, Paul Celan and Theodor Adorno, Salcedo approaches political violence obliquely, maintaining a fine line between art and horror.

Since the end of the Second World War, psychological, legal and moral understandings of repair have been accompanied by transitions to democracy, ranging from military defeat to coup d'état, negotiated transition, civil disobedience and social movements. Within the language of justice, repairing brokenness appeals to a deep need to balance the scales, to make amends to the victims through reparations and public apology and to punish the perpetrators. Democratic debate about political violence is linked with the restoration of public trust and community. Moreover, democracy is strengthened by open discussion in the public sphere – whether through history books, art, literature, film, memorials or museums. While Salcedo's work is part of this desire to come to terms with the past for the sake of a democratic future, she is even more demanding because, like Levinas and Dostoyevsky, she feels an acute sense of responsibility to others.

> The Lithuanian philosopher Emmanuel Levinas has helped us understand that the other precedes me and claims my presence before I exist . . . As a result, everything precedes me, everything makes its presence felt with such urgency that I am not the one who chooses; my themes are given to me, reality is given to me, the presence of each victim imposes itself. (Salcedo 2000: 134)

Disremembered (2014) is comprised of shirts woven from silk and raw needles to represent the grief of mothers whose children have been killed by gun violence. *Neither* (2004) commemorates prisoners detained without appeal in Guantanamo Bay by installing a white room with barbed wire embedded into its walls. *Shibboleth* (2007) depicts the subterranean space of strangers and immigrants in Europe with its cracked fissure in the Tate Modern's Turbine Floor.

While many of Salcedo's installations focus on mourning, it is particularly in her public art that the theme of repair is most salient. Immediately after the ceasefire was broken in Columbia in 2016, Salcedo arranged for a white shroud to cover the town square of Bogota. Sewn together by volunteers, the name of a victim of political violence was written in ashes on each white square to form a single shroud. In the end, 2,350 names were inscribed onto the stitched white fabric to express public mourning for the victims of Columbian state violence. Salcedo's curator, María Belén Sáez de Ibarra, summed up the reason for *Sumando Ausencias* (Adding up Absences): 'The act of sewing together each piece of cloth in an act of reparation, of knitting our own peace and is especially important at this time of uncertainty' (Saez, quoted in Brodzinsky 2016).

Salcedo's art cannot be separated from the 'politics of mourning'. She mourns for those killed by acts of political violence and provides a space in which to think about their absence. Recognising the impossibility of this task does not mean that artists should be silent. On the contrary, as Salcedo maintains, we are compelled to respond to the suffering of others. Her work remains true to Levinas's argument that ethics begins with the face of the other person. 'The face of a neighbour signifies for me an unexceptional responsibility, preceding every free consent, every pact, every contract' (Levinas, quoted in Salcedo 2000: 128).

Silence is part of Salcedo's artwork. Finding inspiration from Franz Rosenzweig's reflections on the silence of art, she recalls how art can bring individuals together from very different places. 'Art is the transmission without words of what is the same in all human beings' (Rozenzweig, quoted in Salcedo 2000: 137). Salcedo's art creates a space for the victims of violence and the public to come together in silence. Offering an artistic encounter with the possibility for change, Salcedo is part of the long tradition of *tikkun olam* as repairing the world. Otherwise, by choosing not to respond, we resign ourselves to the fate of political forces beyond our control, thereby abdicating any possibility, no matter how small, to halt the violence that tears our world apart.

Siobhan Kattago is Senior Research Fellow in Practical Philosophy at the University of Tartu.

References

Brodzinsky, Sibylla. 2016. 'Columbian Artist Creates Enormous Shroud to Honor Country's War Dead', *The Guardian*, 12 October. Retrieved 16 February 2018 from https://www.theguardian.com/world/2016/oct/12/colombia-war-art-project-bogota-doris-salcedo.

Salcedo, Doris. 2000. *Doris Salcedo*. London: Phaidon.
——. 2015. 'Doris Salcedo: Artist Talk', 2 October. Retrieved 16 February 2018 from https://www.youtube.com/watch?v=EfhuzMkKfM8.

CHAPTER 11

Social Repair and (Re)Creation

Broken Relationships and a Path Forward for Austrian Holocaust Survivors

KATJA SEIDEL

Oh, those memories
They are like naughty gnomes. They play with us. They emerge without asking beforehand.
Then they hide or fade.
. . .
They do not respect time or space.
They dress up, become tiny, mocking, confusing. Sometimes they disappear,
To come back as giants, ready to crush us.
Some make us happy, others sad,

They are with us at every moment every hour of every day of our lives.
It is essential to learn to live with them and not for them.

—Lisa Seiden, in *Die letzten Zeugen: Das Vermächtnis der Holocaust-Überlebenden* (translation by the author)

Relationships are broken in war and genocide. Things and people are lost, and memories are contested in the battle against oblivion of names and the horrors that should never be repeated. Reason enters the realm of the absurd and violence destroys what makes us human(e) (Nordstrom 1995). Those who survive cannot but face the gnomes of the past, asking to remake ontologically, experientially and discursively perceptions, relationships, narratives, and a world that has crumbled under atrocious horrors. Postwar societies live haunted by ghosts and build their being and becoming on the relation of time and present absences. What has been torn needs stitching, so that future generations will not repeat the horrors and will not forget the suffering. It is in small acts, in the everyday, the mundane and the human that a shattered world can be rebuilt. And so, social repair is a never-ending process, which surpasses time and generations, and which entails official apologies, legal and moral accountability, financial and material compensation, material repair and bodily as well as psychological healing.

Drawing on one of the key ideas of the volume, namely that repair entails responsibility, care and expectations about the future, this chapter discusses the experiences and reflections of Austrian Holocaust (child) survivors, now living in exile, on the intergenerational memory project *A Letter to the Stars* that was conducted in Vienna in 2008. In it, more than two hundred mainly Jewish survivors/guests, most of them accompanied by one of their grandchildren, returned to Vienna for a week to share with the young generation in contemporary Austria their life stories of suffering, exile and renewal. In their narratives and in the organisers' intention, repair featured centrally as an organising albeit contested theme. With agents from various generations and in the absent presence of the deceased, direct and indirect experiences of suffering and each with their role in the narrative process, repair turned into a highly complex experience of diverse perceptions.

As Lisa Seiden suggests, memories are like 'naughty gnomes' and the ghosts of the past remain among the living, especially after violent extermination and mass persecution. In the present absence of the deceased and the horrors of the past, Horkheimer and Adorno remind us about the importance of acknowledging the relationship between truth, memory and the living, stating that 'only when the horror of annihilation is raised fully into consciousness are we placed in the proper relationship to the dead: that of unity with them, since we, like them, are victims of the same conditions and of the same disappointed hope' (Horkheimer and Adorno 2002: 178). The *A Letter to the Stars* project brought to our awareness many ghosts, friendly and hostile, present or denied, liberated and defeated, especially on 5 May 2008, the most important day of the so-called 38/08 invitation project, when an event took place on the Heldenplatz in Vienna, a place strongly associated with Adolf Hitler's speech and the cheering crowds that supported him at the time of the Anschluss (annexation) of Austria.

One of the most eclectic and well-known squares in Vienna, the Heldenplatz is a symbol of imperial power, the Habsburg monarchy, the signing of the Austrian State Treaty and, of course, the coming into power of Adolf

Hitler and the National Socialist Party in 1938. Haunted by the past, the square thus not only symbolises monarchist power or liberal thoughts of the Austrian republic but also inhabits the memories of the beginning of the Holocaust as well as the beginning of the persecution of those who now came back at our invitation. Countering the ghosts of the past, our guests transformed the square during the public event as they gave new meanings to and spoke out in the same location once occupied by those who would have become their future tormentors. Reflecting back on her experience, Dorit Whiteman, psychologist and survivor, referred to the powerful transformation she felt in the following way:

> When I was on stage, it seemed unreal that I should speak from the same place Hitler had spoken from and even more: He was dead and I was alive! The symbolism of the occasion was immense. I was sure Hitler would turn in his grave – and I thought of the proverb: Whoever laughs last laughs best.

Like Dorit, many other guests presented their thoughts and changed the meaning of the Heldenplatz with their presence and in the presence of their beloved ones, both dead and alive. Their narratives on past, present and future revealed a truth that, as Hannah Arendt (1962) reminds us, the Nazis had sought to exorcise. Hence, guest speakers such as Dorit, who has resolved her relationship with the past, or Erwin, who provided some detail of struggling with his (and Austria's) ghosts, or Otto, who with the help of a photograph connected the living with the dead (Favero 2018: 102), made felt and heard many manifestations of the horror of annihilation, but also contributed to the future of potential renewal.

Building on the description of visual and discursive details of the project, some biographical vignettes and survivors' reflective narratives, this chapter interrogates the meaning of social repair in the context of ghostly matters (Avery 2008), loss, an idea of home and intergenerational re-creation. Some of the other contributions to this volume have also engaged with this matter. For instance, Siobhan Kattago notes in her snapshot that the term repair equally contains elements of hope, or even messianic redemption. She asks if repair happens through words, and not just through actions. Furthermore, in the introduction to this volume, Francisco Martínez situates the discussion within the Western psychoanalytic tradition, in which verbal recounting helps to heal past wrongs. Then he proposes material repair as a way of complementing or 'updating' traditional approaches towards collective recuperation. This chapter contributes to these discussions by arguing that repair and reconciliation do not always go together, yet when they do, they might generate different kinds of pairing and, in the presence of absence, can create new hope for the future.

A Letter to the Stars

Between 2007 and 2009, I worked on the intergenerational remembrance project *A Letter to the Stars*, the largest Holocaust school project ever realised in Austria. Led by the organisation 'Learning from Contemporary History', a society (*Verein*) made up of a team of nine, we organised various events throughout the years. Among these, visiting witnesses in their new homes was one of the most rewarding. While two travels (to Israel and New York) had been conducted previous to my participation, in 2007 I joined the third week-long visit, this time to London, where I accompanied another group of students as 'ambassadors of remembrance' on their encounters with former Austrians. The rich experiences of these empathetic encounters made it possible for participants to go beyond the narratives of suffering and survival and beyond dichotomising categories of victim versus perpetrator. These meetings enabled friendships between people of different generations and life experiences, in which those taking part learned to perceive each other as individuals with strengths and weaknesses, pain and laughter, questions and answers.

Based on the compelling experiences of exchange, storytelling and personal encounters, the team decided to follow up with the by then biggest project conducted by *A Letter to the Stars*, the invitation project 38/08. In 2008, seventy years after the 'Annexation' of Austria into the Third Reich, we set out to invite 250 Austrian Jewish Holocaust survivors now living abroad to visit their former hometown of Vienna for one week. For the endeavour, each guest was invited to come with a companion, and as organisers we encouraged the idea to travel with one of the invitees' grandchildren, hence seeking to address the long-term effects of violence (Argenti and Schramm 2012) and to build relationships not only between those directly affected but also between the survivors' descendants and adolescents in Austria. The invitation enabled a continuation of already established relationships from a previous project and widened the meetings through contacts with new school classes, teachers and pupils, who, over the course of six months, wrote letters to their future guests. They did so in preparation for the meeting in May, in which they would meet their guests in person, listen to their life stories, learn from their experience, accompany them to their former homes and get to know each other. Additionally, participating school classes and our team organised a collective event on 5 May 2008, the day of the liberation of the Mauthausen Concentration Camp in 1945 and today Austria's Memorial Day against Violence and Racism in Memory of the Victims of National Socialism. At first, government representatives invited our guests as honorary guests to a commemorative session in the Houses of Parliament. Subsequently, we had prepared a public performance event at the Heldenplatz and the temporary exhibition *Denk.Mal!*, which together facilitated a visible temporary renewal of a place burdened with social trauma and history.

The intention of the 38/08 project was threefold. First, it sought to facilitate and deepen personal encounters in which young Austrians would be educated about the Holocaust, which all too often is recalled in the abstract number of six million victims. Second, it intended to connect new generations by inviting the survivors to travel with one of their grandchildren, who would learn about their roots and their own family history and would potentially find new friends in their grandparent's former home country. And third, the organisers hoped to contribute to a form of reparation by providing a space to enact agency and build new affective associations in the act of giving testimony.

Thus, in the intergenerational remembrance project, social repair, transformation of places and relations and the layering of memories featured as a guiding theme of the week-long invitation. Ethnographies of political violence have provided excellent examples of the importance of social repair, be it through the power of monuments, the reconstruction of destructed material worlds, the recognition of memories and the deceased, trials that hold perpetrators accountable or the recovery of broken relationships (Fletcher and Weinstein 2002). As a metaphor, the rebuilding of the bridge in Stari Most in the aftermath of the Yugoslav War comes to mind. The bridge in Bosnia-Herzegovina was built during the Ottoman period and was later destroyed by Bosnian Croat soldiers in 1993. Rebuilding that bridge stands symbolically for the ways in which the act of reconstruction – of things, memories and connections – can encourage the repair of social and economic damage from the past (Armaly, Blasi and Hannah 2004).

Commemorative events, performances and the installation of memorial sites constitute similar public statements, often highly political and connected to questions of reconciliation, apologies, renewal or reparation. *A Letter to the Stars* as part of the long-term politics of reparation attempted a related effort of social reconstruction – the rebuilding of relationships and a present that through the hope for a transformed future will make a difference to those participating in it. By means of the 38/08 project and, more specifically, the Heldenplatz event, I thus describe and analyse social repair in the context of recovery, reconfiguration, closure and healing seven decades after the beginning of the National Socialist terror regime in Austria. What does social repair mean seventy years after the Holocaust, and how can we understand it in the context of trauma and coming to terms with the past? What is its meaning in a non-material context in which fixing is impossible? Is it presumptuous to discuss the process of repair in a context where scars will never disappear and where those who endured them have found their own ways of remaking their worlds (Das and Kleinman 2001)?

These questions had been discussed at length among the organisers previous to the invitation and are also reflected in this chapter. How did notions of memories and repair enter the experience of former Austrian Holocaust child survivors now living all over the world? I cannot answer all those questions sufficiently, and certainly not for everyone. I will try, however, to find some responses in my experiences in 2008 and in the comments and reflections of the survivors themselves. As such, this article discusses the effects of the *A Letter to the Stars* project and the various levels – bodily, visual, discursive and cognitive – of presence that powerfully transforms places and people and thus, perhaps, remade a world that cannot be repaired but that can be built anew in a collective creative effort (Nordstrom 1995).

Rewind: Expectations and Purpose, before the Journey

When we decided to organise the 38/08 event, one of the first tasks was to contact Austrian survivors whose names had been provided by the Jewish Welcome Service two years previously. I remember the strength it took every time we picked up the phone – four women in our late twenties ringing up people as old as our grandparents. We were aware that each of our calls meant an interruption of people's everyday lives and potentially the elicitation of painful memories. What does it serve to insist on not forgetting? And what were the expectations that we produced by calling elderly people around the world, inviting them to Vienna and to share their stories with the new generation?

While most of our contacts had visited Austria at least once since the end of the war and some had dedicated their lives to teaching the young generations about the Holocaust and sharing their experiences through books and talks (for instance Levi [2003] and Knoller [2005]), others had indeed sought to bury the past and never returned to their former home country. Although surprised by the invitation, most were eager to hear about the project and responses were overwhelmingly positive and embracing. For example, when I called Lisa Seiden, who, after being saved by the Kindertransport, lived in the UK for seven years before reuniting with her parents in Buenos Aires where she has lived ever since, I was careful, believing that I would have to address her and this highly emotional topic in Spanish. When I finally found the courage to call and she picked up the phone, I tentatively started the conversation: 'Hola Señora Seiden. Me llamo Katja, le llamo de Austria, Vienna', only to hear a reply in perfect

German with a touch of a Viennese accent from the 1930s: 'Oh, aus Wien! Na dann können wir auch Deutsch reden!'

For us, every first contact was an act of courage and hope. Nearly always, our counterparts on the other end of the line were quick to tell us about their Holocaust experience, how they suffered humiliations, how hunger and thirst nearly killed them and how their family members met a less fortunate fate. And so, while hardly any conversation went by without tears on either side, a breath-taking trust equally filtered through the medium of the telephone and relations were being built. And so, for those who agreed to travel, the journey to Vienna began months before their plane took off. For instance, Erwin Auspitz and his family fled the Nazi regime in 1939. He now lives in Buenos Aires, where he arrived in 1941 after having passed through Cuba, Peru and Brazil. A few weeks after his visit to Vienna he wrote:

> The preparation of the journey, whereby I mean the constant rethinking of the task that awaited me, occupied me completely. In particular the suggestion to communicate my life story inspired me. But I wanted more. I was aiming to get them to think. It was clear to me that most of the ancestors of these young people were certainly active Nazis, or, at best, passive and probably sympathetic to the circumstances of the day. I was absolutely unwilling to conceal these facts. On the contrary, I wanted to bring them to light, of course, without hurting anyone. This project filled me completely, and hardly a day passed without me thinking about it.

Gerald Watkins (from Pacific Palisades) expressed a similar sensation and motivation: 'The invitation from the *Letters to the Stars* organisation to visit Austria and talk to students touched me deeply because I consider this a very important element in the process of remembering. The youth of today must see the holocaust [*sic*] as an example of the fact that hate and brutality destroy not only the victims but also the perpetrators'.

Lisa Seiden was among those hesitant to accept the invitation. Too many ghosts (see also the poem at the beginning of this article) inhabited the place she calls her first home. After many weeks of meetings in Buenos Aires with eleven other invitees, many phone conversations in which we got to know and trust each other, and with the support of her grandson, who eventually accompanied her on the journey, she decided to accept. To her, speaking to young Austrians in the same school she attended as a child was what she later called 'probably the most rewarding journey of my life'. And so, for many survivors, accepting the proposal to participate in the project was a task connected to a purpose rather than a 'cost-free travel'. As in the words of Gerald Pollack (from Old Greenwitch), 'I accepted participation in this project not only because the expenses would be paid, but because I believe that the more people understand about the Holocaust, the less likely it will be that they could ever be persuaded to take part in such a tragedy, as surely some of their grandparents did. It is not "Arbeit Macht Frei", but "Wahrheit [truth] Macht Frei"'.

However, not all stories and moments created by our phone calls were easy to digest. Some of our guests generated questions that shocked me to the core, such as when I was asked by London-based Hans Spielmann one day: 'So what is it like in the Austrian countryside – do people still think of Jews as horned?' Some of our guests furthermore decided to accept the invitation, but declined to share their experiences with students. Rather, they used the opportunity to return to Vienna with their families, spend the time on activities of their own choosing and only attended collectively organised programmes such as the Heldenplatz event or the visit to the synagogue in the first district in honour of their deceased parents.

Repair: Place and Memory

During the invitation week, a public event was organised, as mentioned above, on 5 May 2008 on the Heldenplatz. In previous years, the organisation had acted on the square with various artistic and commemorative activities. Probably aware that one of the most striking features of monuments is that we do not notice them (Musil [1927] 1985), the *A Letter to the Stars* installations, performances and memorials were not intended as a permanent monument. Rather, the politics of repair and the transformation of space and history were enacted to produce meaning and narratives that would transcend time. The permanency of the monument was sought on a cognitive level, which, while the events were fleeting and inclusive, would allow for open discourses and renewal.

For instance, in 2005, fifteen thousand students came to the historical square in Vienna's first district to release their letters to murdered victims of the Nazi regime. Later, in 2005, twenty thousand white roses were displayed behind barbed wire. And in 2008, eighty thousand candles were lit by citizens on the Night of Silence to remember and honour the victims of the Nazi regime (Verein Lernen aus der Zeitgeschichte 2008). Projecting their names onto a big screen in the centre of the square, the installation and candles created presences that countered the intended eradication of the Holocaust. And so, while a variety of happenings had already imprinted new meanings on the Heldenplatz, these activities were mainly intended for those living with the legacy of a genocidal regime and potentially the guilt of a transmitted historical shame.

The active encounters of former victims of persecution and their descendants with the children, grandchildren and great-grandchildren of former perpetrators were an intervention that worked on a different level. Taking

Figure 11.1. The *A Letter to the Stars* stage at the Heldenplatz, 5 May 2008; Holocaust survivors and students reclaiming a historical place in their appeal: Never Again. Photograph by Katja Seidel.

on an active role, both the new generations and former victims presented their hopes and worries and constructed new relations not only in their stories and words but with the physical presence of those whose death was sought seventy years previously.

And so, in 2008, all around the square, posters of the *Denk.Mal!* project (meaning, at the same time, *monument* and an *invocation to think*) were presented in an exhibition, designed by survivors, telling their stories or short sentences of what they had wanted to transmit to the Austrian public. Students had produced small pieces of art that additionally complemented the posters and statements of the survivors. At the centre of the square, a big stage had been built with a large screen from which our guests spoke to the audience and where young Austrians performed small acts in the spirit of remembrance, anti-discrimination and anti-racism. Reflecting afterwards about this place and its ownership, Dorit Whiteman added:

> The highlight of the week was the event on the Heldenplatz. The impression was enormous. Everyone who had experienced the time of the Anschluss remembers the ecstatic crowds and Hitler's speech held at this very place.
>
> Now we were here, so many years later, surrounded by pupils who were expecting us with fresh, young, eager faces.

Figure 11.2. Holocaust survivors and artists Lucie and Peter Paul Porges' comment on meaningful transformations of space and memory. Poster exhibited during the *Denk.Mal!* show, May 2008. Photograph by Katja Seidel.

With the event and the *Denk.Mal!* installation throughout the square that is implicated so strongly in the horrors of the Nazi regime, the Heldenplatz was inscribed with new meanings and memories. Images of former survivors now taking back this place from historical trauma not only changed the present moment but also created mental images that endured after the actual moment. The practices of visualisation and enunciation of memories (Macé and Zauner 2016: 16) enabled visions that created narratives of a new and hopeful future, one that allows for some closure with the past through the action of those who formerly were deemed the object rather than the subject of the politics of reparation.

My own memories of the events at the Heldenplatz could perhaps be explained with three words: pain, joy and hope. Pain of having grown up in, and being a part of, a society that for decades silently accepted the historical burial of its own complicity; joy at being able to counter the paralysis that for too long, and probably still far into the future, keeps us from engaging truly with the meaning of repair: the belief and the attempt to face what is broken, and the strength to admit one's own role in it. Because even if the past cannot be fixed, we have an obligation to work with the pieces and create something new. Responsibility in that sense is always there, and hope too. Just as I learned from Robert Singer, a man who survived three concentration camps and a death march, who, upon his return to Israel, wrote us the following lines:

> Thank you very much for the days in Vienna, which you organised so kindly and cordially. After I suffered the persecution in Vienna in the years 1938–42 at the age of 10–14 years, this visit organised by you and your colleagues changed my stance towards Vienna somewhat. I express my respect for you, for your courage to denounce and educate people about the crimes of the Nazis, even if it did take many years.

Reconstruction: Images and Memories

Active participation in commemorative events potentially transforms places and produces new layers of memories inscribed in them. But it also encompasses the power to engage in cathartic moments of sharing one's own trauma by bringing back to the collective present those who were murdered through genocide. One of the speakers on the afternoon of the 5th was Otto Deutsch, Austrian Jewish child survivor, then seventy-nine years old. In June 1939 his mother told little Otto: 'Otto, I have very good news. You are going to England'. Excited at first about his journey to this foreign island, he asked, 'When are we going?' only to hear: 'No Otto, not we, you go'. Saved by the Kindertransport organisation, Otto left two

Figure 11.3. Otto Deutsch with his sister Adele and his mother Wilma Deutsch (photograph taken in June 1939; Adele and Wilma were murdered in an extermination camp near Minsk). Courtesy of Otto Deutsch.

days later, never to see any of his family members again. The day before, he, his mother and his sister Dele went to take a picture of the three of them, for him to take on his journey into a new life. It is this picture that is dearest to the old man, his biggest treasure; the only material belonging from his childhood and the only visual trace of his beloved ones, whom he never fails to talk about. In Otto's words: 'I wouldn't be human if my thoughts did not wander into the past, to my parents and to my sister. Time is not healing. As the years go by, these images only get clearer and clearer'.

While time for Otto Deutsch was not healing, that afternoon on stage was a form of redress, as he was given the chance to talk about his family and to show that photograph on a large screen to an audience, who most likely will now never forget his sister Dele and her beautiful white shoes he adores so much. Through the photograph, we can access present absences and perceive an emotional awareness of pain and suffering beyond words. Through the image, Otto's family entered the Heldenplatz, my life and the memory of many people in the audience. In that moment, 'in looking at us', the photograph as a preservation of memory from a distant past forced us 'to truly look at it' (Didi-Huberman 2012) and critically engage with the normalisation of terror with which we often perceive images of the Holocaust. But more than that, as a means of visual communication it allowed for Otto and everyone present to bring Dele and his mother to the Heldenplatz, for them to be with him on stage and to speak to us with their gaze just as much as Otto did with his words.

I remember the moment when I heard Otto talk about his family. Interrupting myself in taking pictures of the event, I looked up from my camera and to the big screen that transmitted a close-up of the speakers to the large audience. On it was captured the image of the laminated photograph that had been prepared for installation on Otto's *Denk.Mal!* exhibit. Seeing the three people in the picture, and Dele's white shoes which Otto never fails to mention, I had to sit down. Tears were falling from my eyes. I was taken over by a mix of joy and sadness: joy that Otto was able to share this moment with the audience in the presence of his absent family on the one hand, and sadness that the present absence of his murdered family members constitutes the very everyday of Otto's life.

There is no way to bring back what has been taken from victims in the past. For Otto Deutsch, presenting that photo to a large audience was one of the most moving moments in his life. It provided him with a chance to bear witness and bring back to the present those he held so dearly in his heart. Breaking with oblivion, he became an active agent against 'memocide' (Shaw 2007), the intended eradication of memory that often goes hand in hand with genocidal crimes.

Repairing the Future: Never Again

The burden of survival leaves victim-survivors with the obligation to bear witness, to present their stories in the name of those who will never have the chance to do so. Stored outside the usual event-memory-time conundrum, these traumatic memories become locked in time (Langer 1993), or remain as if recorded on tape (Agamben 2003). Yet there is another burden that survivors hold – to make sure that it never happens again. Just as Priscilla Hayner (2001) explains when arguing that the politics of reparation always addresses past and future as well as the importance of 'the guarantee of non-repetition'. When talking about the *A Letter to the Stars* project, expectations and hopes for the future provided an important reason for survivors' participation. This becomes visible in Erwin Auspitz's speech in which he connected the Holocaust with the Argentine state terror in an appeal to the young generation:

> I stand before you in mourning and tears. The six million innocent sisters and brothers of the Shoah provide the frame of our meeting.
>
> However, at any time, in any place, man [*sic*] has always understood how to torment, to humiliate, to murder his brother. Argentina, the country in which my family and I found a new home when we had to leave Austria and our beloved Vienna, suffered a terrible military dictatorship thirty years ago. Thirty thousand people disappeared. *Los desaparecidos*. They were not alive, but no one dug them a grave.
>
> What to do in the face of so much violence?
>
> We survivors may know better than some: violence only leads to more violence. Not to solutions.
>
> But there is a way. The search for truth. I would like to say, true, naked and unshaded truth. Let us look at ourselves. What would we have done if we had been the other? What would we have thought, done, felt? So many questions. And no clear answer.
>
> But our painful and honest search for the truth will bring success: decency and humanity, this will be our success. And then, let us rejoice so that we can look into each other's eyes, take us by the hands, and dream: NEVER AGAIN!

Taking on an active role, Erwin and many others actively chose to return to Vienna and to share their painful stories, their experiences of exile and renewal and the importance of kindness and honesty. Aware of the dangers of Othering and racially, religiously or ethnically motivated exclusion and scapegoating that have once again become fashionable in Europe, he addressed the young generations in connecting personal experiences with worrisome anticipations. Transcending the past, his speech created awareness of the importance of different kinds of pairings with truth, tolerance and the future.

Repair or Break: The Curse of the Good Deed

Analytically, one of the key questions of this chapter is connected with responsibility in repair – just as the introduction to this volume states. Conversations around potential effects of the invitation kept us company throughout the many months in which we developed the concept, whenever we got in touch with survivors, their families and the teachers and students engaged in the project. Definitions of repair include 'the action of making amends for a wrong one has done, by providing payment or other assistance to those who have been wronged' and 'to restore (something damaged, faulty, or worn) to a good condition'. In the context of political violence, however, repair is more often used as a noun – 'reparation' – which, in a more narrow legal-economic sense, means 'to compensate victims of earlier wrongdoing' (Torpey 2003). Such compensations mostly depend on states and include financial reparations and the restitution of material goods stolen from the victims in the past. In Austria, these different kinds of monetary compensations and reparation payments have come far too late. The narrative of Austria as 'Hitler's first victim' (Beniston 2003) prevailed until the 1980s and not only allowed the country to deny its genocidal complicity but also hindered monetary compensations and payments. Important changes took place with the report of the Historikerkommission implemented by the government between 1998 and 2003, which – addressing the crime of 'Vermögensentzug durch Arisierung' (Deprivation of property through Aryanisation) – contributed greatly to untangling the chaotic regulations from 1945 and 1950, and provided more financial reparations and pension schemes to the victimised.

As a non-governmental organisation, *A Letter to the Stars* worked on a different level of amends, one that in anthropological studies on peace and conflict is referred to as social repair or the politics of reparation. These forms of repair belong to the realm of transitional justice and describe various forms of redress that encompass a whole field of interconnected activities and measures on the micro and macro level, both individual and collective, structural and symbolic (Hinton 2010; Seidel 2017). The aim is to 'make up for' past injustice, engage with the long-term effects of mass violence, take responsibility and actively contribute to memory reconstruction and rehabilitation collectively (Robben 2000), and work towards facilitating recognition (Povinelli 2002), or possibly even healing.

Similar to the word 'Wiedergutmachung' in German, reparation however is a highly contested term. In the context of mass political violence, what is dearest to those who suffered can never be 'made up for' – the loss of family members, one's childhood, one's home, the possibilities of education. Nor can these efforts undo the traumatic memories survivors carry in their hearts. While we were aware of the limitations any remembrance project has, imposed critical discussions in Austrian media and newspapers additionally challenged us to think about the risk of potentially re-traumatising, damaging and breaking the fragile stitches that cover the wounds inflicted.

Months before the May invitation week, Austrian newspapers as well as a variety of Holocaust remembrance institutions started campaigning against the *A Letter to the Stars* initiative. Partly, the criticism was to do with the usage of the list of names provided by the Jewish Welcome Service, a political issue, largely connected with the privileged position of the Jewish Welcome Service to stand as the sole organisation to organise invitations to those expelled from their former homes.[1] Another criticism was related to the 'commercialisation of remembrance' and the apparent 'pop-style character' (*Kirtagscharacter*) of the events organised by *A Letter to the Stars*.[2] To this, Andreas Kuba from *A Letter to the Stars* responded: 'in the remembrance project 38/08, Austrian Holocaust survivors from all over the world are invited by dedicated schools. We are committed solely to the needs of the survivors and the participating schools'.[3] And so, while in the organisers' minds and the survivors' experience education, social repair and healing formed the centre of the attempt to contribute to Holocaust remembrance, criticisms voiced by often pretentious experts harmed the project in the public perception.

However, while the above debates were unpleasant, another response of the media was much more disturbing. The invitation project was not a good idea, argued two articles in *Der Standard*, a well-known Austrian daily newspaper, claiming that the event would 'overwhelm the survivors'. The young hosts, both organisers and students, would endanger the mental balance of the survivors, the critics claimed, exposing them to more psychological pressure than they could handle. The organisers would not have considered that their guests would have to be accompanied by professional caregivers, because the meetings would probably lead to emotional outbursts and delicate scenes due to their emotional state.[4] Not surprisingly, in reaction, a debate unfolded in the dialectic of unexpected contributors. On the one hand, a critical 'elite' that warned of 'conceptual deficits of *A Letter to the Stars* project' and accused its operators of 'irresponsibility, naivety or even the "marketing of suffering"'; on the other hand, Jewish displaced persons, who protested, vehemently 'protecting the action because these invitations have great emotional value for them'.[5]

What concerned us the most, as organisers, was the pain that these articles brought to our guests, who felt appalled by the ways in which they were described from the outside – damaged individuals in need of protection, of psychological support, trauma counselling, psychological and physical assistance and so on. In a very critical tone, the articles questioned the competence of the organisers and the intentions of the project itself. For example, historian Bertrand Perz was cited commenting on the planned invitation of survivors: 'it sounds like a field-experiment. The event is unacceptable and undesirable'. According to the article, Perz resented the fact that 'aged survivors are being piloted (*gelotst*) into their former home country without psycho-social care and assistance (*Betreuung*)'. In the same article, Eva Blimlinger, research coordinator of the Historikerkommission, was cited to have thumped on the need for 'professional (psychological) expert monitoring' for all invited guests and disparaged the project, stating that it was 'more a PR action for the organisers than actual interest in the survivors'.[6] As a non-Jewish organisation and with a lack of trained psychologists,[7] who would 'take the traumatised individuals by the hand' in order to help them through the process of returning to Austria and facing their past, we would endanger survivors. Rather than 'remaking them', we could break them.[8]

It was this aspect that was hurtful (if not to say harmful) to those who were the intended beneficiaries of the event, the survivors themselves, reducing our guests thus to solely the Holocaust experience and dismissive of more than six decades building lives, memories, families, careers, new homes and relations, and a future somewhere else. Many concerned people who, all around the world, had followed the debate in Austria sent their responses to us as well as to the newspaper agencies. Expressing his anger towards experts' critiques, Maximilian Lerner from New York defended the invitation project and claimed his agency, writing:

> I am outraged that others want to speak for me. I am a former Austrian who managed to escape to America and then joined the liberation of Europe as a soldier in the American Army. I am now a lecturer at the Museum of Jewish Heritage in New York. . . . We who have survived the Shoah need no caretakers (*Pfleger*) to visit Vienna again. (translation by the author)[9]

Furthermore, the critics were countered by the stated intentions of survivors, such as Bianca Gross, who wrote: 'as for myself, I never considered this proposed trip as a pleasure or reconciliation trip to the country of my birth. I have and can do this on my own and spend the time the way I wish if I do it. With the *Letters to the Stars* trip, I consider giving service – an educational experience to students which they cannot glean from history books'. Equally, Gerda Albert, today living in the USA, who had already taken part in the Ambassadors of Remembrance project in New York, further expressed her disappointment about the lack of respect, stating: 'The young people who give their time and efforts to this project have shown a genuine interest in the lives and personalities of those survivors they have contacted. . . . [The criticism was] probably written by someone who has/

had little or no contact with any of the remaining survivors' (correspondence with Gerda Albert, 2008).[10]

Another comment, this time sent directly to the newspaper agency, was published on 25 January 2008. In it, outraged by the media coverage, Holocaust survivor and psychologist Dorit Whiteman from New York, who had returned many times to Austria, often invited by the University of Vienna to hold talks, wrote:

> I would like to respond to the detailed critical reactions of historians and other experts to the *Letters to the Stars* campaign, whose initiators had invited survivors of the Holocaust to a meeting in Vienna in a very touching and generous gesture. . . . I wonder how well these critics are familiar with the daily lives of the survivors. Both as a survivor and as a psychologist I found their comments completely out of place. We are not faded wrecks that need protection. Those of us who survived the Holocaust spent our years working, producing, and writing – in the business world, in art and science, and in humanitarian initiatives. We worked, raised children and made other contributions to society. Many of us have come back to Vienna before . . . Nobody has to be afraid of hysterical outbreaks. We carry our wounds in the heart and not as a badge on the lapel. (Dorit Whiteman, translation by the author)[11]

In the end, while survivors engaged strongly with the debate that lasted for a few weeks, unfortunately, the journalists and experts who in advance of the May invitation had denounced our team for acting irresponsibly, never bothered to return to our event and see for themselves the reactions of our guests to the effects of their own agency in remembrance.

Recap: Redemption and a Path into the Future

Considering that repair potentially functions as a mediator between a carefully revisited past and a tentatively expected future, this chapter has explored how anthropological notions such as reparation, healing and reconciliation help further our understanding of social repair in its manifold manifestations. After our guests had returned home, we received dozens of letters reflecting on their experiences, with responses overwhelmingly positive and moving. For those who came with their grandchildren, the creation of interpersonal ties for their descendants was a significant aim. Encounters between the second (or third) generations enabled new friendships and reconstructed lost connections between former neighbours (such as in the case of Lisa Seiden and her three grandsons, who have all been back to Vienna since). The combined intergenerational effort of survivors and hundreds of students was experienced as one way to contribute to some form of reconciliation. Furthermore, many emphasised the importance of having been 'invited' by a new generation as someone who has invaluable experience and knowledge. In Sigi Jehoshua Hoffman's words:

> Although I have been to Vienna a few times – as the city in which I spent my childhood and part of my youth was always close to my heart – I have never tried to connect with those living there, because the Nazi times still bore in my heart. This was cured through the encounters with you, with the school, the pupils and the teachers. I came back to Israel as a redeemed (*gelöster*) man.

The *A Letter to the Stars* project thus worked on various levels of the politics of reparation for people who had lost their homes, their families and their country seventy years earlier. Their archives of sorrow (Murphy 2011), filled with memories of dispossession, destruction, loss and pain, turned into repertoires for a new generation. Sharing their memories of ghosts, stories of survival, their childhood experiences and their experiences of reconstruction with students in Austria turned absences and pain into productive contributions for the future. And hope was established in interpersonal encounters.

For Otto, social repair meant standing in the company of his deceased relatives (Favero 2018) and sharing the memory of his sister Dele and his mother in a powerful act against oblivion. For Lisa, returning from Argentina to visit the places of her childhood with her grandson meant building lasting friendships for him and for herself. Erwin used the project to express his deeply felt humanity in the intention to connect two experiences of genocidal destruction and the postulation of non-repetition. And Dorit as much as everyone else who followed the invitation faced the ghosts from the past and ensured the recognition of her own agency. Many more examples could be given of the possibilities (and responsibility) of giving educative testimony in a society that in the past had taken from individuals as group members the right to speak, and in which those who suffered now had a chance to remind us in the current political climate that hate, discrimination and genocidal Othering have to be addressed every day to maintain repair beyond the past and into the future.

In the end, however, it is difficult to sum up what repair means in a situation, when each life story is different and each person's journey brought about distinct encounters. Speaking to the relational and transformative quality of social repair manifested in interactions between people, the process works both ways; for me, it was a privilege to get to know inspiring, warm-hearted individuals full of courage and hope, and to do my part in intervening in history. The project transformed my perception of the world, of what it means to survive, to feel beauty and to live a life with, but not for, the gnomes of the past. It was rewarding to know that I could give something back; coming from the society responsible for suffering, terror and silent acceptance, I was doing something. But more than that, my experiences during the project and the memories people shared with me emanated into my family and initiated conversations at home, where absences that had been silenced for decades were finally talked about and listened to. And so, my own family background slowly appeared and was put into words in an effort of truth, learning and connecting.

Pain will never disappear fully, and no single project, no apology or any form of reparation can fix the harm done. Notwithstanding that insight, the bridges built by the enacted and embodied monument of recognition have the power to create new relations, transform places and people and reconfigure memories to a certain degree. And so, while the journey of life and living continues in the mundane everyday of all participants, some exigencies have come to an end and closed the spiral of terror to which survivors are bound. None has said it better than Dorit, whose words shall conclude this chapter:

> When I told my daughter about my Heldenplatz experience she said: 'Now you have come full circle. Even if you will not do anything anymore, you have done everything that you had to do'. And so I reached the end of my emotional journey. I cannot say 'All is well that ends well', because the bad and hurtful memories will never dissolve. But when it comes to me, I can say that the organisers of *A Letter to the Stars* enabled me to go as far as I possibly could. And for that I thank them.

Katja Seidel is Lecturer of Anthropology at the University of Vienna.

Notes

1. For example, Wolfgang Neugebauer, former director of the DÖW (Dokumentationsarchivs des österreichischen Widerstandes), was angrily criticised: allegedly, '*A Letter to the Stars* wants to compete (*Konkurrenz machen*) with the exemplary work of the Jewish Welcome Service with a mass event' (https://derstandard.at/3130182/Charakter-von-Shoah-Business, retrieved 15 March 2019).
2. See https://derstandard.at/3151625/Event-mit-Kirtagscharakter (retrieved 30 April 2019).
3. Andreas Kuba, cited in Peter Mayr and Nine Weißensteiner, *Der Standard*, print edition, 15 December 2007.
4. See https://derstandard.at/3130182/Charakter-von-Shoah-Business (retrieved 15 March 2019).

5. Historian Margit Fritsche, in *Der Standard*, 25 January 2008, https://derstandard.at/3162474/Letter-to-the-Stars-Wider-die-Monopolisierung-des-Gedenkens (retrieved March 2019).
6. Eva Blimlinger, in *Der Standard*, 8 December 2008, https://derstandard.at/3130182/Charakter-von-Shoah-Business (retrieved 15 March 2019).
7. The team was composed of two journalists, one historian, four anthropologists, one psychologist in training and one project manager as well as seven supporting members who joined our efforts during the invitation week. As a team, we had worked with teachers and students as well as survivors and their families all over the world for the last five years. In response to the criticism, we had made sure that six trained psychologists were on call at all times during the invitation week; luckily, as expected, no intervention was required. Additionally, in advance of the event, the organising team met with a psychotherapist for group supervision and psychological preparation as well as team strengthening.
8. Eva Blimlinger, in *Der Standard*, 8 December 2008, derstandard.at/3130182/Charakter-von-Shoah-Business (retrieved 15 March 2019).
9. See the different letters sent in this link: https://www.ots.at/presseaussendung/OTS_20071214_OTS0280/oesterreichische-holocaust-ueberlebende-zum-projekt-a-letter-to-the-stars-3808 (retrieved 15 March 2019).
10. See https://www.ots.at/presseaussendung/OTS_20071214_OTS0280/oesterreichische-holocaust-ueberlebende-zum-projekt-a-letter-to-the-stars-3808 for more examples (retrieved 30 April 2019).
11. https://derstandard.at/3151744/Letter-to-the-Stars-Der-Fluch-der-guten-Tat (retrieved 30 April 2019).

References

Agamben, Giorgio. 2003. *Was von Auschwitz bleibt: Das Archiv und der Zeuge*. Frankfurt am Main: Suhrkamp.

Arendt, Hannah. 1962. *The Origins of Totalitarianism*. New York: Meridian Books/The World Publishing Company.

Argenti, Nicolas, and Katharina Schramm (eds). 2012. *Remembering Violence: Anthropological Perspectives on Intergenerational Transmission*. Oxford: Berghahn Books.

Armaly, Maha, Carlo Blasi and Lawrence Hannah. 2004 'Stari Most: Rebuilding More than a Historic Bridge in Mostar', *Museum International* 56(4): 6–17.

Avery, F. Gordon. 2008. *Ghostly Matters: Haunting and the Sociological Imagination*. Minnesota: Minnesota University Press.

Beniston, Judith. 2003. '"Hitler's First Victim"? Memory and Representation in Post-War Austria: Introduction', *Austrian Studies* 11: 1–13.

Das, Veena, and Arthur Kleinman. 2001. 'Introduction', in V. Das, A. Kleinman, M. Lock, M. Ramphele and P. Reynolds (eds), *Remaking a World: Violence, Social Suffering, and Recovery*. Berkeley: University of California Press, pp. 1–30.

Didi-Huberman, Georges. 2012. *Images in Spite of All: Four Photographs from Auschwitz*. Chicago, IL: University of Chicago Press.

Favero, Paolo. 2018. *The Present Image: Visible Stories in a Digital Habitat*. London: Palgrave Macmillan.

Feldman, Allen. 1991. *Formations of Violence: The Narrative of the Body and Political Terror in Northern Ireland.* Chicago, IL: University of Chicago Press.
Fletcher, Laurel E., and Harvey M. Weinstein. 2002. 'Violence and Social Repair: Rethinking the Contribution of Justice to Reconciliation', *Human Rights Quarterly* 24(3): 573–639.
Hayner, Priscilla. 2001. *Unspeakable Truths.* New York: Routledge.
Hinton, Alexander. 2010. 'Toward an Anthropology of Transitional Justice', in A.L. Hinton (ed.), *Transitional Justice: Global Mechanisms and Local Realities after Genocide and Mass Violence.* New Brunswick: Rutgers University Press, pp. 1–24.
Horkheimer, Max, and Theodor Adorno. 2002. *Dialectic of Enlightenment: Philosophical Fragments.* Stanford, CA: Stanford University Press. [German original *Dialektik der Aufklärung*, published in 1944].
Knoller, Freddy. 2005. *Living with the Enemy: My Secret Life on the Run from the Nazis.* London: Metro.
Langer, Lawrence L. 1993. *Holocaust Testimonies: The Ruins of Memory.* New Haven, CT: Yale University Press.
Levi, Trude. 2003. *Did You Ever Meet Hitler, Miss? A Holocaust Survivor Talks to Young People.* London: Valentine Mitchell.
Murphy, Fiona. 2011. 'Archives of Sorrow: An Exploration of Australia's Stolen Generations and Their Journey into the Past', *History & Anthropology* 22(4): 481–95.
Musil, Robert. (1927) 1985. 'Monuments', in Burton Pike (ed. and trans.), *Selected Writings.* New York: Continuum, p. 323.
Nordstrom, Carolyn. 1995. 'War on the Frontlines', in C. Nordstrom and A. Robben (eds), *Fieldwork under Fire: Contemporary Studies of Violence and Survival.* Los Angeles: University of California Press, pp. 129–55.
Povinelli, Elizabeth. 2002. *The Cunning of Recognition: Indigenous Alterities and the Making of Australian Multiculturalism.* Durham, NC: Duke University Press.
Robben, Antonius. 2000. 'The Assault on Basic Trust: Disappearance, Protest, and Reburial in Argentina', in A. Robben and M. Suárez-Orozco (eds), *Cultures under Siege: Collective Violence and Trauma.* Cambridge: Cambridge University Press, pp. 70–101.
Seidel, Katja. 2017. 'Peacebuilding, Locals and Academia: A Call for Reciprocity and Participation. Comment on Special Section "Peacebuilding and the Local"', *Social Anthropology* 25(4): 485–92.
Shaw, Martin. 2007. *What Is Genocide?* London: Polity Press.
Taylor, Charles. 1994. *Multiculturalism: Examining the Politics of Recognition.* Princeton, NJ: Princeton University Press.
Torpey, John (ed.). 2003. *Politics and the Past: On Repairing Historical Injustices.* Lanham, MD: Rowman Littlefield.
Verein Lernen aus der Zeitgeschichte. 2008. (Barbara Foglar-Deinhardstein, Marie-Christine Hartig, Andreas Kuba, Markus Priller and Katja Seidel). *Die letzten Zeugen: Das Vermächtnis der Holocaust-Überlebenden.* Brno: Neografia.

SNAPSHOT 12

LIVING SWITCHES

WLADIMIR SGIBNEV

At the busy Sadbarg intersection, Dushanbe's main boulevard, the Rudaki Avenue, makes a turn towards the railway station. Pedestrians, private cars, taxis, *marshrutka* minibuses, big buses and the city's distinctive green and white trolleybuses juggle their way through the dense traffic. Trolleybuses bear – as post-Soviet scholars and travellers very well know – the mark of tapping electric current from two overhead wires suspended above the streets, by means of their distinctive trolley poles. These poles are attached to trolleybus roofs with a spring mechanism, intended to provide enough pressure to keep the poles firmly in contact with the wires. On intersections, where overhead wires cross, electromagnetic switches are provided in order to enable the poles to safely quit one pair of overhead wires for another, leading in the desired direction.

Yet at the Sadbarg intersection, the picture looks somewhat different. Surely, trolleybuses abound, yet magically cross the street and carry on, with decent speed, towards the railway station with lowered poles. But how? Public transport geeks may instantly think of dual-mode trolleybuses, equipped with some off-wire capability, like regenerative brakes feeding into supercapacitor units, or basic diesel-electric auxiliaries. The ethnographer, however, untarnished by propulsion-based nerdiness, stands by and lengthily observes human–technology interactions unfolding.

Teenage boys in purple waistcoats – otherwise working as fare collectors – stand on the small ladders at the rear of trolleybuses. With one hand, they clutch the ladder staves, and with the other, firmly hold the rope dangling from the trolley poles. Some metres prior to the intersection, the trolleybus boy would tear down the rope, and thus lower the contact poles.

Figure S12.1. Trolleybus boy in Dushanbe. Photograph by Wladimir Sgibnev.

The trolleybus keeps rolling, through inertia – without electricity supply, brakes aren't working anyway – while the boy holds the poles down with the help of the rope. Once the trolleybus has reached the other side of the intersection, the boy would jump onto the street and run after the rolling bus, firmly holding the ropes, in order to prevent the poles from rebounding and becoming entangled in the overhead wires. The boy carries on, half running, half jumping, enjoying the poles' ever-rebounding springs,[1] and, still in motion, dexterously releases the rope, so that the poles, sparklingly, rejoin the overhead wires. The loosened rope in hand, the boy jumps back at the ladder, the engine restarts, and the bus carries on towards the busy terminus in front of the railway station.

The reason behind this stunning, skilful, graceful dance, starring a boy and a bus, is fairly simple: the switches at the Sadbarg intersection broke down a while ago, and the boys double as living switches, helping the buses to cross the intersection. Switches are among the most fragile parts of the wiring system, and thus among the most labour-intensive in terms of maintenance and repair.

Almost all public transport networks throughout the former Soviet Union have shed feathers following the economic decline and the political turmoil of the 1990s – most saliently in Central Asia and the South Caucasus, where only a handful of systems have survived out of the many dozens back in Soviet times (Sgibnev 2014). With the collapse of the USSR, responsibility for running urban transport was transferred from central ministries to municipalities, without any appropriate transfer of funding (Gwilliam 2001). The ageing rolling stock was decaying and no funding was available for the purchase of new vehicles, spare parts or the maintenance of overhead lines. Privatisation of investment-heavy tram and trolleybus systems largely failed, and most municipalities opted against maintaining the high level of subsidies, leading to widespread closures (Finn 2008) and the subsequent surge of informal minibus-based transport offers, the renowned *marshrutkas*.

In spite of this hostile environment, large-scale investments were injected into Dushanbe's trolleybuses from the 2000s onwards (Sgibnev 2014). Roughly US$15 million were spent on trolleybuses from 2005 to 2010, a gigantic sum considering the country's otherwise dire budget. In Dushanbe, forty-five trolleybuses built in the 1970s–80s had survived the 1990s turmoil, enough to provide a basic service on a rudimentary network. In 2001, four engines were purchased from the Russian TROLZA plant – the first investment in the electric transit system since independence. Starting from 2004, one hundred buses were delivered to Dushanbe. A follow-up contract in 2008 ensured the delivery of sixty vehicles more, and further ones are upcoming. The older engines were immediately sold for scrap after the 2005 delivery, despite being in good shape. Even those four vehicles delivered in 2001 were put out of service. Currently, Dushanbe's rolling stock is among the youngest in the whole ex-USSR, yet this large investment has proved to be excessive and unsustainable. Out of 160 engines available, barely ninety are in daily service. What is more, funding aimed at rolling stock replacement had no maintenance counterpart, either for vehicles or the infrastructure. Drivers have to shoulder maintenance costs themselves, or brand new trolleybuses are cannibalised for spare parts to keep the rest of the fleet running.

The decision to modernise the trolleybus fleet seems therefore driven to a large extent by show-off symbolic policies. These policies come at the expense of those at the very bottom of the food chain: the teenage bus conductors who are compelled to perform these risky manoeuvres. Cheap juvenile labour, coupled with adroitness and recklessness, thus seems more cost-effective than sending out repair troops. This constellation urges us to draw attention to the too-often neglected labour factor, when discussing infrastructures (Rekhviashvili and Sgibnev 2018). Indeed, other examples abound in the region. Students are compelled to push trolleybuses from roads when electricity provision is failing. Underage conductors are being employed on Tajik *marshrutkas* for the simple reason that their salary is cheaper than replacing vehicle doors, which inattentive passengers brutally slam at every entry and exit. Looking at the back-end of infrastructures thus may open up attention to the emergence of new and different orders (Alexander, Buchli and Humphrey 2007), and reveal their underlying contradictions: linking societies (Tonkiss 2013), objects and technologies (Larkin 2013) and ensuring connectivity for the masses, all while fostering splintering (Graham and Marvin 2001) and inequalities (Hirt 2012) at the same time.

Wladimir Sgibnev is Senior Researcher at the Leibniz Institute for Regional Geography.

Note

1. Technical norms, reportedly, stipulate for a rebound capacity of the poles equivalent to a weight of 24 kg. With boys weighing roughly double, the poles would not lift them high up to the air, but the springs are strong enough to allow for lengthy jumps. This is also revealing of the sheer strength required to hold down the poles with one hand during the first phase of the dancing performance.

References

Alexander, C., V. Buchli and C. Humphrey (eds.). 2007. *Urban Life in Post-Soviet Asia.* London: UCL Press.

Finn, B. 2008. 'Market Role and Regulation of Extensive Urban Minibus Services as Large Bus Service Capacity Is Restored – Case Studies from Ghana, Georgia and Kazakhstan: Reforms in Public Transport', *Research in Transportation Economics* 22(1): 118–25.

Graham, S., and S. Marvin. 2001. *Splintering Urbanism: Networked Infrastructures, Technological Mobilities and the Urban Condition.* London: Routledge.

Gwilliam, K. 2001. 'Competition in Urban Passenger Transport in the Developing World', *Journal of Transport Economics and Policy* 35(1): 99–118.

Hirt, S. 2012. *Iron Curtains: Gates, Suburbs and Privatization of Space in the Post-Socialist City.* Malden, MA: Wiley-Blackwell.

Larkin, B. 2013. 'The Politics and Poetics of Infrastructure', *Annual Review of Anthropology* 42: 327–43.

Rekhviashvili, L., and W. Sgibnev. 2018. 'Placing Transport Workers on the Agenda: The Conflicting Logics of Governing Mobility on Bishkek's Marshrutkas', *Antipode*, Online first. https://onlinelibrary.wiley.com/doi/abs/10.1111/anti.12402.

Sgibnev, W. 2014. 'Urban Public Transport and the State in Post-Soviet Central Asia', in K. Burrell and K. Hörschelmann (eds), *Mobilities in Socialist and Post-Socialist States.* Basingstoke: Palgrave Macmillan, pp. 194–216.

Tonkiss, F. 2013. *Cities by Design: The Social Life of Urban Form.* Cambridge: Polity.

CHAPTER 12

Brokenness and Normality in Design Culture

ADAM DRAZIN

Something is wrong with normality. Studies of repair presume there is a problem that needs addressing, but often the brokenness can be clearer than what the new normal should be. For the most part, repair concerns very ordinary situations, not extraordinary ones, and the re-establishment of ordinary predictable routine. So, in order to re-establish what is normal, it is necessary to establish conceptually what normal might be. In this concluding chapter, I consider the implications of forms of 'brokenness' in a London ethnography, undertaken to inform a design project, and in commentaries on design culture. By design culture I mean the infusion of a sense of professional intentionality that haunts most of the manufactured goods and services in the world, which concerns popular understandings of how design in industry relates to the use of goods and services in everyday life. Since professional design skills of many kinds are increasingly influential, ideas of brokenness usually reference design intentions. Anthropology has thought about brokenness culturally in several ways: as political or economic marginality, as dislocation, as disruption of routines, or as the shortfall of life against expectations. I suggest thinking about brokenness and repair in terms of belonging and alterity, which together create a sense of authority within the everyday relationships where normality is constructed and understood.

'Some stuff just makes you look like a really lazy, bad person if you don't have it fixed . . . That stuff tends to get fixed quicker', said Jenny, about her home in London. Brokenness can reflect what sort of a person you are.

Sadly, Jenny did not actually feel able to fix everything in her home herself. She did, however, know people who might: 'My boyfriend's dad is really handy. He is super, super handy . . . I feel like I am surrounded by people who do that and I think that if I was very serious, I know there are ways I could do it and I know where to get information or who I might ask'. Jenny's reflections show how conversations about brokenness and repair can quickly lead to talking about relationships, and drawing comparisons between oneself and the people one is intimate with. Brokenness can also seem pervasive, it has a materially leaky quality: her otherwise idiosyncratic possessions, when broken, become 'stuff', and one broken thing impacts on others because the domestic routines are disrupted.

But ideas of brokenness vary. In a conversation elsewhere in London, Bettina was much more assertive, and did not necessarily want to be more like the other people in her life. 'My husband thinks they are rubbish and he tries to get every opportunity to throw them away', she said of some of the broken things in her home, which she carefully collected for repair and reuse. 'For me, I believe I can use them in the future, no matter what they look like right now.' What seemed in Jenny's home a vulnerability seemed a strength in Bettina's.

Even in these two short examples, the experiential and intimate connection between brokenness and peripherality is already evident. People can feel peripheral to cultural processes, often through comparing and contrasting themselves with other people they are close to. This relativity makes peripherality about who we are, not only where we are. Studies of design culture in recent years have reflected on these notions. Some studies debate the relative centricity and peripherality of professional designers and 'design users' to ways of working on the material world. Other work, meanwhile, has argued that humans in general are becoming 'peripheral' to design processes, and hence rejected the idea that the design of goods and services should put people at its heart. The brokenness study discussed here is the work of Adjoa Armah, Kelsey McClellan, Sarah Gazzaz and Xu He, postgraduate members of the Studio of Material Life at UCL (University College London). They worked with Daniel Charny of the organisation Fixperts. Building on their work, I argue that processes of brokenness and repair are not only about re-forming material things and places, but about re-establishing the centricity of people. Many kinds of work are understood as 'repair', often for different reasons, but a common thread is that people feel a sense of 'returning' to the centre of otherwise abstract cultural processes. A human purposiveness is restored to environments and to objects. The anthropology of repair is, I believe, profoundly humanist. This means that it is capable of changing how we perceive the operation of global capital within everyday situations.

This chapter proceeds in four sections. I first consider how repair is of particular cultural relevance now, not only because of material decay and dysfunction, but because the very idea of human action in the world has been compromised. I secondly outline the UCL Fixperts project, which illustrates how 'being broken' is not a straightforward idea, and unpack some of its dimensions. Some kinds of repair are actually about belonging in a place enough to have the social authority to act to fix something. This discussion of belonging leads thirdly to a consideration of peripherality in anthropology, and how anthropologists including Gregory (2013) and Harvey and Krohn-Hansen (2018) have thought about feelings of dislocation. Fourth, and finally, I draw on Bateson's theory of schismogenesis to frame everyday normality as problematic, and repairing as offering ways towards new normals, while also offering a feeling of return to places, to routine, and to a sense of self.

Brokenness in Global Design Chains

Why is it that repair has assumed particular importance in the contemporary world, in so many different ways and places? One of the recurring themes of the research in this volume is the compulsion that can be encompassed in feelings of abandonment. When first presented in Göttingen in 2017, these papers led to discussions deeper than simple, self-contained acts of repairing things. Many field sites have the feeling of being picture frames out of which the human subject has just stepped, if only for a moment (see especially Errázuriz and Martínez, both in this volume). Some sites are profoundly nostalgic, where repair is a defence against the possibility of human absence and loss (Frederiksen, this volume). Repair work is often an alternative to acquisition, investing objects with the value of work. In many projects, the experience of brokenness as abandonment thus evokes the imagination of a social person, as memory, as neighbour, as labour.

Anthropological accounts of peripherality commonly propose understandings of the problematic ways that people and material things intersect in different places. These frameworks include seeing a condition of peripherality as decay, hybridisation, movement or inequality. Decay presumes simply that material change is inevitable, a property of the world. Things decay and break in and of themselves, and over time material environments tend towards obsolescence. Hybridisation is more subtle, conceiving of ever-increasing dependence of human culture on artifice and technology. Human–artefact entities necessarily develop, and while some embrace this, others experience their own human nature as ever more peripheral (Haraway 1990). Approaches that emphasise movement suggest that we need to rethink the agency of people. Traditionally, people are thought about as active and motile, and material things inclining to passive stasis, but in a globalising world of accelerating flows, we experience ever-increasing disjunctures (Appadurai 1996), or alternatively frictions (Tsing 2004). Approaches to peripherality as inequality, meanwhile, retain an idea of privileging persons above things, but see material things as politicised mediators of notions of equality among a frequently divided humanity. There are therefore many ways of accounting for how a 'broken' material environment can be experienced as peripherality.

Work in the field of design throws a different light on the nature of these problems. Design work, undertaken by professional design teams and companies, is now recognised as a key component in global infrastructures that shape material objects and environments (Julier 2017). This is to say that there is an increasing consciousness of design work at the same time as companies' and governments' capacities to orchestrate material change accelerates, such that material things are implicated as indices of acts of thinking (see Drazin 2012). In design, value is often created through the thinking work by which global industrial actors anticipate and consider the specifics of local conditions. Fry (2008, 2012), however, argues that there is a need for a drastic shift in how design has been undertaken up until now, and that professional design's role as the brain of globalised industrial manufacturing and services, designing to support local social and practical concerns, is dysfunctional. In recent decades, rather than being led by the development and refining of things, forms and technologies, design has become more 'user-centred', led more by an exploration of human needs, requirements, relationships and experiences (see also Buchanan 1998). Fry, however, points out how this very humanisation of design work has been environmentally destructive. Responding to human lives on the small scale, as through ethnography, is a relatively short-term project that in the longer term can ignore the environments in which humans live and upon which we depend. He understands this in terms of processes of 'de-futuring', such that design work involves re-futuring humanity:

> the unsustainable nature of human beings, past and present, is a structural condition of negation. Unsustainability essentially names human-initiated processes hostile to our future being and the being of many nonhuman others. (Fry 2012: 4)

This implies that the problem for people is, in many ways, design as currently practised. Acts of repair exist as one link in longer design chains by which there is always prior artifice and design intentionality. Goods and environments are understood as professionally designed, by people who in turn have often tried to consider the projects, aims and intentions of local people (who are 'designing', in lower case). One reason why repair comes to assume a much more prominent role is because *most* kinds of work are now understood as about re-forming what others have done before (see Berglund, this volume; and Drazin et al. 2016). Where the problem is the legacy of prior purpose, all work becomes an act of repurposing, and hence repair. In Fry's terms, brokenness concerns how people understand de-futuring, and repair concerns how people respond, which can involve re-making or unmaking.

There are therefore several reasons for understanding cultures of repair as not only about getting material things working again, but about addressing more profound senses of social brokenness lying at the heart of ordinary, normal ways of conducting everyday life. Humans are here the problem as well as the solution. Repair comes to be a kind of action that assumes its nature and significance according to its positioning in the chain of other human actions and intentions. One of the mediators of this sense of centres and peripheries is design, creating a constant sense of global innovation centres where futures happen, and de-futured peripheries (see Suchman 2011). By exploring the Fixperts research at UCL, we can unpack the diverse experiences of brokenness that can emerge in localised design conversations.

Brokenness as a Design Problem

Fixperts is an organisation that works to promote design education, by helping design students to work on real issues in people's lives. It does this by helping 'fixperts' (who are usually design students) connect with 'fix partners', who have a problem that needs solving. Through this arrangement, design comes to be very much a personal activity, which is first about understanding life as it is lived, and then secondly about building an understanding of the relevant 'design problems'. This is a form of human-centred design, but importantly it works at a face-to-face level when most such work is more abstract. Establishing a relationship diffuses the feeling of what designers often call 'ownership of the problem', so the feeling of responsibility for the design response is shared. The brokenness project, undertaken at UCL in 2014, comprised four postgraduate anthropologists working with Fixperts. As I will elaborate, when undertaking a range of ethnographic case studies in people's homes, they quickly reframed the work as being not about fixing but brokenness. Brokenness, not repair, was what people talked about, and was a protracted, intriguing, diverse, compelling and profoundly human topic, compared with the subject of fixing or repairing, which was less verbalised since it seemed to speak for itself.

We might presume that we know what brokenness and repair are, and how they are mutually constituted. Let me outline some of the possible assumptions. Brokenness might appear to be an unusual, distinctive state that sets a thing apart from other (unbroken) things, so not a part of, but a divergence from, ordinary life. We might presume that repair work maps fairly directly onto breakages, such that one repair addresses one condition of brokenness. Repair, it might be presumed, comprises an aspiration for stasis and continuity, a return to how things were, so as to preserve similar routines. We might also make presumptions about the morality of repair: that brokenness is not only problematic but wrong. And that repair is morally right and hence always compelling.

It quickly became evident to the team that many of these self-evident presumptions could be challenged. A modern designer, like the students involved in Fixperts, is called upon to be a kind of mixture of a thinker, handy maker, crafter, psychologist and social scientist. Many designers think about problems in a highly abstract and social fashion, and a conversation with a fix partner can produce a wide range of alternative definitions of what needs to be addressed. If somebody has a mobility difficulty, the problem could be interpreted as mobility, or loneliness, or provisioning, or self-confidence. Some designers will design a transport solution. Others may ask what they need mobility for, and consequently propose designs for better at-home shopping services, family communications, exercising, ways to organise social events, or how to be a better grandparent. In addition, informants talked a lot about the broken things in their homes.

The team therefore, as a part of refocusing on brokenness rather than repair, researched domestic material culture around London. They asked about broken things in homes, about whether and why and how they were seen as broken, how they came to be that way, and what was planned for them. They acknowledged that many people go on for years without actually seeing any aspect of their lives as needing repair. The research took a narrative approach, trying to elicit the stories behind material things, and in doing so, it aimed to elicit such dimensions as routines, practices, ideals and aesthetic inclinations. This was not a major long-term project, capable of a conclusive holistic viewpoint on brokenness. Rather, it was a small-scale ethnographic work aiming to be an experimental, hypothetical interrogation of brokenness using diverse approaches.

Four themes emerged from the ethnographic discussions, and these were presented as 'types', figures with whom a fixpert might find themselves working: the Reminiscer, the Recycler, the Reinventor and the 'Removed'. These are not a definitive set of categories, but serve to unpack the diverse forms of brokenness and fixing, and how different themes intersect and contradict, such as the distinctiveness of broken things; working to re-establish continuity in lifestyles, or change; the relative 'goodness' of repaired or broken things; and the importance of relationships in the mix.

Reminiscing reflects situations in which a sense of nostalgia drives repair, the compulsion to evoke, or return to a more ideal situation remembered from the past. Yet that does not mean that a desire for stasis or continuity drives repair. Reminiscing does not mean that one would necessarily repair an object, because remembering can be more important than actually using something. What it means is that there is a sense of decay and ruination surrounding certain things, and that they appear almost as items of personal heritage. Frequently, these broken objects evoke people, relationships and experience. When 'repaired', such souvenirs might also be 'preserved', the state of brokenness maintained in perpetuity, and so creating permanent souvenirs.

By contrast, recycling is a form of repair with a systemic and utilitarian function, where brokenness concerns problems of value. If reminiscing involves a perception of brokenness as decay or ruination, but preserves value, recycling by contrast acknowledges the possibility of things becoming 'rubbish', a term that was once defined as when things are in a state of zero-value (Thompson 1979. When people work to constantly reuse, they are considering what they do in relation to broad, systemic values. People may talk about repairing something just to get it working again, but nonetheless there are trade-offs being made against wider impacts in the system of material goods and substances. So, the choice to recycle rather than buy new brings short-term and long-term aims into elision and comparison. Because there is a more systemic consideration in recycling, frequently mutual relationships and responsibilities feature strongly, and these intimate social connections assume a microcosmic quality, where one small act stands for grander collective work.

Reinvention is different again. It takes the form of upcycling, actions to fix things that makes them more valuable. 'This could be better', or 'this could be different' was how brokenness was being perceived in this instance. Reinvention celebrates the skill and vision of the person doing the work, an optimistic stance to repair in which things that no longer function become resources. Broken mugs become flowerpots, defunct furniture is put together in new ways and becomes something entirely different. The transformatory dimension of reinvention reflects a more aesthetic side of repair, in which the stylistic vision for the home of the person doing the repair becomes highly important. It also means that things at some level remain evidently broken. The act of repair into something which now functions has been achieved through a sort of sideways step, so that it is evidently a broken thing, out of order but reused.

Hence these three stereotypes, the Recycler, Reminiscer and Reinventor, show how, when asked for the stories behind broken things in their homes, stories emerge that reflect more profound social states. Fixing is not always about re-establishing a normal lifestyle, but positions people across time and space. Very often, brokenness is understood within sequences or chains of thoughts, intentions and empathic acts of consideration. Yet importantly, all three of these stereotypes are figures who have both the capacity and inclination to undertake repairs. By contrast, the people whom the team called the 'Removed' were different. These were people and moments that epitomised brokenness in that simple things needed straightforward repairs, and yet often there was no repair. There was a puzzle waiting to be unpacked here in moments that seemed to be about maintaining the status quo. Typically, somebody might say they just wanted to 'take care of' material things, not change them, or as one woman said, 'I want to leave things the way I found them'. If something was broken when a person first encountered it, they would feel that to fix it would be wrong, a trespass beyond their role. Yet the same person, if something broke while they had it, might make a huge effort to fix it. An object might lie around for a long time – vacuum cleaners, appliances or home fittings – clearly broken, for

Figure 12.1. An informant shows some of her accessories, whole and broken, and her accompanying fixing kit. Photograph by Adam Drazin.

months or years. Often, this situation applied in rented or shared (student) housing, but it could be objects inherited from parents. These were instances devoid of vision, lacking in desire or aspiration, but nonetheless deeply considerate. It was not laziness, but in many ways closer to a sense of propriety, or even respect for others' property, that made repair inappropriate.

Brokenness is diverse, relative and socially situated. What appears to one person as broken may not appear so to another. This is not only about individual wishes, preferred aesthetics or ideals, it is also about the social relationships and responsibilities in which people are enmeshed through their homes. Brokenness is pervasive, with multitudes of things and assemblages in every home. It is not a divergence from normality, it is very normal and ordinary. Brokenness does not mean repair must follow. There are instances when the right thing to do is *not* to fix. Broken things confront people with the issue of whether they belong in a place, and in effect ask people whether they have the authority, not just the capacity, to repair. This also means that there is an immediacy or intimacy in the relationship of people and things, where repair occurs. It is in this situation of everyday belonging and intimacy with objects and places that peripherality comes to be important.

Brokenness and Peripherality

Brokenness is something people live with, and seems pervasive. Sometimes people collect broken things, preserve them and transact them. Sometimes the brokenness is a part of their value. Two people can have different capacities for repair, opening up the possibility of exchanges. At other times, there is also the question of belonging, the consideration of which is a more permanent fixture in a home – the person, or the thing. In these ways, brokenness is not only about perception, but the negotiation of the sorts of relationships that occur around places and things. Brokenness, abandonment and ruination seem to be mutually intersecting phenomena, such that one can ask which comes first, abandonment or brokenness? (See Frederiksen and also Reno, both in this volume.) There are two particular issues to be considered here. One is how anthropology can think about dislocation. A second concerns the question of whether humans can still be considered culturally central, around places and things that resonate with this sense of incipient or actual abandonment.

There are two accounts of brokenness that are inadequate for describing how brokenness and peripherality connect. The first is the Heideggerian assertion that brokenness is how the material world asserts its agency, or what Steven Jackson calls 'the world-disclosing properties of breakdown' (2014: 230). Bill Brown especially develops this idea:

> We begin to confront the thingness of objects when they stop working for us: when the drill breaks, when the car stalls, when the windows get filthy, when their flow within the circuits of production and distribution, consumption and exhibition has been arrested, however momentarily. (Brown 2001: 4)

This argument positions breakage as fundamental to material culture, as 'things' swim into human consciousness, emerging from the background of culturally predictable, passive material objects. Brokenness becomes fundamental to cultural change and reconstruction. Fry, as we have seen, extends Heidegger's thinking to examine the intrinsic brokenness of the designed world, problematising what it means to become human.

A second stance extends this approach to argue for a posthuman understanding of culture. Jackson (2014, 2015) argues that global human life has become ever more dependent upon global technical infrastructures, without which life would become unpredictable day by day. Infrastructure only 'becomes visible when it breaks' (Leigh-Star and Ruhleder 1996: 113). Human action, then, increasingly becomes relevant only as those moments when these tremendous technological networks demand to be repaired. Potentially, the material world is capable of circumventing the need for humans at all (Callon and Muniesa 2005).

Neither of these versions of brokenness adequately accounts for the importance of relationships between one person and another, nor do they consider the role of places and contexts. As the Fixperts' work and various studies in this volume make clear, brokenness often entails a negotiation of relationships, with families, landlords, councils, companies and governments. Anthropologies of labour and peripherality take a very different approach, suggesting that it is possible for human work to be viewed as valuable in itself, and helping us to reformulate our point of view on brokenness and repair. Gregory (2013) takes issue with post-humanist thinking and the tendency to ascribe agency and value to objects and things. He proposes that anthropology should redirect its attention not to material infrastructures, but to 'the 99%' (Gregory 2013: 63). In directing attention (back) to the periphery, one is then also directing one's attention to people, and to human-centred definitions of value. This has always been anthropology's primary methodology as a discipline, to seek out peripheries as a way to encounter people and their contrasting ways of living. Harvey and Krohn-Hansen (2018) argue that this exercise requires a global sensibility. Since contemporary material culture is contingent upon design and manufacturing centres distributed across the planet, people are always a labour force in the process of leaving in pursuit of employment or returning from it. Labour, knowledges and technologies must engage with global flows of information. A growing design sector is one of the phenomena that facilitates this distribution. The conception of labour as always incipiently moving facilitates a sense of a ubiquitous need for repair:

> Dislocation thus refers to the spatial movements of refugees and migrant workers, but also to other senses of disruption, such as the sentiment of feeling out of place, or of losing your bearings as things move and change around you. (Harvey and Krohn-Hansen 2018: 10)

Peripherality in this analysis is partly a function of the perception of value in material places and things. For example, when a home or hometown is seen as infrastructure, it appears as normative and fixed, but when it appears as capital (whose prime quality is the capacity to be exchanged), it is constantly shifting and transforming. Redevelopment or changes of ownership can literally pull the floor from under you. So, when we begin to think along the lines of repair as a form of work or labour, then the problem of brokenness in everyday life is less about perception, or the demands made upon humans by objects, and more about the unending work of disconnection and reconnection to places (Munz, this volume).

In this volume, the periphery implies in many instances a self-conscious sense of marginality, a kind of liminal alterity that is assumed, not only ascribed by the cultural observer. Living in an explicitly globalised world implies gradient flows that are mediated through metropolitan centres, governments (as for Yildirim Tschoepe, this volume), multinational companies and infrastructures. Holst Kjær's work in Vanse, Norway (this volume) illustrates a community that has a history of being 'peripheral' in the world system, in the sense that people would migrate to work in the USA, moving from 'periphery to centre'. The re-adoption of the historical American global centre back into Vanse celebrates but changes this sense of peripherality. The gradients of global flows, once experienced through the unfolding narratives of travel and journeys, are collapsed into instantaneous local manifestations, meaning that everyday life is produced as peripheral. What is very important to remember in this world of moving people and things is the capacity to achieve a sense of returning.

Returning to Normality

When we think about brokenness and repair, we therefore have a lot to take account of. People develop a sense of self in relation to objects, but may also draw comparisons with other people. Repair manifests very clear personal purpose and intention, and yet from a different perspective human design intention is why there is a problem. Brokenness can manifest the agency of objects in an animated world, and yet repair should also appreciate a human-centred way of thinking, privileging people above things. Perhaps most intriguing is the apparent contradiction of consciously living with brokenness. Actually acting to repair something can be a question of feeling one belongs, of having the capacity or authority, of recognition of brokenness not in things but in relationships, of a change of value, or other reasons.

I want to emphasise two particular aspects of brokenness and peripherality. One is that the sense of value is especially high in brokenness, and it really matters how one reacts to it. The second is that the capacity to repair is not uniform, but unevenly spread through society. The subject is pervaded with the micropolitics of everyday life. The social stakes are exceptionally high in situations of repair at the periphery, because the difference between broken and fixed is both a small step and also worlds apart. The studies in this volume explore disturbing themes of abandonment (e.g. Frederiksen), dereliction (e.g. Reno), emigration (e.g. Holst Kjær), corruption, and post-industrial decline (e.g. Khalvashi). They illustrate how these themes are not limited to a few places, but are the norm in much of the world. Peripherality is not fun. At the same time, studies of repair show how it can be transformative, more than simply an increase in value. Homes are made, towns are turned around, communities are forged.

High social stakes, combined with a differential and unequal sense of authority to act, direct us towards a somewhat counter-intuitive suggestion that repair can be highly politicised and involve a sense of competition between people who envisage different responses and have differential senses of belonging. To explain this, we can turn to the concept of schismogenesis to try to understand a sense of brokenness within normal ongoing community and family life, not divergent from it. Bateson ([1936] 1958, [1972] 2000) developed the theory of schismogenesis to consider how a society can deal with the ever-present risk of social fragmentation, specifically the Iatmul community in 1930s Papua New Guinea. His concept, in essence, is that people's normal identities, which are manifested in their everyday activities, ways of talking, work and behaviour, tend towards exaggeration through the mutual personal politics of relationships. So, two Iatmul men who work or socialise together might tend over time to behave ever more like Iatmul men should, according to various mutually understood principles. Over time, this competitive cycle tends eventually to unsustainable stereotypes. This is 'symmetrical schismogenesis'. Alternatively, a man and a woman in Iatmul society might also in their everyday interactions assume ever more exaggerated identities ('complementary schismogenesis'). Even though Bateson observed a tendency towards submissive behaviour among women, relative to men, the effect is the same. In their interactions, men and women tend to diverge and drift apart.

In many ways, Bateson's interpretation was exceptionally pessimistic. As far as he could see, Iatmul society and culture, the everyday identities, relationships, routines, homes, environments and ways of living, would inevitably lead towards social fragmentation. He argued, however, that a society would often develop cultures and behaviours that would mediate against the dangers of 'normality' and social fragmentation. The Iatmul villages had a range of rituals and events where, every so often, people would behave abnormally. In rituals and festive occasions, there would be an inversion of stereotypically gendered behaviour, where men adopted more feminine ways of behaving. This restored a sense of balance. Bound up within these important ritualised behaviours was a sense of purpose, made more apparent in the layering of behaviour as ritual and as choice, making the minds of people more evident and visible.

In contemporary anthropology, schismogenesis is often understood in terms of selfhood, a feeling of drift within everyday circumstances (Tacchi 1998; Feld [1982] 2012). So long as the usual conditions apply, no matter what individuals think of it, simply by behaving normally, with full appreciation of one another and out of respect for one another's authority, people can drift apart. It is in the light of this 'drift', I suggest, that we can understand brokenness and repair. Some acts of repair may be understood not as 'invisible mending', but as acts which, counter-intuitively, are able through very visible transformation to achieve a re-establishment of the status quo, meaning a more realistic normality.

Repaired things, places and communities, which are true to themselves and yet different, in this way manage to re-establish people, not things, as a focus of social life, and re-infuse a sense of human purpose. It is not so much the present condition of things and relationships as the sense of directionality or steerage that repair is able to produce. We began this chapter with Jenny and Bettina in the Fixperts research. Jenny tended to make comparisons with other people in her life: 'Some stuff just makes you look like a really lazy, bad person if you don't have it fixed . . . That stuff tends to get fixed quicker'. She was one of the people whom the group considered an example of a Recycler. She aspired to have a home in which everything worked and functioned, and felt it would be a waste to have to buy new things when one should repair and reuse the things one has. Comparing herself during the discussion to her mother, her partner, her partner's family and her friends, she aspired to be a certain kind of person.

Bettina, by contrast with Jenny, was described as a Reinventor: 'For me, I believe I can use them in the future, no matter what they look like right now'. Unlike the people whom the researchers characterised as Removed, who saw things as broken but did not act to repair them, Bettina felt fully able to assert both her authority and capacity, above other people in her life, to repair her things and home. Unlike Jenny, she aspired to transform things, often into wholly different kinds of objects with new purposes. Bettina's home seemed to be pervaded by things that had become flowerpots, cushion covers and artistic garden furniture. A 'second life', she called it; 'it is easy to make the broken objects alive'. Bettina's version of domestic normality is built from unexpected transformations, a veritable masquerade of objects. Repaired objects in this schema retain their sense of being broken. Both broken and fixed, their significance often lies in being what they are not.

In thinking about brokenness, we can witness moments when, simply through everyday routine and normal behaviour, the ordinary comes to appear almost grotesque, both in stasis and in repair, oscillating between exaggerated states of being. As we have seen, a sense of 'what is broken' very often resides not only in material things and environments, but is perceived as occurring in the social relationships, identities and experiences that are 'read into' things and environments. For many people (and in many of the examples in this volume; compare especially Seidel's work), brokenness is a sign that 'life' is in some way broken, and that it is normality that needs fixing.

Questions of Brokenness

Brokenness is pervasive, ordinary and normal. Brokenness is rarely seen as being connected to dramatic, one-off moments of breakage, rather it refers to normal ongoing ways in which the material world is constituted. Through the concept of schismogenesis, we can go some way to explaining this persistent incremental drifting kind of breakage and sense of dislocation. It is repair that tends to be remembered as the extraordinary, singular event. Acts of repair concern how one can re-establish humans as central points in a drifting world. It is, I suggest, a profoundly humanist phenomenon. The fact that repair establishes normality does not mean that it is the prevalent condition of social life. By contrast, brokenness may be more usual and repair more occasional. In this sense, repair constitutes in multiple ways a phenomenon of 'returning', but not necessarily nostalgic reconstituting.

I have argued that brokenness and repair do not necessarily converge, or have a straightforward connection, but have a manufactured relation. Repair can be about heritage and memories, building value, utility, maintaining the status quo, or any number of other aims. Sometimes, repair preserves a sense of brokenness. Brokenness is about the previous purposes and designs that we and others have cast over material things and places, and how we react to those designs inherited from the past. Brokenness can be collected and valued. In the spaces between brokenness and acts of repair, and how people bring these two ideas into a layered elision, lies the capacity of a person to position themselves, to locate and dislocate themselves in places where they belong, and establish positionality, capacities and responsibilities, with respect to others.

Studies of repair at the periphery should ask about the nature of alterity, significant others and inversions in everyday life. The idea of peripherality in anthropology traverses a spectrum of people as exotic or as marginal. As globalisation has gathered pace over the decades, the discipline has tended to reframe exoticism as marginality, in recognition of mutual involvement in relationships of globalised equality and inequality. Repair is a process that is capable of achieving the reverse process, whereby a socioeconomic marginality, at least for a time, can be rediscovered as exotic.

As so many chapters have argued in this volume, the importance of brokenness and repair is on the increase, and is embedded within these senses of peripherality. Design is one of the increasingly important cultural elements in this package, and should be considered more in order to understand it. The growing infrastructures of design mediate global labour relations. Professional design, and the ownership of design concepts, enables the separation of manufacturing from a company and subcontracting to distant labour forces. The perceived peripherality of global labour to global design is one of the currents that favours local responses to build recognition of human value and belonging. An Anthropocene world, popularly recognised as pre-designed, also means that prior purposes and design in material environments are often assumed. At one level, repair becomes a form of design itself, just the next link in the chain of artifice and remaking.

Adam Drazin is Teaching Fellow in the Department of Anthropology, University College London.

References

Appadurai, A. 1996. *Modernity at Large*. Minnesota: University of Minnesota Press.

Bateson, G. (1936) 1958. *Naven: A Survey of the Problems Suggested by a Composite Picture of the Culture of a New Guinea Tribe Drawn from Three Points of View*. Stanford, CA: Stanford University Press.

———. (1972) 2000. *Steps to an Ecology of Mind*. Chicago: University of Chicago Press.

Brown, B. 2001. 'Thing Theory', *Critical Inquiry* 28(1): 1–22.
Buchanan, R. 1998. 'Branzi's Dilemma', *Design Issues* 14(1): 3–21.
Callon, M., and F. Muniesa. 2005. 'Peripheral Vision: Economic Markets as Calculative Collective Devices', *Organization Studies* 26: 1229–50.
Drazin, A. 2012. 'The Social Life of Design Concepts', in R. Smith, W. Gunn and T. Otto (eds), *Design Anthropology*. London: Bloomsbury, 33-50.
Drazin, A., R. Knowles, I. Bredenbröker and A. Bloch. 2016. 'Collaboratively Cleaning, Archiving and Curating the Heritage of the Future', in R. Smith, K. Tang Vangkilde, M. Kjærsgaard, T. Otto, J. Halse and T. Binder (eds), *Design Anthropological Futures*. London: Bloomsbury, pp. 199–214.
Feld, S. (1982) 2012. *Sound and Sentiment*. Durham, NC: Duke University Press.
Fry, T. 2008. *Design Futuring: Sustainability, Ethics and New Practice*. London: Bloomsbury.
——. 2012. *Becoming Human by Design*. London: Bloomsbury.
Gregory, C. 2013. 'On Religiosity and Commercial Life: Toward a Critique of Cultural Economy and Posthumanist Value Theory', *Hau: Journal of Ethnographic Theory* 4(3): 45–68.
Haraway, D. 1990. *Simians, Cyborgs and Women: The Reinvention of Nature*. London: Routledge.
Harvey, P., and C. Krohn-Hansen. 2018. 'Introduction: Dislocating Labour, Anthropological Reconfigurations', *Journal of the Royal Anthropological Institute* 24(S1): 10–28.
Jackson, S. 2014. 'Rethinking Repair', in T. Gillespie, P. Boczkowski and K. Foot (eds), *Media Technologies: Essays on Communication, Materiality and Society*. New York: MIT Press, 221–40.
——. 2015. 'Repair', *Cultural Anthropology Blog*, 24 September. Retrieved 15 March 2019 from https://culanth.org/fieldsights/repair.
Julier, G. 2017. *Economies of Design*. London: Sage.
Leigh-Star, S., and K. Ruhleder. 1996. 'Steps toward an Ecology of Infrastructure: Design and Access for Large Information Spaces', *Information Systems Research* 7(1): 111–34.
Suchman, L. 2011. 'Anthropological Relocations and the Limits of Design', *Annual Review of Anthropology* 40(1): 1–18.
Tacchi, J. 1998. 'Radio Texture: Between Self and Others', in D. Miller (ed.), *Material Cultures: Why Some Things Matter*. Chicago, IL: University of Chicago Press.
Thompson, M. 1979. *Rubbish Theory: The Creation and Destruction of Value*. Oxford: Oxford University Press.
Tsing, A. 2004. *Friction: An Ethnography of Global Connection*. Princeton, NJ: Princeton University Press.

SNAPSHOT 13

And Then You See Yourself Disappear

Jason Pine

You take this path and then you see yourself disappear. That's how the hiking guide at the river-rafting excursions office explains it – is it his idiosyncratic English, or does he actually mean to say this? I'm looking for a way up Mælifellshnjúkur. I came here to disappear although only now do I know that. I've been working for years on a project that dwells in human horror. Home methlabs, the decompositioning of lives and landscapes and objects – an exuberant, melancholic, promiscuous mixing of bio and industrial chemicals and the place they make and that makes them. Being in it is hard and you get burned. 'Nothing is deeper than the skin', wrote Paul Valéry.[1]

Writing is also a hazard because words are always insufficient while also too much; you have to resist their drive to compose.

Iceland too is uncapturable and ineffable and this is good. The mosses, the mountains the sea the lakes lava fields heaths hillocks sands sky say more, and less, than I ever will; the only thing to do is to be here and then you see yourself disappear.

There are places here where it seems no human should live. In the far north region of Skagafjörður and outside a tiny town, a gravel road winds slowly and balancingly along a steep ridge where far below a rushing river takes all it knows to some far-off destination, never to be heard from again. If you follow the gravel far enough with no guarantees you eventually reach a kind of end. There are no real ends, not on gravel roads that somewhere become something else like rocks and pond-size puddles and brooks, or on mountain ascents where there is always another ascent that appears just when you make your way to a place of rest, or in valleys where the distances dilate as you labour over grassy hummocks or green-daubed lava rock, never have you imagined so much moss and rock. Nor is there an end to water flows, water that rushes wildly along valleys, tumbles abundantly over boulders, turns gently around grassy knolls, slips into sharp cuts in a fen, varnishes flat basalt, and distributes itself impatiently down ravines to meet and join other waters. Nor are there ends to vistas that always encompass yet one more feature, like another mountain, a weather pattern, another lake. Nor are there ends to the days and nights as they accumulate like a palimpsest in the sky and wash the earth below, leaving tracks of light and shadow and colour and texture and scent and sound, outrageous and unanswerable.

. . .

There are no real ends to roads and mountains and valleys and waters and days and nights and there are no real ends even to people. There is a house across the deep, steep gorge perched even hundreds of metres higher than where you find yourself on the gravel road that disarticulates into rock and mosses a world away on the other side. You squint to see how to get there, but there is no way, only the empty cold air of the precipitous gorge and the icy glacial waters running through it. People in the small town a half hour north know about the man who owned the house. He lived alone and happy and he loved life where he was. He was in his seventies when one day they found his body on the floor of the gorge. Some believe that he was happy even when he threw himself into the deep fold.

If you want to see yourself disappear, there is a lot of surface to cover first. Hours in the car will only take you so far and then you have to trudge across tall fields of sedge and through sponge-soaked bogs, past alarmed whimbrels and over splintered rocks, across gurgling rivulets, to the slow long moss heath slopes and then at last it begins. You descend into the folds and the mosses take you the rest of the way. All other sound and sight and sense and the waters and winds disappear. You see and smell and feel only warm moist mosses. No one knows you're there. No one knows you.

. . .

In 2010, Iceland appeared. Eyjafjallajökull erupted and people from around the world came to watch. The tourist boom was welcomed by Icelanders after their country's economy went bankrupt. The value of their money had plummeted, unemployment had shot up 10 per cent, and the life savings of thousands of Icelanders had vanished. Now Iceland has appeared to two million visitors each year, six times the number of Icelanders, who at least have recuperated their livelihood.

. . .

Iceland is always appearing. Magma is emerging from volcanic eruptions occurring at a mantle plume on the Mid-Atlantic Rift, the boundary of the North American and European continental plates, creating new land. This began twenty-four million years ago. Humans appeared 1,100 years ago and lived by fishing and farming. Then, only a quarter of a century ago, Iceland's liberalised banking system transformed the island into a global financial centre.

. . .

Deep, slow geological time and the lightening clouds of algorithmic finance, derivative time. Their asynchrony creates ontological rifts with a human signature. This happens in the boundary layer, the small space where rock and air meet, the space mosses inhabit (Kimmerer 2003: 15).

. . .

SEND NUDES. This someone carved in aerial-view letters by ripping out the mosses from the side of a hill. The message will remain for decades, as the grow season is short.

. . .

And then you see yourself disappear. Maybe he means your personhood, that which makes you ultimately indistinguishable from the moss graffiti artist – your inability, despite all efforts and total will, to descend into the fold alive.

Jason Pine is Professor of Anthropology and Media Studies at SUNY Purchase.

Note

1. "Ce qu'il y a de plus profond en l'homme, c'est la peau . . .", *L'Idée fixe* (1932: 21).

References

Kimmerer, Robin Wall. 2003. *Gathering Moss: A Natural and Cultural History of Mosses.* Corvallis: Oregon State University Press.

Valéry, Paul. 1932. *L'Idee fixe ou Deux Hommes à la Mer.* Paris: Les Laboratoires Martinet.

EPILOGUE

This Mess We're in, or Part of

PATRICK LAVIOLETTE

> Over the skyscrapers (Sweat on my skin, oh)
> The city
> This mess we're in
> —PJ Harvey, *Stories from the City, Stories for the Sea*

The distinct smashing sound of glass breaks the silence of a Baltic midsummer night. It's the noise made by a bottle shattering violently on the tarmac – at a time of year during which the skies are never completely dark. Peeking out of the half-open window of my fourth-floor flat, I see an older man throw a paper bag over the fence, shuffling away quickly but quietly. There's an admission of guilt in his clumsy stumbling gait, as he looks over his shoulder repeatedly. Even without seeing this, there would be no doubt as to it being him who has caused this penumbral perturbation. It's only a question of why? With the throw of the bag, there's not much to suggest it was a complete accident. Maybe he was venting some steam after losing a bet at football this evening. England did actually win earlier, by scoring on the stroke of the ninetieth minute – that always confuses some pundits. Or maybe he was simply aiming to throw his beer bottle into the recycling bins and missed. But even if they'd been open, which they are not, they face in the opposite direction to the pavement, so again this seems an unlikely interpretation. Besides, his sheepish demeanour indicates intent. Breakage for breakage's sake.

Wallowing in my own intolerance at 2 a.m., I'm tempted to shout out at the bottle breaker, who is now escaping unscathed into the half-night. There's a lingering sense that I should cause him some alarm for his lack of worldly respect. To what end though? He's a local and I'm just a semi-resident, someone who cannot even chastise him in his own language (either Estonian or Russian, judging by his approximate age and fairly worn-out clothing). This, however, is only the most basic attempt at a Holmesian process of deduction which Chris Pinney (2012) has playfully argued is intrinsic to any material culture approach. Those who were so inclined might go on to 'fantasise' further about this petty vandal. To ask what other deeds this man (largely silent, but far from gentle) will go on to achieve during these wee hours of the morning. Will he redeem himself by kissing his children lovingly on the forehead as they sleep? Or by kindly feeding the cat before it wakes everyone else up at dawn, begging for breakfast?

What a crazy world we live in, I think to myself, as the song 'This Mess We're In' springs to mind. Even though the lyrics refer to the breaking up of a short romance, it does seem most apt since the subject is loveless love, and that somehow captures this moment well. This little incident of everyday life occurs around the same time that Francisco has sent me Eeva Berglund's chapter to comment on for this very volume. I'm pleased to read that she has reflected on the messy entanglements of activism and apathy, whereby the unordinary character of breakage allows for a socially accepted ethos in which the iconoclastic is fetishised to the point of reigning as the motif that best represents the twenty-first century's consumer-driven, neoliberal economies (Latour 2002).

This short epilogue serves as a concluding 'stream of consciousness' statement – in keeping with some of the strategies of a book that strives to be different. Rather than providing a summary, or offering a mini-ethnography, or arguing for any particular conceptual position, it situates itself somewhere in between the former two aims. Far from making any original argumentative contribution of the comprehensive sort, the semi-arranged musings that follow should nonetheless say something more than a fragmented mêlée. Otherwise, we'd still be in the terrain of breakage – clearly missing the mark.

Anyway, returning to my story, I'm especially annoyed about this pseudo-sacrificial bottle fracas because there will now be some shards of glass on the road and I'll likely cycle right through them tomorrow when using that route. Or nearly as irksome, a car might crush the bottle fragments later on, causing some high-pitched noise just as I'm falling asleep. Perhaps what's most irritating of all is that I can't see any real repair occurring as a result of this senseless act, except perhaps the man's own catharsis in having symbolically destroyed something noisily at this hour. This still leaves me unsatisfied though, disrupting my thoughts in the way that it epitomises many acts of callous entropy. And such a late-night observation stands quite some distance away from any sophisticated ethnographically informed recollection. Nor does it reside in the vicinity of a breakthrough –

other than being a sound that's broken through a relatively peaceful night. Still, it hardly allows us to consider any significant clash of cultures. Nor does it provide a cosmologically shifting catalyst in any way reminiscent of that bottle that fell from the heavens into the Kalahari Desert, as poignantly and humorously depicted in Jamie Uys's *The Gods Must Be Crazy* (1980). Now that's a bottle, unbroken it should be stressed, worth remembering – worthy of several messages.

Yet even such a banal anecdote raises some questions for our times – and for our purposes here. Who else is disturbed by noticing such acts of carelessness, if not outright malicious contempt? Who will have to clean up the mess and is their labour not best invested elsewhere? Of course, such 'public' messes usually clean themselves up, so to speak. The glass gets broken down into ever smaller pieces by the passing traffic, until it ends up in a drainage sewer, or brushed away by some kind soul. Does your average citizen really care so little for their own immediate environment? If so, how do we remain optimistic when imagining the future of humanity? It's all very well to ponder over the relationships between form and functionality, brokenness and reparation, the whole and the malfunctioning, but if this is the default attitude for most people, then we really are facing an uphill battle. So it's worth reminding ourselves that such 'academic' inquiries need to matter. It is for this reason that we've chosen to align short personal micro-insights alongside longer, more conceptually developed macro-discussions, the aim being to pair certain case studies with (auto)biographical narratives of a more evocative and thus perhaps compelling style.

And so, contrary to the diverse contributions to this volume, such an incident as the bottle in the street is not pursued ethnographically. If it is at all useful heuristically, this is only insofar as it can remind us of the value in the type of studies published herein which have sought to contextualise, problematise and give some in-depth *longue durée* to their respective subjects. Hence, there's not much point going on with any fanciful description of nocturnal bottle-breaking here. What I can take up, though, is the potential bike journey that this broken drinking container could potentially disrupt, if I were indeed to puncture a tyre because of the glass on the street. As someone who has never taken a driver's test, I perhaps have more bicycle stories than many people. Happy, silly, even quite traumatic. Indeed, only days after submitting my dissertation, I was nearly killed on the Marylebone Road near Baker Street by a jeep going through a red light. The driver did not even bother to stop after I ran into the rear passenger door at over fifteen miles per hour. That hasn't deterred me from cycling, however. Around the time of being officially recognised as an adult, I bought a second-hand silver Peugeot racer from a friend. It was exceptionally light, with tyres less than an inch wide. It had been well loved and so was in good nick. I used it myself with much affection until stupidly leaving it overnight in the dodgy setting of an inner city back-alley. The solid chain hadn't been cut, but an easily breakable padlock had been smashed apart.

I cannot think right now of many 'objects' over the course of my life that I've spent more time buying, finding, borrowing, cleaning, loaning, mending, storing, injuring myself with, swapping parts over, and even transporting around the world. This is the case, especially recently, when not actually using a bike all that much for extended periods of time. And yet it was through having a bike repaired that Francisco demonstrated his generosity this past spring when, at his own expense, he restored a blue Peugeot racer for me. I'd found this near-antique abandoned in my apartment complex a few weeks after mine had been stolen.

I had intended this found bike as a gift for Fran, but was unable to have it fixed when an expert mechanic had told me the rear axle had been broken so severely as to make any future repairs unsafe. Dissuaded, I gave up. But Fran's perseverance has resulted in a different outcome. One that shows a fundamental feature of repair – the best ones are often 'invisible', they go unnoticed, or rather, unnoticeable. This bike also reminds us of several features addressed in Simon Batterbury and Tim Dant's comparative chapter on bicycle repairs. For one, such objects have kept a simplicity in their design, their hands-on maintenance and their interchangeability of parts. Additionally, they have an intrinsic power to stand outside normative market economy systems – consistently standing as icons for utopian visions of self-reliance, sustainability, social justice and community-building. Indeed, Tomas Errázuriz's chapter in particular, in which he links love, home and the movement of domestic objects through kinship networks, reminds us that for many people in many circumstances, repair is a way of establishing or reinforcing relationships. The gifting of time and/or labour in order to mend something for someone is frequently an act of the most sacrificially intimate sort.

These are all fundamental concepts when thinking of how we can contribute to fixing the planet in this age of the Anthropocene. Or as Jussi Parikka (2016) prefers to call it in his little manifesto, *The Anthrobscene*. His extended essay was published around the time when there was a buzz within media and digital culture studies that started focusing on the relationship to deep geological time and the brokenness of our global energy dependence as a species. He cites sociologist Jennifer Gabrys (2011) as an intellectual canon for considering e-waste, fracking mineral extraction and other globally impacting resource exploitation regimes, as well as mega-scale accident sources, in order to begin comprehending the mess, the obscenity, we're in.

Parikka offers a fresh look at the 'Gaia' debate by emphasising not just technology, but particularly the relationship between media industries and the vast energy/virtual footprint that they leave in their wake. He talks of an alternative, underground way of understanding a global onset for 'human extinction', thus advancing ideas about deep time, to the point where palaeontology becomes incorporated within the 'ontological turn'. He's therefore interested in a geological rather than archaeological study of our media-driven societies. Similarly, the recent book *Staying with the Trouble* by Donna Haraway (2016) is among the more powerful academic attacks on the hubris of thinking in terms of the Anthropocene. Hers is therefore a critique not simply on what we do, but how we think – or fail to:

> The unfinished Chthulucene must collect up the trash of the Anthropocene, the exterminism of the Capitalocene, and chipping and shredding and layering like a mad gardener, make a much hotter compost pile for still possible pasts, presents, and futures. (Haraway 2016: 57)

Even though most contributions to this collection have not employed such terms so explicitly, this book is a catch bag for all these types of concerns. So, if this volume truly aims to be more than the sum, it must stand up to competing attentions on the topic, of which there are many at the moment (Jackson 2014; Dittmar and Tastevin 2016; Graziano and Trogal 2017). And for good reason, since this is not only a hot (perhaps overheating) area of concern, it is more importantly something that is crucial in this day and age (Eriksen 2016). Even over a decade ago, Elizabeth Spelman (2002) had labelled our era as the age of *homo reparans*. Since then, we have been made aware of such things as broken Britain, or the museum of broken relationships as a top tourist attraction site. Repair surely provides us with many forward-looking tropes and memes. Hence, the value of memory repair work in terms of healing and forgiveness when it comes to violent conflict or cultural atrocities does not seem like too far a stretch, as Reno and Seidel have demonstrated here in relation to a relic warship and Holocaust survivors. A suitable analytic framework for repair raises many significant issues. Some of the more important ones have been addressed by the contributors to this volume when dealing, for instance, with ruin and abandonment (Frederiksen), the materiality of infrastructures and cheating the system (Khalvashi), political upheaval or excessive economic austerity (Tschoepe), identity translation and transmission (Munz, Holst Kjær).

As co-editors, we would really like to think of ourselves as a 're'pair – a paired duo of rebels and remakers. There is another book dealing with ethnographies of breakages and fixing (Strebel, Bovet and Sormani 2019), but their anthology is rather inspired by Actor Network Theory (ANT) and more about tinkering with things. These themes are present here too. But the present collection fits more in the vein of ethnographic anthropology in the sense that we draw more heavily on time and the metaphorical dimensions of brokenness. The upshot would be to suggest that while one forthcoming volume on repair deals with a Latourian ANT approach, the other is more political and holistic. And since Latour himself has a knack for synthesising complex ideas into relatively straightforward sound-bites, his words capture some of the iconoclastic themes embedded within many of the texts presented here:

> Thus, we can define an iconoclash as what happens when there is uncertainty about the exact role of the hand at work in the production of a mediator. Is it a hand with a hammer ready to expose, to denounce, to debunk, to show up, to disappoint, to disenchant, to dispel one's illusions, to let the air out? Or is it, on the contrary, a cautious and careful hand, palm turned as if to catch, to elicit, to educe, to welcome, to generate, to entertain, to maintain, to collect truth and sanctity? (Latour 2002: 20)

The great Pacific plastic patch is surely an indication that the pace, scale and impact of waste production now appears almost insurmountable. Yet innovative corrective means are sought and coping strategies continue to persist. Humour, irony, and even sarcasm where necessary, provide such critical mechanisms for reflection and, let's not forget, as an incentive for taking action. In their auto-recollections, Kathleen Stewart and Caitlin DeSilvey embody phenomenological storytelling and non-broken prose. In other words, there is a consistent concern with how embodied affectivity relates to repair knowledges, whereby real and imaginary care gives some hope to the social life of waste, rubbish, damaged goods and breakthroughs of both the conceptual and practical sort.

Stewart's description of the generic character of Comfort Inn roadscapes is reminiscent of the film director and author John Waters' book *Carsick* (2014), when he draws rather humorous (if somewhat bleak) accounts of America's highway 'non-places' during real (and imagined) hitchhiking journeys across the US, from Baltimore to San Francisco. Such a comparison is especially relevant given that Stewart makes two passing references to pop culture in her opening paragraph. Such imaginative techniques seem to be exactly what Haraway is calling for when evoking, in a deliberately non H.P. Lovecraft (1928) way, the mythological aegis of the Cthulhu.

So even if the ebbs of the rivers need mending with walls and floodgates, and even if the air we breathe is no longer uncontaminated, no matter how far one travels, we need to start existing as well as thinking within paradigms of repair. In this we must invest our hopes. Our lives are entangled with successes and failures, fixity and scrappage. To invent and to make is human. To break, to curse, to despair, repair and mend, perhaps all the more so. While addressing many levels and types of breakage/repair, as well as regional and disciplinary perspectives, this volume has not sought to highlight any particular theoretical position. Yet one could conceivably argue that what draws these diverse ethnographic contributions together is a focus that highlights two main features: creativity and care. It should therefore be remembered that to mend is part of the haptic and cognitive processes of making. Fixing is a key ingredient in what it means to be human because things, relationships, concepts and dreams are indeed always breaking.

Patrick Laviolette is Editor-in-Chief of the *Anthropological Journal of European Cultures* and visiting fellow at UCL.

Note

This chapter has been supported in part by the Estonian Research Agency, Project IUT 3-2.

References

Dittmar, Pierre-Olivier, and Yann-Philippe Tastevin. 2016. 'Réparer le monde, ce qu'il en reste (Éditorial)', *Techniques et Culture* 65/66(1): 10–13.

Eriksen, Thomas Hylland. 2016. *Overheating: An Anthropology of Accelerated Change.* London: Pluto.

Gabrys, Jennifer. 2011. *Digital Rubbish: A Natural History of Electronics.* Ann Arbor: University of Michigan Press.

Graziano, Valeria, and Kim Trogal. 2017. 'The Politics of Collective Repair: Examining Object-Relations in a Postwork Society', *Cultural Studies* 31(5): 634–58.

Haraway, Donna J. 2016. *Staying with the Trouble: Making Kin in the Chthulucene.* Durham, NC: Duke University Press.

Harvey, Polly Jean. 2000. *Stories from the City, Stories for the Sea.* Island Records.

Jackson, Steven J. 2014. 'Rethinking Repair', in T. Gillespie, P.J. Boczkowski and K.A. Foot (eds), *Media Technologies.* Cambridge, MA: MIT Press, pp. 221–40.

Latour, Bruno. 2002. 'What Is Iconoclash? Or Is There a World beyond the Image Wars?', in P. Weibel and B. Latour (eds), *Iconoclash: Beyond the Image-Wars in Science, Religion and Art.* Cambridge, MA: MIT Press, pp. 14–37.

Lovecraft, Howard P. 1928. 'The Call of Cthulhu', *Weird Tales* 11(2): 1–49.

Parikka, Jussi. 2016. *The Anthrobscene.* Minneapolis: University of Minnesota Press.

Pinney, Chris. 2012. 'Sherlock Holmes: Father of Material Culture?', *Material World*. Retrieved 15 March 2019 from http://www.materialworldblog.com/2012/11/sherlock-holmes-the-father-of-material-culture/.

Spelman, Elizabeth 2002. *Repair: The Impulse to Restore in a Fragile World*. Boston: Beacon Press.

Strebel, I., A. Bovet and P. Sormani (eds). 2019. *Repair Work Ethnographies: Revisiting Breakdown, Relocating Materiality*. Cham: Palgrave MacMillan.

Uys, Jamie (dir.). 1980. *The Gods Must Be Crazy*. 20th Century Fox.

Waters, John. 2014. *Carsick*. New York: Farrar, Straus and Giroux.

INDEX

Lightning Source UK Ltd.
Milton Keynes UK
UKHW021819080922
408463UK00008B/178

9 781800 736436